Children of Coercive Control

INTERPERSONAL VIOLENCE SERIES

Children of Coercive Control

EVAN STARK

OXFORD
UNIVERSITY PRESS

Oxford University Press is a department of the University of Oxford. It furthers
the University's objective of excellence in research, scholarship, and education
by publishing worldwide. Oxford is a registered trade mark of Oxford University
Press in the UK and certain other countries.

Published in the United States of America by Oxford University Press
198 Madison Avenue, New York, NY 10016, United States of America.

Library of Congress Cataloging-in-Publication Data
Names: Stark, Evan, author.
Title: Children of coercive control / Evan Stark.
Description: New York, NY : Oxford University Press, [2023] |
Includes bibliographical references and index.
Identifiers: LCCN 2023011410 (print) | LCCN 2023011411 (ebook) |
ISBN 9780197587096 (hardback) | ISBN 9780197587119 (epub) |
ISBN 9780197587126
Subjects: LCSH: Child abuse. | Abused women. | Psychological child abuse. |
Control (Psychology) | Family violence—Psychological aspects.
Classification: LCC HV6626.5 .S73 2023 (print) | LCC HV6626.5 (ebook) |
DDC 362.76—dc23/eng/20230501
LC record available at https://lccn.loc.gov/2023011410
LC ebook record available at https://lccn.loc.gov/2023011411

DOI: 10.1093/oso/9780197587096.001.0001

Printed by Sheridan Books, Inc., United States of America

Contents

Introduction

This book identifies coercive control of women as the most important cause and context of "child abuse" and child homicide outside a war zone, including deliberate injury to children, nonaccidental child death and the sexual abuse, denigration, exploitation, isolation, and subordination of children. I critique the current approaches to domestic violence and child maltreatment, provide a working model of the coercive control of children, and closely examine three recent forensic cases involving coercive control of children. In most instances, the coercive control of women and children run in tandem. In these cases, children are abused to further entrap and exploit their mother, a form of "secondary" victimization. But I also provide examples of cases in which abused mothers harm their children to survive or to protect them from worse (examples of what I term "patriarchal mothering") and where children are "weaponized" or are otherwise implicated in the coercive control of their mother. In all these instances, the child is the victim of coercive control.

Global services for children are predicated on the assumption that the fatal and serious nonaccidental harms children suffer fall on a continuum of problems rooted in some combination of maternal deficits, behavioral problems, immaturity, poverty, and environmental stressors. This book directly challenges this assumption by highlighting a criminal cause of nonaccidental child fatality and child maltreatment and promoting a justice response rather than a child welfare response. My contention, supported by a growing body of evidence, is that a small minority of persons, consisting mainly of fathers and male partners, is devastating the lives and life-chances of millions of children worldwide and that this population can be identified, effectively policed, and contained. Over the last two decades, many countries and over a dozen US states have upgraded laws protecting women to encompass coercive control and some, Scotland, for example, have extended protection to children. I would make these protections for women and children universal. By shifting the cases of "child abuse" that are the major cause of deliberate child fatality to the justice system, we would relieve the child welfare

Children of Coercive Control. Evan Stark, Oxford University Press. © Oxford University Press 2023.
DOI: 10.1093/oso/9780197587096.003.0001

systems of their broad protective and punitive functions, hence removing any rationale to extend these functions to the vast majority of "neglect" cases, which are optimally served by in-home supportive, therapeutic, and restorative services located in the community.

Outline of the Book

Children of Coercive Control challenges the prevailing liberalism, which approaches child abuse as a social policy problem rooted in a combination of environmental and maternal deficits, as well as the current enlightened alternative, to prevent the effects of "adverse childhood experiences" (ACES) through screening and early therapeutic intervention with children. Both the punitive and "early intervention" models are premised on the false presumption that the major childhood "trauma" associated with domestic violence (including the physical, sexual, and psychological abuse of children) are effects of circumscribed and time-limited events that can be elicited and managed distally, apart from the events themselves. This book argues that domestic violence, child abuse, and child sexual abuse are not experienced by children as "trauma," or not primarily, but rather, in the vast majority of instances, are experienced alongside myriad other harms, insults, and constraints as facets of an ongoing and predatory pattern of coercion and control that jeopardizes their rights, dignity, liberty, and psychological well-being as well their physical health. To the two current alternatives, services to mothers and removal of the children or early intervention with children, I propose a third, to reframe serious child abuse, child sexual abuse, and related harms to children as the effects of the crime of "coercive control," a course of conduct implemented to appropriate and command the privileges and resources available in a family space, primarily by controlling the mother, but not only. I propose to interrupt this course of conduct by targeting interventions at the (mainly male) partners and ex-partners responsible for coercive control, and neither at the supposedly "immature" or "inadequate" mothers nor the children on whom current social investments in child abuse prevention focus. Children are "secondary victims" of coercive control because the primary obstacle to an abuser's control over the household is their mother. But this reflects the logic of victimization, not the relative importance of interventions that protect children, a point which I emphasize repeatedly. Children play varied roles in coercive control in addition to being "secondary" victims. But even when children forge a "traumatic bond" or "identify with the aggressor" and collude in a mother's abuse—as in the cases I review in chapter 7—I emphasize the protective role of their strategy rather than children's culpability.

The chapters in Part I set the context and illustrate the problems as we found them. Chapter 3 depicts an important point in the "domestic violence revolution," when our research at Yale identified woman abuse as the most important context for child abuse. Chapter 4 takes us to *Nicholson v. Williams*, the outer boundary of the domestic violence revolution, where the significance of domestic violence as a context for child maltreatment became the rationale by which New York City and dozens of other municipalities cited abused mothers for "neglect" and removed their children to foster care. Our victory in *Nicholson* made it imperative that "domestic violence" and "child abuse" be conceptualized and managed as facets of a single course of conduct.

The chapters in Part II outline the experience of children of coercive control, including "child abuse as tangential spouse abuse," a dimension of coercive control that is unique to the abuse of children. Although the child is "weaponized" by the abuser in this dynamic in order to intimidate, isolate, and control his partner, the child here is no less a victim than when they are directly targeted.

In Part III, three cases from my forensic caseload are closely examined to show how coercive control was "lived" by Daniel Pelka, whose abused mother and abusive father were convicted of his starving death in Coventry, England, in 2012; Rachel,[1] who was charged and acquitted of multiple counts of risk of injury to her four children in New Jersey in 2016; and Carmen Barahona, who accepted a plea deal in 2020 in the Florida kidnap and murder of her adopted thirteen-year-old daughter, Nubia. These are extreme cases and will be difficult for some to read. But I know of no better way to illustrate the complexity and urgency of the issue before us.

Some children fall outside my purview. Infanticide is beyond my scope. Though the killing of unwanted children at or near birth may not be nearly as significant a global issue as it once was, infanticide remains a concern, particularly in countries where strict limits are set on family size and male favoring is still a norm.[2] Apart from infanticides, I also exclude the small proportion of children who are killed each year by other children or by adults unrelated to their parents. Conversely, my criticism of the child welfare function is not meant to minimize the importance of national social agendas for children or the need to address vast disparities in life-chances for young people that result from persistent global inequalities in wealth, health, resources, and opportunities. My concern in this book is specifically with children who are harmed in the context of interpersonal life, and with the expenditure of national justice resources so that children in each of our societies have the chance to flourish in their personal/family lives to the limits of their possibility, whatever that is.

Domestic Violence Revolution

Fifty years ago, at Yale Medical School, Anne Flitcraft, MD, made a discovery in the hospital's emergency medical records that helped put "woman abuse" on the map as a major social problem: "domestic violence" was the leading cause of injury for which women sought medical attention, more common than falls, rapes, mugging, and auto accidents combined. During the ensuing decades, an historically unprecedented domestic violence revolution circled the globe, with millions of women (and several million men) in hundreds of countries, at all ages and in all walks of life, coming forward to seek shelter, call police, or simply talk for the first time about the physical and sexual assaults they had suffered, mainly from husbands or other men with whom they'd shared a presumption of intimacy. By the 1990s, most US jurisdictions required police to make an arrest for a domestic violence offense, the only misdemeanor crime in which police were "mandated" to do so. By 2000, England was spending more on policing domestic violence than on national defense. In August of 1975, Anne Flitcraft and I visited Woman's House in St. Paul, Minnesota, one of the first of several thousand "shelters" for women and children in the United States. By 2023, support and services for victims was a robust part of the social budget of over 100 countries. This book builds on this base of support.

As the refuge/shelter movement has matured, so has our understanding of the core concern. From an initial small base of women in our research samples and shelter programs, we developed a picture of "woman battering" that mapped the road ahead for a considerable distance. As our experience base extended to millions of women surveyed, sheltered, and counseled worldwide, and to hundreds of thousands of offenders arrested and rearrested for similar offenses, our appreciation of the complexity of abuse deepened. The physical violence that once held our attention is now seen as one among several means that many men deploy to usurp and maintain power and control over women's personal lives. The intractability of "domestic violence" in the face of the massive availability of shelter and policing forced us to appreciate that what once was conceived as a pernicious form of assault, possibly in response to family conflicts or sexist beliefs, often has more in common with a much more serious "capture" crime such as kidnapping and imprisonment. In coercive control, the domestic violence "incident" is typically one of dozens of assaults which abusers combine with attempts to hurt and demean a woman sexually; frighten her; take her money and exploit her resources; isolate her from friends, family, and other sources of support; and subjugate and control her. The criminal intent involved in coercive control is predatory, calculated, and self-serving, no different from the incentive for trafficking or sexual slavery, and is almost never attributable to mental illness, behavioral problems, or ill-breeding. So widespread a criminal behavior stands as a social fact, borne by sexual inequalities rather than by individual biases, personalities, or predispositions, and supported by social institutions, including those, such as the hospitals, courts, and the police, currently charged with managing the problem of domestic violence. Today, in country after country, "coercive control" has replaced "domestic violence" at the top of the equalities agenda alongside "sexual violence" as the primary societal threat to women's health, safety, dignity, and liberty. As coercive control becomes the prevailing lens through which we view abuse, the focus of interdiction shifts from violence interruption and "safety" to the cessation of oppression and subordination in personal and family life and the preservation of basic rights and liberties. In contrast to domestic violence offenses, which are considered relatively minor, where enacted, crimes of coercive control carry the most serious penalties.

What about the children? While the picture of domestic violence was being enhanced to encompass coercive control, at Yale, we were extending our assessment of domestic violence to children. The research that provided the initial spark for this book was the finding, summarized in chapter 3, that "domestic violence" against the mother is the most important context in which children are being seriously injured or killed. This is true globally, not merely in the United States. Another finding from our research was equally remarkable at the time. The children were being hurt and sometimes killed by the same men who were abusing their wives and partners. This was an astounding discovery, because until then services responding to children knew nothing about "the men" in these homes. For instance, well into the 1990s, despite being considered "cutting edge" in child-abuse prevention, Yale's

"Dart" Committee for Child Abuse kept no information on the fathers or other men caring for the children they investigated. Yale was not unique. In the case discussed in chapter 4, when New York City removed the children from Mrs. Nicholson and the other mothers for "engaging in domestic violence" in 2005, none of the men responsible for the violence was identified, let alone charged. Fathers and abusive men were equally absent from the vast medical and psychological literature on child abuse. The men primarily responsible for hurting and killing children were invisible to the agencies responsible for detecting and protecting children from abuse. One result of the invisibility of men to child protection was fifty years of intervention that failed to reduce child abuse and nonaccidental child death. The field of child abuse was responding to an offense whose perpetrators it would not identify.

Our Yale findings were replicated and widely disseminated. By century's end, programs for children had universally acknowledged the importance of domestic violence. By 2010, every US state and many countries had incorporated domestic violence into its child welfare assessments and response; most state and many national shelter systems had integrated or separate-track funding for children's services; from New Jersey and the District of Columbia, through Hennepin County in Minnesota to Santa Clara in California, from Toronto, Canada, to Sydney, Australia, and Stockholm, Sweden, entire family court systems mandated domestic violence training for family judges and/or adapted best practice guidelines in these cases. In New York City and some other jurisdictions, the new response to children included the language of coercive control. When it introduced its new offense of coercive control in 2018, Scotland included the "exposure of children" to violence and coercive control as an aggravating factor in sentencing.

The implications of our research should have been transparent. Since the two events—domestic violence and child abuse—occurred in roughly the same family space, involved the same actors, ran in tandem and lead to a single compounded outcome, the subordination of women and children to a criminological will, outcomes would have significantly improved if justice and welfare resources had been consolidated around protecting women and children and interdicting abusive men. With the victim women and children, it *should* have been, as my Ukrainian grandmother would say about sex, "when two are as one." Had this happened, *Children of Coercive Control* would not been written.

Instead, what happened was this. With a few marked exceptions, the two problems, "domestic violence" and "child abuse," remained separate and developed on opposing tracks. Women's advocates did our part to reach children. Between 1980 and 2023, the narrow focus on physical violence against women was replaced by an appreciation of coercive control in the movement to stop woman abuse. In about a dozen countries and a number of US states, the low-level crime against women was upgraded as the serious offense of coercive control. Thousands of programs in dozens of countries broadened their perspective to encompass the range of women's abuse experiences beyond physical violence; colocated "shelter" and warning systems at schools, workplaces, gyms, other community sites to which abusers had access; and extended their support services to children and other vulnerable persons targeted alongside adult victims. During these same decades, however, the pediatric, child welfare, and child guidance apparatus moved in the opposite direction, removing child abuse and child fatality from its sociopolitical context, casting domestic violence as a "family problem" devoid of agency, but in which mothers became "engaged" in ways that resulted in their children's "exposure." Public health and children's services identified "witnessing" and the "exposure" of children to domestic violence as among the "trauma" that put them at high risk for subsequent behavioral, mental, and physical health problems and promoted early intervention to relieve the effects of ACES.[3]

Interdiction with men was at the center of the movement to stop coercive control. But the pediatric, child welfare, and child guidance establishments manage child abuse through a combination of sanctions and services for mothers and placement and early therapeutic intervention with children. Even as it officially adapted the domestic violence framework toward child abuse, the children's establishment turned it from something that happens *to* women to something that happens *to* children because their mothers haplessly engage with violent men. The inversion of domestic violence and child abuse was a global phenomenon. Suffice it to say that the response that the US District Court found unconstitutional in 2005—and that violated the 5th and 13th Amendments against indentured servitude, among others— is still the preferred option: the punitive removal of children because their mothers have experienced abuse is reported from England, Australia, Canada, Holland, Poland, Russia, and elsewhere. While the burden of the punitive State response falls most heavily on abused women and children of color, migrant women and children, and indigenous women and children, this is not wholly so. The family courts in all of these countries routinely contract with abusive fathers for protective custody of children they had formerly victimized and, except where coercive control laws are in place, allow perpetrators to cross-examine and denigrate their victims in child custody proceedings. Here, middle-class, affluent, and Caucasian women are common victims.

The treatment of child abuse as a clinical manifestation of maternal neglect is not only bad science. It abrogates fundamental rights of women and children. Chapter 4 recounts the federal case brought by Mrs. Sharwline Nicholson, her children, and other welfare mothers and children against the City of New York because the policy of removal for domestic violence violated their Constitutional rights. I preview Nicholson's predicament here to highlight a major purpose of this book, to pick up the story where we left it off at Yale, with the finding that domestic violence was the leading context and cause of child maltreatment. Millions of children languish in foster care worldwide because their mothers were abused, and millions more remain trapped in abusive homes because what I call "the institutions of secondary socialization"—e.g., the school, child welfare, child guidance clinics, police, and pediatric medicine—continue to regard "domestic violence" and "child abuse" as separate problems, attribute their persistence to some combination of immaturity, environmental stressors, and maternal deficits, and alternatively proscribe punitive responses, including placement, and behavioral management. Because of circumstances specific to their situation, including their race, affluence, or national origin, millions of abused women elude administrative notice from police and child welfare, though their experience with schools and the family courts can be similarly controlling. For all abuse victims, regardless of their race, social class, or national origin, once their fortunes become enmeshed with child welfare, the family court, the pediatric guidance clinic, the schools, or police, coercive control can become a process of "social" as well as individual entrapment, in which individual strictures of male control and deference are complemented or even replaced by Court orders, bench warrants, supervised visits, "treatment" plans, and other formal means of exacting obedience from women with respect to their children. The informal process of social entrapment is part of the story of how children are coercively controlled.

When she was asked to "talk about the violence," the first abused woman who took refuge in our home in 1976 told us, "violence wasn't the worst part." A direct plumb-line connects this observation to my development of the coercive control framework for recognizing and responding to partner abuse, my writing the book *Coercive Control* (2006; 2022) and this book. There is a significant overlap between domestic violence and coercive control. An estimated 75 percent of the domestic violence reported to police occurs in the context of coercive control.[4] But violence may be minimal in many cases and is likely to be nonexistent or to consist of frequent but low-level assaults in many other abusive relationships. Nevala's EU-wide data found that 45 percent of women who reported experiencing high levels of control from their current partner were not being subjected to any violence from this partner.[5] Similarly, as our Yale research demonstrated, most of the injuries "darted" for suspicion of child abuse are actually the consequence of children becoming the "secondary victims" of men's coercive control. While occasionally fatal, these injuries are rarely serious enough to prompt intervention on their own. To get at these cases, where violence is experienced as "subjugation" rather than a physical threat, we have to listen to women and children talk, together and separately, about the cumulative effect of "a thousand cuts," and harms to their dignity, safety, autonomy, intelligence, and liberty, not just about physical safety. The case material I present in this book is a simulacra for this conversation.

We have reached a point in our social development when guaranteeing their physical survival no longer meets our minimal societal obligation to children. The model of coercive control is rights-based, not harms-based, and is premised on the supposition that each of the elements of constraints limit the expression of an activity that is vital to full and equal personhood.

Coercive Control

Children of Coercive Control starts from two widely replicated empirical realities, that the vast majority of child abuse takes place in the context of domestic violence and that the vast majority of domestic violence incidents reported to shelters, hospitals, and police occur in the context of coercive control, a pattern where repeat, "ongoing" but typically low-level physical abuse occurs in concert with a range of sexual offenses and tactics to denigrate, isolate, intimidate, exploit, and control female partners. The importance of domestic violence as a context for child abuse and child mortality has been recognized for decades. The book takes the next step, showing that the criminal strategy of coercive control extends to children both directly, in that children are victims of the same coercive and control tactics as their mothers, and indirectly, when "child abuse" becomes a form of "tangential spouse abuse." Many cases of coercive control also involve "social entrapment," where child welfare, the family court, the school, or other "institutions of secondary socialization" enter families via child-saving interventions that reinforce coercive control and undermine the resiliency and strategic capacities of all victimized parties, including the children. This process is illustrated by the experience of the *Nicholson* mothers described in Chapter 4. Where children are present, children are almost always the "secondary" victims of coercive control and are harmed, "weaponized," used as surrogates or "witnesses," or enlisted as allies in the strategy to control the "primary" victim and so to monopolize the privileges and resources available through the household. While the coercive control of women and children overlap, the harms children experience because of coercive control are distinctive. So are the ways in which children cope with, accommodate, and resist coercive control.

Since we published our original child abuse research in the 1980s, several dozen books and hundreds of monographs confirmed the significance of domestic violence as the leading context for child maltreatment. I would surmise that today it is the exceptional health, education, or sports program globally for youth that is *not* alert to violence "at home" as a common source of a child's problem. Yet, the men who are hurting the women and children are no more likely to be the identified clients, interdiction targets or patients today at the points where children are served than when our research was conducted two decades ago.[6]

Faultlines in the Domestic Violence Model

I will assume as proved an argument I make in *Coercive Control* (2007; 2022), that the domestic violence framework failed to provide a coherent account of woman abuse that captures the nature or scope of the harms being inflicted in the vast majority of relationships for which women seek help or that supports effective intervention or prevention. The working premise of this book is that the fault lines in the domestic violence model with respect to child abuse are equally glaring. In particular, in tracing children's risks from woman abuse primarily to the dangers of "witnessing" or "exposure" to their mother's physical abuse, the domestic violence framework trivializes children's experience of harm and diminishes the basis of a rights-based claim to redress and justice. As we'll learn, the response of even very young children to coercive control suggests that children's senses are affected and actively engaged with their oppression and that even "witnessing" can be a strategic gambit for a child rather than a sign of passivity or indifference. As I have emphasized, the "secondary" nature of children's abuse does not mean the abuse of the child is less severe or intentional than the abuse of the mother. To the contrary, once a child is selected as a target, the types of abuse deployed, and their frequency, duration, and severity, are comparable to those deployed against a primary partner. Indeed, insofar as the coercive control of children often involves their use as "witnesses," couriers, spies, surrogates, and comrades in crime, the array of effects on the child is often greater than on the primary victim. However, the role assigned to the child in coercive control may mean that the risk that the child will be killed is not visible until the abuser's final act to punish the mother. Our cases repeatedly illustrate that children are often and unexpectedly harmed or murdered by abusers without warning because their primary animosity lies elsewhere. Recognizing the secondary role of child abuse in the criminal logic of coercive control is critical to protecting children.

Coercive control involves a long-standing, spatially diffuse, multifaceted pattern of abusive behavior designed to subordinate its targets, isolate them from sources of support, and exploit their capacities and appropriate their resources for personal gain. Coercive control is deployed in all types of relationships and in many social settings other than abusive relationships. For example, David Guterson's *The Final Case* depicts a "homicide by abuse" in Washington State of "Abeba," an Ethiopian girl, by her adoptive white fundamentalist Christian parents and sibs, as the direct result of coercive control imposed in the guise of homeschooling.[7] The fact remains. The most devastating effects of coercive control result where it builds on preexisting sexual inequalities in families and relationships to further disadvantage women and children in ways that men who are coercively controlled are not already disadvantaged. Because coercive control involves ongoing behavior that is multifaceted, self-serving, and almost always "crosses social space" to engage partner-victims at multiple settings, it can be identified and interrupted, its perpetrators apprehended, and the integrity and rights of its victims restored. Protecting women and children by stopping coercive control is a matter of political will and justice resources.

My Approach: A Forensic Analysis

The coercive control of children is a new area of investigation. I base the model of coercive control on dozens of real-life cases, mainly from my forensic practice, my work with women and children in shelters, complemented by news accounts.[8] This is a substantial group, but heavily weighted toward more serious cases. Almost a thousand research monographs have applied the coercive control model since the first edition of my book appeared in 2007. This body of research affords an invaluable empirical overview of what women are experiencing, but it will probably be another decade before a similar body of research extends the spectrum to children. Until then, I largely confirm my clinical impressions with whatever case material I can garner from popular media like film, fiction, Netflix, and online personals. In lieu of social science, this is the best social ethnography has to offer.

I have already suggested why traditional academic and professional sources of information are little help. The vast research literature on domestic violence and child abuse is of little use because it focuses on instances of physical and/or sexual abuse rather than the comprehensive and ongoing crime to personhood, liberty, and dignity women and children recount to me. Abusive men are poignantly described by the women and children I work with, but have no corporeality in medical records of child abuse (chapter 3) or child welfare records (chapter 4), even if the mother is deceased and the man is the only adult in the home.

Since state intervention in families to prevent child abuse was controversial historically,[9] a certain reticence toward abusive men in academic and clinical circles is not surprising. What I find intriguing is the sharp contrast between the silence in the ameliorative sciences about men as a significant source of pathology in women and children's lives and the proliferation of images of angry, violent, brutal, terroristic, and controlling men in the various media consumed regularly by tens of millions of adults and children around the globe. One has merely to recall *Tosca* or *The Brothers Karamazov* to appreciate that the portrayal of brutal and controlling fathers/husbands is not a unique feature of popular culture. The fact that cases of coercive control are portrayed more often in fiction, film, and popular lore than in clinical journals is a matter of public record, not a quirk of my forensic approach.

Cases of coercive control are also all around us in everyday life. When I stopped redirecting my clients to "talk about the violence" and listened to the experiences they considered "abuse," I realized that I had come across stories like the ones I was being told in my practice throughout my career, not only in memoirs or fiction or film for example, but also from friends and classmates in my childhood and school years. When I thought back, my friends in grammar school had described being bullied, stalked, and tormented by fathers or father surrogates; junior high school classmates had told us how their movements, money, dress, and speech had been micromanaged; our children's friends complained that their social sites were regularly pillaged, their phones had been stolen, they were kept in curfew for months; and their high school friends confessed to being locked in rooms, in basements, in attics; tied to a sink, denied toilet paper, beaten with boards; made to sleep in the yard or the car; and been given the silent treatment for an entire summer. Offenders in these cases were usually male, but extended to a range of relations, "friends" of the family, caregivers, coaches, teachers, and clergy. Added to the cases, the catalog of behaviors emitted similarities and the similarities yielded the typology. I did not go hunting for sexual perversity on YouTube. When my clients walk into my office, I set out to draw a power map of their lives based on the worlds already recorded in snap shot in my boyhood in the Bronx and Yonkers, in novels for the Fruitvale Section of Oakland; Belfast; or Rosshire, Scotland.

Other than what I know from the women I work with, the children I've grown up with, and what I've gleaned from literature, media, and sparse social science data, I talk to children. Not *de nuevo*. I start off by confirming what someone has told me about how an abusive male has harmed them, usually their mother or an older sib. I am not an objective observer. I meet the people I work with at a family court or a lawyer's office or a daycare or a shelter or a prison visitor center or the Department of Social Services because someone has been hurt or arrested, even killed, often a parent or child, and something about the situation needs a "fixer." Or someone comes to my office or calls with some other crisis related to abuse. Truth be told, I also want the "story." That's how I learn, by sharing what I know en route to solving unfamiliar problems, like how to stop an ex from getting his former's wife's address from their son's boarding school. Or how to get a protective order for a mother and child hiding in New York under the nose of a senior police official in Belfast, who is the target of the order. I ask even young children why things came down as they did, often discovering that simple reasons make the most sense.

At first I thought my cases were the outliers, similar to cases captured in autobiography, memoirs, or fiction, because they were extreme. Pretty soon, I realized the tragedies I'd read about had been normalized among a huge subset of families in real life in which women and children suffered similar if not identical forms of depredation. Some mothers spewed venom at abusive men when they talked about their children. Others acknowledged shame at their own participation in abusive rituals with their children. Still others showed the stoic resignation I've come to associate with sheer survival. I'm direct with children. But, I don't confront them with what I've been told if they deny something happened. Nor do I accept children's claims of what happened at face value. Children lie. And they lie frequently. Most people do. But with children who are in abusive situations, I take what they tell me seriously, even when I know it is false, particularly when it comes to sexual abuse, where children are most often doubted, because I've seen parents manipulate both affirmations and denials. My primary responsibility is to make it safer for children to live with their truth, whatever it is, usually by expanding the mother's options to do so. Once I make it clear that I lay sole accountability for coercive control with the abuser, women usually offer exacting detail about their children's torment. Children can be more reticent than adults, often because they find our assurances of safety unreliable. As they often are. Nor do I have the power to wrench a child back from even the cruelest foster home or dad. I cannot assure a mother or child that a judge will listen objectively if they explain what really happened. I am no Robin Hood with merry men. The evil sheriffs will outlive me.

My office is not a court of law, and I do minimal fact checking. Other than the usual tests to detect prevarication, I rely on the fact that the basic dynamics of coercive control have been part of women's underlife in most cultures for over a century and known well by me for almost half that long. The patterns are never identical. But they are similar enough to narrow most gaps in information down to a few options. It takes me about forty minutes to tell when someone is filling in details of their lives from a film they've seen or a website. I listen to stories that have been shared at funeral parlors, beauty parlors, nail salons, living rooms, school yards, backyards, laundromats, and gyms for centuries. Edited out of this book are some of the nastiest scenes of physical cruelty as well as some of the betrayals that hurt most deeply. Children are just now learning to share these stories with adults. It is time the family and social sciences took notice. Male violence against children may be officially invisible to our institutions of social administration and protection. But it has hardly been out of sight or mind. From every corner of our community, in parks, laundromats, school yards, gyms, movie theaters, sandlots, playgrounds, city streets, and in cyberspace, clubs, hair salons, cafes, sports contests, and supermarkets, young boys, women, and children talk continually about the violence, harassment, stalking, bullying, sexting, and mistreatment of children by related adults in their midst, most of it by males. The "noise" of street talk finds an outlet in street music, children and young adults plugged into iPods, roblox, and the like seeking resonance through white-noise catharsis of gangsta rap for the surface terrorism that pervades their living spaces.

This said, while the overall validity of the experience I describe comes from popular lore and the media, it is not these popular sources to which I call readers attention in this book. My final point is that the immediate evidence I use is "clinical." As a forensic sociologist, I read legal cases with the same eye for hidden meaning and detail that a medical specialist brings to their physiological inspection. My argument emerges from forensic analysis of law cases, many of which involve abused women who were criminally charged in the death or serious injury of a child caused by a man who is also abusing her. I draw on the general knowledge gleaned from popular media to interpret the complex clinical realities we confront in the forensic context.

The stories in this book may initially feel shocking. But they should not feel unfamiliar. The men who haunt these pages are known to us in some guise even if we do not immediately recognize them. If, nonetheless, we do not "know what we know," this is probably because we are so accustomed to the tyranny over women and particularly over children in our midst, that we confuse its familiarity with its insignificance.

PART I
THE CONTEXT FOR COERCIVE CONTROL

1

In the Beginning

There Oughta Be a Law

Edinburgh, August 2013

This was to be our first real vacation after thirty-nine years of marriage. Or so I was thinking. Anne Flitcraft and I had established research, writing, and training careers in the domestic violence field. I had retired two years earlier from Rutgers University, where I'd taught public health and public administration. I'd always wanted to "travel." I was scheduled to have a heart valve replacement. How many more chances to travel would I have? No children were home—a respite that proved brief. Our cat had "disappeared" in the woods near our home a few months earlier, and our dog Becky had recently died, at nineteen. More pets were not on our agenda. I presented Anne with my offer: a free postsurgical spring in Edinburgh, where I had been offered a Leverhulme Visiting Professorship for the term at the university. I was surprised when Anne jumped at the chance. Having never had as much as a sabbatical, she took early retirement from the University of Connecticut School of Medicine, where she was a primary care physician and clinical director of the Berghdorf Health Center, a pioneering health provider for Hartford's inner city. She too felt there was a risk our time together might be limited.

A prolonged recovery forced us to delay arrival in Scotland till August 1. By a pleasant coincidence, this was also the opening day of the Edinburgh International Arts Festival. Since the university was mostly empty in August, we could settle comfortably into our West End neighborhood, test my new heart valve walking to art venues, and find the best cafés to fetch Anne's morning "double" macchiato (with a shot of a caramel) and luncheon soups. It all seemed so relaxed. Friends posted a photo on Facebook in evening dress "On the Red Carpet at Cannes," where their son's new film version of *Macbeth* was screening. We countered with a "selfie" bundled in winter coats from the charity shop "On the Red Rug in an 'Edinburgh (movie) Theatre.'" If I went to work, for the exercise, I returned to "home cooking," a first in our

Children of Coercive Control. Evan Stark, Oxford University Press. © Oxford University Press 2023.
DOI: 10.1093/oso/9780197587096.003.0002

family history. After our wedding, we'd stayed at a local motel so my parents could use our bed. At seventy-odd years, could this be the honeymoon we'd never had? Not likely. The absence of rain that August in Scotland gave us no hint of the weather up ahead.

Anne had barely mastered Edinburgh's complicated recycling schedule when the news broke. In the weird world we inhabit, this is the sort of news feminist policy wonks dream of. We awoke to find the everyday travail no one seems to notice suddenly in the headlines.

Sheriff Katherine Mackie vs. Bill Walker, MSP

On August 13, 2013, all national media in the United Kingdom featured the same story. Based on complaints by three former wives and a step-daughter, Bill Walker, a long-standing Labour Member of the Scottish Parliament (MSP), was convicted of breach of the peace and twenty-three assaults. The assaults stretched over twenty-eight years (1967–1995) and included punching his wives in the face, leaving one with a black eye, brandishing an air rifle, repeatedly using a saucepan to hit another ex-partner, and putting all his partners through "systematic physical and emotional abuse." Walker was also convicted of an assault on his sixteen-year-old step-daughter with a frying pan. In an astoundingly frank public statement she read from the bench, Edinburgh's Domestic Violence Sheriff Katherine Mackie outlined the chronic and heinous nature of Walker's "controlling, domineering, de-meaning . . . behaviors." Sheriff Mackie also spoke openly about her frus-tration with the one-year sentencing limit in Sheriff's Court without trial because "however unacceptable," this would make his behavior seem not to amount to a "criminal (i.e., 'serious') offense." Even if she sentenced the seventy-one-year-old Walker to prison for the maximum, she complained bitterly, he could remain in parliament, where removal was automatic only for members sentenced to more than a year. He could voluntarily resign be-cause of the shame. But nothing in the law compelled him to do so.

I was paying particular attention as Sheriff Mackie pointed to the large gap separating Walker's "cruel, terroristic and immoral behavior" toward his wives and children and what the law defined as the crime of partner abuse. It was unprecedented for a man to be charged with a single act of abuse committed years earlier, let alone to be held to account for multiple acts committed against multiple partners and children years earlier. Domestic violence was no longer ignored by law enforcement as it had been in the not too distant past. But in the United States, United Kingdom, and much of the world, an abuse offender might be only detained or arrested and charged with one of dozens of his assaults on a partner against whom he'd been conducting a terroristic campaign of violence and intimidation and control for decades. Few of the offenders who were arrested spent time in jail, even if they were charged with a crime. In my 2006 book, *Coercive Control*, I described the constellation of tactics deployed over time to subordinate partners. I coined the term "coercive control" to characterize the vast majority of abuse relationships, which were not limited to "domestic violence," as it was conventionally portrayed. And I documented the huge gap separating the lived realities of coercive control from the normative regimes through which the abuse of women was known and managed. At most, the law's narrow focus on domestic violence had produced incremental gains in safety and accountability at an enormous cost. At worst, framing coercive control as domestic violence reinforced women's entrapment in abusive relationships. Just as with Bill Walker here in Scotland, so too in the vast majority of cases where offending men were arrested in the United States: applying the calculus of physical harms to individual assaults trivialized and normalized the common pattern of frequent, ongoing but generally low-level violence that went on for years while masking the accompanying strategy of coercive control, in which this ongoing violence was typically embedded. Only a tiny proportion among millions of men arrested dozens of times for similar offenses against the same women and children had been convicted of a single serious crime. In fact, imprisonment for a domestic violence offense was no more likely in Britain or the United States after a man's fiftieth arrest for a domestic offense than after his first. To be sure, the reforms implemented had led to sharp drop in the incidence of injurious partner assaults. But this very positive outcome was overshadowed by increases in the proportions of women reporting historical abuse and coercive control. To close the gap that produced tragic statistics such as these, countries like the United States, United Kingdom, and Scotland had to expand working and legal definitions of domestic violence to include coercive control. This was what I'd advocated in my book and on my lecture tours.

Sheriff Mackie knew she was not speaking in a political vacuum. Acknowledging that partner abuse involves far more that discrete assaults, in 2003 Scotland became the first country to adopt a broadened definition as the basis for its national strategy. Drawing inspiration from the UN's

Declaration on the Elimination of Violence against Women, the Scottish executive identified domestic violence as a pattern of "gender-based abuse" perpetrated by partners or ex-partners that "can include physical abuse (assault and physical attack involving a range of behaviour), sexual abuse (acts which degrade and humiliate women and are perpetrated against their will, including rape) and mental and emotional abuse (such as threats, verbal abuse, racial abuse, withholding money and other types of controlling behaviour such as isolation from family or friends)." But, as Sheriff Mackie knew, this broad definition carried no weight as yet in her court or in any other court in Britain. Or elsewhere in the world.

Apart from a series of public lectures I had committed to deliver, my major responsibility as a Leverhulme Scholar in Edinburgh was to "build bridges" between Sottish Women's Aid and its indefatigable executive Lily Greenhan and key constituencies whose support was needed to turn the strategic definition into law. Since our first visit to the Glasgow Women's Refuge in the 1970s, I had returned to Scotland many times, most recently in 2015, when Dr. Marsha Scott had brought me in to train service teams in and around Edinburgh on coercive control a few years earlier. As was true throughout the United Kingdom, here too frustration with the current approach was high among police, prosecutors, the judiciary, and the range of statutory and voluntary sector service providers. But the opportunity for meaningful reform was also reflected in the strategic definition and the transparently opportunistic search of the governing Scottish Nationalist Party (SNP) for an issue to broaden its political base. Could this be the spark?

Sheriff Mackie's sentencing statement got at the heart of how abstracting individual assaultive episodes (any of which may be trivial in themselves) from their historical context can lead to the mistaken conclusion that the abuse of women and children need not be taken seriously. She weighed the "cumulative effect" of Walker's "pattern of abusive behavior" toward his wives and daughter against the single act of assault that would have been dismissed as "just a domestic" in the past. In his defense, Walker claimed "various conspiracies among former wives, political opponents and the media."

How often had I seen US judges accept transparently absurd plaints or rule in favor of fathers accused of abuse in disputed custody cases? A month before coming to Scotland, I'd rushed to a Stamford, Connecticut, court to support a woman's petition to extend the terms of a civil "no contact" order after her husband followed her to her bedroom, broke through a locked door, and raped her. On the submission of my support letter by the woman's attorney, the judge declared a "mistrial" and effectively dismissed the woman's motion by setting a rehearing well after it would have led to effective protection. The judge had already found "truthful" the husband's claim that he "could tell" his wife "wanted sex" by "the way she walked" to the bathroom (the only working toilet in the house) through his master bedroom. Even the lock he shattered in entering her bedroom was an "obvious" provocation since, he had assured the Court, his wife knew full well from past experience "what I was like when she put me *in that mood*." As apparently did Her Honor.

Fortunately, Walker was in a Scottish criminal court not a US family court. The Stamford housewife told me that the judge in her case had attended to her abusive husband's lies "like she was listening to Kenneth Branagh read *Hamlet*," a deliberate reference to a recent TV showing of his 1996 film that had bored her silly. By contrast, Sheriff Mackie rejected Walker's claims out of hand. Instead, she identified his incredulity at being convicted and his repeated claims of victimization as "further indications of your abdication of responsibility for your behaviour." Though the crimes for which Walker was charged had occurred eighteen years earlier, she noted his open expressions of "contempt for your former wives and your stepdaughter and the derogatory manner in which you refer to them," highlighting the fact that the teenager "thought it necessary to protect her mother from you and that you professed to be unaware of any injuries sustained," even though these were both visible and documented by medical records.[1] Again and again Sheriff Mackie identified and condemned the narcissistic behaviors for which abusive fathers are often rewarded in family cases. She observed that the only "remorse" Walker seemed to feel was for himself and further noted that his extreme denial and minimization, even in the face of extensive media coverage, made it unlikely domestic violence counseling would help. In the few instances where Walker acknowledged using physical force, she added, he had justified his actions.

With respect to sentencing, Sheriff Mackie insisted that the overall or cumulative effect of Walker's course of criminal conduct merited a lengthy custodial sentence, even if some of the individual acts did not. Sheriff Mackie recognized what the law in Scotland would not fully comprehend until legal reform in 2018, that the seemingly diverse pieces of Walker's course of conduct were joined by a decipherable and singular behavioral logic, the bespoke offense of *coercive control*, and it was to the various expressions of this ongoing strategy to which Walker's wives and children had responded. Thus, Sheriff Mackie found that it was Walker's behavior that led his children to want no further contact with him, not the fact that his wives had turned them against him, as he alleged. To put it crudely—how often have I wished to hear an Officer of the Family Court put it so crudely—Walker's children hated him because he'd behaved hatefully toward them and toward his wives. Sheriff Mackie sentenced Walker to fourteen years' imprisonment, the longest sentence permissible in Scottish law. Because of the standing of her Court, however, the effective sentence was reduced to one day less than a year. The signal was clear.

Our campaign for new law in Scotland was launched the day after Sheriff Mackie's delivered her sentencing speech.

* * *

Had SMP Bill Walker acknowledged his guilt, expressed remorse, and quietly withdrawn from Parliament, the episode might have been quickly forgotten. Given his age, he would not have spent a day in prison. This outcome would have set our campaign back; it would not have been a death blow. But Bill Walker did none of these things. Like so many of the other men in my practice and the world we inhabit whose narcissism is malignant, once he was challenged and his lies exposed, Walker doubled his efforts to preserve his (false) positive image through even more bluster, accusation, and cover-up, adding Sheriff Mackie, his children, the press, and several of his colleagues in Parliament to his list of targets.

I never underestimate the risk a narcissistic abuser poses when cornered; their willingness to terrorize their ex-wives and children through endless litigation can exhaust all parties involved (including their own attorneys) into surrendering what they had previously held most precious. Men in my cases have battled unyieldingly for sole custody of children whose grade level or birth dates they "don't recall" until their wives abandoned lucrative property settlements or gave up custody altogether, denuded of hope of ever having their children apart from surveillance. Lest this obsessive behavior be confused with purposiveness, consider this. Three abusive husbands of women in my practice completely abandoned their families once they "won" sole legal and/or primary physical custody and after extremely costly multiyear battles. In a recent Connecticut case, my client's husband declared "total victory" when a nine-year court battle ended with the Court denying unsupervised visits by the mother to her girls. Two days later, he dropped the teenagers off at their mother's house with their suitcases, then disappeared. Several months earlier, an evaluating psychiatrist to whom the girls had been describing their father's impulsive jealous rages suddenly admitted the father unexpectedly from an outer room from which he'd been eavesdropping. "Here's the man," the wily MD announced, "Now, does he look like an ax murderer?"

Instead of saving his political career with a public apology, Bill Walker filed an appeal and continued to publicly rail against his wives, his children, the sheriff, and the media. This was his gift to us. And over the months between his conviction and his going to jail, it kept on giving. For the remainder of that August and until Bill Walker finally resigned in mid-September, just days before he went to prison, ever larger demonstrations focused the country's attention on the new level of justice needed in the land.

I should have been paying closer attention. I was so intent on the comprehensive way in which she charged Walker with his crimes against this wives, that I barely noticed the inclusion of the step-daughter's allegations.

Edinburgh Redux: June 2015

Daniel Pelka, Magdalena Luczak, and Mariusz Krezolek

I meant to be provocative.

I was back at the University of Edinburgh, the first stop on a UK lecture tour about coercive control. I had projected two large photos from the tabloids. One was a facial close-up of Magdalena Luczak above a question I intended to be rhetorical: "Killer or Victim?" The second photo pictured her son, four-year-old Daniel Pelka, as the *Mirror* put it, "Innocently running after the mother who would murder him.[2]

My return visit to Scotland in 2015 was prompted by two developments that could revolutionize support for abused women and their children. During the earlier visits to the United Kingdom, I had helped Women's Aid and other grassroots women's organizations and charities in Scotland, Wales, England, and Northern Ireland build support for legal reforms that responded to coercive control. As the result of the 2013 visit, the Scottish executive had appointed a draft commission to come up with an ideal reform law. That same year, the British Home Office had rolled out a "New Cross-Governmental Definition of Domestic Violence," designed to subsume the fourteen other *nonlegal* definitions in the health, human, and social care services under the government auspices. The new definition explicitly identified coercive control as a form of partner abuse alongside domestic violence, doing so in the specific language of a "consultation" that I had submitted with Davina James-Hanman on behalf of AVA (Against Violence & Abuse). Then, in April 2015, the British Parliament made "coercive and controlling behavior" a criminal offense in England and Wales, the first governments to specifically identify a partner abuse crime as a pattern of control-based subordination. Because of its progressive tradition, Scotland could be expected to adopt even broader statutory language. But even before the new level of legal accountability became a lynchpin for any victim-based service intervention in Scotland, statutory agencies like health and child protection would be accountable for identifying and managing a range of abusive behaviors other than violence. If offenders were actually taken off the streets, as we hoped, victims could stay in the homes and remain actively engaged in empowerment within their communities.

This was the context for my charge from Scottish Women's Aid. En route to broadening the base of support for a new offense of coercive control in Scotland, still in the "study" phase two years after the Walker trial, I had been asked to explain to an audience of social workers, health professionals, justice personnel, and advocates how adapting the new definition of coercive control in conjunction with the new offense could improve their work with children. To start, though, I had to reinforce what many in the room sensed intuitively, that something about their current approach to women and children was perilously off base.

The images on the screen had been as inescapable in England during Magdalena Luczak's 2013 trial for Daniel's murder as had been the pictures in the United States of OJ Simpson handcuffed, unshaven, and head down after his arrest for killing Nicole Brown and Ronald Goldman in 1994. Equally shocking were seemingly daily revelations during the trial of the role Magdalena had played in the starving and beating death of her son by Mariusz Krezolek, her live-in boyfriend. The Mail was typical, identifying the woman whose photo I'd put on the screen as "The evil mother who put love of drugs, alcohol and vile boyfriend before Daniel's basic needs." It was also well known that she was abused. So how did this audience see her? Did the fact that the mother was abused elicit sufficient sympathy to win her support, if not sympathy? If not, why not?

Born and raised in Lodz, Poland, Magdalena Luczak had settled in 2006 at age twenty in Coventry, England, where she worked as a cleaner and at a Parcel Post depot. There was no allegation that Magdalena struck Daniel. She had, of course, failed to prevent Mariusz from murdering her son, a fact she readily admitted, that was obvious from the outcome, about which she felt an almost paralyzing responsibility. Taking this felt "sin of omission" as its opening at her trial, the prosecution reframed her "responsibility" as legal guilt by highlighting critical junctures during Daniel's deterioration when Magdalena concealed the realities at home. The judge identified two heinous instances in his sentencing statement. Though she was aware Daniel was so hungry that he would take food from the school dumpster, Magdalena told his teachers to limit Daniel's food intake at school to the cheese and bread she provided. Moreover, she not only had failed to tell his caregivers about his abuse. Just a week before his murder, when she had taken Daniel for a pediatric exam, she had kept from the clinician the vital and potentially life-saving information that abuse by her live-in boyfriend was the source of Daniel's enigmatic medical and physical problems. I ask readers who are swayed by these facts to take on faith that I will reframe Magdalena's ostensible "collusion" in chapter 8 as instances of her resistance and refusal designed to expose Mariusz's abuse while minimizing harms to herself and Daniel, what I term "control in the context of no control." In that chapter, I locate Daniel's theft of food, his admission of those thefts to Mariusz, and the other behaviors used to portray him as a tragic innocent in his own demise as intentional and strategic vis-à-vis the spectrum of coercive control. Against this background, I go to great pains to explain the studied complicity of dozens of well-trained and generally well-intentioned professionals (including said teacher and pediatrician) in keeping the predicaments created by Mariusz for Daniel and Magdalena hidden until the situation resolved and/or a suitable scapegoat emerged for professional malfeasance. If we ultimately fail to fully explain why these and other "good" people do such "bad" things, we can, at least, point the way for them to do less harm in the future.

Much of the media reported Magdalena's claims that Mariusz had beaten, raped, and repeatedly threatened to kill her. But neither the legally required Serious Case Review (SCR) completed by a host of service professionals before the trial nor any of the commentators in the press connected this "admission" of abuse to Daniel's murder, let alone suggested that Magdalena's victimization might reduce her culpability for Daniel's death. To the contrary, several papers reported the testimony about her abuse beneath a photo of "the killer couple holding hands outside the courtroom."

I asked my audience, "What was the 'strongest' emotion evoked by the images?" I'd projected. Unsurprisingly, a large majority endorsed "outrage,"

"anger," "disgust," "revulsion," and similarly "very negative" views of Mariusz, with a small minority, a handful of men and several older women, offering "pity" or a slight variant. A much larger minority offered terms that fell into this latter category when I tapped Magdalena's photo, with some identifying "curiosity" or "puzzlement" as their strongest feeling, possibly anticipating what I had yet to say. Interestingly, at least when viewed with a jury in mind, men were as likely as women to feel "sympathy for Magdalena," though the majority of comments were negative. In fact, my nonscientific polling technique revealed that universal expressions of anger at Magdalena were more overt, even vengeful, than when I tapped her boyfriend, with at least two in the audience, one a woman in a police uniform, shouting "Shame!" Pockets of discontent persisted in the audience for several minutes. I let the room go quiet. Then I wondered out loud. Were these the same feelings that framed the responses to Mariusz, Magdalena, and Daniel by the more than fifty police, social workers, nurses, physicians, teachers, and school officials who interacted with the family in the year before the murder? How well could this family have been served by people harboring these images? After all, I would show, the family was seen by dozens of professionals who knew substantially the same details we now know about the family. The only thing they lacked was the final outcome, though this was predictable or *should* have been predicted from what was known. Even in the wake of Daniel's murder, neither the media nor the trial court showed the slightest appreciation of what it had been like *to be* Magdalena or Daniel in that home.

The "Knowledge" of Women as "Mothers"

The battered women's movement (as the shelter movement is known in the United States) had spent decades garnering recognition for abused women as legitimate claimants of public sympathy, services, and support. So, I was perplexed. As soon as Magdalena was categorized as a "mother," whatever benefits of doubt accrued in her favor because she was recognized as an "abused woman" gave way to an uncritical assessment of her failings. This was true even in an audience brought together under the rubric of Women's Aid and trained to place a premium on wife abuse. When the adjective "abused" was applied to "mother," instead of evoking the constraints on parenting Magdalena faced or the significance of her corresponding efforts to protect Daniel in the face of those constraints, it appeared to evoke deficits in her role or character as a mother. From the vantage of my professional audience, an "abused mother" was someone who was tragically fated to get herself into the sort of trouble that leads to the deterioration in parenting so often remarked on in these cases. This juxtaposition of two social ideas that should have been contradictory, abuse as a deliberate constraint on liberty and "motherhood" as the free development of feminine personhood through parenting, robbed both of their subversive content, thereby denuding subjects of political agency. As an abused mother, Magdalena could function neither as an "abused woman" nor as a "mother who was being subjected to abuse."

This look at how one professional audience in Edinburgh responded to a child who was murdered in the context of wife abuse opens the discussion of the predicament posed to children by coercive control. Note, an abused child faces a predicament not simply because of coercive control but also because of how those responsible for protection "recognize" what women and children are experiencing and respond. The composite responses I critique throughout the book are drawn from my experience with dozens of such audiences, those that were physically and virtually present at lectures, trainings, webinars, workshops, classes, and the like and those whose proxy was a ruling, judgment, recommendation, and/or production of a body of research/writing that bears directly on our subject. In each instance, what is marked is that the prevailing way of seeing or knowing the child and their mother as "abused" serves to simultaneously conceal the significance of what is happening to them, effectively rendering them—and the man who is subordinating them—"invisible in plain sight." In some cases, one has to read between the lines to appreciate the extent to which abuse was "known" by the professionals involved in a case.[3] But in most instances, the fact of an abusive history was not in doubt. And yet, after reading these files, it would be easy to conclude, as it had been apparently in Luczak's case, that the meticulously documented deterioration of these women and children caused by abuse was instead the inevitable byproduct of an unknown force of nature, however tragic, something akin to the rare metabolic disorder for which the pediatrician searched during Daniel Pelka's last medical visit.

Most of those in my Edinburgh audience had been trained to sympathetically identify the sort of domestic violence occurring in the Luczak case, to recognize the associated risks to children and to intervene accordingly. The point my lecture-in-reverse had demonstrated was that something about Magdalena's status as an abused mother, that is, a subtype of mother with particular deficits, kept the myriad professionals involved with the family from recognizing her as an "abused woman," taking into account that she also happened to be a mother, and responding as they'd been trained to do. Note what a critical difference this alteration in perception makes. If we start from the premise that Magdalena's maternal role and her related choices are contingent on her feminine personhood, then maintaining her integrity as a woman with needs-in-her-own-right is taken as the essential ground for the successful performance of all secondary roles, including parenting. In layperson's terms, this simply means that strengthening her capacities as a woman will probably make her better at everything she does, including parenting. In practice this meant stopping the abuse in the most direct way possible. Daniel would almost certainly be still alive had Mariusz been held to account for his abuse of Magdalena. But if we start instead from the presumption that "abuse" is a "condition" rather than a criminal act and signals maternal incapacity, what options have we short of emergency rescue?

Like Daniel Pelka, most of the children you meet in following chapters could have thrived had the men who killed or severely injured them been properly held to account for their *prior known abuse* of their wives or partners *who were also mothers.* As in Magdalena's case, so too in many of these others: Once feminine identity was viewed through the narrow window of the maternal role, the woman's needs and capacities in her own right took on diminished importance. From there forward, attempts by these women to meet their own needs in ways that were not perceived as tied directly to their child's needs, or worse were interpreted as aggravating their children's problems, were thought to constitute willful obstruction of the child's well-being.

All of the women in this book were abused. And all were also mothers. When a woman is coercively controlled, all her decision-making is contingent on establishing the ground where the least constrained choices are possible, including her decision-making as a parent. The extent to which their coercive control *as women* also compromised the *parenting* of the "mothers" in this book is an empirical question examined in chapter 4 and in the particular case studies. Nothing I say is meant to deny that coercive control undermines a woman's capacities as a mother or to minimize how harmful the resulting deprivations are for children. Nor do I downplay the direct effects on children of being coercively controlled. These effects can be extreme even when the mother is not being physically abused. To the contrary, I examine at length "child abuse as tangential spouse abuse," a devastating but common scenario in which the core dynamic involves hurting, intimidating, and constraining the autonomy of children as a primary means to coercively control the woman who is the children's mother. In such cases, even though the mother remains the primary victim, the child can be the object of serious, even fatal, harm. The cases also examine how the women and children subjected to these constraints responded to coercive control and with what lasting scars to flourish as individuals and nourish others. My story is about overcoming adversity through continued struggle and survival, not through its conquest, let alone avoidance or the absence of suffering. Those who survive coercive control carry the scars of endurance throughout their lives. In several cases, I track the costs for children who survive coercive control into the next generation. Even broaching the question of how women can "mother through domestic violence," as my friend the feminist scholar Marianne Hester puts it, is impossible if we start by portraying "abused mothers" as the sort of women who have already made poor choices for themselves and their children to start (including, in at least one instances, the choice to mother in the first place) and so are unable to do anything protective now by definition.

2

The "Abused Woman" and "The Invisible Man"

This chapter provides case illustrations that highlight two obstacles that confound recognition of coercive control as the context for child maltreatment, the belief that an "abused mother" is a contradiction in terms and the willful disappearance of abusive men as the source of harms to women and children. These cases, each in a different way, also illustrate a common theme in the book, how the narrow focus of criminal and family courts on "domestic violence" has the effect of trivializing the abuse-related offense of coercive control, masking both the extent of the offense involved and its scope, particularly the degree to which it encompasses children.

Introduction

When police and the courts fail to recognize the predicament of the child as a covictim of coercive control, courts unjustly blame victims, make the perpetrators of abuse invisible, and contribute to the entrapment and death of children. In 2015, after nearly two years of demonstrations, numerous consultations, initiatives by police and Scotland's chief procurator fiscal (prosecutor), the Scottish government unanimously adopted (132-0) a new serious offense that fully incorporated the coercive control definition that encompassed children. That battle was engaged. This chapter considers five cases, four that are relatively current and one, the case of Hedda Nussbaum, that is considered a classic in the field of child maltreatment.

On July 7, 2015, the father of seven-month-old Aedan Moreno threw him off a bridge in Connecticut after his mother turned him over for visitation. The transfer of the child had been ordered by Judge Pinkus of the Connecticut Family Court.

Aedan Moreno was killed as part of a campaign of coercive control. But the death would have been prevented if the courts had correctly interpreted the

Children of Coercive Control. Evan Stark, Oxford University Press. © Oxford University Press 2023.
DOI: 10.1093/oso/9780197587096.003.0003

elements of abuse presented by Aedan and his mother, Adrianna Oyola. By this time, Connecticut judges had coercive control in their toolbox. Instead, they applied stereotypes of domestic violence and abused mothers. Unlike the Court, Adrianna was only familiar with a domestic violence account of abuse. Nevertheless, she did everything she could to bring Judge Pinkus's attention to the elements of her experience that felt abusive but were not strictly physical. No matter. All the Court cared about was whether the physical abuse had been emergent. It was not. So the Court not only ignored the broader context of the abuse; it responded punitively to the mother's pleas and in ways that directly contributed to the boy's murder.

Next, we look at the case of Santos Miranda and the biological double-standard applied to excuse him for his child's death because of his youth (age twenty-one years) while holding the mother fully accountable at seventeen. Without a biological link to the child, he has no legal obligation to "protect"; but nor is his abuse of his partner recognized as the reason she "allowed" him to hurt the child. This case highlights the extent to which the "coercive control of children" crosses social space behind "the assumption of intimacy" regardless of legal marriage.

The third case I consider is Tondalo Hall, a woman serving a thirty-year sentence in Oklahoma as the result of serious injuries inflicted by her husband to her two-year-old son. Like Adrianna, Tondalo did everything she could to protect their son. Again the Court only attached importance to the physical assaults against the mother, which were deemed not that serious. As a result, the husband, who coercively controlled Tondalo and the boy, whom he nearly killed, received a short prison term and was back at home with the boy when Tondalo went to jail.

The next case comes from my forensic practice. Frank K., a Vietnam vet, is the only father who makes a live appearance in the children's files I review for this book. Following a recommendation from the Connecticut Department of Child Welfare, the Family Court gave Frank K. custody of my client's two teenage daughters, whom he admitted having physically and sexually abused. Sarah, the mother, refused Frank K. access to the girls, in large part because of his ongoing coercive control of her and the girls. This infuriated Child Welfare and the Court. To them, Sarah's "abuse problem" was "in the past," ended with the separation, and it was her intransigence, not Frank's abuse, that threatened the girls' happiness." Again, we find Child Welfare and the Court—but not the abused mother and her children—confounded by the spatial dimension of coercive control. Whether because of naïveté or

malevolent intent, we find Child Welfare and the Court coercively controlling the children.

I close the chapter by resurrecting the feminist screeds leveled at Hedda
Nussbaum in 1987 as a "killer mom" after her live-in boyfriend Joel
Steinberg tortured and murdered seven-year-old Lisa Steinberg, their
adopted daughter. The public excoriation of Hedda Nussbaum in this notorious case illustrates how deeply ambivalent many erstwhile supporters of
women's rights become when the defense of those rights exposes the relative vulnerability of children. At the root of this confusion is the failure to
recognize coercive control as a situated pattern of domination of all parties,
including children, with a manifest interest in women's independence in personal space.

Courts are most likely to trivialize abuse-related offenses against the
mother when violence against the mother has not been dramatic—as in
the Hall case. But even when violence is extreme, as it was against Hedda
Nussbaum, the courts project their own failure to recognize and manage the
course of abusive conduct onto the victim as a "failure to protect" the children. The case analyses presented in this chapter are meant to illustrate how
police, child welfare agencies, schools, and other "institutions of secondary
socialization" respond to abuse cases, namely by simultaneously masking
and legitimating the dynamics of coercive control in families.

None of the mothers in these cases had harmed their children. Yet they
were either held equally responsible for the child's harm or more responsible
than the men who perpetrated the harm, as in the Hall and Frank K. cases.

In each of these cases, the evidence that the mother and children were
being subjected to coercive control was transparent early on, and today, in
a number of countries and some US jurisdictions, would be sufficient to remove and charge the offenders with coercive control. Had the courts been
operating with an understanding of coercive control or had a spectrum offense of coercive control been in place, these women and children would not
have suffered as they did.

Adrianna Oyola and the Killing of Aedan Moreno

Another week. Another headline. This one, more clearly than the others, was
directly attributable to a failure to protect, though not on the part of the usual

suspects. The CNN headline (July 15, 2015) read, "Father Charged in Infant's Death after Jumping off Bridge."

On the evening of July 7, 2015, the body of seven-month old Aedan Moreno was found in the river by a person canoeing near a bridge in East Haddam, Connecticut. Two days earlier, the boy's twenty-two-year-old father, Tony Moreno, had thrown him into the river before jumping in himself. Moreno's jump had been reported and he was rescued by police, revived, and charged with murder aggravated by his child's age.

The infant's mother, Adrianna Oyola, had made her first documented attempt to limit Tony's access to their son three weeks earlier. On June 17, 2015, her request for a temporary restraining order was heard by Superior Court Judge Edward Domnarski. In her application, Oyola wrote that her husband had become abusive when he learned she was pregnant. She detailed his physical violence (which was mostly low-level); his threats against herself and the baby, including a prophetic threat to make both of them "disappear"; his attempts to monitor or stalk her; and his attempts isolate her and control her life. He called her "ugly" and "stupid" and shoved, pushed, and "forcefully poked" Oyola's chest. When she told him to stop hitting her, she wrote, "He told me, 'if you want me to show you hitting I could show you.'" She also described how he yelled for the baby to "shut up" when he was making too much noise and told her "he could make my son disappear any time of the day." She reported she was sometimes "too scared to sleep." He also told her how he would get away with killing her, "by putting me in the ground . . . (with) something to make me disintegrate faster." She was not allowed to bring (the baby) around her family without his approval, "but he could do anything *he* wants without letting me know." She insisted her husband posed a danger to herself and their child and asked the court for a Protective Order and full custody. "I'm afraid he's going to do something to my son," she wrote. "He's angry and . . . isn't thinking straight." It would be hard to manufacture a more complete and straightforward description of coercive control, its consequences, and the potential risks it poses for serious or fatal harm to targeted women and children.

Coercive control was once covered, but then was removed from the domestic violence education provided for Connecticut judges and was only incorporated into Connecticut's Protective Order statute in 2020. So, Judge Domnarski may have been unaware that frequent, but generally low-level violence of the sort described by Oyola is the hallmark of physical assault in coercive control cases; that her description of the other abuse tactics, the stalking, isolation, name-calling, and threats against her and the baby, fit the pattern of coercive control; and that such a history, in combination with the threats to kill the baby and high level of reported fear indicated the child was at the gravest risk of homicide from the father. Connecticut is one of the few states that has no requirement with respect to the consideration of domestic violence evidence in family cases. Nevertheless, a few years earlier, Connecticut Family Court judges were introduced to a system of "dangerousness assessment," developed by Professor Jacqueline Campbell and her colleagues at Johns Hopkins University, that identifies the highest level of risk with stalking, violence during pregnancy, a recent separation, specific threats against the child, and other elements that Oyola described. The DAS is close enough to a picture of coercive control to have alerted the Court. The judge could also directly observe Adrianne's extreme fear and was compelled by this direct evidence to take the threats to make the child "disappear" and to put Adrianna "in the ground" literally. Judge Domnarski responded within his responsibility; he signed the temporary order.

Other critical factors that indicated that Mr. Moreno posed a serious threat to Adrianna and Aedan were identified by a state marshal who served the restraining order on June 17. The marshal reported that Mr. Moreno had no car and no job and had smashed his cell phone earlier in the day. What is obvious in retrospect should have been apparent to seasoned professionals. Moreno was cutting his ties to the outside world; he had nothing more to lose, and might carry out his threats or take his own life.

The same day as the court hearing, child welfare authorities received a report regarding Mr. Moreno, "the father." According to a spokesperson for the Department of Children and Families (DCF), they "conducted a complete safety assessment" that found the husband no longer in the home (because of the temporary court order). After three subsequent visits between June 19 and June 26, they reported the mother had moved the baby to the home of a relative, was complying with the DCF recommendation she seek counseling, and was "taking all appropriate and necessary steps to protect the baby."[1] But DCF did nothing to help ensure the child's long-term safety. Official policy of Connecticut's DCF in such cases is to "hold the offender accountable." Here, Mr. Moreno might as well have not existed. He lacks an "address" sociologically speaking, an example of "invisibility." Note: Though Mr. Moreno was the subject of the report, there is no record that caseworkers interviewed or even contacted the father, let alone took steps to direct him to appropriate services (such as batterer counseling) as they did Adrianna. Had they done even a minimal investigation or risk assessment, they would have at least been able to document what the state marshal had learned about Mr. Moreno and so provide critical testimony on behalf of mother and child at the hearing for a permanent order. Any of these steps would have significantly reduced their risks and would possibly have saved the child's life.

A reader might share the relief caseworkers felt to learn Moreno was out of the house. But caseworkers in Connecticut are trained to see abuse as an "ongoing course of conduct," which almost always continues when a couple is separated or divorced. In fact, a majority of partner assaults are against women who are single, separated, or divorced rather than "married." While the move may have made the child temporarily safer, a more accurate assessment would have viewed his risk as high because of the mother's risk. In coercive control, physical separation changes the means by which power is exercised, but it does not change the illegitimate use of power to control, exploit, and subordinate a partner. An appropriate response to the separation would have been enhanced advocacy to enforce an OP with "no contact" with mother and child.

On June 25, Oyola reported that Moreno had contacted her in violation of the restraining order and police applied for an arrest warrant. The warrant was returned for revisions. But police saw no need to rush the order since, according to Middletown Police Lieutenant Heather Desmond, "the two of them just talked" and "there was no imminent danger." Of course, it was precisely through his "talk" that Moreno had conveyed his intention to make her and the baby "disappear." Had they perceived, assessed, or understood the nonviolent coercive and "control" elements in the case, assessed risk based on Oyola's relative vulnerability as well as the child's, Moreno's self-isolation, the tactics he used to intimidate Oyola, or even the verbal threats in the original petition, police would have personally walked the warrant through the process, significantly reducing the risks Moreno posed to mother and child. Note, the danger Moreno posed to Aedan and which the boy faced was a function of his anger at his wife and was not reflected in his relation to his son. This dynamic holds the key to the coercive control of children, that the child's risk is a function of the total level of power and control being exerted on the dyad, irrespective of how it is allocated, if only because the child is the visible symbol of the wife's resilience.

The final opportunity to save the child came on June 29, 2015, when Oyola and Moreno came before Superior Court Judge Barry C. Pinkus to hear Oyola's petition to make the restraining order permanent. The plaintiff in these hearings alleged that the defendant had hurt her in the past and was likely to do so again if not constrained. Abusers frequently interpret the order itself as a provocation. If he has obeyed the spirit of the order (even if not its letter), the court hearing can be the first opportunity to confront his partner since she got the order and reassert his power over her. If the abuser has violated the order—as Moreno had—he has very likely intimidated or attempted to intimidate his partner by informing her of the consequences of persisting. In either case, a major challenge courts face is how to bridge the seeming contradiction between allowing a defendant his constitutional right to confront his accuser in a case where a judge has already issued a "no con-tact" order based on evidence that such a confrontation may be extremely dangerous to the woman the court order is designed to protect. Conversely, the court must get accurate information about abuse from a mother who has undoubtedly been warned about the consequences of challenging her partner, let alone shaming him publicly. The abuser, meanwhile, has been told to "cool it" by his lawyer and knows that a calm demeanor can con-vince the new judge that he has either calmed down or that the first judge "overreacted." The disquieting effect of the woman's exposure to her abusive partner in court and the related possibility that she will minimize his abuse makes it imperative that a judge put her remarks in the context of events described in written statements, reports by third parties or agencies, and other proceedings or venues.

Even with Moreno present, Oyola repeated her allegations about his abuse, though they were muted, particularly with respect to his physical vi-olence. Oyola told the judge she was "sometimes" afraid he would beat her and feared "he was always there" when she heard cars stop in front of her house, a reference to his earlier stalking. Neither lead was explored by the judge. Instead, following the letter of Connecticut Law, Judge Pinkus was only interested in whether Oyola felt she was in immediate physical danger, which she did not, in no small part because of Moreno's relative compliance with the TPO. When the judge asked her about the physical violence, Oyola emphasized that Moreno's abuse was mainly "mental," though she added that he was constantly "pushing me around and just abusive" and added that he had slapped and punched her. Though he may have done so, there is nothing in the record to suggest that Judge Pinkus reviewed the written or oral tran-script of the earlier hearing, the DCF report, the report by the state marshal or the police warrant application for violating the restraining order. He asked no specific questions about the basis for Oyola's fears for the child or for herself. Nor did he ask Moreno about his threats or his violence. Given his sole focus on physical violence, however, it is unclear whether Judge Pinkus would have responded differently even if he was aware of the threats to kill her and their infant son.

Judge Pinkus delivered his orders in a Connecticut Family Court in 2015. Today, coercive control is recognized by statute in Connecticut as a basis for an order of protection. Family judges in Australia, Canada, England, Northern Ireland, France, or Scotland, and in California and some other US states would recognize Oyola's description of "mental abuse" as an indicator of possible coercive control and would be prompted to open questioning about degradation, intimidation, and asking, "how did he control your life?" in areas like money, eating, sleep, childcare, and going and coming. In addition, the threats to Aedan could have been framed as facets of the coercive control warranting a protective order in California, Connecticut, Hawaii, Massachusetts, New York, and several other US states. Instead of eliciting the extensive history of coercive control, Judge Pinkus addressed the couple's age and immaturity. He told the couple:

> "You're not giving me grown up behavior . . . . You're parents now. Okay? And if you want your child to grow up to be healthy and well, you need to grow up and deal with each other as adults, and you're not doing that right now."

Judge Pinkus addressed Oyola as if she could achieve the equal playing field she sought through the protection order simply by growing up. Not only is seeking court protection for oneself and one's child a constitutional and legal right but also it is the first-line remedy most often recommended by police, child welfare, and shelters in abuse cases. By defining Oyola's effort to secure court protection for herself and her child as "immature," Judge Pinkus substituted his own moral compass for steps DCF has rightly identified as "necessary" and "appropriate." This was a variant on what we'd heard in Scotland in response to the insistence that Magdalena Luczak could not be both an "abused" and a "good" mother. The TPO had worked to significantly reduce the danger to mother and child, by creating a physical separation that her husband could breach only at a legal risk to himself. The coercive control framework anticipates that abusers will change their tactics in this circumstance, deploying means to "cross the social space" created by the TPO such as stalking or electronic surveillance or by changing his target to the minor child. Had Judge Pinkus put the de-escalation into the perspective afforded by the record, he would have recognized the need to reinforce the TPO, not to suspend it.

In 2015, Judge Pinkus found that Tony Moreno did not pose the "imminent" or "continuous threat of present physical pain of physical injury" required by law and denied the request. Even as he noted the relationship was not "good" (*sic*) and in "chaos," he instructed the couple to work together to forge a parental rights agreement. The probability that Mr. Moreno would or even could engage in any sort of "rational" negotiation about visitation (or any other facet of the relationship) was belied by his past violence, threats, stalking, acts of control, his depressed and obsessive state, and his declarations that he could do what he wanted with her and the child, but that she would need his permission just to bring the child to her parents' home. Thus, the judge's order placed the entire burden on Oyola (whom he deemed "immature") to negotiate with a man who had no desire or capacity to do so about access to her and their child that would endanger them both.

Apologia and Response

After Moreno killed his son, Connecticut's victim advocate, Michele Cruz, published a sober, but scathing critique of Judge Pinkus's behavior in the *Connecticut Law Journal*. In response to the article as well as to other questions raised about the judge's behavior by myself, legislators, advocates, and the press, Connecticut's Chief Court Administrator Patrick L. Carroll, issued a vigorous defense of Judge Pinkus. After extending perfunctory condolences to Aedan's family, Judge Carroll described the "difficult choice" Judge Pinkus faced as "representative of the difficult decision that judges must make each and every day." This difficulty, according to the judge, reflected having to balance the safety of abused women in issuing restraining orders against the constitutionally protected "liberty rights" of alleged offenders. Judge Carroll III said nothing about the standards that should be applied in such cases, let alone about whether Judge Pinkus had, in fact, applied these standards.

I never testified before Judge Pinkus and have no reason to think he is less sensitive or knowledgeable than other sitting magistrates in Connecticut or elsewhere. Nor am I personally acquainted with Judge Carroll. But if Judge Carroll is right, if Judge Pinkus's decision-making process is "representative" of how even a minority of Connecticut family judges approach cases involving domestic violence or the issuances of protection orders, it is deeply worrisome. As we saw, Judge Pinkus failed to conduct even the most cursory review of the record, focused his questioning on the letter of the statute, but ignored its legislative intent and public purpose, and substituted his parochial moralism and irresponsible advice for the types of instructions that are recommended even when a motion for an order is rejected (such as telling a plaintiff that his decision should not discourage her from pursuing making subsequent motions). My guess is that Judge Carroll has little idea what the standard of practice is with respect to domestic violence matters because, until a public relations nightmare like the murder of Aedan Oyola occurs, there is little oversight or accountability. It is no secret here in Connecticut that even the most robust judicial leadership is at risk if an acknowledgment of an internal failing in the courts catches a political eye. Even so, it behooved the chief court administrator, to reassure the child's surviving family and the public that he would review the child's death—such a review is a legal requirement in the United Kingdom—and ensure full cooperation in any investigation.

Judge Carroll would not have had to look far to find an instance where his use of "discretion" in assigning custody to an abusive dad had led Judge Pinkus to a "difficult decision" with equally tragic outcomes. In a 2007 Family Court custody case, this time brought with the support of the Connecticut's DCF as well as the Department of Probation, Joshua Komisarjevsky sought full custody of his daughter, charging the teenage mother with "alienating" the girl's affections from her father and with drug abuse, though neither charge was substantiated. Komisarjevsky came to court with an electronic bracelet because of his abuse of Jennifer Norton and had a long criminal history and history of psychiatric and behavioral problems that included molesting his adopted sister. Nevertheless, with DCF at his back, Judge Pinkus stripped Norton of custody, citing her "immaturity" as a factor, and awarded full custody to Komisarjevsky. Not only had the Court missed evidence that Komisarjevsky coercively controlled Norton, but also the extension of the coercive control to the child. Had Komisarjevsky been charged with coercive control of Norton, his case for custody of his daughter would never have come to court and he would likely have been convicted of a serious offense before committing his most serious crime.

In June 2007 the judicial branch's family relations counselors reviewed Komisarjevsky custody case and determined that he and Norton were appropriate candidates for a "conflict resolution conference," which they scheduled for August 2007. The date is significant. A month before Norton was to meet with him for "conflict resolution," on July 22, 2007, Komisarjevsky and another parolee committed a robbery in which they raped and murdered a mother and her two teenage daughters while the father, Dr. William Petit, lay tied up and brutally beaten in the basement. Komisarjevsky left his daughter with his mother during these family murders. Later on, his mother was the person he blamed for his problems.

The "Protectors": Santos Miranda vs. Connecticut

As described earlier, Judge Pinkus displayed a shocking degree of insensitivity to the predicament Oyola faced because seeking protection for herself infuriated Moreno, increasing Aeden's danger. Each year in the United States and United Kingdom, several thousand women who face similar predicaments when their children are hurt or killed by their father, stepfather, or father-surrogate are charged criminally with "failure to protect," "risk of injury," or a variant. In seven US states, convictions for this crime carry a possible sentence of life in prison. The crime is heavily gendered. Fathers or other male partners are almost never charged with "failure to protect," even when they were present and failed to prevent a mother from killing a child.

Another Connecticut case is instructive because, in reversing a conviction in 1996, the Appellate Court made its gendered rules explicit.[2] This case did not involve allegations of wife abuse.

Twenty-one-year-old Santos Miranda moved in with his sixteen-year-old girlfriend and her children, a two-year-old and a newborn, in January 1993. Four months later, he called 911 when his girlfriend's four-month-old daughter was choking on milk. At the hospital, it was discovered the baby had broken ribs, two skull fractures, and other injuries, which Santos had caused. Miranda's girlfriend accepted a sentence of seven years in a plea agreement for "failure to protect." She denied hurting the children, and there was no evidence that she had. Neither was there physical evidence that Santos hurt the children. Nevertheless, the trial court found that the nature of the injuries, the prominence of the child's suffering, and the role he assumed as their surrogate caretaker gave Miranda responsibility to protect the children from abuse and he received a ten-year sentence for risk-of-injury as well as a thirty-year prison sentence on six counts of assault in the first degree. Miranda appealed, arguing in part that, since he had no biological relationship to the child, he was not legally obligated to protect.

The Connecticut Supreme Court upheld the appeal and threw out the assault charges and sentence, concluding that Mr. Miranda's constitutional rights to due process had been violated since "he couldn't be expected to know he was violating the law when he failed to protect the victim, secure medical attention for her or to report the situation to authorities." They cited his age (twenty-one years), the fact he was unemployed, and that he was not the biological father of either child. The Court upheld the "risk of injury" conviction, however. Although there was no direct evidence he had inflicted the injuries to the child, there was overwhelming circumstantial evidence that he had either done so and/or was aware of the child's suffering during the months they were occurring.

This double standard that will surface repeatedly in this book, where a child dies or is seriously hurt, almost certainly as the result of a man's action, and the mother and partner are charged. Here, the Appeal Court excuses Mr. Miranda because of his youth (twenty-one) and the absence of a biological relation to the children, whereas the mother's biological status mitigates any advantage to be gained from her youth (seventeen). No one asked my opinion in the Santos case because there were no claims of wife-abuse. But even in cases like this one, where we have bare facts and no mention of wife abuse, there are two forensic "mysteries": Why did the mother "allow" torturous abuse of the infant on her watch? And why did the twenty-one-year-old partner brutalize the newborn but not harm the two-year-old? In our subsequent discussion of coercive control, we learn that selective victimization is an intimidation tactic in evidence where one child becomes the surrogate for the partner, the "whipping boy," who is punished to discipline her. "Scapegoating" a child is particularly common in abuse cases like this once, where the partner's "offer" to share parenting responsibilities is really a threat to take a child hostage, in this instance so Santos could ensure she would do his bidding at work, keep the secret, and return home promptly. Santos's defense, that he had no biological relation to the children and therefore was not emotionally invested in his care, is precisely what puts the child at high risk from his coercive control in this case. Had the prosecutor been aware of coercive control, the mother would have been a key witness in strong case against Santos from which neither his youth nor his lack of ties to the children would have protected him.

Battered mothers are held to the standard of *strict liability*. The Connecticut Court excused Santos Miranda because, since he was neither husband nor father, he could not be expected to protect and seek prompt care for a victim child simply because he was aware of the child's injuries or *should* have been aware. By contrast, his girlfriend is responsible despite her age since she is the mother regardless of whether she was present when the injuries were inflicted or was even aware the child was hurt. Strict liability cannot mean what it suggests, that there are *no* circumstances in which a mother is excused from her duty to protect.

As readers may suspect, the reality in these cases is often complicated: the coercive control of children, like woman abuse generally, rarely involves an isolated act, but almost always involves a pattern of mistreatment that occurs over a period that can last days, weeks, months, or even years and is "known" to some extent to everyone in a household as well as to many others in contact with persons in the household. Later in the book, I return to the murder of Daniel Pelka, a case in which several hundred people, including dozens of health professionals, teachers, and police, had access during critical periods to a child who was being killed, including dozens of professionals qualified in child protection. Not all personal or even "clinical" knowledge is legal knowledge of course, and it is too glib to suggest that identifying signs of trouble retrospectively means a child could or should have been saved. My point here is that with nonoffending victimized mothers, the answer to whether a victimized woman was aware of a threat to her child is rarely a simple "yes" or "no." Every victimized woman is aware that the man who is hurting her is also harming children in the house, though she rarely is a party to the extent of the harm even if she is willing to acknowledge it. The forensic challenge—and the question readers should ask—is whether, in a particular case, the constraints under which a person is operating can reasonably be expected to prevent them from "knowing" and acting effectively on what they know. Were the same constraints that limited her information about other key aspects of their lives—such as their savings, his children by other women, or her husband's drug use—also limiting her information about her children? Moreover, if she could "see" what was happening to the children—that her daughter was losing weight for example, or that her son was obsessing about a video game—could she bring that knowledge to awareness without experiencing the risk associated with feeling compelled to do something? At the extreme, in coercive control cases where surveillance and threats of harm are pervasive, abused mothers self-censor "dangerous thoughts" and perceptions before they surface, including the perception that their child is dying, a condition known as "perspecticide." In this condition, they truly do not know what they know. This is illustrated in the Barahona case, in one of our final chapters, when Carmen shifted her attention from the twins, whom Jorge was torturing and starving, to her other children, and focused on her protective instincts rather than on what could happen to her if she intervened. The point I emphasize throughout is that stopping the coercive control of the woman/mother in these cases almost always protects the child and avoids the ethical thicket created by trying to balance a victim's accountability for her child's harm against her capacity for safe, deliberate action.

Given the reality, that the most common scenario involves interventions by mothers that are sadly inadequate rather than an absolute paralysis of cognition and action, the courts allow a woman charged with "risk of injury" or "failure to protect" to claim she was acting under "duress," and faced threats of violence against herself or other family members that made her too fearful to report promptly or rendered her otherwise incapable of preventing the abuse. I've had little success with these defenses, however, even with clients who suffered horrific, long-standing physical abuse and faced hostage-like levels of entrapment replete with comprehensive financial regulation, stalking and other forms of surveillance, and extreme isolation. In theory, terroristic forms of coercive control can be as paralyzing as physical constraint. But the duress defense retains a substantial subjective element: since both the threat and the response are identified on a gradient, supernatural standards of maternal resiliency are brought to bear that can present a barrier to sympathy that is nearly insurmountable. The standards of harm applied in these cases are drawn not to a transparent legal norm, least of all one rooted in the notion of women as full persons with the same rights and liberties as other equal persons, but to a retributive standard of gendered justice based on popular sentiment that "someone must pay" when a child is harmed.[3] That "someone" is almost always the woman, because she is deemed the "only (responsible) adult" in the room by default because she is also "the mother." By contrast with a duress defense, a coercive control defense sets out objective descriptions of coercion and control such as "entrapment," "isolation," and subordination ("He made me into his servant"), etc., that correspond to specific deficits in personhood, liberty, autonomy, and dignity that are incompatible with legal responsibility. Here, "will" is conceived as a political attribute requiring the space for action provided by "rights," not only as a physical or psychological space.

In this book, I return repeatedly to the challenges posed by the propensity for social agencies, police, and the courts to blame mothers when their children are hurt or killed regardless of the extent to which their capacity for independent action has been eviscerated. To Judge Pinkus and the many judges who share his views, "the abused mother" doesn't describe an existential predicament in parenting created by an "abusive father," but a form of "immaturity," a failure of femininity that invites the sanction of law (as a "failure to protect"), with none of the subjective historical weight we associate with justice. Suffice it to say that the abused mother appears as an oxymoron only so long as she stands with her child alone in the room, and the abusive man remains invisible as a source of power.

Most of the women in my caseload fail to attract public notice. But among those who do, those charged with failure to protect or risk of injury invariably are demonized by the press, much in the same ways as was Oyola, the mother in the Santos case, Luczak in England, or Nussbaum in New York. The numerous strategies these women devised to protect their children go unnoticed. They are not only convicted at very high rates but also often punished more harshly than the partner who has actually inflicted the serious or fatal injuries. One example is illustrative.

Tondalo Hall

In September 2015, I sent one of several thousand letters received to urge the Oklahoma Pardon and Parole Board to commute the thirty-year sentence of Tondalo Hall after the nine years she'd already been imprisoned.[4]

In 2004, Hall brought her two-year-old son to the hospital with serious injuries. When police investigated, they found that Hall's three-month-old daughter had also been abused. She and her husband, Robert Braxton II, were arrested, then interrogated together. Braxton repeatedly threatened his wife before, during, and after the interrogation. He admitted he had hurt their son, and Hall took a "blind plea." This meant she accepted responsibility for allowing the abuse to happen and left her sentence to the judge's discretion. She told prosecutors that Braxton had abused her as well. The prosecutors promised her leniency if she told the truth about her husband's abuse of her and the children. So far so good. The only possible confounder was that the prosecutorial motive in seeking Hall's testimony about her own abuse was to pursue Braxton for the child's abuse, which carried the more serious penalty.

During the trial, as she'd promised, Hall testified against her husband. This took considerable courage, since he had threatened to kill her if she turned against him. But the judge excluded the testimony about his abuse of her as prejudicial, because she also faced charges with respect to the child, and as irrelevant to whether he had hurt their children, including her claim that he had strangled her during pregnancy. Without the evidence that she was being constrained by her husband, Hall appeared to be culpable for failing to stop him from hurting their son. Because of the judge's ruling and the prosecutor's failure to build a strong case against Braxton apart from Hall's testimony, the prosecution case against him collapsed and Braxton was allowed to plead guilty to the crime to which he'd already confessed. He was sentenced to two years and promptly released from prison for time served. However, the prosecutors were furious at Hall because, they believed, she had minimized Braxton's violence against the children. They asked for and got a sentence that was fifteen times greater than her husband's.

The Oklahoma Pardon Board rejected the petitions and our letters. Hall was released in 2019, after serving fifteen years, after a national campaign identified nineteen women serving sentences of ten years or more in eleven states for "failure to protect."

The Hall-Braxton case presents an all-too-common scenario in which preconceptions about the "abused mother" lead to her being sanctioned when a child is harmed even more harshly than the man who committed the offense. Hall was not home when Braxton hurt their child. But nor, in the public's mind, was there anything about *him* that motivated the crime. To the contrary, news coverage of the trial juxtaposed reports of the injuries Braxton caused his two-year-old son to descriptions of him as an otherwise "caring" father and as "reserved," i.e., nothing like the man we conjure as the typical "child beater." Like so many similar stories where journalists provide the proximate context for school shootings or other horrendous crimes with facile observations from neighbors who possess only superficial knowledge of the killer, coverage before and during the trial left the impression that Braxton had simply "cracked." But why? What drove him to it?

Braxton did not look like a child abuser because he may not have disliked his son. Braxton hurt his child as a way to dominate his wife. The abuse in the Hall-Braxton home followed the logic of coercive control. To start, Hall was the victim of a pattern of coercive control that included physical abuse, but whose primary components consisted of intimidation, degradation and control, exploitation of time and money, deprivation of basic resources, and the regulation of her daily life. Braxton "abused" the children and controlled her access to them and how she spent time with them as a means to manipulate and control her, the pattern I call "child abuse as tangential spouse abuse." Hall took the stand prepared to describe the full range of deprivations she had suffered. Had she been allowed to do so, she could have helped a jury understand both the extent to which Braxton was solely responsible for harming the children and, as importantly, his motive for doing do, to control her and the household. Recognizing his "secondary" motive for hurting the children also explained the apparent inconsistency between Braxton's brutality toward the children and his being a "good" and "caring" father. By contrast, if the jury was allowed to see him only as a "father," they could reconcile the description of him as "caring" with his relatively minor physical abuse of the children. Apart from the assault that led Tondalo Hall to take their son to the hospital, most of his abuse of the children *was* minor. This was because Braxton hurt the children largely to get his wife to comply with his demands. In this scenario, all of which Tondalo witnessed, he would mainly shake his fist as *if* to hit the child, become passive-aggressive to the extreme while offering to caretake (the posture mistaken as "reserved") or would smack a child inappropriately, the occasions for the less serious abuse. This was almost always sufficient to elicit the response he wanted from Hall. It is Hall's ready compliance that limits Braxton's abuse of the children, the dynamic that indicates it is "tangential spouse abuse."

Had the prosecution envisioned Hall as a fully empowered woman, it could have conjured an imago of her in the jury's mind that matched the foe Braxton sought to bring low by hurting the children. As it was, judge, jury, and the prosecution grew impatient with the emphasis Hall placed on the humiliation she suffered. Race is not mentioned as an issue in the case file, nor in the appellate briefs. But Hall is Black, and there is strong anecdotal evidence that racial bias prevented the prosecution from assigning her the same honorific status as they would have a white woman, and so with crediting the harms caused by her being abused.[5]

At home, Braxton could keep Hall subservient by degrading her and with relatively minor assaults on the children. When Hall returned to work outside the home, however, a seeming necessity that had been the topic of endless family negotiation, the precarious status quo was ended. Countless phone calls to Hall at work elicited promises and reassurances that were too distal to placate Braxton's torrid fantasies of her transgressions and omissions, acts of disloyalty to him, most imagined, for which his wife had to be punished.

Whereas in the first scenario the violence against the child was somewhat proportional to the response it was designed to elicit; in the second, the aim was terroristic. The violence was arbitrary and "unsupervised," i.e., when he was alone with the children. Again, however, Braxton's level of harm to the children had nothing to do with animosity toward the children—as Braxton's character witnesses confirmed—but was designed solely to hurt Hall. His character witnesses supported his absence of malevolence toward those he hurt most seriously. A secondary gain of violence-while-babysitting was to ensure Hall's continued vulnerability at work as well as her isolation from the support of coworkers, issues to which we return in later chapters. Surely, readers familiar only with child protection will see that without appreciating the spectrum nature of the coercive control offense, the motive, dynamic, and potentially fateful consequence of the Braxton's child abuse would be missed. Things may be improving slowly. In 2020, another Oklahoma child, Rebecca Hogue's son Jeremiah "Ryder" Johnson, was killed while he was in the care of his mother's boyfriend, Christopher Trent, who subsequently killed himself. Although there was considerable evidence that Hogue had been subjected to coercive control, including gaslighting and other forms of intimidation, a domestic violence expert was barred from testifying in her trial after prosecutors argued Hogue wasn't a victim of abuse as Oklahoma law defined it. Both the prosecutor and the jury recommending a life prison sentence with the possibility of parole, which she received, though with all but thirteen months of the sentence suspended. The presiding judge said in Hogue's sentencing hearing that she was a victim of her boyfriend's abuse—just not under state law.

On February 20, 2022, State Senator Kay Floyd, D-Oklahoma City, introduced Senate Bill 1446, which would add "coercive control" to Oklahoma's domestic abuse definitions. If passed, predatory behaviors such as isolating a victim from loved ones, depriving them of necessities, and threatening them violently or sexually would be prosecutable by law. If coercive control is enacted, women like Hall and Hague would be considered covictims with their children rather than perpetrators and would presumably be entitled to protections from abuse before their children were targeted.

Braxton held his wife responsible at home and at work. As did the prosecutors. And so, to some extent, did she. Hall believed that had she not returned to work, Braxton would not have abused their son. While I cannot know what was on the prosecutor's mind or the judge's when they too turned on Hall, it is certainly objectively true that their action reinforced

Braxton's own position that, while he alone harmed the child, his behavior was constrained by her decisions. The press also left the impression that this "reserved" "caring" dad was broken by an "abused mother." This is a difficult juncture for a forensics of coercive control. Apart from the economic incentives that caused her to return to work, Hall was undoubtedly aware that doing so provoked Braxton's jealousies and that he might displace his notorious insecurities on the children. At the same time, the theory of coercive control is predicated on a partner's unconditional right to make self-interested decisions that do not objectively constrain another's capacity for choice or action. The choice to earn a living is among the key liberties whose constraint is punished under coercive control law. This is one of those instances that must be placed in the context of an ongoing course of conduct: Braxton's strict liability for his controlling behavior reflects his use and punishment of the children to serve his selfish personal interest, not the family's well-being. The fact that Braxton might not have hurt the children as badly if Hall had stayed at home doesn't change his accountability here and is merely indicative of the normative level of unfreedom in the household.

Let there be no misunderstanding. When I argue that Braxton's or Kent's interest in hurting or controlling their children was "secondary" to coercive control or their partners, I do not mean that the harms they inflict on children are secondary to "woman abuse" in importance.[6] In point of fact, as here, in a custody dispute, the secondary victim may be hurt more severely and require emergent intervention precisely because they are not the primary target of control, though the threat to the child has only been implied. But unless we recognize the structure of criminological intent, it is easy to miss the risk children and other secondary victims face from coercively controlling men who may have no ostensible animosity toward those they hurt or kill. Children become secondary targets of abusers in the same way an invading army may alter its route to level a defenseless village because the enemy has reinforced its primary installation.

Recognizing that child abuse in the context of wife abuse is a form of *secondary victimization* simply means that the *primary* goal of coercive control in the arena of sexual inequality is the continued exertion of male privilege in personal life through the establishment and maintenance of a fear-based regime of domination over *all* resources and capacities available through the relationship. I am focusing on children because, next to women, they are the most common targets of coercive control. But unrelated household members, grandparents, neighbors, adult siblings, in-laws, coworkers—are all vulnerable. The spectrum of coercive control may extend to claims on the resources, capacities, and liberties of all members of the extended family and/or its friendship network. The adult female partner is typically the major creator and carrier of resources and capacities in the household not already possessed by the male partner as well as the ex-officio keeper of children to whose resources and capacities the abusive partner lays claim. But this may not be as true in other cultures and societies as it is in the West. Wherever it appears, coercive control is effective so long as the perceived costs of compliance are less than the costs of refusal, resistance, or escape. In a later chapter, I address another form of child abuse as "secondary victimization," where the abuser enlists the child(ren) in his strategy to control the mother.

Thus far, we have reviewed the victimization of children when the outcome was known, allowing us the wisdom of hindsight. In the cases in the second half of the book, the children we meet are in the throes of negotiating in and around the interstices of coercive control of themselves and their mothers as they try to retain the modicum of maternal resources and capacities they need to thrive. We will also see the converse process at work, where women contest the coercive control of their children to preserve some vestige of their femininity through and apart from mothering.

To reiterate: the "secondary victimization of children" in coercive control is often the most dangerous context for child abuse. The abusive adult may or may not have a personal connection to the child. But insofar as the child has become a means to his end, which is control over the woman, the child is disposable and what happens to the child is solely a function of the parent's rage, regardless of whether he feels animosity toward the child or not. Most child homicides, which are committed by men, are examples of "secondary victimization" in the context of coercive control. Again, think of the soldiers that attack the defenseless villagers with the force that should be held in reserve for the armed fortress.

In the Braxton-Hall case, the mechanics of injury and the vulnerability of the child make an emergency rescue, regardless of the actual power dynamics involved. I do not hesitate to recommend that child be rescued in such circumstances, even if it entails a temporary separation of the child from their mother. As a general rule, however, identifying the secondary role of children in the spectrum of coercive control suggests that the most effective way to ensure the child's well-being is to remove the abusive partner who is threatening the woman.

The court sentencing Hall wanted to hear none of this. How could Hall explain that the logic behind the fact that Braxton had hurt the child most seriously outside her purview lay in his motive and rationale for hurting the child, namely to terrorize *her*, in no small degree by establishing an incongruity between his normally "good father" persona in her presence and the unpredictable "beast" he became when she abandoned him. By parsing his violence and dominance across time and space along the spectrum of coercive control, Braxton had effectively deprived his wife of her singular identity as a "battered wife," at least in the eyes of the State of Oklahoma. There is another paradox. The State of Oklahoma punished Hall for not stopping Braxton from hurting their child. There was probably nothing she could have done that would have completely protected their child. In theory, however, had she capitulated more completely to his coercive control, he would have had fewer occasions to take out his displeasure on the child. The cost would have been her imprisonment. As it turned out, Hall *was really abused*, just not in the stereotyped ways the State imagined.

The Invisible Man

Until now, men's voices have remained largely off-stage.
The coercive control of children has remained invisible in large part because the institutions responsible for monitoring and managing harms to children in personal life—police, the family court, the child welfare system, and pediatric medicine—approach their charge through the narrow prism of "child abuse and neglect," a broad conceptualization of children's risk that is defined almost exclusively in terms of women's responsibilities for caretaking and protection. In this approach, which defined the family space as consisting of exclusively of women and children for administrative purposes, the experience of domestic violence is considered a failure in mothering, in no small part because victims have "allowed" themselves to be harmed in ways that jeopardize children. Chapter 4 focuses on the case of Mrs. Nicholson and her children, et al., where New York City's Administration for Children and Families (ACF) responded to women's victimization with draconian policies that punished abused mothers by removing their children to foster care while taking no notice of their male partners, a practice the federal court compared to indentured servitude. The underlying conceit behind the Nicholson policies and much else in legal and social services for children is that women

are the only effective agents in families with respect to children. A key aim of promoting coercive control as a framework for examining harms to children is to bring abusive men back into the picture and give them a speaking part.

In the next case, Frank K. made a cameo appearance because his presence became essential for Child Welfare to take the children from the mother. Although male partners and/or husbands figure centrally in all the cases of women and children I examine, they almost never appear in the same courtroom as the women who are charged, they are rarely interviewed by police or hospital social workers, and they leave few written records. In chapter 8 have much more to say about Mariusz Krezolek, the man who starved Daniel Pelka to death in Coventry, England, and whom we met in chapter 1. But everything I surmise about Krezolek is secondhand; at key moments, I had to infer Krezolek's presence at a scene by his effect on those whose reactions are recorded. We sense the presence of men in cases involving children the way scientists initially intuited the presence of molecules and atoms, by watching things move about, in this instance women and children, according to a logic not their own. Thus, there is no mention of Krezolek's presence during Daniel's last visit to the pediatrician, and we know about his intimidating presence only from the MD's cross-examination at Magdalena Luczak's trial for murder. I explore this point at length in the case chapter on the murder of Daniel Pelka (chapter 8). To me, the absence of men from academic, organizational, and legal accounts of child abuse is the most astounding thing about them, given the omnipresence of men in the unfolding family dramas. This is particularly astounding given the prominence of men historically in the fields of child protection, child psychology, and pediatrics. Like the child establishment, for much of the social service, policy, and legal apparatus dealing with families, men are assumed to be absent from their children's lives in hundreds of countries long before they physically leave the home.

Google "women and child abuse" and pages of entries unfold. Google "men and child abuse" and the first ten entries refer to "child *sexual* abuse" and then to parenting manuals. A scan of recent articles, chapters, and texts devoted to "child abuse," "child welfare," "domestic violence," or "abused children" reveals only a handful of references to men, even when the search is extended to the relevant medical fields of psychiatry, pediatrics, and family medicine. Although men frequently author articles on child abuse and appear prominently among those footnoted, they are conspicuously absent as research subjects. Why is it remarkable that men are absent as a focus in the child abuse literature? It is remarkable because, as I reiterate in my discussion of the Yale research in chapter 3, the vast majority of children who are intentionally and seriously injured or killed in their homes or families are harmed by men (fathers or father-surrogates) not by women. Moreover, this fact has been well established and widely replicated in journal articles for decades.[7] A slightly less damning reality is that men abusing women is far and away the single most important context for serious and fatal nonaccidental injury to children, and possibly accounts for 45 to 50 percent of *all* such cases.[8] Thus, it is not just "men" who are mainly responsible for hurting children, but a specific subset of men, men who are also abusing women. This fact, that the subset of abusive men who are abusing women are responsible for the majority of nonaccidental child deaths and serious injuries to children is an important empirical foundation for this book. If this fact has been known by least a substantial subset of researchers, educators, and policymakers in the child field, however, what has not been known until now is that the primary context in which children are harmed in conjunction with woman abuse is coercive control, a pattern that, because it is ongoing, and multidimensional and "crosses social space," can also be identified, interrupted, and stopped, preventing further harm to women and protecting children.

As things presently stand in most jurisdictions, unless and until they are eventually charged with a child's murder, the abusive partners in these cases are conspicuously missing from the interventions in the child's world. Sometimes they are physically absent. Chapter 4 concerns the case of the *Nicholson* mothers, whose children the ACS in New York had removed for "engaging in domestic violence." But with whom did they "engage?" Mrs. Nicholson's husband makes a cameo appearance in the opening scene of the ACS narrative, when he breaks into the apartment and assaults her, breaks her arm, then exits. He is presumed to have returned to North Carolina from whence he came, though we have only Mrs. Nicholson's best guess for this, since no search was conducted, warrant issued, or attempt made by ACS or NYC police to contact him. Though neither child witnessed the attack—the baby was asleep and the older girl in school—once it was determined that *she* had exposed the children to harm, his role appears to have been little more than an agent provocateur. But in all the other *Nicholson* cases, the men responsible for abusing the women and children are in and out of the house, court, and even the Welfare Office, but never identified or questioned, let alone retained.

In the Pelka case (chapter 8), Mariusz Krezolek was arrested for domestic violence and on several occasions for sexual assault. But for practical purposes, he might as well have been invisible. He was never removed from the home in these cases, and, though police were also involved in investigating Daniel's home situation, Krezolek was not interviewed as part of the child abuse inquiry and his role in the family's downward spiral was never identified. He remained the elephant in the room even after the pediatric visit. He was arrested and charged after he killed Daniel. But he was largely unknown and invisible until then. When "oversight" occurs in the presence of a valence in power of this magnitude, with this consistency and with this level of tragic consequence, we are in the presence of systemic blindness or bias that requires a fundamental restructuring of how problems are defined, investigated, and solved. The terrain on which child abuse occurs is largely hallucinatory as to how harms occur and who is responsible.

In the *Nicholson* case, discussed in chapter 4, Nicholson's husband was the assailant who broke her arm. But New York City and ASC were alone responsible for the multiple harms the Nicholson children suffered in conditions the Federal Court found analogous to indentured servitude. If his mother, Magdalena Luczak, was not responsible for Daniel Pelka's death, who is? Krezolek alone is guilty. But is he the only one responsible? Or do the dozens of professionals who disregarded his presence over the years as if he was a specter share responsibility? And can we really let the buck stop with the professionals? Readers will consider these questions closely in the case chapters.

I raise the specter of "the invisible man" early in the book to alert readers to a facet of the problem we are considering that might be overlooked, that an "erasure" occurred at key junctures in the history of research on child abuse and services to protect children whereby the persons responsible for harming women and children and depriving them of basic rights and liberties were made to disappear by the agencies and institutions charged with oversight, assessment, protection, and the administration of justice. The sum result of the interactions with these institutions over time was that a web was cast over these families where abuse occurred that ensnared the women and children while leaving the men "outside." As political scientist Kathleen Arnold points out in *Why Don't You Just Talk to Him?*, when the family is seen by child welfare or the family court, it appears the "mother" is the only adult in the room and therefore responsible for both protecting her child and any harms to the child.[9] Since the force that is disabling her is invisible, her stasis appears to reflect incompetence, which, lacking an obvious organic cause such as blindness or mental illness, is held to be willful. Institutional myopia may be by design—as when ACS in New York classified all child welfare cases in the mother's name even if she was deceased—or by implication, as when Judge Pinkus instructed Adrianna Oyola to "show me maturity" by reasoning with a man who has beaten and stalked her and is threatening to kill her and her son. Until countries adopted a serious offense of coercive control, the situation was only slightly better on the criminal side, where the focus was on the offender. Here, as I showed in *Coercive Control*, the cloak of male invisibility was laid on by the level of justice administered: the assumption that domestic violence was a low-level misdemeanor combined with an emphasis on efficient case processing to generate dismissals, nolo contendere pleas, and light sentences that made a mockery of the men whose coercive control has been experienced by the victimized partner. These men often carried long rap-sheets, which could eventually earn them a jail sentence if they were arrested for a "serious" offense such as robbery but had no effect on their tyranny in the home. A side effect of the revolving cell door on criminal processing is that many women withdraw their complaints rather than put themselves at risk for a charade of justice. Rather than recognize how shocked their erstwhile clients are by the level of evil the State can dismiss, many prosecutors in my acquaintance read such withdrawals as acts of ambivalence or worse and retreat into cynicism. The next case illustrates what happens when an abusive man is actually processed with his victims.

Invisible in Plain Sight: The Case of Frank K.

A repeated theme in this book is the complicity of institutional actors in the entrapment of women and children. The example of Frank K. illustrates how institutions maintain the invisibility of abusive men, even when the men are transparent about their motives and behavior.

Frank K., a Vietnam vet, the abusive father of twin nine-year-old girls, Tanya and Sasha K., stayed on the scene and acknowledged his difficulties with violence. There was no secret that Frank was a danger to his family. Sarah M. had reported her husband's terroristic threats, violence, and control over her and the girls to local police more than ten times; her psychiatrist traced her symptoms of depression and other problems to his abuse; Frank K. told the supervising agency about his outbursts; the hospital at which he was an outpatient had a record of his violence against his wife and daughters; the girls had described his violence against them to police; and the Family

Court had given her an Order of Protection that limited him to supervised visits with the twins at their school cafeteria. Everyone knew Frank K. was violent and abusive, including Frank. I first encountered Frank at the VA, in a group I co-ran for men suffering from PTSD.

Frank was given a holiday overnight with his girls over Christmas, but failed to pick them up. The last week of vacation, the girls were scheduled to attend a break program at their school designed for working mothers. When the girls refused to dress for the program, mom became frantic she would miss her job and possibly lose employment, phoned the school, and was told to bring them in with their clothes and "all would be taken care of." Reassured, Mom brought them to school, they dressed in the car, she dropped the girls off and left. The girls promptly undressed and refused to rerobe. The school called police and Sarah was charged with "indecent exposure" (the charge was withdrawn) and the girls were transported to the Yale Child Study Center for observation. From there, the case was referred to DFYS, Connecticut's child protection agency.

Frank had a long, well-documented history of abuse. Connecticut had agreed to abide by the consent decree in *Nicholson* (chapter 4), to wit that no mother could be charged with "neglect" stemming from their own abuse and that the focus of intervention should be on holding abusers accountable and supporting victims. No matter. From the vantage of child welfare, Frank wore a cloak of invisibility.

By the time I came onboard, the agency had removed the girls from the "out of control" mom and was seeking to do so permanently and had transferred primary physical custody to dad. Sarah had only limited supervised contact with her daughters. The girls, who claimed to have been beaten by dad and an elderly aunt in whose care he left them, had run away several times and were currently inpatients at a psychiatric facility. Each time the girls ran, threatened suicide, begged mom to rescue them or reported their father or his aunt, Sarah was blamed for their "deterioration."

Sarah's situation illustrates a key point, that restoring men to the story of child abuse often involves making visible what is already in plain sight. I have described the men as "invisible." But this is not because they have literally left the scene like Mrs. Nicholson's husband in chapter 4. The old joke is that it only takes one psychiatrist to screw in a light bulb, but "it has to *want* to turn." Similarly, bringing men into the picture is less about shaking up professional consciousness than creating a political climate in which it is possible to know what we already know about how power works in families and relationships. Frank K. went everywhere we asked him to go and made no pretext of either his motives for wanting the girls or punishing Sarah. As we will see in chapter 8, Krezolek was in the home when police, social workers, the school nurse, and others visited. Komisarjevsky came to the Family Court in shackles. The sheer presence of the men and evidence of their cruelty is not enough. The professionals have to *want* to change. Men are here to be seen. We have to be willing to look into their eyes.

Patriarchal Mothering

First and foremost, restoring men to the picture allows us to see women and children in relation to men: we are reminded that, outside the fictional Gilead, "mothering" (like "fathering") is among the more complex biosocial role choices available in modern relational systems that retains a modicum of decisional autonomy. The exercise of this autonomy, evident in deciding whether to become a mother, for instance, with whom, and then, once a baby is born, how to "mother," presumes the prior existence of a reflective feminine self (a "woman") and implies the existence of one or many other external interests with claims on decisions about mothering with varying degrees of legitimacy, including the partner's and now also the child's. I emphasize decisional autonomy because I assume a malevolent external logic such as coercive control is at work whenever mothering appears to be "all there is," i.e., when it lacks the reflective element (whereby a person's needs as a "woman" and mother are distinguished) and the relational element (through which she distinguishes her needs from those of the child). The cases in this book repeatedly confront us with a condition I call "patriarchal mothering," where an element of the partner's coercive control involves micromanagement of the woman's interactions with her child, including her use of discipline, at the same time that his influence remains hidden and these practices appear to emanate from her. Women in this predicament appear to be occupied by an alien ("patriarchal") spirit and enact harms ritualistically, usually with little discernible hostile affect, and in ways that are inconsistent with past parenting behavior. Without an awareness of coercive control as the force providing the "patriarchal" logic behind the alien parenting, we are left puzzling over the Netflix scenario, to wit, "Soccer Mom becomes Killer Mom." In the Connecticut case, the girls deteriorated because their mother couldn't protect them from Frank. Sarah couldn't protect the girls, because

DCF and the Family Court insisted on his having unsupervised visits. When the girls deteriorated, DCF and the Court held Sarah responsible because, frankly, there wasn't another responsible adult in the room.

Sarah eventually regained custody of her girls. But this was a notable exception. Most of the cases I discuss involve children who were killed or seriously hurt and women who faced criminal charges because of things they were alleged to have done as "mothers" that lent themselves to a singularly malevolent interpretation, crimes of commission, and/or crimes of omission, things they did not do or did not accomplish in at least two significant examples, which it was assumed a reasonably protective mother would or could or even should have done. My forensic goal is straightforward, to redirect the malevolence that now targets abused women at the men whose illegitimate use of power has constrained the women's choices. This is not a moral claim. The accusations against these women I hope to neutralize involve criminal guilt and should not be confounded with the feelings of personal responsibility and even psychological guilt expressed by all of the women/mothers in these cases for not having prevented the harm to their children and irrespective of whether they had directly assaulted the child. Unfortunately, in charging nonoffending mothers with "failure to protect" or its variants, courts often deliberately misread or play off these commonplace feelings of psychological guilt, as if someone who feels responsible for making bad decisions should accept legal accountability for killing her child. An innocent defendant can be so overwhelmed by their sense of personal responsibility that they become ineffectual in their trial. This is what happened to Magdalena Luczak. The overwhelming sense of guilt that the media and court interpreted as "cold indifference" led to her suicide in prison on what would have been Daniel's seventh birthday.

Readers may recall that the unsympathetic reception of Luczak as an "abused mother" was accompanied by a sociolegal account of someone who had "failed" in her obligations as a woman. Presumably because she made the ("bad") choice to be abused, it was assumed she was unable to make good choices (i.e., protective) now. What disqualifies her is not the sort of mental incapacity that might excuse her from legal responsibility, but a moral disqualification, a seeming incapacity to behave decently and honorably.[10] The projection by an officer of the court or a case worker of shame for being abused can devastate anyone, but it is particularly painful to women whose marginal status because of race, sexual identification, or immigration is already stigmatized. A corollary of the belief that abused mothers are incapable of protective parenting is that, when a child is killed by an abusive partner, the female victims are assumed to be guilty unless they meet very high standards of protective action. The default assumption in many of the cases we've reviewed thus far was that the female defendant "colluded" with their partners (as Luczak was said to have done with Krezolek) or, "did nothing to stop him," like Tondalo Hall, which amounted to the same thing.[11] The charge of "exposure" to domestic violence leveled at the Nicholson mothers is a perverse variant of collusion, because "exposure" implies that the victim welcomes the abuser's performance. What is most apparent in *Nicholson* is also true of the criminal cases: nothing is more difficult than to locate a specific man in the social work, medical files, case files, or court records with sufficient corporeality to constitute a coconspirator, let alone someone who can be put on the stand to be questioned. We may have a general image of "those men" from our case practice or from a cable TV crime procedural. We may even have seen his photograph, as we did Krezolek's, as he is hauled off to jail. But where has he been until now?

Lest readers conclude that the stereotypes of "the abused mother" and "the invisible man" are byproducts of conservative ideologies, I close the chapter by reviewing the reception of Hedda Nussbaum, an abused mother, by New York feminists when she was being considered a codefendant in the trial for murder in the killing of Lisa Sanders, age 6 years.

The Case of Hedda Nussbaum

"Failure to protect" statutes are ill-advised, applied inequitably, and allow criminal, family, and child welfare courts to punish women based largely on their compliance with gender stereotypes, in this instance the belief that mothers (but rarely fathers) bear ultimate responsibility for childcare, regardless of their own circumstance. But these statutes and their enforcement reflect an important reality, that few events elicit more revulsion and outrage or a quicker rush to judgment than when a child dies or suffers severe injury on a mother's watch, even if, and sometimes particularly if, she is also a victim. Older readers will recall the systematic beating to death of six-year old Lisa Saunders (Steinberg) in New York City in 1987 and the conviction of defense attorney Joel Steinberg for manslaughter. But condemnation of Steinberg was as nothing compared to the vilification of Hedda Nussbaum, his live-in partner, for not protecting Lisa, at one point staying alone with the suffering child for ten hours without calling for help. Steinberg was never charged with his abuse of Nussbaum. But Joel Steinberg subjected Hedda to the same tactics of coercion and control he applied to Lisa, causing Hedda permanent facial and spinal injury, raping her repeatedly, making her beg for basic resources or exchanging them for sexual and other services, and locking her in the apartment so that she had to literally crawl out of the house with a ruptured spleen to get to the hospital for help at one point. At the time Lisa died, Hedda's status was less than that of a slave whose labor remains essential. Had he not been arrested for Lisa's death, he almost certainly would have caused Hedda's as well. Lisa was his "whipping post." Steinberg's torturous treatment of Lisa was designed to subdue Hedda. With Lisa's death, he had no more hope of affecting Hedda, who had no thoughts left for herself. Lisa's mistreatment was not on the authorities' radar. But they had ample knowledge of Hedda's predicament. Even a cursory investigation of Hedda's abuse would have saved Lisa.

None of this mattered. Neither the media nor the public found anything about how she had suffered that relieved Hedda Nussbaum of responsibility for Lisa's death any more that the crimes against Tondalo Hall or Magdalena Luczak relieved their guilt for the death of their children. Instead, the paralysis caused by Steinberg's brutality was registered as collusion and concealment by infuriated outsiders.

Ironically, two of the most damaging responses came from sources that should have been sympathetic. I had worked closely with Safe Horizon and Sanctuary for Families, the organizations mainly responsible for sheltering abused women in New York City. Yet, Hedda Nussbaum was denied access to a battered women's shelters in New York City, apparently because she refused to identify herself as a "battered woman." Meanwhile the most damning portraits of Hedda were drawn by authors with impressive feminist credentials, the antirape activist and author Susan Brownmiller and the *Grove* editor and novelist Joyce Johnson. Brownmiller's thinly fictionalized account, *Waverly Place* (1989), recognized the parade of outsiders who had witnessed Lisa's abuse, and Johnson's *What Lisa Knew* (1990) condemned the indifference of teachers and child welfare to obvious signs of Lisa's suffering. But in both books, Nussbaum rather than Steinberg is the villain, an active witness and participant in Lisa's torture and death who sustained her injuries as a willing coparticipant in sadomasochistic rituals. This was the same transparently fabricated and self-serving argument made at trial by Steinberg's defense counsel.

Conclusions

Professionals who work with women and children are no more immune to prejudice against abused women than the public. There are few greater emotional or ethical challenges to professional objectivity than when a child in our caseload is seriously or fatally harmed. In such circumstances, it is hard to resist the temptation to relieve the sense of impotence, the magical belief that something they *could* or *should* have done would have protected the child, by making the mother their proxy-by-projection, even to the point of blaming her for not realizing the risk her own abuse posed to her child. I have been caught up in this process more than once. Despite decades of exposure to violence in my work, I felt such deep despair and helplessness when I reviewed cases of child fatality for the State of New Jersey that I resigned from my appointment from the Regional Child Fatality Review Board in just over a year. Had I served even another month, I believe my capacity for empathy in these cases would have died. The problem is made worse if we have children of our own. These cases drive home our children's vulnerability and our own, puncturing any fantasy that "it can't happen here." When I first began working in criminal cases on behalf of women whose children were seriously injured or killed on their watch, I shared the same initial revulsion, however defensively, as well as the propensity to rush to judgment. But once you "walk in the shoes" of those who survived the terror, your resiliency is steeled and you can never again settle for accessing a case solely through the records of the tragedies it produced.

My cases are always ethically challenging and emotionally draining. But my feelings ricocheted between outrage and impotence in 2013, during those months in Great Britain when the media, the Royal Court of Justice, and the Serious Case Review Panel of experts eviscerated what was left of the self Magdalena Luczak had fought so hard to salvage from Krezolek's coercive control. I watched her emerge from her trial as "the killer mom," whose character and motives could be deduced from the stock adjectives the media keep on file for such villains. At no point was there any sense that she had a personhood whose loss was worthy of grieving alongside Daniel's, that she was a woman in her own right, not merely a "mother," a woman who, if allowed to speak in her own voice, might mine her unique historical address to make sense of her behavior. Instead, her image as a monster hid the real monster in the proceedings, and provided a scapegoat to absorb the blame deserved by all those who had walked through a home filled with the detritus of Krezolek's rage without noticing his presence. In 1987, Hedda Nussbaum was described similarly in a report as "a dark form, huddled in a corner" by a social worker who came to the apartment and then left, without either acknowledging her humanity and recognizing that little would soon suffer Hedda's fate. Not only did the demonization of Hedda Nussbaum in the mass media set the stage for Steinberg's relatively short sentence; it provided the scapegoat for the failure to protect Hedda; and supported by negation, the core argument in the "sexist" screeds, that women's natural endowment was to mother. Had I had access to her defense team, I would have willingly been Magdalena Luczak's proxy. She was too traumatized to tell her own story, and I longed to tell it for her. Magdalena, Adrianna Oyola, Tondalo Hall, or Hedda Nussbaum. I want to say: Had these women been treated like their lives mattered, their children would be thriving today.

3

The Old Model

Domestic Violence and Child Abuse

Child cruelty remains all too common. So do violent family conflicts. My concern in this book is not with these universal phenomena but with "child abuse" and "wife abuse" as social facts that arise when particular forms of conflict receive official notice; become a matter for public surveillance, record and interdiction; and so lay claim on fiscal, social, and moral budgets. In the twentieth and twenty-first centuries, these social facets of personal life came to public notice as "problems" when the quality of life for women and children took on new significance for an expanding economy and overall social development. In our era, this happened in two waves: the recognition of domestic violence as the most important context for child abuse—the focus of this chapter—and the recognition that both "domestic violence" and "child abuse" are elements of coercive control, the topic of this book. The core thesis is that the persistent intractability of "domestic violence" and "child abuse" as social problems is a direct result of the failure to confront their common source in coercive control, a "failure" due to the privileges that accrue to families, which allow the exploitation of children, and to men in particular, which allow the exploitation of women and children.

My key informants in the book are women and children who are being victimized. When they first encounter a school, a hospital, the police, or child welfare, most of the ordinary people who inhabit these pages are "sorted" as the English say, as microdots on a hard drive held in a storage tent somewhere in Ohio and Birmingham or Taiwan. If I meet them, it is sometime later, when they come to a shelter, appear in Family Court, or are remanded to an quasi-judicial setting like a child welfare hearing, where the women are brought before the docket and, with their children's futures at stake, face the equally dangerous option of either denying they're being abused or acknowledging abuse and being censured by losing their children to foster care. Or I meet them in the course of a criminal proceeding. A woman has been charged because a child has been killed or she has killed an abusive partner, or she has been implicated in some other crime that she committed

Children of Coercive Control. Evan Stark, Oxford University Press. © Oxford University Press 2023.
DOI: 10.1093/oso/9780197587096.003.0004

as a result of being abused. It is at this juncture that those who personify so-cial facts "talk back" out of the agony of the Great Refusal to accept the given alternatives. For the first time in the modern era, these women and children have a third option. Under the rubric of coercive control, a woman can ex-plain how she can be a victim of abuse, a mother of an abused child, and an effective parent at the same time. Or, in a criminal trial, she can both be a victim and mount a vigorous defense of her rights. To reconcile these contra-dictory positions, the person who is wreaking havoc on the household must be prevented from doing so. The "abused mother" ceases to be a contradic-tion in terms only when the abuse of her and her children is stopped.

This chapter describes two important empirical data sources on the appli-cation of coercive control to children, the Yale medical studies that revealed the duration, scope, and prevalence of woman abuse, including its extension to children, and the study of hospital "Dart" records that demonstrated the singular significance of domestic violence as a context for child abuse. Taken together, these studies showed that "domestic violence" and "child abuse" are composite harms that emerge and develop in personal life in tandem in ways that resist single-point interventions by medicine, police, or Family Court. The chapter concludes with a critique of "witnessing," the conventional ex-planation offered of how children are harmed by exposure to violence against their mother apart from being deliberately assaulted or injured acciden-tally. I will show that, for children, "witnessing" is more often a form of en-gagement than a passive effect and is only one of the many ways in which children's senses become engaged with coercive control.

Recognizing that child abuse in the context of wife abuse is a form of *sec-ondary victimization* simply means that the *primary* goal of coercive control in the arena of sexual inequality is the continued exertion of male privilege in per-sonal life through the establishment and maintenance of a fear-based regime of domination over *all* resources and capacities available through the relationship. I am focusing on children because, next to women, they are the most common targets of coercive control. But unrelated household members—grandparents, neighbors, adult siblings, in-laws, coworkers—are all vulnerable. The spec-trum of coercive control may extend to claims on the resources, capacities, and liberties of all members of the extended family and/or its friendship network.

* * *

Our story begins almost fifty years ago, in the summer of 1976, when a grant to visit shelters for battered women and their children brought me and Anne

Flitcraft to the Chiswick section of London. We passed a cobblestone wall with the words "A HOUSE FOR WOMEN" scrawled on it in large letters and knocked on the red wooden front door of "Chiswick Women's Aid," the best-known refuge for abused women in the world. A large woman filled the doorway. This was Erin Pizzey, the founding "mother" of Women's Aid. Pizzey bent down and hugged me, greeted Anne with a kiss, and waved us in with none of the wariness we'd experienced at other refuges in England. This was defense by numbers. We entered an extraordinary scene. Women and children were everywhere, in and out a kitchen door, unloading supplies, traipsing up and down stairs, two girls and a younger boy playing darts in a hallway, a half dozen other children huddled around an old pinball machine; one woman, her back hunched on the fourth stair held in her arms another woman, whose weeping was audible. Amid the noise and chaos, a meeting of sorts was being conducted. Five women, tightly set on a sinking coach, leaned forward, attentively listening to a woman sitting cross-legged on the floor in front. A group of children played a game of jacks, oblivious to their mothers' unfolding drama nearby. "There are 90 women and children staying at the house at the moment," Pizzey bragged. "If they can manage this, they can manage anything." What struck us about this scene, even back then, was that whatever had happened to these women and their children that brought them to Chiswick, they had experienced it together and had "managed" together as well.

That night, after we'd finished a potluck West Indian meal, a Jamaican lawyer who was staying at the Refuge organized a group of about eight "volunteers." We took rolls of toilet paper, a portable toilet, cans of paint, rags, and some roll-on brushes, and crossed town in an old minibus that doubled as a youth hostel for older boys. We parked near a station, at what looked like an abandoned Railroad Hotel. One of the women entered through a back window, opened the front door and we marched in. Having "squatted" the hotel, we had the paper up, the floors washed, and the first coats on the shelves before we rolled out our mats. The next afternoon, the first carload of residents of the Chiswick II Refuge arrived. We were ready.

Played over and retold again and again, the Chiswick scene reminds us that, despite the emphasis in movement posters and literature on "violence *against* women," women and children always came as a unit. This is not only because they often lived together and fled together. It was also because, more often than not, they had been jointly targeted by a single process of oppression. As much as the refuge/shelter supported the empowerment of individual women, it also provided an experience of women and children doing-for-themselves that became a template of self-determination for the cohort the generation to come.

The images of women and children doing for themselves were fresh in our minds, when Anne returned for her last year of medical school and asked Dr. William Frazier, director of the emergency room (ER) at Yale–New Haven Hospital, if she could do her required medical school thesis on battered women who used the surgical emergency service.

"What's a battered woman?" Dr. Frazier asked.

The Yale Trauma Studies

To answer Dr. Frazier's question, Anne Flitcraft focused her medical thesis research to determine the significance of domestic violence among women who visited Yale's ER during a single month with complaints related to injury. The results were so surprising that Dr. Flitcraft, Dr. Frazier, and I received federal support to spend much of the next two decades replicating Anne's methodology among a much larger population of ER patients as well as among obstetrical patients, general medical patients, and other groups, in each case distinguishing the clinical profile of the abused from nonabused women at the site and assessing the appropriateness of the medical response. What became known collectively as "The Yale Trauma Studies" are described at length elsewhere.[1] For our hospital sample, we reviewed the complete medical records of a random sample of 3,676 female trauma patients who had used the ER in a single year. To identify the distinctive clinical syndrome associated with abuse, we compared the histories of the group we identified as "abused" with an equal subsample of 600 nonabused women.[2] Tens of thousands of pages of medical notes, thousands of years of medical history, hundreds of medical records were hauled into freight elevators, transferred to offices, key punched onto cards, sorted by machine, and fed through a wall-side computer to print out sheets for reading.

Suffice it to say that by the time we finished our analysis, "domestic violence," which previously had no significance in medicine, was identified at the cause of visits for almost 20 percent (18.7%) of the women who used the ER; these "battered" women (so-named because of the frequency with which they were injured), accounted for 40 percent of *all* injury visits to the hospital ever presented by their cohort of female patients; and their average abuse history was 7.2 years, though we had no way to tell whether this represented a single relationship or several. Abuse had myriad medical, psychosocial, and mental health effects, including injury. For example, the women with a history of abuse were seven times more likely to abuse alcohol than the nonabused women and much more likely to have attempted suicide, often multiple times. Forty-eight percent of African American women who had ever made a suicide attempt made at least one and often multiple attempts in the context of an abusive relationship. A third of the 174 rape victims reported at the hospital had a previous medical history of abuse; meanwhile, among the rape victims over thirty, almost two-thirds (58%) had a history suggesting the sexual assault had occurred during a history of abuse.

Our main headline was that domestic violence was the leading cause of injury for which adult women sought medical attention. But this could be misleading. To those who read only the headline, it would easy to draw the erroneous conclusion that wife-beating was much more extreme than was thought. In fact, most of the physical abuse women suffered was low-level and noninjurious. Behind the headline was the real story, that the most harmful and frightening facet of physical abuse was not that it was severe or life-threatening, but that it persisted for a considerable period—7.7 years on our study—and was punctuated by sexual assaults and who knows what other tactics whose *cumulative* effects over time were to evoke a behavioral and psychosocial profile that included suicidality, alcohol and drug abuse, depression, and a host of other symptoms more commonly associated with victims of kidnapping or terrorism than partner assault. We had unearthed the terroristic nature of the physical abuse used in coercive control. But we didn't know it at the time.

The above paragraphs summarize a decade's worth of research that generated dozens of monographs on the medical sequelae of domestic violence. Our research became a small part of what today is a vast global research literature on violence against women.

In the Yale medical records we reviewed, there were numerous notes expressing nurses', doctors', and social workers' "concern about 'child abuse.' " But there was no clinical or narrative corroboration.

Coinciding with our work at Yale, at the University of New Hampshire, a research team headed by sociologist Murray Straus and PhD student Richard Gelles was questioning a sample of families drawn from the general

US population. From a burgeoning field of family sociology and therapy, the New Hampshire sociologists brought an acquired belief that "violence" and "abusive violence" constituted the extreme end of a range of "conflict tactics" family members used to address their differences. From their standpoint, it was the physical valence and probable effect of "violence" that made it inappropriate, so that any use of "violence" as a "conflict tactic" was inappropriate, regardless of who used the violence and who was targeted. To get their results from the national population sample, they juxtaposed answers to questions about intracouple conflicts to answers about which adult hit the children "how" and "how often?"

Both the Yale and New Hampshire studies revealed rates of domestic violence and suspected child abuse that were far higher than expected. The New Hampshire Study asked men whether women also hit them, a question we couldn't answer from our base in women's medical records. The medical records we were using had evidence of injury and other actual health consequences of abuse, which the New Hampshire study lacked. They could speculate that a reported "kick" or a "punch" might be worse than a "hit," but they had no information on what outcomes actually occurred, if any. Self-proclaimed "men's rights" organizations would later insist that reports of women and men being "hit" in similar numbers in the New Hampshire study meant there were no sex differences in "abuse." But of course, since New Hampshire studies had no evidence on actual consequences, there was no way to tell anything about "abuse" from that research. Still, the disproportionate frequency with which men assaulted women was sufficient to distinguish a subgroup of female victims as "battered wives." The empirical results of the New Hampshire research supported what we held going in, namely that male-on-female partner violence was far-and-away the most prevalent form of "abuse" in couples.[3] About this there was no disagreement.

What about the children? The large-scale empirical studies gave us the big picture. The couples questioned for the New Hampshire study acknowledged using a range of "conflict tactics" with their children, including violence. But it was unclear what proportion of these tactics fell under an operational heading of "abuse." The abused women in the Yale medical population were far more likely than the nonabused women to tell their clinicians they were "concerned about child abuse." But this too was only a clue. Neither we nor New Hampshire had any reports from children or records on children to corroborate suspicions.

The Yale Child Abuse Study

To get a closer look at the actual dynamics at work with the children, Dr. Flitcraft and I drew a year's sample from a Yale–New Haven Hospital "Dart" Team population of "abused" children and then accessed the records of their mothers to see how many were also being battered.[4] This represented all 116 of the children "darted" anywhere at Yale during a year who were assessed for abuse by the specialist team of pediatricians, social workers, nurses and psychiatrists. Since Yale's Hospital is the designated referral point for child abuse assessment in the region, the year sample approximates the total number of children identified as abused in the New Haven metropolitan region, a catchment area of close to 300,000. Today, once he'd accessed the confidential records, my grandson could draw our sample with his iPhone in an afternoon. So it's hard to imagine what our challenge was like. To create our data set, it took four of us working for several month locating, drawing, hauling, reading, abstracting, coding, key punching, and sorting volumes and volumes of medical records. So straightforward were the findings, so signifi-cant were the absolute numbers, that their meaning seemed unavoidable: do-mestic violence ("wife abuse") emerged as the most important context for child abuse. More, as its most important *cause*. Nothing even came close.

To start, we had to identify victims of domestic violence. At that time, neither domestic violence nor woman battering was part of a medical vo-cabulary. In order to identify battering from women's medical records, Dr. Flitcraft adapted an "index of suspicion" she had applied to the larger trauma sample drawn from the emergency medical sample. The first step was to abstract the "trauma history" from the medical records of the sample of mothers. Next, based on the description, location, nature, and stated cause, each injury episode in the medical history was ranked as "positive," "prob-able," or "suggestive" for abuse or abuse was ruled out as a cause ("negative"). Third, a woman was identified as "positive," "probable," etc., based on the highest ranked injury she's experienced. Finally, psych notes and other facets of the women's charts were explored to elicit additional information about any abuse experiences. A similar strategy had been adapted by Henry Kempe when he set out to find the population of "abused children" hidden in the medical population in the 1950s.

Combining information abstracted with this tool with other information in the records revealed that 52 of the 116 mothers "darted" for child abuse by the hospital's specialist team for a single year were in abusive relationships

(45%). Another six (5%) had a history of marital conflict, though we couldn't tell if they were being abused. Soon after we completed our study, a research team at Boston Children's Hospital used a similar identification approach to reveal that the abuse of the mother was the context for 60 percent of cases of identified child abuse at their facility.[5] It was highly unlikely that two unconnected teams working in pediatric settings wholly lacking in knowledge of domestic violence would come to this finding by chance.

Our studies were hospital based and so technically only applied to women who used a medical system. Yale–New Haven Hospital is a large University–City Hospital that draws on a diverse multitown patient population. The Boston study drew on a more ethnically diverse population. The findings raised the distinct possibility that domestic violence was implicated in half or more of all reported cases of child maltreatment. Domestic violence might not be the *cause* of child abuse in these cases. But it was far and away the most common context yet identified, outweighing all other medical, behavioral, or environmental factors combined. Once researchers looked, they had no difficulty identifying domestic violence in these families. Yet, despite an extensive literature on child abuse, neither the medical nor social work literature mentioned domestic violence. Since domestic violence had been in the news for at least a decade when we pulled our sample, this was an example of what I term "invisible in plain sight." Since the child welfare system takes its lead from medical experts, it is no surprise that the services responsible for monitoring child abuse in the community had nothing about domestic violence in its policies and practices. Adding a single, simple question about the mother's experience had apparently exposed a major factor in child maltreatment that had been "neglected" by experts in children at Yale and Harvard/Boston, two of the nation's most prestigious pediatric centers of research for over a century. Our findings about domestic violence and children remain unchallenged. This book extends the earlier research by identifying coercive control as the most important dynamic that governs the interplay of domestic violence and child abuse, child sexual abuse, and other forms of maltreatment in these cases.

Our differences with the classic child abuse paradigm go a good deal further than its neglect of "domestic violence" (now coercive control) as a context for child maltreatment and child killing. Ever since Henry Kempe provided the first radiological description of the "battered baby syndrome" that became the foundation of the modern child protection system, many of the most progressive child advocates in the United States and abroad have distinguished the admittedly small proportion of "real" child abuse cases with which society should be rightly concerned, which are the proper domain of ERs and pediatricians, from the large caseload of child "neglect" cases in which serious injury and nonaccidental death are highly unlikely and where underlying causes are associated with poverty and inadequate housing. A greater awareness of domestic violence in these families may be relatively recent historically speaking. Bur followers of the classic child maltreatment model—such as the social workers and pediatricians who were involved with the *Nicholson* mothers—are not completely surprised that domestic violence" is so prominent in the "neglect" caseload because they see it as one of among the many problems disproportionately associated with poverty and disadvantage. In the minds of these child professionals, there is important distinction between the risks to children posed by the range of "environmental" factors disproportionately associated with poverty, including now domestic violence alongside homelessness, and "real" child abuse which they claim is the byproduct of female incapacities, such as immaturity, alcohol and drug abuse, and mental illness. As discussed in chapter 4, the *Nicholson* mothers were charged with the crime of "neglect" by New York City's Administration for Children's Services (ACS) because they had "engaged in domestic violence," even though their "engagement" consisted largely in their being coerced and controlled by abusive partners. Followers of the Kempe model would not be surprised that none of the children in the *Nicholson* families suffered "real abuse."

But if the child abuse establishment is right to separate cases typified by "real" violence from cases where children present with general malaise linked to "neglect," our research at Yale showed that it has been dead wrong about which cases these are. In fact, we found that, contrary to what is what widely claimed to support current child welfare and child abuse policies, domestic violence of the mother and coercive control are far and away the most important cause and context for "real" child abuse involving deliberate serious injury and child fatality. These cases, where serious physical abuse was more likely, were distinct from cases of child "neglect" that tended to involve environmental stressors such as unemployment, a death in the family, mental illness, poor housing, and poverty. Typically, "neglect" cases did not involve domestic violence. Ironically, from the vantage of its effects on children, domestic violence in the home was more direct and toxic than other stressors (such as poverty, substance abuse, chronic illness, and unemployment) and far more susceptible to intervention than the "neglect" cases that were typically byproducts of the racism, unemployment, poor educational opportunity, and inequality that are endemic in the neighborhoods from which Yale draws its patient population. To be clear, many children do suffer because their parents are immature or because of maternal mental illness or alcohol or drug abuse. Among this population is a small subgroup where maternal and/or child deficits merit emergent intervention. But neither the abused mothers who were "darted" for suspicion of child abuse not their children shared these characteristics. Their risk arose entirely from the abusive partner, a factor exogenous to the characteristics of mother and child. If cases of "child abuse" due to domestic violence were managed by criminal justice, as I propose, and "neglect" cases managed through social justice interventions and social work, only a relative handful of true pediatric emergencies of the kind Henry Kempe envisioned would remain to manage. But this takes us too far ahead in our argument.

In the ensuing years, research, interviews with protective mothers, and testimony in family and criminal court cases greatly clarified the dynamics of child harm in abusive relationships. But our early findings left no doubt about the exercise of power in relationships and households or the general contour of the dynamics among the children in the Yale study. To start, the abuse by men in these families was "ongoing." Like many of us who are not abused, the nonbattered mothers of abused children averaged 1.1 trauma-related hospital visits as adults. By contrast, the battered mothers averaged 4.2 injury visits. In other words, the children were being "darted" amid an assaultive process that was "ongoing" at the very least. In the nonbattering families, mothers were typically identified as the parent responsible for the child's maltreatment. This is hardly surprising, since women were often single mothers in these cases and, even in the best of times, the levels of teen-births, poverty, racial discrimination, unemployment, sexual terrorism, drugs, and alcohol in the neighborhoods surrounding the hospital made a certain number of "failures" in parenting inevitable. Not only was "real child abuse" more likely in the "domestic violence" cases than in these households but also the typical child abuser in the abusive relationships was the same man who was abusing the mother. Fathers or father surrogates were identified as responsible for the child abuse in approximately 50 percent of the cases where mothers were also battered; the victimized mothers were identified as the responsible parties in 35 percent of the cases, and "both" parents were identified as responsible in the rest. This was more than three times the proportion of men identified as child abusers in the nonbattering families.[6]

By identifying men as the cause of frequent nonfatal and nonserious injuries to women, this finding added a crucial missing dimension to survey findings implicating fathers and father surrogates in serious and fatal child abuse. It is highly likely that, as many of the examples in the book illustrate, a majority of these crimes against children occurred in the context of abuse of the mother and could have been prevented by interrupting the coercive control. This hypothesis was supported by another finding, that a history of domestic violence was well established before the child abuse was reported. If this dynamic proved to be generally true, it confirmed what the women in the shelter were telling us, that abusive partners hurt the children as part of their strategy to control them. What did this imply about the larger dynamic of coercive control? Apparently, children generally became the focus of a man's abuse *after the mother*, possibly because the rewards of abusing the mother alone proved suddenly insufficient. Was this because the presence of a child steeled women's resistance to abuse or merely broadened the field of opportunity? In either event, this was the first signal that, when it occurs in the context of coercive control, child abuse is a form of secondary victimization. This is a major finding of this book.

Let's briefly review. We know that the child abuse caseload can roughly be subdivided into cases of "real" abuse (serious injury or other threatening harm to the child) and "neglect" (poverty, loss of housing, drugs, alcohol, mental illness, and immaturity); that the mothers of abused children are also the victims of "domestic violence," but not the mothers of children darted for "neglect"; that this abuse is typically long-standing and antecedes the identification of the child abuse; and that the abusive men are identified as responsible for the child abuse solely (50%) or jointly with the mother (15%). With these findings in mind, consider the next finding from the Yale Child Abuse Study. At Yale, many of the children from battering families were darted because "mother needs support," an implicit recognition of the domestic violence in the home. Our coders learned about the abuse largely because the women had spoken about it to a medical provider either at a visit for abusive injury, another abuse-related problem, or for a problem unrelated to abuse. The coders also learned about the domestic violence in the home because they brought their *index of suspicion* to bear on the women's medical record. In other words, they suspected a mother was abused because on another occasion, she had presented at least one injury at the hospital we could identify with abuse. Did the social workers on the "Dart" Committee also know what our coders suspected? Since there is no record of the domestic violence in their files, we can only surmise that if they had taken the time to ask women why "mother needs support," the women would have disclosed, a safety plan could have been developed and, if need be, the woman and child could have been removed to safety or put in touch with justice services to hold the perpetrators accountable. Though there is no evidence women were ever asked about abuse at home, what was fascinating was this: *regardless of whether the nurses, social workers, and pediatricians on the Dart Committee were aware of which mothers were abused, they responded differently to the children of battered mothers than to other children even when all else appeared the same.* Note, however, their differential response was more punitive, not more sympathetic. The most common response was to remove the children. I call this differential response to a class of patients an "implicit diagnosis"; it amounts to a diagnosis because it has real consequences, and is "implicit" because it is based on the differential treatment of a group of patients with no basis in fact. Because of the negative connotations of the response, the terms applied to the children of abused mothers function as what sociologists call a "label" whose only function is to elicit a hostile response from providers who read the code later in the service chain. Something is telling social workers and nurses to treat the children from abusive homes differently and more harshly than other abused and neglected children, but what that something is not apparent.

The consequences of "the label" were clear, even if the knowledge from which it drew was not. The hospital team was more likely to report the children of the battered than of the nonbattered mothers to Connecticut's Department of Children and Families (DCF). This was true even when the level of harm to the child was identical. In sum, one of the premier child protection units in the country—Yale New Haven Hospital's "Dart" Committee—selected children who were injured pursuant to their mother's abuse out from other children with identical injury presentations for referrals to the Department of Children and Families. Regardless of what prompted these referrals, their effect is frankly punitive because they initiate costly, disruptive investigations, administrative proceedings, and intrusive visits that send families on a downward spiral. As we will learn in chapter 4, this punitive response also exacerbates the effects of the abuse the children are already experiencing the home, a process I call as "social entrapment." The point is that this punitive response by clinicians and social workers is due not to anything that the mothers or children have done or that is "wrong" with them, but to what has been done for them. Fathers or father surrogates were not referred, although in 65 percent of the cases men were identified as solely (50%) or jointly responsible for the child's injury. We will step into the river a bit later in the next chapter, when we consider the *Nicholson* mothers, a group of women whose children were removed after they were referred to child welfare by a "Dart" Team such as Yale's solely because the mothers had "engaged in domestic violence." But they remained invisible at Yale. In the hundreds of case files and agency records I reviewed in preparing to testify in *Nicholson*, I found repeated references to the men who had abused the women and children in those cases. But they do not make a physical appearance. Nor did the abusive men ever show up at Yale.

We will recall that the Yale research and New Hampshire teams began from a common interest in mapping a family drama in which children and women were the victims of violence. Both sets of studies identified the male partner as the most common source of serious harm to the children as well as their mothers (and pets), contradicting a belief at the time that transmission in these families was a "pass-the-parcel" game where man-hits-wife, wife-hits-kid, kid-kicks-dog, and so on down the line. By the late 1980s, however, the Yale and New Hampshire teams had moved in different directions and separate specialized subfields had developed around "domestic violence" and "child abuse" as if there had never been a common ground. Men had never been a central concern in the child abuse field. By the late 1990s, men had disappeared from the child abuse and child welfare literature altogether, as perpetrators of both child abuse and domestic violence. In the rare monograph where "domestic violence" was acknowledged, mothers were held accountable as the source of "exposure" and the actual offender was not identified.

As a new PhD working with the New Hampshire team, Richard Gelles had shared honors with "other feminists" for discovering "battered wives" in the 1970s and linking men to child abuse in the early 1980s. We will encounter Professor Gelles again in the 1990s, in chapter 4, as the lead expert in defense of New York City in the *Nicholson* case, where the City was held in contempt for removing children solely because of their mother's abuse.

With respect to the abused children, my career was no less circumspect. The Yale Child Abuse Study should have led logically to an exploration of the source and operation of men's illegitimate authority in these families and the points at which it was most vulnerable to interruption. But the children had a low priority, in my professional life at least. Instead, Dr. Flitcraft and I focused on the arenas in which our research was having the greatest impact, on the response of the health system to abused women and the criminal justice system to men. My earlier book *Coercive Control: How Men Entrap Women in Personal Life* (2007, 2023) recounts our "march through the institutions" of health and justice circa 1980–2010. For my purpose here, two institutional responses to the "news" about the significance of domestic violence are most relevant. The first involved legislation introduced by President Clinton and many US states pursuant to the recommendations of the Attorney General's Task Force under President Reagan that made domestic violence the only misdemeanor offense in which arrest was mandatory. The second development, initially outlined in a US Surgeon General's Task Force Report under C. Everett Koop, recommended that child welfare programs and medical facilities responsible for child abuse screen for domestic violence.[7] Meanwhile, in large part due to the Yale research, the Centers for Disease Control (CDC) helped make physical injury the generally accepted demarcation for when cases should be considered "high risk" and the US Department of Justice recognized injury as a prompt to a jail sentence or restrictive court order. The domestic violence model made similar headway in eliciting support for Refuges throughout Europe, Canada, and Australia and for enhanced police and health intervention throughout much of the world, including parts of South America, Africa, and Asia.[8]

Children were rarely mentioned in our campaigns. For one thing, few women's advocates in the battered women's movement, refuge movement, or the larger movement to end violence against women and girls approach children's well-being and child custody issues with the moral clarity they bring to men's physical and sexual violence against women. For another thing, there are important race and class differences in how evidence that domestic violence harms children is used. As we'll see in chapter 4, the *Nicholson* case illustrated how the presence of domestic violence was used to justify the removal of children from poor and minority mothers, one reason many shelter workers distrusted child protective services after the 1980s. At the same time, the presumed risk domestic violence posed to children could be used to advantage in custody disputes with abusive men (including women of Color) in family court and by the predominately white and middle-class women who sought stay-away orders. Similarly, evidence that children are usually resilient to their mother's physical abuse can be used to mitigate criminal charges against women for "failure to protect" or to bolster an abuser's claim that he spewed his venom at his partner with no intended harm to the children. Attitudes toward battered mothers were further confounded because shelter workers often felt deep ambivalence about how women in refuge mothered their own children. Under Presidents George Bush and then again President Trump, as track funding for support and housing were limited, many programs for abused women and their children nested within broader social service coalitions. As the feminist policy analyst Paige Sweet astutely observed, "After, 2000, many more shelters in the U.S. became players in the social service game they originally hoped to change, providing 'parental surveillance'[9] for the child welfare watchdogs, and emphasizing . . . 'therapeutic citizenship' where women learn to perform psychological wellness through racialized tropes of respectable motherhood."[10]

Without belaboring the point, the fact remains. After a brief moment when it appeared that a single paradigm of household abuse by a dominating male would unify diverse perspectives in the antiviolence movement, the fabric was rent and the "child abuse" and "domestic violence" subspecialties went in separate directions, both losing sight of the larger familial context that was an important original source of our concerns. The New Hampshire researchers were among the first to recognize the particular prevalence, frequency, and severity of men's violence against female partners. Riding an antifeminist backlash during the Reagan presidency in the 1980s, however, the New Hampshire team shifted to forms of "family violence" that were less controversial than sexual violence, such as "mutual violence" in couples, female-to-male violence, and the "transmission of violence" witnessed in childhood to the next generation. By the Biden presidency in 2018, this line had spawned a cottage industry and become near gospel in the field.[11]

Our work on children drew more narrowly focused attention, primarily from child welfare systems and the family court. Many state children's registries added "domestic violence" to the factors that put children at risk for abuse and qualified "mothers" for services; I worked with child protective service agencies in about fifteen US states to devise and implement training protocols to sensitize caseworkers to abuse. There probably wasn't a single major forum for custodial decision-making or policymaking in child welfare to which our research findings were not disseminated.

Before turning in chapter 4 to *Nicholson*, the case that moved us decisively to approach child maltreatment in the context of coercive control, it is necessary to revisit and reject a core assumption that guided our research at Yale, that apart from being physically injured during violent domestic conflicts, children are harmed as "witnesses" largely because of how exposure to extreme events affects their undeveloped aural, visual, and emotional sensitivities. Over 1,000 monographs document the traumatic effects of witnessing violence on children.

"Witnessing": A Misnomer for the Experience of Coercive Control

Children "experience" coercive control as if it is happening to them, even when they are being forced to play the role of spectator. For children, witnessing is always at the same time a form of participation and an experience of victimization, and participating is equally a form of spectatorship. Some children become a witness by happenstance. Many more children are assigned to witness abuse or assume the role of witness as a strategic way to support their mother or to intimidate their father.

The heady reception of our early research on domestic violence as a women's health issue led us to expect similar gratitude when we announced that the huge establishment constructed to save children by bolstering motherhood (through welfare) and child protection was based on a false premise, that women held the key to the suffering of children, not men. Things changed. Only not in the direction we hoped.

I was not surprised that domestic violence and child abuse and fatality were linked. What surprised me was the strength of the association. I had naively assumed that the presence of millions of households headed by women in the United States and abroad meant that a huge number of children were being raised without the presence of a significant man in their lives, hence that rates of child abuse and domestic violence would be far lower in these households. Two things turned out to be true. Where no male involvement is recorded in a family, there are very few cases of serious child abuse and almost no child fatalities. When sole women physically abuse or kill their children, it is largely in the context of mental illness, a situational depression, or substance abuse rather than under conditions of immiseration, immaturity, or "stress," as the children's literature claims.[12] These cases are serious, but are far too few as a proportion of the children at risk to merit an entire intervention subsystem. More relevant for my purposes is the second truth to emerge from our research at Yale, that the women we supposed would be at the lowest risk for domestic violence and child abuse, those who are "single, separated and divorced" actually report the *highest* rates of both problems, with married women, whom we assumed to be at highest risk, reporting the lowest rates of both problems next to widows. This finding has enormous implications for understanding the nature of abuse and for intervention. The fact that child abuse and fatality (primarily perpetrated by men) is highest among abused women who are "single," "separated," and "divorced" means that the means used to coercively control women and children—what I refer to as the "technology" of coercive control—must be designed and deployed to "cross social space," i.e., the distance/difference in time/space that physically separates them. When an abusive father tracks his son's movements on his iPhone or geocodes his paper route, he is deploying stalking as an element of coercive control. Separation and concealment can be effective ways to reduce or end vulnerability to domestic violence. But the "spatiality" of coercive control mitigates the efficacy of separation as a strategy for protecting women and children from abuse. The spatial dimension of coercive control is critical to providing safeguards for children in custodial disputes involving coercive control.

Because of its spatial dimension, social proximity—courtship, dating, separation and divorce, and court-mandated visitation—defines the period when women and children are at greatest danger from abuse in coercive control, not *physical* proximity as defined by marriage or a shared living space. Surveys have consistently shown, for both men and women, that divorced or separated persons were subjected to the highest rates of intimate partner violence, followed by never-married persons. The trouble with these statistics is that they are based solely on reported physical violence, which tends to be more severe, whereas the pattern typical of coercive control is frequent, but low level and more diffuse violence. More pertinent to the situation of children is that separation and divorce often signal the beginning but almost never end the coercive control of the children. As we will see shortly, regardless of whether violence continues in a relationship after a physical breakup, so long as coercive control tactics continue, the children are likely to be targets, even if the abuser has never shown any previous animosity toward the children.

Regardless of whether violence continues or escalates postseparation, the overriding risk to children in this period is likely to reflect their vulnerability to the use of intimidation and control tactics "through social space," such as stalking and the use of geomapping and electronic tracking devices. Previous iterations of domestic violence—think of Marlon Bandon in *Streetcar Named Desire* (1951) or Bradley Cooper stuffing cake in Lady Gaga's face in *A Star Is Born* (2018)—portray the male abuser's as "a king in his castle," a combination of bluster, drink, anger, and growl. But the reality women and children face is more often like the young lions on the prowl. Their presence is not a matter of any public record; their names, faces, and addresses do not appear in child welfare reports, or pediatric records on child abuse. These men seem as elusive to the systems responsible for monitoring children's well-being as they do to their partners. And yet, to hear the children tell it, these men haunt the schools, playgrounds, football and soccer fields, and game malls in every suburban center and town. As the title of the novel by Native American Tommy Orange suggests, they are *There, There* (2019).

Just as cyber-technology allows abusers to pursue women and children through social space, so is it helpful to conceive of "leaving abuse" as a process of migration rather than a simple matter of separating and relocating. This was illustrated by the experience of a twelve-year-old boy who listened intently at our dining room table while a young Hispanic woman from Waterbury, Connecticut, described an incident where the boy had hit her with a wooden board at his father's instruction. The woman fled with her son. She described hiding with him for days in fields, then in bus stations, in restrooms, in all-night rest stops, and in abandoned cars. She was among a number of mothers who recounted how men had followed them when they fled with children on foot, on bikes, across fields, in cars, across state lines; how they hid with friends, police officers, gang members, old girlfriends, ex-wives, coworkers, coreligionists; how their partners had their children follow them or had their children kidnapped from school, from friend's homes, from the homes of their grandparents, from dance class, and from baseball practice. Millions of abused women and their children spend months, even years, migrating across countries and continents to evade detection and interdiction. No matter how long they can remain in one place, the children's lives are often in shambles before long: the children's education is improvised, their social network is limited or confined entirely in cyberspace, their sexual maturation is atrophied and their emotional intelligence is based on anticipating and preparing for exposure and isolation from loved ones. Amid all, after harrowing tales of survival, the child and mother would confess they wish they had done more to keep each other safe. One woman's daughter told her about her father's sexual abuse when they arrived at a safe house, but she acknowledged she was too afraid of the consequences of her anger to follow up.

One consequence of coercive control being extended over time and through social space is that children experience abuse as happening to them rather than as a fixed externality (even when their mother is the only ostensible target) and as continuous, cumulative, and omnipresent rather than consisting of discrete "doses" or events. Consider how poorly a term like "witnessing" captures how Edna's girls processed their father's abuse.

Edna is a thirty-two-year-old woman who was born in Jamaica and lives in northern New Jersey, to which she moved from the Island with her mother and father when she was ten. She has four children, between the ages of eight and twelve.

A short, stocky woman, Edna arrived at the shelter in Newark, New Jersey, in a state of harried disarray with four daughters in June 2019. The family had not bathed nor had a change of clothes in days. The woman's hair, which had streaks of gray, was matted in dreads on her head. Clean clothes and a bath were delivered and acknowledged, but the family sat together at meals, huddled tent-like, quickly finished off the small plates they drew and then rose, rising a blanket of dust, and returned to their room. The third night, another resident called Edna to come down. The girls came down as well, crowding their mother on the stairs as if to conceal her from view. In the living room, a small group had gathered for "haircut liberation night." As Edna sat blushing, the girls were made to step aside. One of the residents, a licensed hairdresser, snapped off a braid and shouted. Then another. As each braid fell, the women raised their voices in unison. And another. The woman was sobbing. The oldest daughter explained that the father and she had had a disagreement about a heating bill six months earlier. Since then, he had forbidden her to bathe or wash or cut her hair. The girls bathed at school when they could, she told us. But they refused to shower or bathe at home so long as their mother could not do so. "We were witnessing her 'shame,'" they told us, mimicking their father's intonation, but with a note of indignation. By now, you could detect a faint smile curling through the woman's tears. The twelve-year-old was weeping, and the little girl was giggling, though she was sobbing at the same time.

While Edna's children decide not to bathe at home in solidarity with their mother, this effect of their father's coercive control on their hygiene is not captured by "witnessing" or any of the other current phrases for child maltreatment. In the ACS case in chapter 4, Mrs. Nicolson was alleged to have "engaged in domestic violence" in front of the children by being hit in their presence, thereby having "caused" the children to "witness" her abuse. Edna could have been similarly charged for forcing the girls to witness her "shame." But note, the "witnessing" here is an experience of the girls staged by the father to have an effect in subordinating ("shaming") the mother, an example of what I called "child abuse as secondary or tangential wife abuse" earlier in the book. We will come across the tactic again in a later chapter, when we meet Jeanette Hughes, whose husband, Keith, shamed her by forcing her daughter, Tiffany, to shower immediately after visiting her biological father, sending the message that she was made "dirty" by contact with the mother's ex. Tiffany told me she was unaffected by the showering ritual. But it devastated Jeanette. Unlike Tiffany Hughes, Edna's girls were frightened by their experience, indicating that the use of witnessing as a tactic to frighten women may not reduce the terroristic effect on children. In a novel, *The War for Gloria* (2021), Atticus Lish portrays nine-year-old Corey's horror, fury, and shame at his mother's abuse by his father. The experience stays with Corey for years, shaping his choice in friends, work, whether to attend school, and ultimately how to define manhood for himself. Corey's attempts to defend his mother against her ex border on the fantastical. Still, by recognizing the degree to which his father has triangulated him with his mom, he is able to differentiate goals for himself that do not implicate his mother. Corey survives because his mother was the direct target of his father's abuse, not him. I call this abuse of the child "secondary" to signify that children are not the principal victims and that offenders may display no open hostility toward a child they kill or seriously harm. If intervention in coercive control is early, therefore, children like Corey can emerge relatively unaffected.

The other important facet of recognizing that child victimization is secondary is that the child can often find security in attachment to the mother, thus avoiding the kind of traumatic "identification with the aggressor" we see in the case of Anna Covlin, in chapter 7. Edna's daughters assumed her victimization as their own and redressed some of the inequity by taking showers at school. In the same way, Corey in the Atticus Lish novel, resolves some of his ambiguous hostility in the marines, recognition by Lish that some of the sexual violence in the military originates in coercive control. Edna's daughters weave their experiences of their mother's abuse and her response into their stories of their own abuse and recovery, no less victims than she is, even if the role chosen for them by their father is passive. Children resist, accommodate, and survive: Edna's children refuse to be played off against their mother; they refuse even to shower at home. But sensitive to their image at school (as well as to their mother's added shame if they are found to be "unclean") they keep up their hygiene as best they can. Edna is at the center of recovery. Everyone at the shelter is aware that the trajectory or abuse and recovery encompasses them all. In the Lish novel, though his father causes the death of a surrogate son and Corey fails to present a coherent picture of his father's abuse to police, he is able to extricate his father's imago from his own as a combat marine and project it onto an enemy warlord in a training video. A less sanguine author might have recognized the extent to which the military redirects the rage it helps to instill at women, in the form of sexual violence.

The effect of being forced into the role of a "witness" by an abuser can be devastating to children, because of the messages it sends about one's efficacy as a person, not only because of the vulnerability a child feels when a protective parent is hurt. Despite his relatively undeveloped physique, in the Lish novel, Corey makes a number of attempts to keep his mother safe (as well as to stave off her amyotrophic lateral sclerosis, or ALS), all for naught. Like Edna's children and so many others, he berates himself for "doing nothing" when his mother is dying. In fact, this common feeling of impotence among children is the direct result of being coercively controlled by their father with as much disregard for their rights and needs as he showed to their mother. I met Joe Torre as part of his "Safe at Home" initiative. I think of Edna's girls and Corey when I listen to former NY Yankee skipper describe how he and his brothers fled to a neighbor's house when they saw their father's black Buick parked at home in the afternoon. Because they knew what he was there to do to their mother. "And then to you too," I tell Joe now, "by making you ashamed at being too afraid to help her." This causes my hero of the 1998 Season to tear up when he recalls those days alone with this brothers. Hiding.

In all of these cases, children's experience of "witnessing" abuse involved far more than a passive reception of an external event of violence. In each case, witnessing was a process of interpretation, affect, mediation, and response. Children are often forced to witness abuse, as numerous case examples in the book will illustrate. The effect can be devastating. Joe and his brothers were forced to imagine their impotence as an attribute of their humanity rather than as a concrete affect they could counter through specific action. The result was that they left their sister to confront their father as the three of them could not. Our literary fiction is filled with stories of Pennsylvania farm boys or children on cattle ranches in Nebraska and Oklahoma who have waited out a cold night in a field with a similar shame. Abusers also force children to witness their mother's abuse to demonstrate how incapable she is of protecting them. Edna's girls felt powerless. But they did not compensate by despising their mother, as their father would have them do. Instead, they become joined with her in escape and shelter as forms of strategic prowess. As children's unfold their narratives of witnessing their mother's abuse, the responsibility of the listener—be she police officer, parent, social worker or psychologist—is to restore the balance of power in the room, countering the voice of the abuser in the child's head, so that strategic behavior becomes an option. I like to think a teacher who was aware of coercive control could have identified the girls as "victims" at their school—was their showering at the school the sign she needed?—and created "the shelter in space" to avoid their having to come to us at the Newark shelter in a disheveled state.

From Child Abuse to "the Coercive Control of Children"

Although seemingly less ephemeral than coercive control, child abuse can't be deciphered in clinical records with the same clarity as "domestic violence." Though a parent or foster parent can cause appalling or fatal injuries to a child, as the practical focus of intervention, "child abuse" extends along a continuum of maltreatment that is less a physical demarcation than a political construction born of decades of negotiations between pediatricians, child psychiatrists, child welfare providers, politicians, and parents. The social problem of "child abuse" for which child protective services and children's services generally have jurisdiction encompasses a broad spectrum of childhood experiences of which Henry C. Kempe's "battered child syndrome" is a small subgroup. Nothing in our Yale Studies challenges the reality Kempe described or the importance of emergency intervention to prevent children from being "battered." What I challenge is the claim, implicit in the administrative jurisdiction of the child protection system and the family and probate courts globally over the broad spectrum of "child abuse and neglect cases," that there is an etiological link between the relatively small number of preventable child deaths caused primarily by maternal deficits, the much larger proportion of child fatalities and serious injuries caused by abusive men, and so-called neglect cases, where children's interests are jeopardized directly or indirectly by abusive tactics against them or their mothers other than violence. In the approach I advocate, "child abuse" is identified as an element of the serious criminal offense of coercive control and is defined narrowly to include the majority of children currently "darted" for physical/sexual child abuse at the hospital whose mothers are also being abused. I reserve the broader heading, "the coercive control of children" to include both physical "child abuse" in the context of partner abuse and all other forms of child mal-treatment secondary to subordination of the mother. This definition extends to the examples I give in the final chapters of children who are enlisted by their father in the abuse of their mother. As victims of coercive control or of "child abuse" under the rubric of coercive control, I do not include the millions of children who are currently darted for risk of "abuse and neglect" almost entirely because of maternal deficits, environmental factors (such as loss of housing, COVID, or toxic hazards) or natural disasters but who have neither been physically abused nor subjected to coercive control. For these children, I believe, resource-based community solutions are almost always more appropriate than those administered by the child welfare system, the courts, or police.

La Lotta Continua

It took several decades before the pattern of punitive referrals we identified at Yale would become official policy at child welfare systems across the country. Ironically, by ringing the alarm about the importance of domestic violence as a cause of child abuse, the Yale studies heightened awareness of the risk to children in these cases without providing an antidote. We may have pushed child welfare systems that were not already doing so to officially "see" do-mestic violence in their midst. But without the political power to broaden the mission of child welfare to encompass the men responsible for abuse, an appropriate response was foreclosed and the result was punitive.

I have already mentioned some of our efforts at dissemination. Over the next decade, Dr. Flitcraft and I presented the findings of our child abuse study before the US Congress, the US Civil Rights Commission, and key committees in five state legislatures. We appeared before several national commissions, including one investigating child abuse and neglect. Our findings were widely recognized as valid, if not always enthusiastically embraced. The research reported in this chapter helped spawn a global awareness of the importance of domestic violence as a risk for children. As a result of our research and hundreds of other studies that validated and superseded our findings, national and state governments responsible for services to children as well as the vast network for child-saving and child-protection organizations in the voluntary sector adapted "domestic vio-lence" screens to identify the population of affected children in their midst.

Unfortunately, the increasing sensitivity of pediatric, children's services, and child welfare to a clinical picture of "domestic violence" had a paradoxical effect. In hundreds of jurisdictions in the United States, United Kingdom, and Europe, being identified as a "victim of domestic violence" by the child health and welfare systems resulted in a punitive rather than an ameliorative response: children were reported to be harmed by being "exposed" to violence or having witnessed it, parents "engaging in domestic violence" was targeted as a cause of child neglect and their children were placed in foster homes. Ironically, the research we report in this chapter became the basis for the welfare Golgotha we faced off in the *Nicholson* case, the subject of chapter 4. We clearly identified abusive men as the principal source of harm to women and children in families and relationships. What we did not anticipate was that the singular focus of family, children, and welfare services on abused women meant that abusive men would remain invisible regardless of their culpability. The epic confrontation between the *Nicholson* mothers and New York City's ACS led to the prohibition as unconstitutional of child removals based solely on a mother's physical abuse. As an advocate and expert witness for the *Nicholson* mothers against ACS, I present my evidence about the children as it was intended. Chapter 5 provides a brief critique of screening for adverse childhood experiences (ACES) as a way to prevent childhood trauma. A critique of the punitive approach, removal to foster care, and the "therapeutic approach," relief of ACES as the salve to abuse, take us to the border of the new frontier of coercive control. The Yale research made it no longer tenable to bifurcate domestic violence and child abuse. The child welfare system identified the connection between domestic violence and child abuse through the mother's "engagement" in an abusive relationship, blamed mothers because children might be harmed by their abuse, and removed the children. ACES purports to head off the long-term effects of childhood trauma caused by abuse through early therapeutic intervention with the children. Instead of this approach, I propose to remove the perpetrator of coercive control, the original source of the child's trauma.

I remember, as if it was yesterday, presenting the child abuse research at a Special Workshop on Violence Prevention convened by US Surgeon General C. Everett Koop in 1985. Ronald Reagan was president and Dr. Flitcraft and I were cochairs at the workshop. Determined to put "violence against women" on the national health agenda for children, the courageous surgeon general had assembled the leadership of the child research, welfare, and protection movement into one auditorium. In the middle of Pentagon City, the full hall remained hushed during a presentation we made accessible through straightforward graphics. We finished. Then, we asked for questions. The hall was silent. We had been talking to dead people. The surgeon general sat aghast. He had called his army to battle and discovered his general staff constituted a fifth column.

A decade passed before the reception improved. The "dead awakened" in 1994 because President Bill Clinton put 1.5 billion federal dollars on the table through the Violence against Women's Act, legislation that remains the foundation for government support for shelters in the United States. For the first time, funding for state child welfare programs was to be linked to "collaboration" with "the battered woman's movement." Overnight, our phones starting ringing. Now, everyone in child welfare wanted to hear what the couple from Yale were saying. Putting money on the table moved concern for children affected by abuse from a sideline to the main show. The bill offered funding to state child welfare agencies that took notice of domestic violence; suddenly, public policymakers could officially acknowledge what had been part of the "known known" everywhere else. I would regularly attend hearings for potential state programs, often one of three or four men in the room of several hundred. I would audibly correct speakers who used the derogatory "mom" when what "you clearly mean to say is 'woman.'" And if there was no mention of the required partnership to our services, I would rise conspicuously and mutter loud enough to be heard, "Then, I will take my 150 million and go home." Or some such.

Is it too cynical to suggest that federal cash did more to awaken the child welfare interest in domestic violence than the sudden enlightenment afforded by our research and the work of others? When I began research in child welfare files in the 1990s as background for the *Nicholson* cases, I found the strongest evidence for my case in Central Office files filled with pleas from fieldworkers begging officials to "do something about the domestic violence" that had flooded child welfare agencies for decades without any response.

As we've seen, our victory proved pyrrhic. I naively assumed that the logical response to the discovery that domestic violence caused child abuse was to remove the source of the abuse. That was the Right thing to do. This is not what happened.

The Yale studies set the stage for the themes the rest of the chapters the book examine in greater depth, the singular impact of male partner abuse on children's well-being; the ongoing nature of the harms children face; the core dynamics when perpetrators use or abuse children as part of their campaign to subjugate their mother; the consequences for children and their attempt to survive and escape these consequences both independently and in conjunction with the victimized mother; and the dilemmas posed for women and children targeted by coercive control when they turn for help. These themes are developed in the context of our new understanding of coercive control. To go there, however, we first have to through the ACS. And to do that, we needed the *Nicholson* mothers.

It started, as such things often do in our business, with a phone call. My world turned upside down. Work I'd thought would spawn a new era of cooperation between child welfare and the women's movement was creating a disaster for our core clientele.

The caller was Jill Zuccardy, (then) a young staff attorney with the Sanctuary for Families and Children, an advocacy group for domestic violence victims, headquartered in the Bronx.

Did I want to want to work on the "*Nicholson* case"? She asked.

Her question was a little like Fredrick Engels selling the *Communist Manifesto* at the Berlin Zoo in 1855 by asking a sucker in the crowd, "Do you know what stage of the class struggle you're at?" No one at the Berlin Zoo had heard of "class struggle."

"Huh?," I mumbled sheepishly, "What's the *Nicholson* case"?

Did I know that New York had a policy of removing children solely because their mothers had been victims of domestic violence? Jill quizzed. And that these mothers are then charged with "neglect?"

"I did not," I admitted.

And that their names are then put on a "black list" that keeps them getting employment in daycare, teaching, or any occupation dealing with children? And did I know this was regular practice at ACS?

"No," again. I should have guessed the line was baited—then came the reason Jill had reached out to me.

Did I know that ACS is citing the research of Yale researchers Dr. Evan Stark and Anne Flitcraft, MD, as supporting the position that being exposed to domestic violence was a form of child abuse?

So began my multiyear involvement in the *Nicholson* case, which ended in 2005, with what remains today the strongest answer by the US Federal Judiciary to the State's punitive treatment of battered mothers and their children.

4

Mrs. Nicholson and Her Children
vs. The City of New York

A minority of homes remain intact during the course of coercive control, particularly in rural areas or more affluent communities where property owners
can readily isolate victims, exploit them and regulate their mobility "behind
closed doors." If an affluent couple is separated, their relations with one another and the children are likely to be regulated by proprietary institutions
with a low tolerance for highly visible "conflict." Until an "escape," murder,
or "scandal" interrupts the oppressive dynamic in these families, outside
public institutions play a minimal role.[1] But for the tens of millions of abused
children in the United States and abroad whose family lives are reproduced
piecemeal in the economic and social marketplace, the interface with the
public world is continual and the experience of coercive control is inextri-
cably bound to how police, hospitals, schools, child welfare agencies, and
other "institutions of secondary socialization" respond when women and
children report, seek help, or resist or escape their abuse. The durability of
coercive control as a major offense is inconceivable apart from the collusive
and unwitting role of public institutions.

This chapter describes the real-time confrontation between abused
mothers and their children with the child welfare, police, and the family court
systems in New York City that came to a head in 2004, pursuant to a class
action to stop the city from responding to abusive situations by removing
"exposed" children from their biological mothers, placing them in foster
care, and charging the victimized women with "neglect" solely for "engaging
in domestic violence." The victory in the *Nicholson* case was seminal to the
reconceptualization of domestic violence as a global offense that deprives
women and children of constitutionally guaranteed rights, resources, and
liberties.

The vast majority of homes where children are subjected to coercive control are headed by women who are single, separated, and divorced. In this
context, where men may be physically separated from a mother and her

Children of Coercive Control. Evan Stark, Oxford University Press. © Oxford University Press 2023.
DOI: 10.1093/oso/9780197587096.003.0005

children or have a tenuous legal connection at best, coercive control can continue only if it can "cross social space." This refers to the propensity for abusers to deploy electronic surveillance, stalking, tracking devices, and other invasive means to "cross social space" during periods of physical separation as well as to the role secondary social institutions play during periods of separation in applying rules, resources, policies, and practices to women and children that replicate patterns of dependence and subordination that are no longer being directly imposed in the home. So critical are the policies and practices of these secondary institutions to the fortunes of female victims and their children that four states in Australia have incorporated the role of state institutions into risk assessments for children.[2] Once introduced, the theme of how the institutions of social betterment enter and reconstitute the personal lives of women and children as dependent is woven into the cases throughout the book. The implications for our reform agenda are unavoidable. Unraveling coercive control entails not simply removing the abuser, but rendering the systemic social support for his aims ineffectual.

The *Nicholson* mothers challenged the usurpation of their children's liberty by the child welfare system in New York City. The *Nicholson* case was the culmination of two decades of conflict about the terms on which abused women who were mothers would be received by the child welfare system. Ever since the campaign to support the Violence Against Women Act of 1994, negotiation for improvement in the child protective services (CPS) response to battered women was guided by three principles: *empowerment* (to treat women as full persons in their own right with needs of their own), *safety* (to give precedence to "safety for women" alongside children, even if this meant excluding and/or incarcerating men), and *accountability* (to acknowledge the existence and agency of "men"). Forced by political pressure to recognize "domestic violence," CPS nevertheless maintained its singular focus on women as mothers by framing the experience as a "problem" that mothers transmitted to children in an emergent time-frame. "Emergency" here referred not to a well-identified predicament in children, but to a condition of administrative paralysis. Confronted with myriad situations that cried out for liaison with justice resources to respond to men, CPS used the "emergency" as a legal conceit so caseworkers could take a child without notifying a court, getting a court's permission, or giving the child or the mother benefit of due process. Emergency removals and placements rationalized a transparently victim-blaming practice as a matter of expediency while concealing the violation of rights as "business as usual."[3]

Starting in the 1980s, CPS and the family courts throughout the United States, with New York City's CPS agency, the Administration for Children's Services (ACS), in the forefront, had a policy of charging battered mothers with "neglect" for "engaging in domestic violence" and removing their children because of the harms allegedly caused by "witnessing" or "being exposed" to domestic violence. Mrs. Nicholson's children were removed and she was charged with "neglect" for "engaging in domestic violence" solely because she was physically abused. Her children were not hurt nor otherwise affected. Along with other mothers whose children had been removed in similar circumstances, Mrs. Nicholson and her children claimed that the removal and allegations violated their constitutional rights. They took the City of New York to federal court and, in 2005, a US Appellate decision in the 2nd Circuit found that removal solely on the grounds of domestic violence violated the constitutional rights of women and children, including their due process rights and the children's right to be free of indentured servitude. The decision provided relief for the plaintiff mothers and a lasting benefit for thousands more. But for our present purpose in this book, the key to the *Nicholson* case is that it made transparent the role of child welfare, the family court, and other "institutions of secondary socialization" in the coercive control of women and children where abusive men had stepped out of the picture, sometimes for good.

The plaintiff women in the case represented a class of mothers who were cited for "neglect" in homes where battering occurred but where children had not been harmed by the nonbattering custodian and where the protection of the children and their best interest can be accomplished by separation of the alleged batterer from the custodian. No evidence was ever presented or claimed that any of the children who were removed in the *Nicholson* families had actually been physically abused or otherwise harmed. To the contrary, there was hard evidence that removal was ACS policy in domestic violence cases regardless of the children's status. In the "Zone A. Pilot" project that assessed ACS's responses to cases of abuse, forty-seven of seventy-eight cases involving allegations of domestic violence were "indicated"; 23 percent of the children in these families were removed. There was no evidence of even one case in which ACS caused or contributed to holding the batterer accountable for his behavior. In fact, in the case of April Rodriquez, ACS not only failed to hold the batterer accountable but also turned the children over to his custody. Caseworker Robert Chamarro admitted that even if he learned of a situation of a batterer with a gun,[4] ACS would remove the child rather than take steps to have the batterer arrested.[5] The unavoidable conclusion was that the removals were punitive and designed with the sole purpose of exerting agency control over the victimized mother. As in Mrs. Nicholson's case, the removals were often effected without benefit of a court hearing, so that the coercive aims of ACS could not be easily countered by legal interventions. Although this meant the separations typically lasted for weeks rather than months or years, the children were often held virtually incommunicado, leaving the women utterly vulnerable, frightened, and dependent. In most of the cases, though not in all, the abusive partners remained in the picture and used the women's heightened vulnerability to their advantage. Whether the children were physically harmed in foster care, suffered health problems, or only suffered the wrenching emotional trauma of being rent from their mothers, the Court and the ACS were the source of the negligence. "Social entrapment" denotes the extent to which the involvement of ACS (police and the family court) increased women's vulnerability, facilitated the abuser's control and, through removal, directly effected physical and emotional trauma in children. When the trial began, the families had been reunited. But the children remained traumatized, and neglect charges were pending against several of the mothers.

* * *

By 2004, when we brought *Nicholson*, child welfare, hospitals, and a range of services for children in the United States and in many other countries routinely screened clients for "domestic violence" and thousands of these services maintained specialist domestic violence functions or teams to manage a clientele that was estimated at 30 to 35 percent of the child welfare population. The NYC practice of charging abused women with "neglect" for "engaging in domestic violence" and removing their children to foster care was not universal, but it was commonplace. Removal can be devastating to children under any circumstances, even when a proximate emergency merits rescue. But when a removal is arbitrary or frankly punitive, as in the *Nicholson* cases, the child's alienation can be compounded by guilt, rage, powerlessness, and self-loathing. With coercive control, the effects are further aggravated by the split siting of control created by placement and the heightened anxiety created for a child who may already fear his mother's loss because she is being abused. With a child removed, the women facing civil action or worse, their partners often escalated the coercive control. We had promised that early intervention to stem abuse would dramatically cut foster placement. Instead of cutting placement numbers, the aggressive pursuit of women and children confronting domestic violence caused foster care demand to increase sharply along with the number of nonoffending women who faced an array of administrative, family, and criminal charges associated with "engaging in domestic violence" and "neglect." Child welfare budgets skyrocketed. Hospital Dart committees expanded, and the chain of referral from an "indication for service" and "emergency removal" and placement shortened. A new approach was called for. But this time, as a psychiatrist might have foreseen, we couldn't wait for administrative agencies and the family courts to change by themselves.

Protection in Foster Care

Step one involved showing that the "cure" was as bad as "the disease." When domestic violence surfaced as a social problem in the 1970s, researchers initially emphasized the risks violence posed in a child's family of origin. From its beginning in the 1970s, the global women's movement highlighted legal accountability for the men responsible for violence and sexual abuse and protection and support for victims. But the mainstream view was more moderate, and highlighted ameliorative rather than incarceral approaches, including removing "innocent" children from what were widely assumed to be "toxic" family conflicts to somewhere "safe." Foster families were thought to be one good answer, particularly if they confirmed the American stereotype of the proper home as white, Protestant, peaceable, and "middle-class." A decade in, however, and certainly by the early 1980s, research had made it abundantly clear that violence against women and children is common in all relational settings; that it is used more extensively against women with children who are single, separated, and divorced than against married women; and that is as common against women with children in foster care as it is in the homes from which children are taken.[6] Moreover, exposure to abuse or neglect in foster care greatly increases the child's risk of being victimized as an adult.[7] The reality revealed by this data confounded the common practice in child welfare of shifting the focus of assessment, once a child is placed in foster care, from the child to the mother's "parental readiness" for reunification and paying little attention to the child's guest environment.

Based in large part on the risks to children in foster care, in 1981, Carolyn Kubichek filed *Doe v. New York City Department of Social Services*,[8] the first case in the country to establish a constitutional right of a foster child to be free from child abuse in a foster home. The ruling was adopted by a majority of federal appeals courts throughout the country, protecting thousands upon thousands of foster children.

The *Doe* decision affected the spectrum of coercive control at two junctures. The first juncture, which lies outside the scope of this book, involves a heightened awareness that foster care is a critical arena for policing because of how abusive fathers exploit the acquisition of foster children and their management by women in their control to bolster their command over economic and domestic resources in the foster home. The abuser's aim in this circumstance is to "game" the system by eking out for personal gain through bullying and exploitation the meager difference between State levels of home support and the bare subsistence required to keep women and children alive. The State is a silent and usually unwitting partner in this process.

The second juncture at which the *Doe* decision touched on coercive control brings us to the *Nicholson* mothers, whose lives were upended when the child welfare system deployed removal and foster placement in ways that disempowered them and enslaved their children, effectively complementing the role of the abuser and functioning as an extension of "the patriarchy" in their lives. So long as it was assumed that foster placement was a benign intervention, foster care was the "safety valve" for the child welfare policy of taking children from battered mothers. Now that placement was known to carry risks, including the risks of exposing a child to domestic violence and child abuse, the intervention would have to be justified on its own terms and in relation to the alternatives available.

The *Doe* decision helped us recognize the rights of children on their own terms, even when not with their biological family. But far from fostering a more catholic approach to family assessment in child welfare, subsequent case experience made the agency more aggressive with respect to removal, not less so, responding proactively to instances of case "ambiguity" or caseworker uncertainty with speedy placement to avoid the admittedly rare worst-case scenario. An important prequel to *Nicholson* was New York City's response to the death of Eliza Izquierdo in 1996.

Child Welfare in New York and Eliza Izquierdo

Six-year-old Eliza Izquierdo was killed by her mother in 1996 while she was an active client of New York's child welfare system. Nearly everyone who had contact with the Brooklyn girl was implicated in the tragedy, including the Family Court judge who had favored the abusive mother over the father in her custody award. Readers who are interested can Google the tragic details. The facts were terrible. Even so, what happened next was hard to fathom.

New York City's child welfare system is the world's largest public agency. Every day, the thousands of caseworkers, specialists, and social workers it employs encounter children at the brink of tragedy. Among the several hundred thousand referrals they receive for suspected child abuse or neglect through their hotlines and other portals each year, more than 10,000 are marked for "investigation." Thousands of these cases are "indicated" because the risk to the child is deemed so high as to require an emergent removal and placement in a foster home. Child abuse and fatality in foster homes is quite common, in no small part because the men who are surrogate "fathers" in these homes are rarely assessed. This reflects the archaic maternalism of child welfare agencies, their historic ignorance about domestic violence and coercive control, and their propensity to avoid accountability when things go wrong. Whether placement causes more tragedies than it prevents is unknown. Even so, the major alternative to placement, keeping children who are a high risk of being abused in their homes through a combination of remedial and preventive services targeted at the primary caregiver, remains an elusive fix. I know of no human service enterprise anywhere whose workers confront a more complex mix of needs, disabilities, and vulnerabilities on a daily basis than those who service families in care with child protection in New York City. The death of a child in care remains tragic. But for those of us who work on or near the front lines, it is a "normal" tragedy, somewhat like learning about another school shooting or that a 500-million-year-old glacier had slipped into the sea.

Based on my past experience with a child death in care, when Elizabeth Izquierdo died, I expected the New York agency to have a modulated response to the public outcry. The chief executive would give a mea culpa that satisfied the mayor, a few lesser executives in line-services responsible for protection would offer to resign; a dozen caseworkers would be reassigned to desk jobs pending investigative review, and a handful of supervisors would take early retirement. Some portion of human resources would be transferred from administrative to protective services. There would be an in-house report to the commissioner and an independent report to the mayor. Normal business would resume in a week if not a manner of days. This is how large child protective agencies *should* respond to tragedy. This is because with life-saving agencies that deal with a huge multitude whose health, economic, and social conditions border on subsistence, a certain number of tragedies are unavoidable and indicate nothing whatsoever about the overall quality or effectiveness of services.

My expectations were far too conservative. Instead of treating the girl's death as business as usual, the agency went into bureaucratic shock. There was a total lockdown. Frozen in denial and self-pity, agency leaders exhibited defensive responses you expect to get from trauma victims rather than hardened generals of the State's health and welfare police. Over the next few months of 1996, the agency closed its doors, reorganized, and reopened under the new name the "Administration for Children's Services" (ACS). The department head was replaced by a new "commissioner," Nicolas Scopetta, an outspoken political figure who had aged out of the foster system but had no prior experience in child welfare. Convinced the girl's death was a harbinger that past misdeeds would return to haunt them, the new commissioner ordered a review of *all* previously closed cases, thousands upon thousands, adding immeasurably to already heavy caseloads and effectively bringing the capacity of ACS to respond to new cases to a complete halt for several weeks. It reminded me of how the Chinese responded to a glitch in the Five-Year Plan in the post-Revolution Mao era: Whole Departments of government shut for a year or more to engage in critical self-study based on a sacred Marx-Engels text. Scopetta's edicts lacked the simplicity of Mao's "Little Red Book." But their effects on ACS morale were similarly confounding.

Symptomatic of the new commissioner's flight from reality was his first practice directive. In December 1996, as if the institutional memory had disappeared with the old agency name plaques, Nicolas Scopetta unveiled his "new Reform Plan" for ACS, including a mission statement and operating principles. Much of the plan appeared to be the byproduct of White-Out and Xerox photocopying of decades-old mimeo sheets. But one unequivocal instruction stood out as a radical change. Workers were "to resolve all ambiguities in favor of removing children from harm's way" and "to refuse to reunite them with their parents until the parents demonstrate that they can keep the children safe." Lest the draconian implications of this order get lost in its saccharin tone, we will parse this. Everything that happened later depended on this directive.

The heart of case management in child protection is risk assessment, whereby skilled professionals appraise the probability that a bad outcome will occur for a given child based on key markers and available supplementary information. Never mind that caseworkers rarely have the education, training, or vital data to handle the cases they are assigned. The vast majority of women and children they encounter cope regardless of what is done to them. Meanwhile, accumulated exposure makes caseworkers more assured, if not always wiser. Constructed on the basis of skimpy evidence from previous tragedies, an index of "risk" is a conservative guide that broadens the pool where judgment is required in worrisome cases by assessing the statistical probability of what *could* be going on from the vantage of a highly unlikely worst-case scenario. Risk assessment is better than the alternative—to wit, eeny, meeny, miney moe, or business as usual, looking out at the diverse child welfare clientele through the narrow lens of personal experience.

In the last chapter, we saw that the presence of domestic violence greatly increases the probability that children will be maltreated. This makes domestic violence a "risk factor" for child abuse and means we should ask a mother who checks a box indicating her own abuse is a concern: Is your child also "unsafe at home?" Scopetta wanted his workers to avoid ambiguity. But "ambiguity" is inherent in domestic violence cases no matter how a woman responds to questions because . . . well, just because "abuse" can cause a lot of distortions in communication and pose future risks that are not predicted by current circumstances. I am *not* suggesting the caseworker *should* suspect an abused mother of lying if she denies her child is in danger; she probably is not. What I am pointing out is that risk assessment is an unreliable tool because the judgments caseworkers make in domestic violence cases always take place in the context of ambiguity. Scopetta or his advisors would have known this had they spent any time in the trenches. The unpredictability of abuse is a facet of abuser terrorism; though abused women and children "know" something bad is coming, the future is always "unknown." Talking about something or someone that makes you afraid of talking complicates every exchange about abuse to make extended communication the only true source of trustworthy information. There *always* comes a point when the worker must rely on gut instinct or take a leap of faith based on her training and judgment. Trial lawyers make their living off such moments because they can result in tragic miscalculations. But for most caseworkers, most of the time, things turn out well enough to allow a night's sleep.

Back to why Scopetta's edict about removal made us crazy. Since first taking on the child welfare Golgotha in the early 1980s, we'd hammered home that the high proportion of battered women in the child welfare caseload hovered between 40 and 45 percent. This had two implications: so long as the violence went unacknowledged, these women were "underserved"; a majority of the highest risk children—probably 75 to 80 percent—resided in this hidden subset of homes. Research suggested that early, effective intervention to protect women from domestic violence in these families would reduce foster placement in New York City by more than half and cut the incidence of serious and fatal child abuse by two-thirds. In child welfare speak, this made cases of domestic violence rife for further inquiry about child abuse, risk assessment, and case management.

Scopetta was putting the agency in reverse, backing away from the cues to saving lives. By instructing his staff to recognize ambiguity as a red flag for placement rather than as a prompt for risk-assessment-based judgment, Scopetta was consigning the subclass of mothers who were domestic violence victims and their children to removal and thereby increasing the risk to both, the mother by further isolation, the child by subjecting them to disruption and abuse in foster care. By enhancing the family's experience of social entrapment, he was reducing the capacity for women to establish free-standing, secure households.

Removal of a child is a frankly punitive intervention that is normally permitted only after a court finds the mother guilty of some offense. This created a dilemma for Scopetta. Since the targeted mothers are victims of domestic violence, they are presumed to be "nonoffending." ACS lawyers resolved this dilemma by adapting a body of case law that applied the Failure to Protect Doctrine (under state neglect statutes) to nonoffending parents in these families. By alleging these mothers had "engaged" in domestic violence (by offering their neck to be choked, e.g.) they had failed to protect their children and so were guilty of neglect.

Commissioner Scopetta's actions affected caseworkers as well as their clients. By denying his staff the opportunity to address the ambiguity inherent in child protection work, he was effectively "deskilling" them, shrinking their realm of discretion to near zero, and thereby setting the bar for government interference in family life extremely low. But he was doing something more. Effectively reclassifying the existence of domestic violence per se as "emergent," he was forcing caseworkers to "open" a far higher proportion of cases than they could conceivably handle, dealing a possibly critical blow to agency efficiency and morale.

Scopetta's edict highlighted the contradiction inherent in the ACS practice of adopting a child-centered response to a woman-focused problem. There was an alternative he could have chosen. As his predecessor had done when a child died in care, the new commissioner could simply have restored the status quo. Like Rudy Giuliani, the activist mayor who appointed him, Nicholas Scopetta believed in taking action that was politically visible regardless of the long-run consequences. The fear of embarrassment at being seen to have "done nothing" by leaving children with abused mothers was greater than his concern for the dangers created for both by separating mother from child. The chance that his actions might have unforeseen or tragic consequences seemed less important than appearing indecisive or ineffectual.

The overall number of children placed in foster care declined in the late 1990s, almost certainly because budgets for placement and in-home support were cut. Even so, between 1998 and 1999, the rate of child removal in NYC was approximately twice the removal rate for the balance of the state. Meanwhile, though the trend in New York City followed the overall downward trajectory, with the absolute number of children placed in foster care declining by almost 20 percent under Scopetta (dropping from 42,000 in 1996 to 34,354 in 2000), almost the entire decline was accounted for by shifting the placement of children from family members (kinship care) to placement with strangers, who actually increased as an absolute number of hosts in 2001–2005.[9]

Nicholson v. Williams

Fast-forward to May 2001, more than twenty years after we drew our sample at Yale. Nicholas Scopetta was still commissioner of ACS. Sharwline Nicholson, April Rodriquez, and a dozen other battered mothers appeared in person in US Federal Court in Brooklyn to complain that their constitutional rights had been violated when New York City charged them with "neglect" and placed their children in foster homes solely because they were victims of domestic violence. All the children had been harmed by their experience in foster care. I was an expert in the case, essentially summarizing in testimony the conclusions expanded in this book. The remainder of the chapter takes the experiences of the plaintiff women and children in the case, *Nicholson v. Williams*, to examine how ACS built on the evidence of domestic violence in the lives of these women to exercise coercive control, first over the children, but ultimately over the mothers as well.

In a Legal Aid Society review of Bronx Family Court cases involving domestic violence, concluded in 1999, nearly one in four children was separated from parents and kin. In these cases, as was also true in the *Nicholson* cases considered here, "domestic violence" (referred to with the euphemism "engaging in domestic violence") was the sole ground for removal.[10] The City's defense was that ACS removed children in domestic violence cases *at the same rate* (approximately 24 percent) as in all other cases. Again and again, ACS repeated a similar argument, that it treated domestic violence cases like every other case of suspected child abuse. Fortunately, in Judge Weinstein's words, this line of reasoning "shocked the conscience" of the Court. *Nicholson* confirmed the child's constitutional right to their mother. Among the other wrongs committed by ACS he cited, Judge Jack Weinstein found that forcibly removing the children to the homes of strangers violated the 13th Amendment's prohibition of "indentured servitude," i.e., was akin to slavery.[11] His point was that, since domestic violence per se was not an indication of child abuse, that removing even one child from their family without cause is an inexcusable violation of the child's and the family's rights, including their liberty rights. In this instance, the State is a conscious purveyor of entrapment, not the slaveowner. While the "slave" metaphor makes us uncomfortable when applied to the status of women in America, as the late Supreme Court Justice Sandra Day O'Connor would remind us, when the 13th Amendment was ratified, it was meant to apply equally to housewives and bonded slaves.

When *Nicholson* began, the conversation about coercive control was still open-ended."[12] The plaintiff mothers and children in *Nicholson* were a cross-section of lower-middle-class New Yorkers. They were relatively young; non-white; ethnically diverse; multinational; embedded in family, kin, and/or family networks; and middle- to low-income. The women were employed at or near their educational level and the children were in age-appropriate care, preschool, or school. These were not women "on welfare," though they more closely matched the recipients of Aid For Dependent Children (AFDC), the welfare program ended by Congress in 1996, than the more predominantly white and middle-class women whose abuse experiences come into public view in high-profile custody and divorce cases in state family courts.[13]

Sharwline Nicholson

The lead plaintiff family immediately affected by Scopetta's policy change was Sharwline Nicholson and her children. In 1999, Nicholson was a thirty-year-old single mother of two young children, living in a poor, tightknit black community in Brooklyn, New York. Nicholson had emigrated from Jamaica after graduating from high school. She was by all accounts a conscientious and attentive mother. She was determined to give her children every opportunity—and at the same time to fend for herself. When her son, K, who was four-years-old, seemed to be struggling, she enrolled him a school where he could receive intensive early intervention. Her daughter, D, was ten months old. Nicholson was attending college, moving slowly but surely toward her degree. A single mother, perhaps, but a single mother with a trusted network of neighbors and friends to help her with the children.

On January 27, 1999, Nicholson was home, D was asleep in her crib in the next room, and K was at school. Carl, her former boyfriend, knocked on the door. Carl had moved "down south," the occasion of their breakup. But he had never been violent or threatening. She let him in.

Carl was angry about rumors that Nicholson was dating someone. She denied it. He wouldn't listen. He threw things. Then, he hit her. She cowered on the floor, covered her head as he kicked and pummeled her. She made it to the telephone. As she dialed 911, he fled. Carl disappeared from the case. But the coercive control of Nicholson and her children had just begun.

Nicholson was bleeding from the head, and her arm was askew. Didi was still asleep. Nicholson called a neighbor, who took Didi and agreed to pick up K from the bus stop. The neighbor, with two children of her own, had helped out before.

When police arrived, Nicholson provided a full account of what had happened. She did not want to leave her children, but she agreed to go to the hospital. In addition to the obvious contusions on her head and body, she had a concussion and a broken arm. She was admitted.

Nicholson arranged for her cousin Michelle in New Jersey to come and take the children. That evening, three police officers came to the hospital and told her (falsely) that her children could not stay with someone who was not a family member. Later she was told Michelle was unacceptable because she lived out of state. She provided contact information for two other relatives who could care for the children while she was in the hospital. Nicholson took pain medication and went to sleep believing the children were safe with Michelle.

Acting at the behest of ACS, the police had already seized the children. They had entered the neighbor's home with drawn guns—allegedly because Carl might be hiding there—terrifying not only Nicholson's children but also the neighbor, her husband, and their children. Finding no danger, the officers took Nicholson's children away in a police car. Nicholson's son, K, who is afraid of the police, says he thought his mother was dead when the police came to the neighbor's apparent and "arrested" him at gun point.

At 6:30 the next morning, ACS called to tell Nicholson, "We have your children." In response to her many questions, the unidentified person on the line told her, "You will have a court date next week. We will let you know when it is." Nicholson was instructed to go to counseling and to take parenting skills classes so she could learn to be a "better" parent. This was because, ACS told her, she was "uncooperative." The head of child protection wanted her to signal her cooperation with ACS by going to police to get an order of protection. A criminal court had already denied her such an order because the father was out of state.[14]

Supervisor Williams knew that the common practice of removing and holding children so that ACS could dictate a mother's every move was illegal. An ACS worker has one business day after removing a child to meet with an ACS lawyers, go to court and file a petition seeking permission to hold the child. A "hostage" is a "person taken by force to secure the taker's demands." Williams had taken the Nicholson children hostage, having seized them at gunpoint from a trusted neighbor and babysitter, in order to effect Nicholson's "cooperation." During the trial, Judge Weinstein noted that when battered mothers are forced to choose between their constitutional rights and their children, they tend to choose custody of their children.[15]

After a week of not being allowed to speak to the children, Nicholson was "whooping and hollering," according to agency records. ACS's first petition charged Nicholson with child neglect on the grounds that she had "engaged in domestic violence in the presence of her children," cited this allegation as a basis for holding her children, and asked the court for an order placing Nicholson's children in ACS custody. ACS included an allegation in the petition that Carl had once hit K. ACS knew all of the allegations were untrue. An order of protection was issued to protect the children in case they would be returned to her. Carl was also cited for neglect, but his citation was sent to Nicholson's address though he never lived there. The court insisted that Nicholson enforce the order of protection, though she had originally called police and he had fled.

Eight days after she had last spoken to her children, ACS permitted her to visit them. When Nicholson found her daughter, she was sitting at a table by herself "with tears running down." Her son had a swollen eye. She filed a police report on behalf of her son, who told her the foster mother had slapped his face. She was not allowed to talk to K on his sixth birthday, twelve days after the separation. On February 18, twenty-one days after the separation and fourteen days after the Family Court had paroled Nicholson's children to her, ACS returned the children. The catch was that the family could not live in its own home, could not live in New Jersey, and would be subjected to random ACS supervision. Nicholson and the children moved in with a cousin in the Bronx. The cousin's apartment was also unacceptable to ACS, they called and harassed the cousin and Nicholson and the children were forced to move out. In the meantime, her son had to leave school because of excessive absences while in foster care. Since there was a no contact order restricting the children's travel, Nicholson sent them to Jamaica to live with their grandmother. In response, ACS issued a warrant for Nicholson's arrest unless she produced the children. On April 7, as she was at the Post Office collecting her mail, two police officers handcuffed and arrested Nicholson and took her to Family Court in Brooklyn, where she sat for six hours in handcuffs.

It was at this proceeding that Nicholson met the attorney who would initiate the class action. The Court allowed her to return to her apartment in Brooklyn, requiring her to cooperate with supervision and services offered by ACS, and she was visited biweekly until August, when the petition against her was dismissed. ACS communicated to the State Central Registry that the neglect report stemming from the domestic violence incident was indicated against her and Carl. As of this writing, she remains on the State's record of persons who are unemployable in work with children because they are "neglectful parents."

April Rodriquez

April Rodriquez was the biological mother of two children, Elijah, age three, and KYL, age two, and the step-mother of Jasmine, age seven. From 1995 to 2000, Rodriquez had a stable living arrangement with Mr. Gamble, the father of the three children. There was no history of wife or child abuse. Rodriquez was employed as the assistant manager of a video store.

In August 2000, while the children were asleep, a verbal dispute in the hall of the apartment escalated and Gamble pushed Rodriquez to the floor, where she scraped her mouth. She reported the incident to the police the next day, Gamble was arrested, and Rodriquez fled with her biological children to her grandmother's house, leaving Jasmine with the paternal grandmother. Rodriquez decided not to go to a domestic violence shelter because she was informed by a hotline counselor she would have to quit her job to do so.

ACS initially told Rodriquez they intended to file a petition against the father and approved of her living temporarily with her grandmother until she could afford a place of her own. But the position changed after Gamble filed for legal custody of the children. At that time, ACS pressured Rodriquez to sign custody over to Gamble for six months although he had been arrested for domestic violence, solely because she lacked adequate housing or daycare for the children while she was at work. The children were placed with the paternal grandparents by the CPS caseworker, "a secure environment outside the father's home." Then, on October 16, a month and a half after the assault on Rodriquez, ACS filed a petition of neglect against Rodriquez for "engaging in serious domestic violence in front of the children," and two police officers removed the children from the grandparents' house to foster care.[16] ACS told Rodriquez her children would be returned if she entered a shelter, which she did, first going to an emergency facility for the homeless and then to a shelter in the Bronx, which was neither confidential nor equipped for domestic violence victims. She had to quit her job. When ACS returned her children, she testified during the trial, "they were not the same kids I gave (ACS)" She recounted,

> (Her) daughter's hair was all breaking. . . . Her shirt was filthy, and her diaper was disgusting. The seven-year old had bags under her eyes. She looked disgusting. And, at the time, he was two years old, Elijah, he had all this (sic) bruises and pus and blood coming out of his lip. I didn't know what it was.

Rodriquez's case is instructive because, unlike Carl, the boyfriend of Shawrline Nicholson, Gamble, the children's father, stayed in the picture. When Gamble attempted to use the fact that his wife could not afford housing on her salary alone, ACS recommended she turn custody of the children over to him, which she refused, and, then, charged her with "neglect" for having engaged in domestic violence and placed the children in foster care in order to compel her to accept a completely inappropriate service referral. Almost all of the harmful consequences of coercion and control in this case for Rodriquez and her children were the direct result of coercive control by ACS.

Egaete Udoh

Ekaete Udoh was a forty-three-year-old working mother of five girls, ages thirteen, fifteen, seventeen, nineteen, and twenty-three. Born in Nigeria, Udoh moved to the United States in 1977, after her family arranged her marriage to her husband, whom she had not previously met. Udoh had worked for the Board of Education as a paraprofessional and teacher's assistant for eight years and supported her four younger daughters on her $23,000 salary.

Udoh reported that her husband's physical abuse began shortly after they married and occurred "as many times as possible" and "so many times, I can't recall all of them." She attributed the premature birth of her first daughter to a beating. She called police "many times" when they lived in Kentucky, and was taken to a shelter when a neighbor witnessed her being chased and beaten by her husband. Abuse continued after the couple moved to New York City in 1984, and she called police again in 1985 after a beating when she also reported him beating the children with his hand and a belt. The police never arrested Mr. Udoh.

In 1995 and 1996. Mrs. Udoh went to Court and obtained an order of protection for herself and the children, but did not exclude him from the house. In response to an ACS investigation in 1996, Mr. Udoh defended his use of corporal punishment to control "so-called unruly behavior of his children, and that this even extends to the disciplining of his wife's behavior," as his Nigerian "heritage." ACS noted also noted, "He is upset over the fact this his wife has not given birth to a son and claims that one of his rights as a Nigerian male is to seek a second wife." In 1997, Mrs. Udoh moved out, obtained a court order to collect her belongings, and secured an order of protection, which Mr. Udoh was arrested for violating when he persisted in contacting her. Due to financial difficulties, Mrs. Udoh returned to the Queens home in 1999, but reported no further incidents.

In May 1999, Mr. Udoh hit their daughter A. in eye because, she said, "I was not able to fit all the dirty dishes in the dishwasher." Mrs. Udoh told the school what had happened when she picked her daughter up to go to the doctors. Two ACS caseworkers came to the house and told Mr. Udoh he had to move out, which he did, shortly thereafter returning to Nigeria for the duration of the case. Mrs. Udoh filed a police report. On May 5, the caseworker found the children were in no imminent danger if they returned home with their mother.

Everything changed a day later. On May 6, the ACS legal department advised the caseworker that she could file a neglect petition against Mrs. Udoh, because she had "engaged" in domestic violence, and remove the children without a court order if it was an emergency. CPM Delamothe testified at the trial that the children were in "imminent danger" because Mr. and Mrs. Udoh might be in Family Court at the return of the children from school and (the children) wouldn't have parents to return to." Despite the children's ages, CPM Delamothe was concerned they might not have keys. Nor had they asked the children. ACS called Mrs. Udoh before she left work to tell her not to come to court because her children had been removed from school and placed in foster care. When they were picked up by ACS, E. Udoh, then seventeen, told the caseworker, "I felt very comfortable staying with (my mother . . . I am safe. . . . I told her I didn't think it was necessary to be removed and I felt a great suffering if I was removed from my house."

On May 7, ACS filed a neglect petition against Mrs. Udoh and her husband alleging that she had "engaged in domestic violence" with him in the presence of the children for approximately twenty years. Page two of the petition, where answers are required for why insufficient time was available to obtain a court order prior to removal and why removal was necessary, was blank.

On May 20, ACS agreed it was safe for the children to return home; the Family Court ordered them paroled to the mother. Yet it took another eight days for ACS to notify the foster care agency that the court had ordered them paroled. E. described her time in the foster home as "very uncomfortable"; the foster mother treated us "like criminals," she said.

In this case, a twenty-year history of coercive control of the mother and children was well documented, the mother had reported the most recent episode of child abuse to the school (and ACS), and the father had returned to Nigeria, at least until the resolution of his criminal case. When they were removed, the children were not only safe but fully capable of caring for themselves at home. The thin pretext used to place the children as well as to charge Mrs. Udoh was solely to terrorize her into not returning to her husband should he return. While the circumstances under which the couple reunited after the earlier split are unclear, any ambiguity about Mrs. Udoh's responsibility for the ongoing abuse should have been resolved by holding her husband fully accountable for the coercive control.

Mrs. Garcia

Mrs. Garcia's case was distinctive because ACS's punitive motivation for removing the children was unusually transparent. When the family first contacted child welfare, ACS domestic violence specialist Cheryl Meyers interviewed them. She found the three children showed no ill effects of either abuse or witnessing. Meanwhile, Garcia was "fully cooperative" in terms of disclosing a past abusive relationship, providing information about her relationship with Mr. Hunter and the attack that took place, and in efforts to help police locate Hunter and protect herself and her children. Myers concluded that Garcia was "a strong woman who would do anything to protect her children," and that removal of the children was not necessary.

ACS verified the history Garcia provided with police reports. These showed two assaults prior to the current incident. Occurring five years earlier, both assaults were linked to a dispute with the children's father about visitation and occurred on successive days. None of the reports involving Hunter prior to the July 6 incident suggested he used or threatened violence against Garcia or the children. Nevertheless, based on the reports they had, ACS determined there was a "long history of domestic violence" in the household," and that the case should be indicated against Garcia because "although she took the necessary precautions of protecting her children by filing complaints at the local precincts," she had let the batterers back into her life and did not "see herself as a victim of domestic violence."

The abrupt decision to remove the children was put into context by notes in the case record that two days before the remand was requested, CPM Lowell ordered the caseworker to file it "based on the fact that [Ms. Garcia] has blatantly refused to cooperate with ACS." G. Reyes, one of Garcia's children who was removed, explained to the Court the callous way in which this motive was conveyed. When she asked the caseworker why she and her siblings were being taken away from their mother, the caseworker replied, "over a phone call, if your mom would have called, you would not have been removed."

Is it too much to suggest that here we have CPM Lowell (for ACS) basically asserting the gambit "my way or the highway" and self-consciously weaponizing the children as punishment for disregarding this irrelevant orders?

Mrs. Norris

Michele Norris was a twenty-four-year-old mother of two-year-old J. and worked at JFK airport in Queens. An earlier ACS visit for suspicion of "drugs and domestic violence" proved "unfounded." Later the same month, Norris decided to break things off with her partner and leave the apartment. Mr. Figueroa attacked her as she was collecting her things. She testified, "(He) dragged me by my hair, threw me into a wall, hit me in the face." Norris couldn't get to a phone, but the landlord called police. Norris showed police her injuries, filed a police report, and was granted an order of protection.

Though the apartment was in her name, after the attack, she moved in with a friend for safety. Although he was not present when she first returned to pick up some things, Figueroa returned while she was still there and attacked her, breaking her phone and hitting her in the face. This time when police arrived, Figueroa locked himself with the baby in the bathroom. The police informed Norris that because of the protection order, either she or Figueroa would have to leave. Since Figueroa refused to leave the bathroom, police escorted Norris out of the apartment without helping her take her son back.

The next day, Figueroa left J. with a babysitter. When Norris returned to take the child, he had a fever, so she took him to the hospital emergency room. On the way to the hospital, Norris received a call from the ACS caseworker telling her she had neglected Justin by "engaging in domestic violence" and "leaving him with an abusive man," She was told the circumstances involving the police were "irrelevant." Although J. was admitted overnight with pneumonia, Norris brought him to ACS the next day as instructed because, as she was told, "as far as we're concerned, your son belongs to the State." She told the Court, "it was the worst part of my life. I mean, I didn't know what was going to happen from there. I didn't know where he was going to go. I had no rights . . . . [ACS] told me, "he wasn't your son anymore."

In early April 2000, ACS filed a neglect petition against both parents for "engaging in domestic violence" and based on information and belief, that both parents used drugs. Three weeks later, ACS filed an investigative summary in which they acknowledged the drug charge was "unfounded," but they never removed it from the neglect petition. A Family Court hearing in June made obtaining the parole of her son contingent on individual counseling for domestic violence, completing a parenting skills class, undergoing drug testing, getting a job, and maintaining a two-bedroom apartment. While

Norris found a private attorney who helped her meet her goals, she had to pay for the classes and the apartment with no help from ACS or Figueroa.

On September 19, the day before her Family Court appearance, the ACS caseworker told her she could get her children immediately if she "went into court and made an admission of domestic violence." She refused. On September 20, 2000, the Family Court ordered that J. be returned. He had been in ACS custody for nearly five and half months.

Norris testified,

> He's very attached to me. He screams (whenever) I even walk in the room. He thinks that I am leaving. Every time the doorbell rings, he gets hysterical. Especially when we go to my mother's house, he latches on to me. He won't leave my sight and he says I don't want to stay here, I want to go home with mommy. I think he's very afraid to be away from me ever again.

The case of Norris illustrates a range of tactics—lying, threatening, kidnapping, blackmail, denigration, etc.—commonly associated with coercive control. But perhaps what is most impressive is the desperate tactic of charging Norris for following police orders by leaving her son with an abusive man where he might have killed the child if there had been a confrontation in the locked bathroom. What is left unsaid here speaks loudly of the ACS predicament that it projects onto Norris and her children—that her partner has no standing in the world of ACES, neither as a person of responsibility nor even as a villain.

Other Plaintiff Mothers

Among the plaintiff mothers, Sharlene Tillet was the only one targeted whose contact with ACS was not prompted by an incident of physical abuse. Like several of the other women, when she was cited for "engaging in domestic violence," she was on the verge of escaping to California, where she believed she could keep herself and the children safe.

Tillet had a nine-year-old and a newborn. Though Tillet reported a long history of abuse, she had broken things off with her boyfriend, he had moved out of the apartment they shared, and she had purchased a plane ticket to California and was planning to leave right after giving birth. The boyfriend was waiting at the hospital. Rather than create a scene that might have culminated in a violent confrontation at the hospital, Tillet allowed him to give her a ride home. This turned out to be a safer choice. Neither child was ever hurt and the boyfriend never re-entered the apartment. But ACS had been alerted. When he dropped her at home, ACS was waiting with the police. They took both children, including the newborn, and Tillet was charged with "engaging in domestic violence," though the boyfriend was not present. He was charged as well, but never arrested. She was also charged with "exposing" the baby who had not yet been born when the boyfriend was around and having no crib. At the trial, her caseworker testified that Tillet should have reported the domestic violence to the police so that "there would be a record."

In this instance, ACS involvement is gratuitous. If the penultimate confrontation at the hospital might have been an opportunity to interrupt a dangerous situation, once Tillet maneuvered the ride home and he had respected her boundary by leaving, the only legitimate ACS concern was whether she needed assistance getting her children and luggage to the plane. Again, whether by design or implication, ACS is continuing and exacerbating the coercive control of the children.

A final case highlights how directly ACS undermines women's safety planning. When Chrystal Rhodes filed for an order of protection, ACE filed a petition to place the children because she had exposed them to domestic violence. However, when police served the order and removed the abuser from the home, they failed to ask him to return his keys. When police left, Rhodes was terrified the abuser would return. Her rational safety plan was to flee the home with the children. But when she told ACS what she had done, they instructed Rhodes to bring the children with her back home and wait there till 7 pm, when the caseworker arrived to remove them.

Note, all of the allegations against the women in the *Nicholson* class involved their having been victims of domestic violence. The only other allegations were that Tillet did not have a crib for her newborn and a Mrs. Berisha had taken a valium without a prescription, on one occasion six months earlier. Neither was grounds for neglect.

On July 9, 2001, a trial began in the Federal Courthouse in Brooklyn on whether the "mothers" identified in *Nicholson* constituted a "class" and were, therefore, eligible to sue the government, and whether and in what form a preliminary injunction should take. The trial extended over 24trial days, 44 witnesses testified, 212 documents were introduced, and extensive briefing and argument followed. The courtroom was packed daily with plaintiff supporters whose often audible responses gave the detailed descriptions elicited of case malpractice the timbre of Greek Tragedy. Our shock at the time was at the incredible callousness on display toward the predicaments created for the women and children by the abuse and the complete disregard for the rights of the children. In retrospect, what is striking is the unintended effect of this callousness, the extent to which the combined response of ACS, the family court, and the police became a surrogate for the control over the mother and the children the abuser could no longer impose directly.

The effect of ACS intervention was to further disempower the abused women and their children. All involved, particularly the ACS caseworkers, felt their lying, bullying, and manipulation of the women and children was justified because the women's capacity to make good decisions—hence also their *right* to make those decisions—had been abrogated when they "engaged" in violence. To ACS, being a victim of domestic violence signified rightlessness. For our purposes, the significance of the ACS actions lay not in their malfeasance, or not only, but in the extent to which assuming the "domestic violence" perspective allowed the agency to play the role of the "extended patriarch" with respect to the women and children in their caseload once the abusive male was no longer doing so, thereby assuring their subordination would continue. As importantly, ACS ensured that the woman's condition of dependence and subordination would remain the context for the parenting decisions, the same logic that underpins coercive control. Thus, in the *Nicholson* case, CPM Williams acknowledged the children were at imminent risk "because she [Nicholson] was not at that time able to protect herself or her children because Mr. Barnet had viciously beaten her." In Williams's mind, when she allowed herself to be beaten, Nicholson forfeited her rights to determine her own and her children's future. Even though Nicholson repeatedly arranged for her children's protection, CPM Williams refused to allow her to decide who would care for her children while she was in the hospital and after she was released. Nor, even though both she and police had established that Barnes had left the State, did he allow Nicholson to return to her home; nor did he even ask why she did not feel she or the children were in danger. Caseworkers repeated that it was "common practice" to declare that a child faced an "emergency" (when they did not), to permit a removal without a court order, or simply to intimidate mothers who were "more likely to comply" (with services) with their children removed. CPM Williams testified he filed approximately two dozen new petitions each week of this sort in addition to filing the petition against Nicholson alleging that she was neglectful although he did not believe she was neglectful. CPM Stewart filed a neglect petition against Rodriquez, although he did not believe she was neglectful. He took the children into ACS custody on January 28, 1999, though he knew ACS lacked judicial authorization to do so, which he sought, but only five days later. CPM Stewart moved Rodriquez's children from their mother to their father's house because he felt she had not provided adequate childcare for the children while she was at work. She made the move even though father had been arrested for domestic violence and had a prior indicated child abuse case and though Rodriquez felt the children were safe where they were. Robert Chamorro removed Rhodes's children before he or his caseworkers even spoke to her. Chamorro explained that he removed the children because when his caseworker pushed the buzzer to an apartment, an unidentified male voice answered, even though Rhodes had moved out of the apartment to escape her abuser. CPM Bonnie Lowell caused the prosecution of Garcia because she did not return a phone call, continued to prosecute Shipe Berisha based on allegations she knew to be false and commenced neglect proceedings against Jessica Valentin and continued prosecution, although ACS had concluded she was not neglectful. Dorabella Delamonthe made the decision to remove the four Udoh children from their mother after her caseworker had determined that the girls could safely remain in their mother's custody, because she planned to summon both Mr. and Mrs. Udoh to Family Court to respond to neglect proceeding and did not know whether the teenage daughters had keys to the apartment in order to let themselves in while their mother was in court.

Note, although each of these caseworkers is theoretically acting independently of one another, given the similarity of their responses, it seems fair to conclude, as the Court did, that it was ACS "policy" to remove children from mothers solely because they had been abused and that, since this response provided no benefits to those affected and caused considerable harm, that this was a punitive response, was therefore unjust, and violated their privacy and liberty rights. The Court was not concerned with our purpose here, namely to situate the ACS on the continuum of coercive control by which men, as a group, dominate and unfairly benefit from the resources and capacities of women and children.

The *Nicholson* Court was rightly concerned that the *Nicholson* mothers be compensated for acts of commission by ACS, including the alienation of their children. But the collusive role of ACS was also revealed by another reality, the failure of ACS to cause or contribute to holding the batterer accountable for his behavior. In fact, in the case of April Rodriquez, not only did ACS fail to hold the batterer accountable. They turned the children over to his custody. In the several cases where ACS brought neglect proceedings against the batterer, this was only in response to pressure from a mother's attorney and after they commenced proceedings against the victim. When challenged to make the official policy of protecting children from domestic violence consistent with never charging perpetrators, case managers placed the burden of prosecution on the mothers. According to CPM Delamonthe, responsible for about 20 caseworkers and 400 cases, Sharlene Tillet should have reported the domestic violence to the police so that "there would be a record." This echoes the dictum "my way or the highway," and put women and children directly in harm's way. Chrystal Rhodes fled her home after an incident of domestic violence, because the police had not taken the keys from the abuser when serving him with an order of protection. Her rational safety plan—to flee the home with the children—was disregarded by ACS, who required Rhodes to bring the children with her back home and wait there until 7 pm, when the caseworker arrived to remove them. This was plenty of time for the abuser to find and kill her and the children.

In fact, although child safety provided the justification for ACS involvement with these families, the allegations against the mother were based solely on the extent to which women accepted safety strategies widely known to be ineffective against domestic violence and coercive control. Before seeking allegations against the mother, the supervising attorney testified, they determined whether she got an order of protection and was willing to relocate, exclude the batterer, or go into counseling. All of these check boxes are functions of the coercive control to which she is being subjected; the fewer she can check, the higher the level of entrapment and the greater the need for critical intervention. Going to a shelter or getting an order of protection can often protect women and children, particularly in the short term and if danger is immediate. But to be usable, a "safety plan" has to be tailored to fit the circumstances the victims are confronting. Otherwise, the "order" to "get safe" is likely to limit options, increasing risk, a form of disguised betrayal. When Rodriquez called the domestic violence hotline, she was told she would have to quit her job to get into a shelter. After the Family Court judge released her children to her, ACS would not return the children until she had secured a place in the shelter, even though the judge's order said nothing about this. She found a shelter that had places for mother and three children, but lost the places to another mother, because all the children have to be ready to enter at the same time and hers were still in foster care. Because she had quit her job and could not get her kids, she was moved by the city over the next few months to various one-room facilities, none confidential or focused on protection.

After a three-month hearing with dozens of witnesses, Federal Judge Jack Weinstein ruled in favor of the mothers, adopted substantial portions of my testimony, ordered the City to stop the unconstitutional practices, and provided certain remedies. The *Nicholson* decision condemned the City's practice of prosecuting battered mothers for child neglect "when she has done nothing but suffer abuse at the hands of another," and concluded that the City's regular practices in cases involving domestic violence harm children much more than they protect them from harm. Harshly criticizing the City's practices, the court noted that "children's welfare, the state interest which is so often the great counterweight deployed to justify state interference in family affairs, has virtually disappeared." Judge Weinstein found that ACS policy violated numerous rights protected by the US Constitution including liberty rights, privacy rights, the protection against malicious prosecution, and the child's right to its caretaker. He also found that arbitrarily removing children from their parents and placing them in foster care without due process violated the 13th Amendment's prohibition against indentured servitude.

Judge Weinstein appointed me to represent the plaintiff mothers on a *Nicholson* review panel charged with overseeing ACS's compliance with the court order. In the few months of cases our panel reviewed after June 2002, nine of ten children from homes where domestic violence was identified remained with a parent and the rest were with relatives. It appeared ACS might have been doing less harm than before.

I met the *Nicholson* mothers with the children still removed or just returned. They described feeling entrapped, isolated, and intimidated, sentiments that resonated with everything I'd heard from women living in domestic regimes of coercive control. As the months passed, their courage steeled. With their lawyer advocates at their side, the *Nicholson* mothers articulated their anger at having been silenced and controlled by ACS with as much vehemence as any of the women I had encountered in my shelter work denounced their male oppressors. Here, also as in their personal lives, their outrage at indignity was rights-based as well as focused on their own and their children's well-being. What change in standing or consciousness supported this new outspokenness? With her children returned, Mrs. Nicholson was slightly worse off than before. She had never been coercively controlled by her partner; the father of her children was gone (again); but the challenges she faced in housing, employment, and education had been aggravated by the struggle with ACS, not alleviated by it. Domestic violence, rape, and coercive control by men continued to factor in the lives of other plaintiff women post-*Nicholson* as they had before. But the women's common experience of disenfranchisement and entrapment was the result not of what individual men had done or were doing to them, not only or not primarily, but of how ACS had seized on their experience of individual victimization to exploit their vulnerability as women, read it in this sense the way a batterer would, and responded by removing the children who were their moorings as mothers. And ACS had done so with support from the Family Court and the police. ACS had exploited a moment of crisis in order to complete the process of entrapment and disempowerment against which the women were struggling, with some success in the case of Mrs. Nicholson at least. With their femininity under attack, at the very moment when their recognition as full persons in their own right required the most vigorous defense, the *Nicholson* mothers were forced to abandon their children. Not unconditionally of course, but with terms that not only included accepting responsibility for their own victimization but also being subjected to a regime of inspections and regulation with respect to work, parenting, hygiene, and the like that was incompatible with their standing as persons and increased their vulnerability to abuse. The coercive control the *Nicholson* mothers were experiencing was not "domestic" but a social construction, established through a web of authority by a State institution with as little regard for the violent men involved as for their female or child victims. By the time the women confronted ACS, some had broken free of the abusive men who generated their original cases; others had not. But with the "war" with ACS underway, their children home, and the State no longer standing unnoticed in their partner's corner, the workaday struggles for survival looked less formidable. With the boot of ACS off their necks, they could once against call for help when they needed it.

Conclusion

We triumphed in *Nicholson*. In legal terms, the ruling in *Nicholson v. Williams* in 2001 simply required New York City to provide evidence that foster care was a safer option than leaving the child alone *before* it placed a child. This seemingly minor requirement had three enormous implications in practice. First, since domestic violence was *not* considered per se harmful to a child, this change put an end to placement solely because there was domestic violence in the home. Second, it implied that the first approach was to take steps to make the family home free of domestic violence. No child could be placed if we could show that the family home could be made safer by removing the abuser from the house or otherwise lessening the risk, e.g., by a protection order or arrest. Third, as a condition for removal, ACS had to show a child had actually been affected by domestic violence in the home and that the risks of further harm outweighed how the child could be harmed by removal and placement. Moreover, the trauma assumed to be occasioned by removal had to be considered. This highlighted the extent to which a child's constitutional right to its mother has a psychological underpinning. By focusing on the institutional violation of rights involved in ACS's unconstitutional behavior, *Nicholson* also touched a more nuanced dimension of the damage caused to children by removal, a dislocation of their social identity as racial beings and citizens for example, or as descendants of genus popularis extending back generations and across oceans. Even seemingly so simple a term as "safety" used in a post-*Nicholson* context carried the implication that some measure of "justice" was involved when a child was moved, not merely a recalibration of the hazards to which they were exposed.

The most controversial implications of the *Nicholson* ruling involved the extent to which it balanced children's rights against one another, including their rights to safety and to "their" family home and their "liberty" right to be kept from indentured servitude, and to which these rights, all other things being equal, were found to be conditional on women's constitutional rights, including but not limited to their rights as mothers to their children. Needless to say, the implications of this decision have confounded proponents of "children's rights."

PART II

THE COERCIVE CONTROL
OF CHILDREN

The New Model

5

Violence, Sexual Assault, and Psychological Abuse

"I've been on this farm most my life. All I did was shoot my wife."
—Van Morrison, "Got My Mojo Working"

Introduction

This chapter and the next describe the strategic "technology" used to coercively control women and children in the general population: violence, sexual abuse, psychological abuse, intimidation, isolation, and control. Chapter 7 identifies "Child Abuse as Tangential Spouse Abuse," a tactical element that is unique to the coercive control of children. In this instance, the abuser enlists or "weaponizes" a child in the abuse of the mother. In all of these instances, even when the child "identifies with the aggressor" partner, the child is a "secondary victim" of coercive control. What this means for intervention will become clear as we proceed. My aim is to construct a forensic model of coercive control that captures the interaction between a partner's intention, the selection and deployment of tactics, the effects on children, and their response.

My description of the elements and dynamics of coercive control is drawn from a limited body of relevant empirical research, my clinical and forensic caseload, and miscellaneous narrative accounts, personal journals, email histories, news stories, memoirs, letters, fictional accounts, and films.[1] The vast research literature on domestic violence, child abuse, and their overlap provides an important window into the frequency with which abusive men also harm their children. This body of work has very limited applicability to coercive control, however. This is because most research on violence against women and children only considers assaults isolated at a single time (point prevalence) or "ever," whereas physical abuse in coercive control is typically ongoing and relationship-specific. Surveys are an equally unreliable gauge to attitudes, which they measure as a static mindset at a point in time, rather as

Children of Coercive Control. Evan Stark, Oxford University Press. © Oxford University Press 2023.
DOI: 10.1093/oso/9780197587096.003.0006

consciousness emerges and evolves in relation to the changing complexity of abuse and opportunities for support and intervention in the community. An example comes from India, where the Tamil Nadu National Family Health Survey (NFHS) in 2016 reported that 70 percent of women justified domestic violence against women. When ethnographic data was collected in the same population, however, the researchers found that women rarely justified violence but rather struggled with violence in three ways—subverting violence, calibrating violence, and collaborating against violence.[2]

Domestic violence research that enumerates harms to women and children as individual or "repeated" acts misrepresents their experience of coercive control in the same way that criminal laws anticipating stranger assaults, rape, or stalking behavior miss the bespoke elements of these offenses in the context of relationships. The coercive physical tactics in abusive relationships cover a broad spectrum from "pushes," "grabs," and "shoves" to shootings, and are significant because of their cumulative effect. But, the vast body of existing research on violence against women and children applies a "calculus" of harms to incidents of assaults to distinguish real violence. I draw on violence research only when the data collected on physical and sexual abuse includes a spectrum of assaults or can be arrayed historically along a timeline to comport with the violence used in coercive control. Meanwhile, apart from a handful of studies that asked about "psychological abuse," the empirical literature on the intimidation, isolation, and control of children is too sparse to be helpful. With the marked exception of Emma Katz's remarkable study of recently separated families, there is no empirical evidence on the deployment of "coercive control" with children.[3]

The primary basis for applying a coercive control model to children is the evidence provided between 2002 and 2022 by the five men, seventy-five women, and thirty-five children in my forensic caseload and contained in my case files in the form of interview notes, court records, letters, emails, diaries, text messages, news articles, and other materials collected during the course of my investigations and reports. Unless a news report or other source is explicitly identified, the vignettes in these chapters are abstracted from my files. I have also sought confirmation, illustration, and insight from social science literature and nonclinical sources that recount the abuse experiences of children, including novels, memoirs, and film. With respect to women, the model provides a framework for new law by delineating "bespoke" elements of behavior that is already criminal (such as assault, rape, and stalking) and highlighting the harmful effects of other behaviors (psychological abuse, isolation, degradation, "economic abuse," "control," etc.) that are not currently crimes. With respect to children, however, where the understanding of "child abuse" is well entrenched and the alternative coercive control framework is in its early development, the model is offered as a heuristic, a framework for formulating a new approach to how children are being harmed in family life, rather than as map for law. In extrapolating the basic elements of coercive control from women to children, I believe I have captured much of breadth of their experience, particularly when you also consider the additional dynamic described in chapter 7, when children are enlisted in their mother's abuse or "identify with the aggressor." I must add two caveats, however. My caseload is diverse, but it does not representative the experience of all groups. There may well be dimensions of coercive control, elements of psychological, emotional, or technological abuse, for example, that do not show up in a forensic caseload or that I overlooked. It is also possible that children are being coercively controlled directly by women and men in situations that do not involve coercive control of a caretaking partner, but are no less devastating. If this is so, I wouldn't catch it.

In *Coercive Control* I explain that, early in my career, I reminded a woman who told me "violence wasn't the worst part" of her experience to "talk about the violence." Fifty years on and hundreds of thousands of women's stories later, we have a model to put the violence that was our singular focus on a spectrum with the broad array of oppressive and nonviolent tactics deployed to dominate them, into an historical context of their entire abuse experience and into a spatial frame that encompasses the multiple settings through which they pass and to which abuse extends. I could "step outside the trees" of an empirical social science and set aside the maps of domestic violence drawn over a generation, because I could turn to the women (and men) in my forensic practice for a new map on which to plot the fault lines of coercive control. From our new map it was easy to trace the way to social science: since the publication of *Coercive Control* in 2007, coercive control has been the conceptual framework for almost 1,000 research monographs.

But where are we to turn if we want an alternative to the violence/maltreatment model of children? Of course, I talk to children when I can in shelters, courtroom settings, and in my practice. But, unlike women, who are increasingly encouraged to tell their stories in person in public venues, there are few social outlets where children's voices can be heard directly, unmediated by the range of formal and informal guardians who dictate, regulate, monitor, and sanction their rites of passage at every point in their life cycle, from toilet training through induction in the military. Children of

Coercive Control would not be needed if those responsible for the protection, nurturance, well-being, and independence of children had attended to their diminution on so large a scale by coercive control. So, in addition to bringing the real voices of children into this book, I have also relied on their imagined voices, how I imagine them, based on other things I know they have thought or done. For example, in my defense of Magdalena Luczak (in chapter 8), I assume the voice of Daniel Pelka, the murdered child; and in the Covlin case in New York, where I was a witness for a girl's aunt and uncle opposing her wishes to remain with her father, I spoke from within what I imagined her voice as best I could. To get an even broader sample of how children experience coercive control, I revisited the classic ethnographic literature on children living with the stress of racial segregation, economic depression, and migration.[4] Finally, to get the fullest possible picture of children's experience, I also draw on the dynamic, psychologically complex character portraits of children under duress created by novelists.[5] None of these sources—not fiction and certainly not my imagination—is a substitute for robust empirical science. But data without a conceptual framework is like water without a glass. Taken together, these sources provided evidence of a sentient reality which the child sciences had not noticed. The terrain on which the ethnographers and novelists encountered children had not yet been overdrawn by a violence template and so they were able to see dimensions of children's experience of abuse which the violence researchers missed, but which we can now also see.

The dimensions I outline—violence, sexual abuse, psychological abuse, isolation, intimidation, and control—apply to the experience of children who are coercively controlled secondary to their mother's victimization. While this is the most common context in which children are coercively controlled, it is not the only context. A significant but unknown subset of children are victimized by one or both parents who are not also coercively controlling another. Although the model described in chapters 6 and 7 would apply in these cases, the dynamic outlined in chapter 8 and illustrated in the case chapters would not. I emphasize early intervention to remove the abusive adult as a means of child protection because, in cases where the mother is being abused, the victimization of children is almost always a secondary stage in a strategy to monopolize the resources and privileges available in a domestic/ social space. If the abusive male is removed early on, the children will most likely be safe. Obviously, removal of the offending adult is more complicated if s/he is the sole source of the child's support.

Identifying the child's victimization as a secondary aim in the abuser's strategy does not mean child protection is secondary in importance. To the contrary, I recommend the prompt removal of a perpetrator, with incarceration if necessary, because I place the highest priority on protecting children. The generation of child savers who built the child protection movement advocated child protection as a form of "harm reduction" or the alternative, the "rescue" of children by their removal to foster care. Arrest for coercive control is a form of prevention because it interrupts abuse before children are ensnared and restores the integral family unit so children can thrive. In conjunction with arrest, I favor interventions that relieve the trauma children suffer because of wife abuse, particularly when, as in the best of such programs, like Witnesses of Woman Abuse, which originated in Canada in the 1980s, "wrap around" housing and other services are also provided for survivors.[6]

The fact remains. Even the best of these programs rest on a flawed premise that the primary harm to the children in these cases results from what has happened to the mother rather than what is done directly to the child. In analyzing the dynamics of coercive control, we are interested not only in the range of harms being directly inflicted on children but also in children's responses, including both those that are deliberated and purposeful and those that are defensive or wholly reactive. With abused women, we now recognize a long-term struggle with "power and control" that unfolds over a broad social terrain that is overdetermined by sexual inequality and the supports men receive from the institutions of secondary socialization, job discrimination, and the like. There are a number of similar struggles by children against oppression depicted in the ethnographic and fiction literature. Recognizing how age is a limiting factor, the coercive control of children should also be framed as an "engagement" with men (and their mothers) rooted in family life that unfolds over time in and away from the home in the school, soccer field, teen center, or cyber-hub, in which children play active and ever more conscious roles.

The recognition that children "engage" coercive control does not implicate them in its occurrence. It simply acknowledges children are engaged with their personality, volition, and "voice" in all encounters no matter how heavily weighted toward their victimization such encounters may be. As we shall see repeatedly, the physical, emotional, and cognitive effects heretofore attributed to "witnessing" or "exposure" of children to domestic violence are far better explained dialectically, as the result of the engagement of children's active subjectivity with a malevolent other. While trauma models have been adapted to encompass the "prolonged" and intrusive psychic assault that typify the coercive control of children,[7] I worry that they leave little room for children's agency. Children experience coercive control much in the way they experience an encroaching fire or a flood. For a moment, they are caught up in what appears to be a fate that is overwhelming and inescapable. Although their survival can seem fortuitous, it inevitably reveals a level of grit and purposiveness that steels them for future challenges. Children miraculously survive when no survival seems possible, what I call "control in the context of no control."

A final word about sources. From women's medical charts, it is possible to extract historical data sets of physical, medical, mental health, and behavioral health problems that emerge in tandem with what we now know are techniques of coercive control. There are no comparable data sets available for children. Based on medical, clinical, or child welfare records alone, we would not suspect that children are subjected to anything other than physical and sexual abuse. But nor is the coercive control of children invisible. Detailed and evocative portrayals of children being subjected to coercive control can be found scattered throughout fiction, memoirs, diaries, the Internet, popular magazines, and streaming media. These accounts suggest that what I'm finding in my forensic cases reflects a broad reality in children's lives, perhaps across generations. Integrating fictional accounts of oppressed children into provider training can sensitize police and other front-line providers to coercive control in the same way that integrating survivor stories into "narrative medicine" enhanced the capacity for physicians to recognize and treat the full manifestations of cancer.

The dimensions and effects of coercive control are also gleaned from talking to children. Generations of children, women, and men have left eloquent records of having endured being made subordinate and denuded of freedom, security, dignity, autonomy, and personhood in their personal lives. If we want to understand how children are harmed when their entitlements to safety, nurturance, autonomy, and sexual development are usurped today, we have to listen to the voices of those who have suffered these indignities in the past, and those who recreate their voices.

I did not discover the coercive control of children. What I am doing in this book is framing a torturous experience others have eloquently described in relation to a newly developed appreciation of rights and subjugation. The mistreatment of children by fathers and father-surrogates in homes and

families had been part of popular lore at least since women's improved social standing allowed them to negotiate the terms of their own and children's
dependence on men in personal life. In the history of the United States, the
"social problem of children" referred to children who lacked proper families
or homes due to moral, natural, or social disaster, such as the estimated
350,000 "orphan children" shipped by train to stolid farm families out West
from Eastern ghettoes (1854–1924) or "children of poverty" placed in foster
care en masse in the 1970s and 1980s. By contrast with the social problems
impoverished children presented to public sentiment and commerce,
children's "troubles" "in" homes have been considered "private" matters for
familial management, for imaginative treatment, or later, for therapeutic
processing, but not the focus of public oversight or formal laws. In fiction,
memoir, or film, the source, experience, and consequence of the child's suffering is outlined in detail, but given a site specific psychological or biograph-
ical explanation, even if the character inflicting the pain is identified. One
example must suffice. In Brian Hobson's novel *Where the Dead Sit Talking*,
a Native boy's predicament is depicted as a function of his social situation—
his abusive father is at large, his mother is in prison, and he is in foster care.
But he suffers his sexual fantasies as a personal burden, which Hobson's
hero conveys to me via his novel, but I relate to the experiences of my family,
friends, and clients. The Native boy is not a victim of coercive control. But
his predicament is identical to the predicaments faced by the children in my
practice and by following his thought process, my children see their own.

Recognizing coercive control requires a new way of seeing and hearing
children, to paraphrase the social critic John Berger.[8] More exactly,
it reframes the old miseries children have recited through the centuries
against the backdrop of new opportunities for rights, dignity, and equality.
A Stamford, Connecticut, preteen proffers an account I have heard in
slight variation from affluent children a dozen times, of being kidnapped,
humiliated, isolated, and nutritionally deprived by his father, a banking executive in nearby Greenwich. Where do we find this boy in our texts on child
abuse, family conflict, or domestic violence? Before I recognized coercive
control, the only place I could imagine such a boy appearing is on the pages
of fiction or Netflix. Coercive control is hiding in plain sight.

A major point of this book is that the "discovery" and naming of coercive control is the result of a political intervention at a particular historical
turn, not a pressing fact of nature that results from "the march of science."
Despite the efforts of reformers like Francis Cobbe and George Meredith in

the 1870s, interest in violence against women had disappeared from public agendas by 1900. The ethnographic enthusiasts who built the burgeoning fields of social work, public health, urban anthropology and family and community sociology between 1890 and 1960 seemingly talked to everyone in America. Yet, they produced not a single footnote to family violence for the first three-quarters of the twentieth century, let alone a monograph. We can be excused if we thought we had discovered domestic violence circa 1970s.[9]

Violence against women and children had neither disappeared nor even diminished significantly in the last century. What disappeared was the visibility of abuse as a social problem requiring an administrative or political response. The historical and anthropological record leaves no doubt that abuse of women and children remains pervasive in all known societies.[10] In fact, it is probable that the abuse of women and children occurred at about the same rate in 1870, when Francis Power Cobbe first addressed "Wife Torture in England," as in 2010, when the British Crime Survey queried victims.[11] If violence was not a matter of public record through much of the twentieth century, we must assume abuse continued to surface during the periods when it went unrecognized, wherever family members found it too much to bear at home, either directly or through its numerous manifestations, at hospitals, police stations, child rescue centers, and other points of service. This is the presumption that led Anne Flitcraft to uncover the "hidden epidemic" of domestic violence inside medicine that was reflected in millions of women worldwide seeking refuge in shelters. Our work at Yale was an early salvo in the burgeoning of a huge literature on domestic violence, including its link to child abuse. But the dearth of literature on the coercive control of women and children today is similar to the relative silence that surrounded domestic violence forty years ago. Here, again, we have to look outside of social science and medicine to find images of how women and children are being oppressed in their everyday lives.

In the 1980s, the "social problem of abuse" was rediscovered and cast as violence against women. In the 1990s, the problem of domestic violence was linked to children, primarily through the co-occurrence of wife abuse and child abuse, the possibility that children would be inadvertently injured during an assault and the risk to children from witnessing domestic violence.[12] Two decades later, in 2007, in concert with the global progress of the women's movement, abuse was redefined again, this time as coercive control, a form of domination in personal life in which violence is combined with other means to exploit a partner's capacities and resources for personal gain. The change occurred not because more detail emerged about women's suffering, but because as women's standing improved, new possibilities emerged to relieve women's suffering that made details about their personal predicament salient. It was women's new opportunities that made fetters of what had previously been considered mere social consequences of inherent differences between the sexes. We now believe it is wrong not merely to physically or sexually harm women, but to treat them, or any persons, as unequal, subordinate, disposable, unworthy, as means to personal ends, however this is accomplished. The same historical currents that made it unacceptable for men to treat women as less than full persons now are extending to children. Although millions of children are identified because they are abused or neglected each year, interventions have failed to make a dent in the problem or in child fatality resulting from abuse. By recognizing the coercive control of children as the primary context for child abuse and nonaccidental child death, we elevate the rights of children from physical rights to life and safety, to the rights of full persons to be free of subjugation and humiliation.

Data management was still in its infancy in the early 1980s. But it was already possible for our small research team at Yale to get an incomparable look through women's medical records behind closed family doors at thousands of the same encounters nurses, social workers, home visitors had with the families for decades. Taken together, this collective record showed how problems unfolded in the lives of ordinary people over the entire period of their family formation. Seeing "child abuse" against the background of woman's complete medical records made it possible, for the first time, to conceptualize the problem as part of a family history rather than as a discrete event, as evolving, "ongoing," or repeated, and to link it to a parallel pattern of abuse to the woman, to see that both the "child abuse" and the "wife abuse" were byproducts of a single household tyranny and that this evolving pattern had a range of medical and psychosocial effects among which physical or psychological trauma were not necessarily the most important. This reading of the medical record as a collective picture of woman and child abuse by male partners was credible because a combination of structural factors (such as the growing importance of women in the economy) and political factors (such as pressure from women's movements in the United States and globally) made it possible to move women and their children into the mainstream as justice claimants.

Among the tomb of published monographs on domestic violence and children, including our own, only a tiny proportion contain historical data sets bearing on violence or sexual abuse, and fewer still contain evidence on elements of coercive control of women and children other than physical and sexual abuse. Moreover, persons responsible for abuse are rarely identified. Even the few useable studies had to be massaged to create a timeline for the violence. What was true of those who made the Yale Records, the case records at ACS in *Nicholson*, and the case file in the Pelka case (chapter 8) is typical of almost all of the institutional records that contain evidence about children: police, physicians, clergy, nurses, and caseworkers who crossed family portals appear to have rushed through the spaces and out again without pausing to notice that they had been to this home before, let alone to challenge or question the Golgotha in the room, the Man holding the reins of coercive control. Women and children were seen repeatedly without any acknowledgment of familiarity. Men were sometimes identified because they accompanied their wife, partner, or "girlfriend" to the hospital. But the abusive men weren't often mentioned and almost never identified. Only because we are working from the template of real life can we extrapolate from the fragmented records of adult injury, punches, rape, "fights," and the like to the responsible and victimized persons so that the violent incidents form a pattern and fall into place alongside incidents of suicidal ideation, miscarriage, depression, falls, "fear of sleeping," and "concern for the children." The discrete instances over many years form a history that is made coherent, as a downward spiral of physical, psychological, and social denigration and subordination accumulated in the presence of doctors, nurses, social workers, and sociologists who saw only the bruises on the mother, "alcohol on breath," and a mental and behavioral health profile of someone prone to fights.

Thirty years after we identified the medical and psychosocial profile associated with deliberate injury to women, we had enough case material to identify coercive control by husbands, partners, and ex-partners as the major context for women's abuse, subordination, exploitation, and denigration in personal life. Another thirty years has passed since we identified woman abuse as the major context in which children are physically abused and killed. We now have enough case material to identify "child abuse" as a "secondary form of wife abuse," the "coercive control of children."

I have no basis on which to estimate how many children are being subjected to coercive control. We do know it is a very high number, in the many millions in the United States alone.

The Model of Coercive Control of Children

Violence

Violence is the first identifying element of coercive control that concerns us with children. Where the female target of coercive control is visible to the community and/or is a significant source of the household income, violence may begin with the use of a child as a scapegoat. More often, violence against a child is initiated when coercive tactics against the mother are deemed insufficient. Our research at Yale (chapter 3) showed that "domestic violence" was the leading context in which children were "darted" for abuse and neglect.[13] This "overlap" has been repeatedly confirmed. The Centers for Disease Control and Prevention report that in homes where violence between partners occurs, there is a 45 to 60 percent chance of co-occurring child abuse, a rate fifteen times higher than the average.[14] When researchers reviewed the medical charts of 570 children of battered mothers, they found that almost all (93%) had been exposed to domestic violence and that 41 percent had been physically abused, almost all by the same man who was abusing their mother. Eleven percent also had been sexually abused.[15] A recent review of studies for the Casey Family Foundation using a conservative definition of child abuse showed a robust link between physical and sexual child abuse and domestic violence, with a median co-occurrence of 41 percent and a range of 30 to 60 percent.[16,17] Where children are present, the extraordinary degree to which violence against women and children co-occur suggests that child abuse is a defining element of coercive control of children by men across personality types and cultures. For the purposes of assessment and intervention, unless proved otherwise, it must be assumed that men identified as perpetrators of *either* coercive control or child maltreatment have perpetrated both.

Physical violence is the most prominent feature of the coercive control of children and the first facet they recall to memory. Data are overlap of "domestic violence" and "child abuse" is a useful indicator of the general risk children face from coercive control. But equating the violence used against children with the conventional picture of child abuse is misleading. The pattern of physical assault typical of the coercive control of children is similar to the pattern of assault used against adult women. It mainly consists of repeated, noninjurious assaults, often beginning when a child is a toddler or before, and extending over a significant time period and may be punctuated by more severe assaults and/or instances of sexual abuse. Assaults can be dramatic. Tiffany told me that, when Brianne was two, her step-father, Keith Hughes, beat her so badly, Tiffany was "horrified." She also witnessed Keith "pull down" Brianne's pants when she was two or three and "spank her hard." She described this as happening on several occasions. Even in this case, however, it was because of the repeated, methodical, and long-standing physical mistreatment of Brianne that Tiffany and her mother felt helpless to protect the child.

Child abuse in these families is usually of shorter duration than woman battering, in part because it is a tactical complement to other means of coercing and controlling a partner, because partner abuse often begins before a woman becomes pregnant or a child is born, and because children often leave the home before the battering ends. Since men typically spend much more time with their wives than their children, their child abuse is usually less frequent than their adult battering. An exception involves cases where the child is the wife's proxy, as in the broker example, where, if she refused to obey his commands, refused him sexually, or displeased him, he beat their son, refused to pay the children's tuition and/or denied her access to their infant. We saw another common scenario in the Hall/Braxton case, where Tony Braxton beat their two-year-old son to ensure his wife's obedience when Tondalo Hall worked outside the home (chapter 2).

The fact that child abuse is less frequent than adult abuse does not mean it is less harmful. The vast majority of all abusive assaults—well over 90 percent—are noninjurious to both adults and children. Again, it is their frequency, duration, and cumulative effect in instilling fear that commands attention, not their severity. However, because a high proportion of children who are assaulted are very young, the ratio of injurious to noninjurious episodes is higher among child than adult victims, particularly in instances where children are harmed "accidentally" during an assault on their mother or when they intervene to protect her.[18] Importantly, the absence of severe injury to a child victim of coercive control does not obviate high future risk. To the contrary, the secondary nature of the child abuse when a child is being controlled as way to control the mother means that a child may be "weaponized" and severely injured and killed as part of coercive control with no prior warning. This dynamic was also illustrated in the Oyola case (chapter 2), when a father drowned his child toward whom he had shown no prior animosity. As with adult victims of coercive control, the main effects of the physical violence to which children are subjected tend to be nonspecific and cumulative rather than episode-specific. The first serious assault on a child is often fatal. The child's risk in these cases is direct result of the disablement of the mother's protective capacity by coercive control.

Because coercive control occurs in millions of relationships in which no children are present and its onset often precedes the birth of children, an outstanding question is whether and how the birth of a child affects the nature and extent of abuse. There is substantial research indicating the increased risk of abuse to pregnant women and in every aspect of pregnancy, including its occurrence, its course, and the greater likelihood of a poor outcome.[19] Some abused women in my practice viewed having a child hopefully; others less so, fearing it might increase their entrapment. Lavonne L. reported that Miguel's violence diminished significantly after the birth of "his" son, though the respite was temporary. Pregnancy and the birth or presence of a child can be the occasion for the onset or escalation of physical abuse. Adrianna Oyola reported that Tony Moreno's first assault occurred when she became pregnant, an example of his use of reproductive coercion discussed in chapter 2. In the Hughes case, as in Lavonne's, the abuser who initially welcomed the presence of a child quickly interpreted their presence as potential competition for their partner's time and affection. Several men in my practice shared intense feelings of jealousy about young children that were comparable to their jealousy about grown men and brooded over their wife's attention to their children during routine activities like bedtime, changing diapers, and feeding. Several of these men acknowledged carrying resentment from their competition with sibs for their mother's love and attention. For others, however, the jealousy toward their children seems to be rooted in a primary narcissism about wanting the partner's attention focused solely on him. Jeanette Hughes hesitated to become pregnant because of her husband's cruelty to Tiffany, her daughter from her previous marriage. She ultimately agreed, largely because Keith seemed so excited about the prospect of his own child. Before Brianne was two, however, he became furious about the time she demanded from Jeanette and beat her, posted pictures of her naked on the web, and found a pretext to punish her whenever his wife failed to comply with his demands, a tactic he later applied to their adopted son, Aiden. There is no empirical evidence that the presence of children leads to an escalation or diminishment of abusive violence or other forms of coercive control.[20] What is clear is that when a child is present, the coercive control strategy will change to take this into account, if only because the abuser sees the child as a competitor for the scarce resources of time and attention in the household which he seeks to monopolize.

When children are interviewed about violent incidents, their account of an accompanying or precipitant event, the abuser's behavior, or the child's experience is often more salient than the description of the assault, an oft-repeated put-down, a tender memory of their mother or earlier innocence, the silent treatment, or looking at photos on an iPhone, or eyeglasses being removed. The combination of the "signal" and the assault gives the child's account verisimilitude. Conversely, the fact that the assaults on children culminate a sequence of events helps explain a key feature of children's response, that children's most intense anxiety is aroused by rituals that tell them an assault is coming. Children often displace their anxiety from the assault to the object or ritual in question, their father's key turning in the door, a cell phone call announcing his arrival home. For some children these moments, recalled many years later or perhaps excited by a random current event or memory, may screen out actual violence or abuse that may have occurred, the way Joe Torre recalls his father's car in the driveway or another man in one of my groups recalled an empty wine bottle in the garage. For children, this defensive adaptation is protective and lessens the intensity of an abusive assault to some degree, much in the way victims of violent sexual assaults protect themselves, by "splitting" off a part of their consciousness. But in displacing the anxiety onto one of its props or its pretext, the child also gives the abuser the power to elicit a paralyzing fear merely by gesturing at something that recalls the scene. Thus, in the middle of an angry spat with his son from whom he wanted money, a partially disabled father in his eighties had only to remove his cap to bring his ex-marine son to his knees in fear.

A significant proportion of parents in the general population acknowledge using physical and/or psychological means to manage their children. But, probably fewer than 1 percent of these involve terroristic violence typical of coercive control. Surveys of how children are harmed by "witnessing" or "exposure" to violence hopelessly confound these two scenarios, resulting in estimates of the proportion of children who are exposed to domestic violence in the general population that range from 6.5 to 82 percent and of the number of children affected from 3.5 million to 15 million.[21] These results are too discrepant to be useful. By contrast, based on Myhill's reanalysis of the data from the Crime Survey from England and Wales (CSEW) a third (30%, $n = 5,791$) of the women who reported some form of DVA had experienced what he termed "coercive controlling violence" (repeated violence combined with isolation, denigration, and other tactics).[22] Forty percent of violent families are characterized by co-occurring partner and child physical abuse of the sort that is consistent with coercive control.[23] This means coercive control affects tens of millions of children annually.

This data could mislead us into thinking that millions of children in the general population are jeopardized by coercive control who are beyond the reach of police, hospitals, shelters, and other services. In fact, a high proportion of coercive control cases are already "in the system" in many countries, particularly where domestic violence laws are enforced or coercive control laws are in place. The coercive control of children is the most serious context in which children are being hurt, almost always as an element of the mother's abuse. Although victims of coercive control may constitute only 30 percent of the abused women who respond to the British Crime Survey, because victims of coercive control call police many times more often than women who are assaulted only, they constitute a substantial majority of police and hospital cases, perhaps as many as 75 percent.[24] A majority of these police cases include children who have been assaulted and subjected to other forms of coercive control. Moreover, the probability of concurring coercive control of women and children increases sharply as abusive violence becomes more frequent, with the probability going from just 5 percent when a single act of partner aggression has occurred in the past year to nearly 100 percent when an average of one act of partner aggression has occurred each week.[25] Because coercive control has been mistaken for a relatively minor violent offense, these children remain largely unprotected. My guess is that by simply identifying and reclassifying repeat domestic violence offenders already in the system as perpetrators of coercive control, police would extend protection to 60 percent of the children who are currently being abused in their homes, perhaps more. Note, this substantial coverage is achieved by a transfer of resources to serious crime enforcement and a corresponding cuts in misdemeanor domestic violence enforcement.

This is not everybody. An additional group of children is being assaulted and coercively controlled by men who are also coercively controlling their partners, but who have not assaulted them.[26] While these cases may surface in Family Court, in a civil divorce proceeding for example, the absence of significant physical violence makes it unlikely that the children will become a focus of concern until they are seriously harmed. Hopefully, this situation will change in the United States as the coercive control of children comes under the radar in California, Connecticut, California, Hawaii, New York,

Washington, and other states. This suggests a paradox in our business, that the most serious *hidden* threat to children may lie in families that have prompted little or no attention because the level of isolation and control is so high.

It is impossible to say based on current data whether child abuse in the context of coercive control involves a significant minority, about the size of the population known to be infected with the HIV virus, already a staple on the chronic disease agenda, or a much larger but more transient population, like those affected by coronavirus. From the slim evidence available, we conjecture that somewhere around 65 percent of the violence that currently results in domestic violence arrest or other intervention by police in the United States and other countries is part of the pattern of coercive control and that similar or even larger proportions of the violence against women and children identified by child welfare, domestic violence services, and the family court also occur in the context of coercive control. As yet, we have no statistical basis to assess the extent to which coercive control extends to children in the 40 percent of cases where it does not include severe or ongoing violence against the mother.

Physical violence against children (classic "child abuse") is an important element of coercive control. But two common assumptions about the risk to children in domestic violence cases are almost certainly wrong when the real dynamic involves coercive control, that the children's primary risk arises from the man's *violence* against the woman and that the child's secondary risk is the result of visual/auditory exposure or "witnessing" the violence. In fact, even infants and small children face a far greater risk of being deliberately assaulted by the abusive assailant in coercive control than of being hurt inadvertently, as a means both to frighten or punish the mother and to control the child. Later in the chapter, I illustrate a common high-risk scenario in coercive control that is rarely anticipated by police or courts in domestic violence cases, where an assailant with no prior history of violence against the children identifies them as an obstacle/opportunity in his campaign to control the mom and uses violence or any other means at his disposal to exploit/remove the obstacle. Nothing in the man's prior relation to the child predicts this scenario. To the contrary, the child's vulnerability is a function of the protective resources available to mother *and* child and determined by a global assessment or the risk the abuser poses to *either* parent or child.

The Complexity of "Witnessing Violence"

Any child present may be emotionally wrought or harmed accidentally during a partner assault. But the supposition that "witnessing" and "violence exposure" are the main receptor media through which children are harmed by abusive violence or coercive control abuse is mistaken. Conversely, it cannot be assumed that a child who exhibits trauma in an abusive situation has been harmed by "witnessing." On the one hand, the recognition that "child abuse" is a common element of the coercive control of women means that many effects now attributed to witnessing and exposure are the result of noninjurious physical assault on the child. On the other hand, the fact that multiple insults are involved in coercive control in addition to physical violence suggests that many observed effects in children researchers attribute to witnessing violence are probably responses to yet to be identified nonviolent constraints, such as stalking, microregulation, threatening, or isolation tactics. Once we recognize that the insult to which children are responding is not fungible like violence, and may have its effect because of fear or by confounding perception, as when a sudden gift or withholding of recrimination elicits terror in a child who has come to expect and cope with punishment, we are forced to entertain a repertoire of children's cognitive, emotive, and behavioral responses to abuse that reaches far beyond the passive implications of "witnessing" or "exposure." Finally, and much will turn on this in case assessment, child "witnessing" is almost never a condition of passive receptivity in coercive control scenarios. Abusers establish children as "witnesses" as a tactic to terrorize children and intimidate women; at the same time, children willingly "bear witness" as a means to support their mother's resolve and display their resistance. "Witnessing" in abuse scenarios is a complex behavior that may have multiple and even contradictory causes and effects, not all of them malignant.

Empirical Support

How much child abuse is coercive control? Teasing out the empirical evidence on the use of violence against children in the context of coercive control is challenging. Women reported that their partner's abused their children in multiple ways on a recurring basis rather than in isolated acts. But since almost all the published research reports assaultive incidents at a single point in time, I could corroborate women's claims only by regrouping data into "historical" data sets. This was possible with only the handful of studies that collected data on the same children at different time periods to start and only with respect to two forms of abuse on which this data was collected, violence and sexual abuse. "Psychological abuse" was the only other element of coercion and control that was sometimes taken into account.

Unlike the instances of severe violence that garner attention in the child abuse literature, the physical assaults against children that occur in the context of coercive control are marked by frequent, low-level violence punctuated by injurious incidents. The first NFVS reported that 50 percent of the fathers who abused their wives three or more times during the previous twelve months also acknowledged they had abused their children with the same frequency.[27]

Two well-designed studies of battered women provided a glimpse of the frequency of child abuse, its link to child sexual abuse, and the interplay of violent and nonviolent tactics against mother and child over time. The first study involved a convenience sample of 111 abused women drawn from four cities[28] ("the urban study"). The second study compared samples of abused women in shelter and living in the community (166) with nonabused controls (199).[29] The "comparative study" was one of the very few US studies in which target children were interviewed as well as their mothers.

The mothers in the "urban study" were asked whether their children were intentionally or accidentally hurt "never," "rarely," "sometimes," "frequently," or "very frequently." The most common abusive dynamics involved batterers who hurt mother and child in separate incidents and/or hurt the child "accidentally" during an assault on their mother. Thirty-eight percent of the mothers reported that their children were harmed in separate incidents at least "rarely" and 15.3 percent of the children were hurt in this manner frequently or very frequently. Meanwhile, 37 percent of the children were hurt "accidentally" and 26 percent "intentionally" during domestic violence, with 13 percent and 10 percent, respectively, being hurt in these ways frequently or very frequently.

As would be expected with coercive control, abused mothers in the comparative study reported histories of nonviolent as well as violent abuse, with both escalating together, and a pattern of violence against themselves and their children that involved frequent low-level assaults punctuated by more severe acts. Two-thirds (62%) of the abused women reported they had been strangled ("choked") at least once; half had been threatened with a weapon. But the modal assaults were "beatings," experienced by 69 percent. Twenty-eight percent of the women reported they had been beaten more than fifteen times during the last year and also reported being pushed or grabbed an average of 12.7 times. Children's reports coincided with reports by their mothers, contradicting a widespread belief that abused women are in denial about the risks to children in these relationships. During the previous year, mothers reported that their partners had threatened to harm the children an average of seven times. Interestingly, a high proportion of the "controls" also reported being abused, though it was more common in the group already identified as abused. Depending on whether we consider reports by mother or child the more accurate, the child was "slapped" or "hit with objects" by the abusive partner 10–20 times as often as the child was "burned." Conversely, most children reported being slapped and over a third said they were hit with an object at least once during the previous year. Interestingly, there was no association between a mother being abused and her use of physical punishment. In fact, according to the children's reports, the abused mothers were significantly less likely than the comparison mothers to slap their children or hit them with objects. This finding suggests that the "pass the parcel" theory of domestic violence— where man hits woman who hits child—is wrong. There is no way from existing research to determine the duration of child abuse in the context of domestic violence. The findings confirm the identification of coercive control with violence against children that is generally low-level (slapped, punched, or hit with an object), frequent, and occurs across space. This is the violence of coercive control.

The urban study also documented the large proportion of children who are harmed accidentally or intentionally by the abusive partner during domestic violence. Younger children are disproportionately represented in households where domestic assaults occur and are often harmed inadvertently during an assault, because the mother is holding the child, for instance.[30] But even younger children often try to intervene and are harmed as a consequence. One large, multicity study found that children were involved directly in adult domestic violence incidents from 9 percent to 27 percent of the time (depending on the city). The dynamics in these cases often involve children trying to referee, rescue their mother, deflect attention to themselves, or otherwise distract the abuser, protect younger siblings, or call for outside help. This suggests *how* children are hurt, but also *why*, because they intervene and resist. It begs the question to suggest that harm to children in these instances is "accidental" or to blame women when children are harmed for "allowing" themselves to be assaulted with the children present, as in the *Nicholson* case.

Like the violence used against women, physical assaults used to control children are designed to instill fear rather than obedience to a command primarily, and may be terroristic—a sudden slap, punch, or kick that seems to come from nowhere; characterized by low-level bullying (slapping, pushing, pinching grabbing, shoving, etc.) or the use of objects. As a consequence of the frequency of the violence used against children, children report violence as "ongoing," "all the time." The results are "cumulative" rather than incident-specific. Children experience being subjected to "torrents of abuse" over time, the "fire" or "flood" metaphor I cited earlier. This, of course, is quite different from the current emphasis in child protection on emergent events. "Death by a thousand cuts" is a more appropriate simulacra.

Despite the common scenario—frequent, low-level violence extended over a considerable period—reported patterns differ widely, in part because the most common context for this violence, men's control tactics over their partner, differs so widely. Some children report being physically abused as part of a predictable ritual where the scene is set, as if in a dream sequence. Others experience "walking on eggshells" whenever they encounter their father. Assaults administered as punishments for specific offenses appear to be the exception, though many children could recite accusations (such as "thief," "slut," liar, "momma's boy") that were often repeated during assaults with no current reference. Some children report they or a sib being a "scapegoat" selected to take punishment for a range of problems at home (as I discuss in the Anwar case in the next section). Several children described an angry, "dark," or crazy demeanor. But a number of other children insisted their abusive parent rarely lost his temper when he assaulted them, or even raised his voice.

The violence used in coercive control is sometimes fatal and often severe. But, its primary intent is terroristic and its aim is to frighten and control, not to cause pain and injury, and the means, timing, duration design, setting, and placement of the violence in relation to other coercive and controlling tactics is critical to assessing its effect on a child. It is easy to misread a coercive control scenario by applying a calculus of physical harms to the violence and assuming, for example, that a child's fears that his father plans to kidnap or kill him are exaggerated because the man has not previously committed a serious assault. An abusive man may feel no hostility toward the child and display none. Thus, on February 8, 2022, a forty-two-year-old divorced, Miami Lakes, Florida, father, Humberto Kovar, posted a smiling photo of his son (age nine) and daughter (age eleven) on social media just two hours before he killed his children.[31] As I've emphasized, the fact that the man had not abused the child in the past and had agreed to cooperate in his care, which experts and Courts frequently see as meriting free access to parenting rights, has no bearing on the risk the man poses to the child so long as he remains intent on controlling his partner. Absent protections for the nonabusive parent, the probability that a child will be seriously hurt or killed is a function of the level of control *in the relationship* and the existence of operational protective measures, including physical protections such as alarms, protected password, and safe homes. Without an appreciation of the larger power dynamic at work, the capacity of even experienced clinicians is confounded to predict dangerousness to children because the classic signals of rage or passive-aggressive hostility do not apply. Once a history of wife abuse via coercive control is confirmed, the children must be considered a target.

Men parse their use of violence with children, as they do other tactics, with respect to its perceived instrumentality within the unfolding strategy of control over the partner and, through her, over the privileges, rights, and resources available through the household. In a small proportion of cases, the child or children in a relationship are the sole targets of violence.

Case Example: Violence against Children as a Tactic of Control

Mr. Anwar was a former bank executive, who had "retired" in his early fifties to live in a luxurious apartment, write a memoir, and depend on earnings from his wife's high-visibility Wall Street job managing bond portfolios. Any marks on her person would have immediately raised suspicions among her colleagues and almost certainly jeopardized her position. So his primary means of controlling his wife were nonviolent, terrorist threats, torrents of insults, physically and sexually humiliating her in front of their son, in-house stalking and the micromanagement of her domestic routines. But the main weapon in his arsenal was the use of their teen son as his scapegoat, literally, keeping her frightened and defferential by kicking, punching, and otherwise derogating the teenage son, usually "for no reason," solely to punish her, get her to give him money, or send her a message that left no "marks." Observing the bruises, the counselor at the elite private school referred the boy to a psychiatrist, who medicated the boy for depression. The psychiatrist was also seeing dad, but said nothing about the physical assaults on the boy, though he must have made the connection. When the wife threatened divorce, her partners at the firm received anonymous emails suggesting she had leaked confidential trading information. Although the allegations were fabricated by the husband, to avoid further embarrassment, she separated from the firm and set up an independent office, exhausting the funds she had set aside for the divorce. Two years later, she had recovered her income, found new clients, and filed for divorce again. This time, despite her husband's threats, she refused to back down. It was at this time that Mr. Anwar committed his first injurious assault in his twenty-year marriage, attacking his wife with a barbell, hitting her repeatedly in the head. Only the children's early intervention made it possible to save the woman's life through reconstructive surgery. At the criminal trial, the psychiatrist testified that Anwar's "emotional imbalance" was the side-effect of one of his medications. What set him "over the top," the MD opined, was the emotional "betrayal" of his wife's decision to initiate divorce proceedings "behind his back." Anwar claimed half of the marital assets earned during the marriage, almost all by his wife while he was out of work and "writing my memoir of a childhood in Pakistan" at home. If the psychiatrist could neutralize the attempted homicide, the conscience of the family court might be similarly salved.

I return to the Anwar case later in the chapter. Suffice it to say here that in the context of his coercive control over his wife and children, Mr. Anwar's act of "losing control" (including his "decision" to stop the meds he was taking for "anger management") was part of this coercive control and the logical progression of a malevolent pattern of behavior designed to "gain control." Note, even in the psychiatrist's eyes, Mr. Anwar's assaults on his son were the byproduct of his problems with "anger management" at his wife and their occasion and escalation reflected the progression of her independence in his eyes, not anything in the father–son relationship. The son talked to the psychiatrist about his suicidal thoughts, which the psychiatrist shared with the school. But rather than get at the heart of the problem, the father's exploitation of his wife and his weaponization of the son, the source of the boy's depression, the psychiatrist chose to medicate the boy's depression, imagining this would fix the situation, an illusion with which the school colluded, an example of "social entrapment."

The case clearly illustrates that the proximate risk to the child and ultimate risk to the mother was a function of the total extent of the father's violence and control, not of his previous threats to the mother. Anwar was using coercive control of the mother and children long before he committed an assault. The school was worried about the boy's risk to commit suicide, almost certainly a reflection of self-loathing because of his father's hatred. This risk was reduced—and the boy reported no subsequent suicidal ideation—after his father exploded at his mother and the boy "rescued" his mother. Conversely, the father's violence against the teenager was other-directed (he had impatience, but no particular animosity toward the son whom he tortured) and so was misinterpreted by the psychiatrist as a problem with "anger management." The psychiatrist was right to an extent: While medicating the son sent the wrong message, that *he* was the problem, medication for Mr. Anwar allowed him to control his rage (and his jealousy of her success and his dependence on her) and redirect it at his hapless son. To this extent, the medication "worked" to give Ms. Anwar the space she needed to build her business and file for divorce. It also allowed Mr. Anwar to continue his coercive control through his son without "losing his temper." Though technically, Mr. Anwar lost control over his impulses when he stopped taking his medication, he lost control to gain control over his wife, as do so many abusive men. Therefore he stopped taking his medicine with criminal intent. We explained this to the Court and they sent him to prison with a significant sentence.

Anwar was an exception. His violence and threats against his children were parts of a self-conscious strategy to elicit specific concessions from his wife, sign over certain properties, and give him specific sums. His use of the son to blackmail his wife was also explicit. This level of explicitness is unusual, though not unique in my caseload, in part because the assets at stake were concrete and visible. Mr. Anwar had all the qualities of an "intimate embezzler." In identifying the coercive control of children as an element of woman or spouse abuse, I am referring to its structural role in the subordination of female partners, not necessarily to the abuser's conscious intent. In most households, coercive control evolves through trial and error over time as oppressive behaviors with observed benefits are formally shaped into tactics.

Sexual Coercion

Sexual coercion is the second defining element of the coercive control of children. Only a handful of studies have considered the impact of these elements in combination. In a study of 120 preschool children (ages 4–6) who had been exposed to domestic violence in the last two years, 38 percent had also been physically and/or sexually assaulted and showed significantly elevated scores of PTSD and developmental problems.[32] In the coercive control of women, sexual coercion occurs along a continuum that runs from inappropriate touching, biting, sexual harassment, and denigrating sexual comments to sexual assault, anal rape, and what I call "rape as routine," where a woman's participation in sex is based on fear. Research has now confirmed the existence of this taxonomy in adult victims.[33] Understanding sexual coercion in abusive relationships as a continuum of behaviors designed to enforce control is a key to intervention and interdiction. Failure to recognize where a woman's experience of victimization falls on this continuum results in the "reality aspirations" gap between victims' report to police and the criminal justice response.[34]

The sexual coercion of children is more difficult to envision because the reality of how children are violated is so far from the common understanding. In my framework, the sexual coercion of children entails rational (i.e., calculated) tactics to monopolize the sexual resources and opportunities in a family space. In contrast to the view of rape or sexual abuse as distinct act, crime or violation, I posit sexual coercion as a "course of conduct" that takes different forms over time and through social space with the common effect of denying a child dignity, confidence, and sexual autonomy.

The case of Jeanette Hughes illustrates the interplay of how abusers use the physical and sexual coercion of women and children to reinforce their coercive control.

State of Penn. v. Jeanette Hughes

After a brief courtship and nineteen-year marriage, Jeanette Hughes shot and killed her husband, Keith, during an assault precipitated by his threatening to "punish" Aiden, his step-daughter Tiffany's nine-year-old son, for "leaving the garage lights on."

Keith had beaten Aiden in the past and had been investigated by child welfare pursuant to complaints of physical abuse by his daughter Brianne and of sexual abuse from Tiffany, the child's biological mother (age twenty-two). In both cases, the daughters told me, Keith had "cleaned up his act" and the allegations were judged "unfounded." At the time of the shooting, Tiffany was living with her boyfriend and Brianne was staying with her maternal grand-mother. Jeanette was terrified of Keith. She slept with a gun under her pillow. Keith had raped Jeanette during their brief courtship (which he blamed on alcohol) and had sexually abused and exploited her sexually on dozens of occasions since. He had strangled and beaten her on several occasions, pointed a gun at her and fired into the wall or above her on two occasions and destroyed a good deal of household property. He had threatened to kill her, her daughter, her ex-husband, her boss, and others. Jeanette saw these threats as credible, since Keith had also told his wife that he had killed people in the past, including children, as part of a criminal gang. Keith's violence had become more serious and his behavior increasingly erratic recently, in part because he had lost the regular supply of illicit and licit drugs he used to self-medicate his obsessive jealousy, rage, and guilt. By the time, Jeanette shot her husband, she was a virtual hostage in her own home. She had left her seventeen-year employment as a dental assistant to work in their gun store; had no social contacts other than her mother; was either with him constantly or reported her whereabouts to him regularly; had no money of her own; had lost both her own money and her brother's to his drug and alcohol habits so that their store was on the edge of bankruptcy; was dressing, cleaning, cooking, and so on according to his rules (see the discussion of Brianne's accommodation below); and had become a slave to his sexual demands.

On the evening of the shooting, Jeanette faced a classic battered woman's dilemma, how to prevent Keith from again harming Aiden without herself becoming the target of his rage. Despite the calculated risk of doing so, she challenged his derogatory and threatening comments about Aiden. He turned his anger on her, accused her of "taking his side" and caring for Aiden more than him. After an hour or so of threats and insults, Jeanette took her dinner into their bedroom. Keith followed, grabbed the plate, and smashed it on the floor, eliciting a memory of her father smashing a brown glass ashtray during an assault on her mother, sending shards everywhere. Keith vacuumed up the food. Jeanette told me, "This was the angriest I ever saw him. He threatened me with the handle of the vacuum cleaner up to my face." Keith then put his forearm on her face and neck, choking her and pushing her cheekbone with all of his weight. She recognized his "blank" look from earlier assaults. She told investigators, "He's yelling how he hates his life and me and how he wishes I would die. He has a dazed look in his eyes and he loses it." Jeanette further told the investigator, "When he put his hands on me, I got the gun out from the safe. I crawled across the bed, grabbed the gun, the Luger. He stood by the dresser and said, 'what are you going to do, shoot me? Then shoot me.' I said 'no, I just want to be safe.'" Keith briefly exited the room but returned after a few minutes. He accused her of taking his pain medication, his cell phone, and the keys from the car to keep him from leaving. He grabbed her phone, telling her if he couldn't have a phone, she wouldn't either. She reportedly replied, "I don't want your phone." At this point, all she recalled was that Keith continued to "scream and yell." She told me she thinks he was coming toward her, but couldn't say for sure. She told an investigator, "I didn't think. I just shot." When he heard the shot, Aiden came downstairs and brought his father a glass of water. Keith told police, "She didn't mean to shoot me," that it was an "accident." He died on the way to the hospital.

Aiden remains an offstage presence thus far, even though his safety and well-being are in both parents minds, Jeanette's to protect him and Keith's to keep his safety in jeopardy so as to control Jeanette. The fatal confrontation is instigated when Jeanette challenges Keith's control over Aiden.

Keith's exclusive access to Jeanette that night was also a function of his isolation and control of her other children, Brianne and Tiffany. Keith accomplished this through sexual coercion. Sex with children may satisfy erotic needs. But as a tactic in coercive control, it is designed to manipulate, intimidate, disempower, degrade, control, and compromise the child's capacity to support the mother, enlist the child as an ally, and divide the mother from her child(ren). At the less violent end of the spectrum, the sexual abuse of children involves behaviors and communications that deny children dignity, respect, and sexual autonomy. These behaviors include denigrating their physical appearance, sexual identity, and sexual choices; controlling their dress, hygiene, and physical appearance; and denying them access to information about sexual health. A high proportion of abusive men both sexually and physically assault their adult partners.[35] By contrast, whereas rape and violence are typically complementary tactics in the abuse of women, because the sexual abuse of children primarily serves an instrumental rather than an affective role, abusive men more often select target children for physical *or* sexual abuse, sometimes alternating these tactics with different children in the same family. This is illustrated in the Hughes household.

Keith Hughes physically abused his biological daughter, Brianne, as well as Aiden, his adopted son. Tiffany also told me that he took pictures of Brianne naked, which she believed was inappropriate. But he chose Tiffany to abuse sexually, Jeanette's daughter from her previous marriage. The first instance occurred when she was a teen and had just returned from a visit to her grandparents, a common occasion for her father's denigration (see below). She told me she had asked Keith to use the computer and he'd said yes, though he'd almost always refused this request in the past. He was drunk. He showed her a photo on his cell phone of her mother in bed naked and told her, "Your mother is a 'dead fish' in bed." He offered to show her a video of them having sex. Feeling embarrassed and uncomfortable, Tiffany turned off the computer and went to her room. Keith followed and offered her a red dildo that "my mom didn't use." He asked to see her underwear and offered to show her how to use the dildo. He then approached her, pushed her against the wall and rubbed the dildo against her groin. Tiffany told Keith she felt uncomfortable and told me, "I was terrified." That night, he came into her room at 2:30 am and retrieved the dildo from the shelf, again terrifying her. Tiffany also told me that Keith would call her when she was at her friend's house, tell her how beautiful she was, "like your mom," and tell her the sexual things he wanted to do to her.

Several years later, after she'd become addicted to heroin, he called to ask her to come along on a drug buy, telling her Jeanette was coming as well. He came alone. When they arrived, Keith ordered her to have sex with the dealer in exchange for the drugs. When Tiffany refused, he sexually assaulted her at gun point.

* * *

Putting Tiffany's experience of sexual abuse in the context of Keith's strategy of coercive control is critical to grasp both its particular meaning to Tiffany and its larger criminological significance because of its effects on the overall vulnerability of Jeanette, Tiffany, and the other children to Keith's control. By way of introduction, suffice it to say that child sexual abuse by fathers and father-surrogates is so widespread and its link to partner abuse and other forms of child maltreatment is so robust that its roots in normative masculinity are unavoidable, as is its secondary role as a means to dominate female partners.[36] Within the context of coercive control, the sexual assaults are terroristic because their function is to disable the child's capacity for self-care and protection as well as to degrade and humiliate her. So-called incest and sexual coercion of children is rife with this sort of complexity. Yet, the sociological and clinical literature has little to say about these links. Instead, like the literature on adult rape, discussions of child sexual abuse, including "incest," are dominated by medicolegal portrayals of offenders as deeply wounded, serial predators whose psychological profile sets them apart as a distinct subtype, a byproduct of disturbed family function, or "lack of spousal sexual activity etc."[37] In popular lore incest is widely associated with sexual deviants, racial stereotypes, poverty, and imbecility. Embracing these portrayals, police, family judges, evaluators, and child welfare workers are prone to discount claims by protective mothers that their "upstanding," psychologically normal husbands have sexually abused their children and to view the claimants as vengeful, alienating, or worse. Of course, there are persons—women and men—who fit the profile of a sexual predator. The fact remains. The vast proportion of child sexual abuse is committed by fathers and father surrogates who do not fit this profile.[38] As a result, child sexual abuse that occurs in the context of coercive control is rarely identified; almost never seriously considered in family, probate, or juvenile proceedings; and rarely punished. In fact, some proportion of the "model citizens" who sexually abuse their children are given primary custody or liberal, unsupervised visitation. The harms suffered by girls like Tiffany rarely elicit justice claims on behalf of the children violated.

As the Hughes case illustrates, the rape and sexual molestation of children by fathers and father surrogates is a common form of child abuse and is widely associated with coercive control among families in all social classes. The link between physical abuse and incest has been known for decades.[39] In a historical study of the records of the Massachusetts Society for the Prevention of Cruelty to Children, Linda Gordon reported that 38 percent of the incest victims were the daughters of mothers who also had been abused.[40] Conversely, "incestuous" fathers are more likely than other fathers to abuse their wives.[41]

The typical man who commits incest is a "wife-beater," not a psychopathic pedophile. Moreover, it is now apparent that in tens of thousands of cases "incest" is one of many sexual insults on a continuum of abuse perpetrated on children as part of a broader pattern of coercive control. Women will sometimes retaliate to defend their children more readily than to defend themselves. The motives here can be complex. In one a case I had in the early 1990s, a Palestinian client who had been beaten and raped by her husband and three of his brothers, retaliated only when he attempted to sexually molest their fifteen-year-old son, hitting her husband with a club so that he lost permanent use of his legs. She told me that raising and protecting her son was the sole point of dignity her husband had respected in her life. She saw the attack on the boy—rightly in my view—as an attack on her. She realized the boy might abuse his own wife as an adult.

In the comparative study described previously, 36.8 percent of the women reported that their partner had sexually abused their child, all but one of these women was also being abused. This included the community and control samples. As with adult victims of IPSA, so too is child sexual abuse typically repeated. Child sexual abuse is limited to a single incident in only 17 percent of cases, and 40 percent of reported father–daughter incest lasts at least a year (though the link between the duration of child sexual abuse and partner abuse has not been made).[42] An important difference between children and adult victims is that, whereas IPSA typically occurs in combination with domestic violence in the coercive control of women, the comparison study found that the child sexual abuse was related to the wife abuse, but *not* related to the incidence of physical child abuse. In other words, as I suggested earlier, abusive men either physically or sexually abuse their children, but rarely do both. Keith Hughes sexually abused his step-daughter Tiffany, but physically abused Brianne. Less it appear that his decision was based on consanguinity, he also took naked pictures of Brianne. In cases of coercive control, physical and sexual abuse of children are functionally equivalent tactics to coerce, control, and/or punish their partners, a motivation whose significance was first identified in interviews with incestuous fathers conducted by Williams-Meyer and Finkelhor.[43] The argument that control of the mother is the typical motive for child sexual abuse rather than a prurient interest in sex or in power over the child is supported by the finding that the perpetrator's biological relation to the child made no difference in predicting his offending. With children as with adult victims, the portrayal of the men responsible for child sexual abuse as a psychological subtype is shown to be false by the extent to which coercive control is the context for sexual abuse, the parallels between physical and sexual abuse in this context, and the apparent function of both as forms of punishment, revenge, or control of a female partner. Child sexual abuse in the context of coercive control is a form of exploitation and intimidation and only secondarily involves prurient sexual interest or psychological turmoil.

Sexual Abuse as an Isolation Tactic

Keith Hughes raped and sexually assaulted his step-daughter Tiffany in order to fracture her bond to her mother and undermine Jeanette's trust in Tiffany, the major obstacle he saw to his total control of the household. Jeanette seem-ingly disbelieved Tiffany, confirming a storyline common in novels and film of a certain genre, where a daughter is "lost" to her mother after the latter disbelieves the daughter's report of rape or incest we know is truthful. Given the ultimate alienation and sometimes suicide of the rejected child in such circumstances, it is hard to withhold judgment of a parent who fails to vali-date a credible claim from a child. Within the constraints of coercive control, however, where sexual abuse of a child is often used as an isolation tactic, with the precise object of stirring animosity or repulsion between the parties, mothers can use denial/disbelief strategically to maintain a bond that is crit-ical to survival. This was how Jeanette used it in the Hughes case.

Jeanette's experience as a girl corroborates the conventional script. When Jeanette was a preteen and living with her family at her maternal grandmother's house, she was sexually abused by an uncle. Jeanette's mother refused to believe her, although the uncle had been sexually inappropriate with her as well as with a cousin. She sent Jeanette to a psychologist, whom she hated. Shortly thereafter Jeanette was placed in "special education" classes and came to see herself as "retarded," although her grades soared as soon as her family got their own place. Her mother's disbelief left Jeanette with deep feelings of resentment and caused a lasting fissure in her relationship to her mother which Keith continually exploited.

When I interviewed Jeanette in prison, she told me that one of her biggest regrets was disbelieving Tiffany's claims that Keith had sexually abused her, in part because she appeared to be recapitulating her mother's response to her being abused as a teen. At the time, she reported, she had accepted Keith's denial and his explanation, that Tiffany was "jealous." She blamed herself for Tiffany's growing alienation—they are currently reconciled—as well as for her heroin use after she moved out. Interestingly, Tiffany's very different ac-count suggests a more complicated dynamic was in play. Tiffany remembers that, when she told her mother about the abuse, Jeanette asked, "Do you want me to leave him?" Whether or not Tiffany's memory is accurate, in her mind Jeanette was identifying the predicament she faced if she accepted her truth, to leave Keith, as a problem for them *both* to solve. Not wanting the guilt at breaking up the family, Tiffany replied, "No, I'll leave." But Tiffany is also taking responsibility for bearing the burden of Jeanette's dilemma because she recognizes the danger she faces if she acts on the violation, a dilemma Jeanette's mother did not face when she rejected Jeanette's report when she was a girl. Tiffany reported being molested to the school. Jeanette told me she warned Keith, "We have a problem." Children and Youth came out that day, but the investigation concluded the allegations were "unfounded." At the time, Jeanette was not ready to confront Keith, but she was aware of the need to protect Tiffany from Keith. While Tiffany views her move to her grandparents' house several months later as her own doing, Jeanette told me "little by little I let her stay more at the house of her grandmother." In either case, Tiffany's move deprived Jeanette of her major source of support in the home, greatly increasing her vulnerability to being controlled. Isolation from Jeanette was devastating for Tiffany. Within a few years, Tiffany became addicted to heroin, a habit she shared with Keith. Despite Keith having created an insurmountable barrier to their relationship, Jeanette and Tiffany continue to take some responsibility for the well-being of the other, an example of "control in the context of no control."

The separation of Tiffany and Jeanette, the direct result of Keith's sexual abuse of Tiffany, harmed both women, isolating Jeanette from Tiffany's support and curtailing the positive role Tiffany played in Jeanette's life. At the same time, their separation reflected the tacit agreement that confronting Keith's sexual abuse of Tiffany would bring the crisis in the household to a premature head with possibly disastrous results for both women. Both Tiffany and Jeanette suffered poor outcomes regardless of their choices, Jeanette in prison for murder and Tiffany addicted to drugs. But arguably, things might have gone even worse had it not been for the resilience they developed because of their negotiation across the thicket of assaults, deception, and control they confronted. Keith did everything he could to isolate Tiffany from her biological father and his family as well as from Jeanette. He demanded she take his family name, but had to defer when her father and she refused. The showers Keith made Tiffany take to clean the "dirt" from her visits to her father had a stronger impact on Jeanette than on Tiffany, as we've seen. It was after one such visit that Keith sexually assaulted her, presumably because each sojourn in the outside world steeled her against his control. Aiden was too young and vulnerable to protect Jeanette, and Keith exploited this fact by hurting or threatening him to win compliance from his wife or to punish her, as he did on the day she shot him. When Brianne's report to CPS failed to get results, she moved out, afraid of Keith's vengeance. With Tiffany and Brianne out of the house, Keith's violence escalated dramatically. By this time the shooting occurred, Jeanette had been forced to leave her long-time position as a dental assistant and was virtually never alone, since she worked with Keith at the gun store 999 during the day. In the lexicon of coercive control, by isolating her, Keith had managed to enter and close the last vestige of Jeanette's "safety zones"; she had no place left to breathe the air of a free woman. If she could retreat no further, a confrontation was inevitable. Absent coercive control, we might envision the stories of Tiffany and Jeanette as a downward spiral of decompensation spawned by childhoods rife with drugs and sexual abuse. Instead, we have a mother and daughter overcoming formidable personal odds and structural barriers to endure.

In the Hughes case, among the many effects of Keith's sexual abuse of Tiffany, was the strategic advantage it gave him, by threatening to break Jeanette's protective bond to her daughter, primarily by creating a double-bind for both victims in which either alternative, concealing or disclosure, led to pain and further alienation. Note, that he eventually raped Tiffany as punishment for her refusal to provide sexual services to a stranger. Keith's move was "strategic" because he went after Tiffany sexually only after numerous other attempts to break his wife's ties to her daughter had failed. Keith knew he was taking a risk when he assaulted Tiffany and "dared" her to report it to Jeanette, hoping her reporting would divide them, if she did. Keith was desperate to retain control of Jeanette. Even if Tiffany did not tell Jeanette what Keith had done, after his sexual assault, he knew she would no longer be able to argue the "tell truth to power" line persuasively that had made her Keith's most formidable opponent. Tiffany's description captures the dilemma framed by coercive control for the abused child. She told me she feared Keith's control over her if she did not disclose—even though doing so meant almost certain rejection from her mother. Until then, she remained the only child outside his control. But Jeanette also faced a dilemma, however she chose to respond to Tiffany: she feared for her life and for Aiden's life if she confronted Keith; but if she believed Tiffany and did nothing, she had failed to protect her children and lost confidence in her capacity to parent and protect them. Disbelieving Tiffany (and forcing her to leave the house) was the safest course of action for Jeanette. But it meant Keith had won, isolating his victims and making them more vulnerable. That his victory would be only temporary was not inevitable.

How much of Keith's behavior was under his control, I cannot say. But in assaulting Tiffany, he also put his control at risk, not least because Tiffany might tell Jeanette and Jeanette respond by throwing him out of the house, reporting to police, or worse. Rather than force Jeanette to make the choice, Tiffany disclosed and then voluntarily left the house, moving to the home of her biological father's parents.[44] Jeanette chose to believe Keith, largely,

I think, because it felt like the safest option at the time She admitted later, she only said this out of fear. She knew her daughter was telling the truth and told her so when they met shortly after Jeanette went to prison for killing Keith.

* * *

"Beyond Witnessing": Conceptualizing the Harms of Intimidation, Isolation, and Control

The dynamic in the Hughes case provides a unique opportunity to appreciate the secondary role of an assault on a child in fostering the devastating psychological effects of "witnessing" on the mother, Jeanette Hughes, much the same effect as if she had seen her child raped or executed by an enemy soldier. Jeanette did not "see" Keith sexually assault her daughter. But the fear and self-loathing instilled by the apprehension of his assault was terroristic, in no small part because it undermined her confidence in her capacity to protect her children. In another case, the abusive partner ordered the older boy (age eight) to put his hand up his sister's vagina (age seven) but claimed the mother "witnessed" the boy do it. "That much is true," Robin B. acknowledged, "because he forced me to stand in the room and watch. . . . He told me, "You're going up to the room to watch him do that to his sister. He said it was my child to watch (RC) do this to teach VC a lesson." Asked what would happen if she didn't watch, she replied, "He said he would beat the shit out of me." This affective dynamic, by which a woman is intimidated by watching her child demeaned and abused, is as much a consequence of the coercive control of children as the effect on the child who is made to feel her vulnerability by bearing witness to a parent's denigration, isolation, and control. Every aspect of coercive control is performative, each prop, each line, each movement, has reverberations and elicits responses from all persons in the "play." It is always being "witnessed" as well as being experienced.

From interviews with 26,229 adults in five states, the CDC estimated that children had witnessed domestic violence in 16.3 percent of US households, a figure acknowledged to be conservative.[45] Fathers followed by cohabiting boyfriends accounted for 78 percent of the abuse these children witnessed, with the percent of male perpetrators increasing with the level of violence.[46] Since partner abuse almost always includes multiple assaults, it must be assumed that *all* children in these homes witnessed domestic violence to a greater or lesser degree. For example, Leighton reported that children were "present" in 81.3 percent of 1,799 domestic violence incidents she assessed but that 100 percent of children were in the same or an adjacent room during at least one incident.[47] Adults underreport children's exposure to violence. Children often provide detailed recollections of events they were not supposed to have witnessed.[48] Meanwhile, 78 percent of the children in a community sample reported observing violence by fathers against their mothers when at least one parent reported that no violence occurred or that their children had not viewed such events.[49]

It is now possible to reconstruct this data so that we not only put the children in the room on multiple occasions when physical abuse occurred but also recognize that in relegating the children to (mere) "witnesses," the CDC researchers are assigning an arbitrary, seemingly passive role to children in what the case materials have shown are active scenarios, involving multiple tactics in addition to violence, where children are engaged victim/participants. Taking the experience of the Hughes children as typical of the CDC sample, we appreciate that virtually all children in the sample were at the scene when coercive control occurs, their experience is multifaceted and complex, confounded by the fact that they are targets and/or participants as well as "witnesses," extends to insults far beyond physical violence, is different for each child and cannot be approximated using conventional psychobiological models of "trauma." Does "witnessing" capture how Tiffany processed seeing Keith stage naked photos of her little half-sister Brianne at age two and how the memory elicited the "suspicion" she harbored that he might be molesting her son Aiden, whom she had to leave behind when she moved out years later and who was the same age as Brianne had been during her "witness"? What exactly is the offense to Tiffany here, who, along with Jeanette, is the target of Keith's assault on Brianne? In fact, to capture the effect and experience on children of the range of tactics that involve chronic, but intangible abuse (such as isolation, control, and subtle forms of intimidation), we have to imagine children as fully sensed and rights-bearing human beings with an imaginative and impressionable brain capable of defensive and strategic responses but also of a persona capable of being denuded of autonomy and dignity. Once we turn from the physical tactics of coercive control, to nonviolent and less tangible abusive tactics, such as "intimidation," "isolation," and "control," we are looking at emotive, behavioral, and conditional effects on children that are no less substantial than physical effects but that are hard to quantify. Moreover, in many instances, children lack the linguistic facility and/or the experiential foundation to associate their feelings of unease or dread with the corresponding control tactic directed at themselves or their mothers. The example below of the father who threatened to make the dog "disappear" is a relatively straightforward intimidation tactic. But what about this example of Keith's control of household finances ("economic abuse")? Because of Keith's scrutiny of her expenditures, Jeanette was terrified of "wasting" money, so she rarely turned the heat on, even in the dead of winter. Tiffany remembered always wearing sweatshirts when she was growing up, but never knowing why the house was so cold or so dark. She would retreat to her room and turn on the light. Tiffany held Jeanette responsible for keeping the house cold and the effect was for her to stay in her room, a response that compounded both her and her mother's isolation. Here, the isolation of Jeanette and the children, a structural dimension of their entrapment, was the result of a control tactic. But the isolation is not the direct effect of control, like turning on a lightbulb, but the indirect effect of a prior disempowerment.

Each child's experience of violence and other elements of the coercive control reflects their placement/vantage within the family system, the developmental challenges they face during the abuse trajectory, and the particular obstacles or opportunities the children pose to the appropriation of the family's resources.

In the Hughes household, each of the children had a different vantage on Keith's physical abuse. Tiffany walked in on or was in the room on at least three occasions when Keith assaulted her mother, Jeanette; she recalls hearing him shout and threaten her on numerous occasions; she saw Keith assault Brianne, her younger sister; she remembers watching Keith take naked polaroid photos of Brianne at age two or three, and she suspects Keith sexually abused Aiden after she had moved out and was living on her own. Tiffany was unaware of the extent of Keith's control over Jeanette and was out of the house when he coercively controlled Brianne. So Tiffany saw Jeanette as "weak" rather than controlled and subordinated and saw her own role as encouraging Jeanette to act rather than as an ally.

Psychological Abuse

The third dimension of the coercive control of children for which there is some empirical evidence is "psychological abuse." Tasmania, and several US states restrict the legal understanding of coercive control to "psychological abuse," usually defined to include a range of nonviolent abusive behaviors many of which, such as degrading, isolation, controlling behavior, and monitoring someone's time, money, or movement, are not already criminal offenses. An alternative approach, which I advocate in this book, has been adapted by Scotland, South Wales and Hawaii, among other jurisdictions. In these jurisdictions, coercive control is defined as a "bespoke offense" that includes multiple elements (such as violence, child abuse, sexual assault, and stalking) that are distinctive in the context of coercive control in addition to psychological abuse. In this book, I have emphasized the violent tactics used to coercively control children in a large majority of cases and referred to tactics such as denigration and ridicule that deny persons respect and can contribute to self-loathing in children. I am now prepared to explicitly distinguish coercive control tactics designed to physically or structurally alter a child's situation (such as when a child is physically or sexually abused, isolated from social contacts, and exploited economically) and "psychological abuse," by which I mean subjected to shaming, threats, belittling, or demeaning behaviors that are designed to make them afraid or feel badly about themselves. Threatening, shaming, and belittling can have devastating effects, particularly when they target a person's core racial, sex, or gender identities. In the context of coercive control, however, psychological abuse is rarely effective in the absence of complementary structural barriers to and/or constraints on person's opportunities/capacities to respond. In other words, psychological abuse alone is rarely sufficient to subordinate a child, though it may be. Conversely, when a child appears to have adapted to an abusive situation, as in chapter 16, it is rarely the result of psychological abuse alone.

One of the few surveys to include "psychological" abuse as well as physical violence was a nationally representative telephone survey of the victimization experiences of 4,549 youth aged 0–17 conducted between January and May 2008. Created by the US Office of Juvenile Justice and Delinquency Prevention, the NatSCEV reported that the proportions of children exposed to psychological and physical abuse were roughly equivalent both during the same year (5.7% vs. 6.6%) and during their lifetimes (16% vs. 17.9%). There is no way to know whether the same youngsters were exposed to both types of abuse. As a general rule, however, the coercive control of children includes both physical and psychological abuse as reinforcing means of oppression. Name-calling and continued denigration by anyone of a child can be devastating, even from another child. But from preadolescence on, the most devastating context of name-calling is one in which the child cannot respond in kind, walk away, or otherwise escape the pain resulting from the insult because s/he fears the consequences of doing so. Psychological abuse is most harmful, therefore, when a child's capacity to respond is also being constrained by isolation and control tactics.

The Special Case of Infants and Preschool Children

The psychological effects of coercive control on children are as various as the tactics deployed and merit years of specialized attention. To date, close attention has been paid primarily to the impact of extreme maltreatment on infants and the exposure of young children to physical violence.

The highest rates of domestic violence are reported by women between the ages of twenty and thirty-five years, so it is not surprising that younger children are represented disproportionately in households where domestic assaults occurred.[50] Researchers believe that the stress-induced fear associated with witnessing violence is sufficient in itself to evoke psychological and behavioral problems in children in these age groups, largely because of separation fears. The healthy development of preschool-aged and young children requires a sense of security in a continuous bond with a caretaking parent who exercises reasonable control over the child's immediate universe, including control over the boundaries separating the caretaking relationship from the outside world. In this view, the main mechanism of trauma to infants is the threat violence poses to their emotional security. The emotional security hypothesis suggests that differential exposure of children to the severity of the abuse will moderate the effect of maternal trauma on infant trauma. Descriptions of infants exposed to domestic violence note problem behavior that is consistent with trauma symptoms such as eating problems, sleep disturbances, lack of normal responsiveness to adults, mood disturbances, and problems interacting with peers and adults. In one study of infants exposed to domestic violence, nearly half (44%) displayed at least one trauma symptom in the two weeks after an episode, and the number of episodes to which a child was exposed was directly correlated with the total number of infant trauma symptoms.[51] A recent study found that childhood exposure to parental abuse, especially before two years of age, was associated with a seven-point drop in a child's IQ.[52] Another study demonstrated that children exposed to parental abuse before age three suffered no behavior problems at first, but by the time they entered school at age five they had become overly aggressive. The researcher labeled this a "sleeper effect" of exposure.[53]

Because preschool children think in egocentric ways, they are more prone than children at other ages to attribute violence to something they did. Physical independence (such as learning to dress themselves) is another developmental task specific to preschool-aged children. The instability associated with exposure to violence has been found to inhibit the development of physical independence and to elicit regressive behavior. Preschool- and school-aged children are frightened and sometimes terrified by witnessing abuse. They tend to express their insecurity through clinging, crying, nervousness, and a constant vigilance over where their mothers are. They may also display a range of somatic problems (including insomnia and other sleep disorders), eating disorders, bed wetting, ulcers, and chronic colds. Exposed preschool children have been found to be more likely to suffer from a failure to thrive, developmental delays, and socialization deficits. A meta-analysis suggested that effect sizes for trauma symptoms in preschool children occurring as a result of exposure to domestic violence were greater than those for other forms of internalizing behaviors.[54]

It is impossible for me to do justice in this book to the vast literature on how violence against their mother affects children. Suffice it to say here that shifting the focus to coercive control changes the emphasis from the fear of physical harm and separation—and annihilation of the self—to an abiding sense that the universe is unpredictable and the moorings of identity are unsafe. But the historical and diffuse nature of the abuse associated with coercive control means that the nature of the stressors involved in abuse has to be reconceptualized to anticipate that children's response will change over time to reflect developmentally specific challenges and the fact that the psychological and behavioral risks associated with their experience will be mediated by the age-specific developmental tasks that are delayed, disrupted, or distorted by the tactics deployed. Despite the scope, duration, and intensity of woman abuse, one comprehensive review concluded that the vast majority of adult survivors of wife abuse test as psychologically normal or only somewhat impaired with fewer than one in five evidencing serious psychopathology,[55] and that the vast majority of the women affected remain unsymptomatic.[56] While there is no basis for premature optimism that assessments of child outcome of coercive control will look similarly positive, this possibility is greatly enhanced by early intervention to remove perpetrators. The rationale for prompt intervention is to bring justice through the door, not amelioration.

Unlike infants, whose capacity to accommodate trauma is constrained largely by their psychic and physiological immaturity, older children are both more resilient and more sensitive to permanent impairment as the result of distortion in the identification process. Thus, despite the finding that children who experience domestic violence in their homes are at high risk for physical injury and psychological or behavioral problems, it cannot be assumed that most children subjected to coercive control suffer long-term or severe consequences. As Crooks, Jaffe, and Bala emphasized, whether serious problems will develop depends on the resilience of a particular child, the available support system, the child's developmental age, and the nature and extent of abuse tactics to which children are exposed, with the probability of harm increasing sharply if physical and/or sexual abuse is chronic.[57]

Even if they do not exhibit behavioral or cognitive difficulties, children who live with abuse are actively engaged: They interpret, predict, and assess their roles in causing fights; worry about the consequences; engage in problem-solving; and take measures to protect themselves, their siblings, and their primary parent physically and emotionally. Intervening to protect an abused mother is a common source of physical harm to children as well as of guilt, when their intervention fails. Psychological defenses might be at work even when children seem unresponsive. For example, Peled offered this chilling account: "I wouldn't say anything. I would just sit there. Watch it.... I was just, felt like I was just sitting there, listening to a TV show or something.... It's like you just sit there to watch it, like a tapestry, you sit there."[58]

Apart from infants, whose fragility may make intervention in any abuse scenario emergent, the main challenge to assessment with children under sixteen is to differentiate the effects of coercive control from how children are affected by other adverse, traumatic, or violent events in the community, including domestic violence. Depending on how violence is defined, most children in the United States are exposed to violence in some form annually, and many are exposed to multiple adverse events. The NatSCEV conducted between January and May 2008 measured the past-year and lifetime exposure of children seventeen years and younger to various forms of victimization, including child maltreatment, conventional crimes, school and peer violence, and community and family violence.[59] More than 60 percent of the children had been exposed in some form. Importantly, compared with the 9.8 percent of children who had been exposed to adult partner violence, almost half (46.3 percent) had been physically assaulted during the year, and more than one in ten had been injured in an assault, with the risk of having been injured rising as children age. Multiple victimizations also were common; 38.7 percent of children reported two or more direct victimizations in the previous year, and more than one in ten experienced five or more direct victimizations. Furthermore, older children were more likely to witness violence at school or in the community than in the family. Indeed, exposure to family or intimate partner violence was found to be a significant risk factor only among infants (where it was third in importance) and in early adolescence (where it was fifth in importance). Moreover, since multiple exposures are typical, children only exposed to partner violence at home might differ from typical children in other respects as well.

The physical and sexual violence experienced by the children of coercive control matters, as this chapter shows, less because of its physical valence than because of its frequency, duration, sexual nature, and use to restrict rights and liberties and access to personhood. Unlike the many forms of violent victimization to which children are subjected, including domestic violence, coercive control jeopardizes the child's autonomous being in the world. It does this with the three tactics that are the focus of chapter 6.

6

Intimidation, Isolation, and Control

Parents and partners hurt and abuse children for a variety of expressive and instrumental reasons. But coercive control is deployed with a single objective, to establish a condition of dependence/subordination in children by making the perceived costs of their refusal, resistance, or autonomy higher than costs of their compliance. In most instance, children are coercively controlled as a means to subordinate their mother. To this extent, children are "disposable in the context of coercive control" in ways that women are in only in the last instance. This fact, that children are usually "secondary victims," means the risk is extremely high that an abuser will kill a child whom he may never previously have harmed to extend control over his partner. Even where a coercively controlling partner has not abused a child physically or sexually, children are almost always subjected to tactics that compromise their autonomy, deny them dignity, and deprive them of the resources and support they need to thrive. Although these tactics have numerous physical, psychological, and cognitive effects on children, I am also concerned here, as I am with the women, with their standing as rights-bearing persons.

This chapter introduces "intimidation," "isolation," and "control," three broad tactics that are key to the successful deployment of coercive control, particularly in combination with violence and sexual and psychological abuse.

To examine how children are coercively controlled, I adapt the heuristic I developed for women. Case evidence and empirical evidence from dyads of abused mothers and their children show that the physical and sexual abuse of children by abusive men is commonplace and follows the same pattern as with the women. The violence and sexual abuse tends to be low-level and noninjurious rather than severe and frequent and is "ongoing" rather than incident-specific. Apart from the important recent work of Emma Katz (2022), the psychological abuse of children in the context of coercive control is largely unexplored.

By contrast with violence and sexual abuse, there is no robust empirical evidence on the use of intimidation, isolation, and control tactics with

Children of Coercive Control. Evan Stark, Oxford University Press. © Oxford University Press 2023.
DOI: 10.1093/oso/9780197587096.003.0007

children in abusive relationships or on the proportion of domestic vio- lence cases in which these tactics are deployed. The following preliminary scheme is gleaned from narrative accounts, the two dozen or so children I've interviewed in my forensic practice, and the half-dozen published sources cited in the text, including the path-breaking books *Mothering through Domestic Violence* (2006), by Lorraine Radford and Marianne Hester, and *Coercive Control in Children's and Mothers' Lives* by Emma Katz (2022). Like many in our field, Professor Katz's interest was initially stirred by a personal experience as a teen with a perpetrator of emotional abuse and control and strengthened by discovering how little such strategies were mentioned or their effects considered in research on children's experiences of domestic violence.

Intimidation

Intimidation is the fourth major element of the coercive control of children. Intimidation tactics used with children include physical threats, taunting, verbal threats, threats with weapons and objects, the destruction of toys and personal mementos, harm to animals, and denigration, abandonment, men- acing looks and gestures, stalking, invasions of privacy, the silent treatment, sensory overload, and deprivation of basic necessities. Intimidation tactics instill fear, secrecy, dependence, compliance, loyalty, and shame. There is considerable overlap in the intent and consequence of violence and intim- idation tactics, and the proximity of fear and actual harm to a child may make a distinction seem unnecessary as for instance, when a father smashes a child's toys with a hammer. Meanwhile, other forms of intimidation, in- home stalking for example, or "menacing" looks, may entrap or immobilize children as literally as if they were imprisoned. In coercive control, both vio- lence and intimidation are experienced as "terroristic" and both are inextri- cably linked to the control, command, and exploitation tactics used against the child as means to monopolize the opportunities and resources available through a family space. Despite the fluidity of the lived experience, however, the women and children with whom I work report they find it useful to sep- arately map tactics used to directly compel their obedience and tactics that elicited compliance because of fear, what I call the "or else" proviso.

Abusers stalk, threaten, frighten, and denigrate children; take or de- stroy homework, property, or things they cherish; and otherwise attempt to intimidate children to get them to say or do something, to stop doing or saying something, or not to say or do something that provides support for their mother or otherwise undermines control over the household. Literal threats against children are illustrated throughout this book and run the gamut in my forensic practice from threats with weapons, exposure to the cold, slapping children at the table, holding a child out a window by his legs, and making the dog "disappear." Because of their relative size differences and dependence, children form a bigger-than-life "imago" of the adult in their mind that gives the adult's statements and gestures much more weight than they appear to merit to an outside observer. For example, what an abused woman might experience as a "tension" at the dinner table, children recall many years later as terroristic.[1] Intimidation tactics are effective because the target imagines what the abuser may do or is capable of doing to them, to someone on whom they are dependent or someone or something they cherish. Children are particularly susceptible to projected fears not only because of their physical dependence but also because the child's world is filled with unknown persons and unpredictable realities of which parents and any number of adults never tire of warning them.

Children are often made to feel guilty or blamed for problems in which they played no role and could not have caused, such as a woman canceling a date because her daughter is ill. By contrast, "shaming" is a specific tactic used to intimidate children in coercive control by continually devaluing a child's opinion of themselves and the opinion significant others have of them. Abusers use child-shaming as a form of intimidation because the effect of making a child feel badly about themselves is to inhibit their wishes, values, and interests, including their interest in opposing the abuser's continued control over the mother and resources in the household. Any aspect of the body, the child's physical appearance, performance, speech, thoughts, or behavior can be targeted for shaming. The emotive context for shaming is self-hatred or loathing rather than fear, but the two feelings, fear and self-loathing, often combine to stifle a positive sense of self. Many families engage in ritual put-downs, and the assumption of a "low posture" is rewarded in some cultures. But shaming as a weapon in coercive control has the specific aim of erasure and immobility, and there is no compensatory emotive reward as there is for "low posture." Nor does shaming resemble "bullying," another common humiliation ritual. In one classic American Western, *The Big Country* (1956), sibling bullying is portrayed as a rite of passage to manhood; in the modern context, bullying is taken out of the family context and the child who is the object of bullying triumphs over his tormenters through superhuman or extrahuman qualities (*Karate Kid*, 2010; *Cyber-Bully*, 2011; *Tormented*, 2009). The most significant difference between these illustrations of "bullying" and the shaming of children that augments coercive control is that the latter is a staged performance directed to the woman and/or about her, albeit indirectly. An example comes from earlier in the book, where the father and two older sons by a previous marriage, heckled, ridiculed, and humiliated the woman's youngest son, until she fled from the table and ultimately from the house, seemingly abandoning her claims to custody as well as household assets.

Examples of how children are denigrated are among the most evocative in our business, no less so when a public figure like Joe Torre or Jane Fonda discloses they felt demeaned and terrorized as children. Here, however, I want to re-emphasize the earlier point, that however impactful it may be on children, in coercive control, men denigrate children for its intended effect on the mother, often regardless of how a child is affected or even whether s/he is affected at all. This is important in two scenarios, when a mother is affected even if a child is not and when a child interprets a mother's lack of response as rejection. Both scenarios are illustrated in the Hughes case. Keith made Tiffany shower immediately after she returned from visits to her biological father or grandparents. Jeanette interpreted these as denigrating behaviors designed to make Tiffany feel "dirty," and Jeanette felt shame that she could do nothing to protect Tiffany from Keith, a clear demonstration of his control over her. But the teenager was relatively unaffected by the showering ritual, which she felt was just "bizarre." By contrast, when Tiffany disclosed to Jeanette that Keith had abused her sexually and essentially dared her to tell her mother, Jeanette was too afraid of what she would have to do to believe her. She pretended to be incredulous and accepted Tiffany's decision to move out, possibly because she hoped Tiffany would be safer, even though Jeanette was more vulnerable without her daughter. In both these instances, denigration is an element of control.

In this book, I highlight a number of cases in which bringing coercive control to light has led to a successful outcome such as the termination of an abuser's parental rights, a reduced sentence, or an acquittal where a woman killed an abusive partner who threatened her child. But a sample of my emails would leave a very different impression and reflect the more realistic status of millions of women and children caught in the matrix. The more typical experience is illustrated by a recent email. This excerpt also reflects the fact that intimidation consists of a composite of tactics rather than single act or strategy.

> My husband coerced my oldest son to place tape recorders in my car and to invade my privacy (i.e., taking pictures of my prescription medication, coercing my oldest son to go through my phone and forward over 240 text messages and pictures), and coerced our children to choose sides to prove their love. Ultimately, because of my love for my children and what I felt was a desperate need to protect my boys, I was willing to go to great lengths to get along with their father, and comply with his demands.[2]

The effects of intimidation can be profound and long-lasting even when children do not witness the abuse directly. Former New York Yankees and Los Angeles Dodgers manager Joe Torre and his siblings were never assaulted by their father and never actually saw him beat their mother. But they overheard his abusive outbursts of anger throughout their childhood. In Torre's case, as with many of the children in my caseload, the images conjured up of what was happening to their mother and could happen to them were probably more frightening than the reality. On the website of Safe-at-Home (http://www.JoeTorre.org), the foundation that Torre started to help children exposed to domestic violence, he describes how just seeing his father's car in front of his house filled him with fear, made him a "very nervous child," and caused him to hide at a friend's house rather than return home after school. Men in my counseling groups still felt guilty because they realized that their taking jobs, joining school clubs, or finding other "safety zones" to avoid their father's violence as teens further isolated their mother and increased her vulnerability. Ironically, Joe Torre's sister, who remained home while much of the abuse was occurring, reports none of the guilt the Torre brothers feel today for not standing up for their mom.

Where do men's images of "control" come from? A comprehensive answer would take us far afield, into mass culture, psychosexual development, religious history, and the rites of militarism. One example must suffice. From the 1950s through the 1990s, millions of men saw fathers interacting with wives and children in the TV sit-coms in which authoritarian parenting was a norm. In era before domestic violence was widely condemned, the most popular sit-com was *The Honeymooners* (circa 1955–1956), in which the bully husband Ralph Cramden's (Jackie Gleason) raised-fist threat to send his wife Alice "to the moon" was funny because her deadpan stare in response appeared to stop his fist midswing. Cramden was displaced by the more re-alistic and racialist father-husband Archie Bunker (*All in the Family*) in the 1970s and in the late 1980s and 1990s by Homer Simpson (*The Simpsons*), a cartoon character father-husband who maintains the bravado of his white bully predecessors Cramden and Bunker but looked more like Charlie Chaplin's "Tramp" than a member of the KKK. You won't have to look far if you missed these shows: Disney purchased *The Simpsons* in 2019—and *All the Family* is still viewed on YouTube by millions. These examples make two points. Nothing in the social science literature in this period comes closer than these TV caricatures to the reality of coercive control faced by millions of women and children worldwide. But the equally important fact about the imagery of the authoritarian husband/father is this: these shows were so pop-ular because even as they made a common reality of American life suddenly recognizable—living with an egotistical bully who sucked all the air out of the room—they mystified this reality, by making the outrages appear spo-radic, transient, penetrable, and followed by . . . "flowers," more like riding a roller coaster than walking on an endless treadmill. Is it surprising that the domestic violence movement named the calm in relationships between do-mestic violence assaults, "the Honeymoon" phase, after the Cramden show?

Coercive control is not a sitcom. The abuser is always on. It is not merely that women and children "walk on eggshells" waiting for the inevitable ex-plosion. The reality of life with coercive control is more surreal: every mo-ment of a child's day is saturated with authority and foreboding, making ordinary routines like brushing teeth or sitting on the toilet feel like critical tests of character. Intimidation is a way of life. Displays of anger set such a high bar for independent thinking that children set to rote tasks or remain immobile for long periods rather than take a chance by opening a new book or playing a video game. When the imagination of millions of children is honed to a tyrannical will, the national imagination is dulled. I believe that the muffled response to one school shooting after another, including the ap-parent lack of resistance by young people themselves returning to schools, is a response to a dulling of sensibility in the home.

Intimidation runs throughout coercive control. Only fear makes it seem rational for children to say "Yes" when they mean "No," to remain silent when it is time to speak, and to give up what is rightfully theirs.

Keith Hughes threatened his children in numerous ways both directly and indirectly, as a way to frighten Jeanette. Keith would scream at Brianne when she was a toddler as if she were much older. Tiffany described him as "always angry," said she overheard him threaten to kill Jeanette on at least three occasions and remembered him taking away her toys and breaking a bow and arrow in half. Brianne also described an episode when Keith was upset at her for playing a record too loudly. He came into her room, gathered up all of her toys, including her dolls, and threw them all out. She told me, "I never played with dolls again." Both she and Tiffany talked about his angry shouting as "all the time" and an "everyday occurrence." Like her mother, Tiffany faced reading challenges in school. She reported that when she asked Keith for help, he would scream at her, tell her she was lazy, and insult her as stupid. Tiffany emphasized how horrible and terrified it made her feel for herself and her mother to see someone Keith's size and weight (6 feet and almost 200 pounds) taking his anger out on her little sister. Tiffany put it eloquently. She described Keith as "So much bigger. . . . His size filled the house." Even after he had driven Tiffany from the house, Keith continued to threaten to hurt her as a way to get his way at home, at one point telling Jeanette to get him pain medications on the black market or he'd give Tiffany and her boyfriend a "hot" bag of heroin to make them overdose.

Intimidation with children is shame-based because its aim is to make children do things they would not normally do or refrain from doing things they believe are right or necessary to protect themselves, their mothers, or their siblings. But the unique status of children because of their age, size, and dependence on adults infuses the imago of the batterer with an omnipotence that extends their fear to all arenas of their lives, including those beyond the abuser's purview or control. Whether or not one accepts Freud's description of father–son conflict as a facet of an Oedipal phase, challenging and even confronting a parent's authority is a normal phase of psychological development and autonomy for children. Because of the "or else" proviso and the corresponding imago, children who are intimidated in the context of coercive control are often unable to mount any sort of challenge to their father (or to external authorities) or do so explosively and often self-destructively. They may remain unduly dependent on a mother or mother-substitute for protection or seek safety through "identification with the aggressor," carrying their father's anger toward their mother into their relationship with her or into relationships with men or women later in life.

An exhaustive catalog of the ways in which batterers intimidate children is beyond our scope.[3] Suffice it to say that abusive adults use most of the same tactics to intimidate children that they use with other adults. Abusive men in my practice have threatened to hurt or kill their children, their pets, or significant others in their lives; destroyed their property, including CDs, iPhones, and pagers; denied them access to food, toileting, and basic hygiene; forced them to shower or bathe several times a day; denied them clean clothes; forced them to go to school and to restaurants unmasked during the COVID pandemic and/or to ride "shot-gun" without a seatbelt. Men exploited their physical size, strength, or the sound of their voice to terrorize young people; persistently degraded and humiliated them in front of their siblings, friends, and strangers; and threatened or imposed severe punishments for minor transgressions or "for no reason." Children in my practice have been dropped off in unknown locations; left without money in the most dangerous neighborhoods; forced to destroy, donate, or give away clothes, toys, or mementos with special meaning; and made to sit without moving for hours on end. Children are stalked by their fathers to school, parties, baseball practice, and on dates. Fathers have enlisted other parents, friends, schoolmates, crossing-guards, a school nurse, and a guidance counselor as proxies, reporting on their children, placing objects with special significance to the father in their locker, and stealing cell phones, diaries, and library books from the locker. Many of these behaviors occur in the presence or in the sight of other people and may appear to have an innocent explanation. But in almost each instance, the children tell me, they were threatened and would have welcomed an intervention, even if they had been unable to accept help. Intimidation is not a tactic; it is a campaign to overcome the courage and destroy the confidence of a child and its aim is terroristic.

The fact that children are dependents by definition blurs the boundaries between abuse and fear-based "discipline," allowing caseworkers to rationalize very high levels of harm by male abusers. In one recent Vermont case, the abusive partner had taken to punishing the child because he believed his mother was having affairs at work. Baby M. (age three) was found with "multiple injuries covering his entire body from burns from water as well as cigarettes . . . metal pellets lodged in his foot . . . [due to] the child being shot with a BB gun . . . numerous hoop like marks staining his skin . . . the child reportedly was whipped with strap, . . . etc." Just above this note is the caseworker's observations about the father (BF) who inflicted these harms. "Despite BF attending parenting training he may not have grasped the different stages of learning for children and to treat each child according to their own growth and development. BF may have been impatient with the child's potty training and following his directions. BF may also be exhibiting learned behavior in striking the child with objects (punching him in the head with his fist as he did his wife e.g.-ES). BF also reported to have anger issues and may not have received the appropriate services to address this concern."

What do we have here? On one side is a textbook example of "child torture" as a form of secondary victimization designed to intimidate the mother who has provoked her partner's jealousy. The children's rights to physical, sexual, and psychological integrity are being repeatedly and flagrantly violated. On the other side, we have a caseworker framing the violations from an ameliorative standpoint, thereby aligning with the abuser's position, that the children have no primary justice claims, albeit unwittingly. By effectively disregarding the child's personhood, the caseworker also legitimates the father's treatment of the child as nothing. The father's attacks on the child originate in his morbid jealousy about the mother. In a classic code reversal, the social worker attributes the father's attacks on the child to his failure in parenting, in this instance, to an impatience with potty training, presumably a "learned behavior" (shoot a three-year-old?) he can unlearn in parenting training. If I am right, the child is merely a fetish for the mother in this case and parenting is not the proper focus. But for the social worker to frame the case in this way, s/he would have to recognize the child as rights-bearing, the mother's standing as the primary victim, and the criminologic intent behind the father's behavior, to subordinate the mother by destroying her children. This corrective requires a paradigm shift, not merely a revised emphasis in training.

In the last chapter, Jeanette Hughes killed her abusive husband only after he had driven her daughters from the house, isolating her from crucial support. This example illustrates an important feature of intimidation tactics, that by increasing the overall level of perceived risk in a household, they increase the risk to the abuser as well as the victim. The fact remains, because the gap in size, strength, and resources between adults and children is normally so great, adults can terrorize children with far less effort than with their partners and with less fear of retaliation. Moreover, the intimidation of children often remains invisible. Threats or punishments may involve things that have specific meaning to a child such as toys, game machines, or pets whose disappearance or destruction may be invisible to other members of the household. It can be equally difficult to recognize coercive control when the intimidation of children is marked by a terroristic reaction to minor rule infraction, change in routine, or invasion of "my space." In one case, a fifteen-year-old girl was left outdoors in a miniskirt during a Connecticut winter night because she had shown a friend a sacred "Doors" concert sweatshirt her father had inherited. It is easy to mistake the sudden escalation of an es-tablished pattern of threats for an "overreaction." In these cases, the child is the proverbial "whipping boy" with the abuse s/she endures a foretaste of what is/will happen when the mother commits a transgression. In response to extreme threats, children withdraw, find safe spaces, or curtail routine ac-tivities, which may include those needed for survival, like eating, bathing, or using the toilet. A variation to the sudden "overreaction" is an extreme cur-tailment of normal family activities over relatively minor matters. Because a mother failed to inform a father about a canceled music lesson, causing the man to lose part of an afternoon's work for an unnecessary pickup, the man refused to talk to his wife or daughter for two years. Both the sudden loss of control and the severe restraint are extreme and unpredictable; their effect is to have everyone walking on pins and needles. Men often exploit the normal emotional deficits they bring to a relationship as a weapon of deliberate emo-tional deprivation.

Samuel W., a contractor in Pennsylvania, was an evangelical Christian who had physically abused his wife, but not his children, a point the family judge held in his favor in awarding him temporary custody of the three older boys who expressed a preference to live with him. Although he had not phys-ically abused his children, he had intimidated, isolated, and controlled them in numerous ways. He had pulled his family out of their church after Jesus revealed to him in a dream that the other congregants were homosexuals. Another command from Jesus involved monthly "house cleanings" that in-cluded his gathering up his children's toys in the front yard along with photos or other mementos of his wife's family and burning them. Samuel had also made the dog "disappear."

I return to Samuel W. shortly to illustrate how the extreme fear of harm to themselves and their mother he instilled, combined with their isolation from outside support (such as friends, schoolmates, or fellow congregants), led the older boys to "identify with the aggressor" and join his campaign against their mother. Suffice it to say here that, all children form imagos of fathers that are bigger than life to some extent and that are usually normalized over time through reality-testing during negotiations over real-world transactions. Under the aegis of coercive control, however, where there is little refuge from the authoritarian regime, the child's initial imago of the father as "bigger than life" is unlikely to be mediated, toddlers feel terrorized and are prone to seek premature closure of their Oedipal anxiety by taking shelter in their mother. Young children are particularly prone to internalize the terror they see in their mother's reactions to her abusive partner as their own, projecting the disruption of her "perfect" nurturance and love onto the surrounding environment, which they now see as unpredictable and unsafe. Families caught in this defensive reaction to coercive control are less likely than other families to participate in community initiatives or programs like food drives, COVID screening, or vaccination, and are likely to appear resistant to community safety initiatives. Here, the family's insularity is a symptom of a regime of coercive control.

At age three, an Indiana client, Jonathan D., had witnessed his father assault his mother and break her nose, and remembered "all that blood." His parents divorced and the father moved to Arlington, Virginia, where he remarried. The court ordered the boy to fly to Virginia for monthly visits during which he recalled being cared for by his step-mother or kept in his room. Otherwise, his only contact with his father was during weekly phone calls which he remembered less because of what was said to him than because of the fear he observed in his mother when she got on the phone. He was unaware that his dad cursed his mother on the phone and threatened to take custody if she persisted in pressuring him to pay court-ordered child support. But his childhood fear of his father was reawakened when he watched his mother tense and then become tearful during conversations. No sooner had the mother relocated to Washington, DC, to join the Clinton White House than the father went to court demanding primary physical custody. When Jonathan told the evaluator (and then the judge) that he was terrified of his dad, the father called as his expert witness psychiatrist John Gardner, the doctor who first propounded the theory of "parental alienation syndrome." Dr. Gardner never interviewed Jonathan D. or his mother and presumably learned nothing about any domestic violence to which the child was exposed. But he nonetheless concluded that since the couple had been separated for almost a decade, the boy's fear of his father could only be the result of "alienation" by his mother. To overcome such alienation, he recommended full legal and residential custody be shifted to the dad. When I got involved, two years later, the mother still only had two days a month visitation, the boy was prohibited from even visiting his own pediatrician, he had gone from an "A" to an "F" student, had cut crosses into his arms, had run away from home on several occasions, and was on the verge of being placed in a residential school. The point here is not the transparent foolishness of Dr. Gardner's pocket diagnosis of "parental alienation syndrome," but the incredible power the fear conveyed to the young boy by the effect of the father's threats on the mother. This boy, who was suffering intimidation by the father by proxy was the direct victim of coercive control of the mother.

A parallel to the "gaslight" games abusers use to make their partners believe they are crazy involves blaming children, making them confess, and then punishing them for anonymous events whose authorship by the batterer is well known but cannot be identified except at great risk. In a number of my cases, such "disappearances" involved pets. In one instance, a dog allegedly "escaped" because the yard gate had been left open. Although the daughter had been on an overnight when this supposedly occurred, her father used her confession of responsibility as the pretext to prohibit her going to the prom. Variations involve forcing children to watch the abused mother falsely confess or beg forgiveness or when mothers collude in scapegoating one of the children. A related scenario is illustrated by the case in chapter 9 when, the mother, Rachel, put her son Marc's hand on a hot stove, fearing that, if she did not, her abusive boyfriend Roberto would hurt the child more seriously. That case illustrates a common facet of intimidation tactics, that a mother and child may be punished jointly for imagined sins committed by either.

Household pets are frequently weaponized to show that helplessness is no defense against authority. A recent Danish study of over 9,000 adolescents ages 12–16 found 5 percent reported "companion" violence against a pet and a strong correlation between violence against pets, psychological abuse of children, and less severe forms of physical abuse.[4] In a recent Connecticut divorce case involving a hedge fund executive, the abusive father demonstrated his power by forcing his wife and children to take their beloved dog to the pound because the animal had entered his study. A pet was also a target in the Hughes case. At one point in their marriage, Keith spent eight months in Alaska on assignment for an oil company. While he was away, Jeanette got a dog for the family, a terrier named Allie. When Keith returned he immediately saw the pet as a competitor for attention. Brianne was frightened by his father's treatment of the pet. He would kick and scream at the dog and yell, "All I do is pick up her shit!" Despite doing everything to make Keith like the dog, one day the dog was gone. Keith said he had taken Allie to the Humane Society.

Intimidation tactics cross social space, following children as they retreat for safety to the homes of relatives and friends and to work. Shortly after CPS decided Brianne's allegations that her father had abused Aiden were "unfounded," she moved in with her grandmother, fearing his retaliation. In December, Keith began texting Brianne during the early morning hours, around 3 am. He would start by telling her he forgave her for calling CPS but then would become nasty and threatening when she didn't accept his apology. He also called her boss at the pizza restaurant and told him that he would kill the owner's business partner because of how he was treating Brianne (she told me there were no problems at work). He told Brianne that he would hire someone to break her boss's legs and that he knew people that would do it. Case evidence such as this also indicates that the coercive control affects persons across a broad spectrum and is widely "known."

Whereas abusers threaten women with hurting their children or having them removed, they often use threats against the mother to terrorize the children. In one Connecticut case, Joan D. shot Jason D. with his own gun as he slept, believing he might kill her because he had asked her to bring him his gun from his truck. In their twelve years of marriage, Jason had assaulted Joan twice, hitting her with a rake and hitting her in the head with a rock, in both instances because he was dissatisfied with how she had cleaned the yard. He repeatedly told her, "I watch C.S.I. . . . and know how to kill you and get rid of the body without leaving any tracks."

On several occasions, Jason D. made his children line up with his wife in the back yard where he told them, "If your mother is not here when you come home, you can find her buried in the ground near the dog." The older boy told me that he was more afraid of being alone with his father than that his mother would be killed.

Batterers use more subtle forms of harassment and stalking with children than with adults. These behaviors are designed to demonstrate omnipotence by showing that the abuser's immediate needs and desires justify his violating any boundary, whether court ordered or imposed by the children themselves. A key element of these intimidating behaviors is the fear induced by unpredictability. Two fathers in my practice showed up unexpectedly at school events and soccer practice, even though they were prohibited by court orders from doing so. In both cases, school officials looked the other way, impressed by the fathers' plaints and their "sincere" interest in their child's activities. Even where fathers just observe at these events, children feel torn between their positive feelings of getting support (often from a person who had shown no previous interest) and betraying their mother. More often, abusers use these occasions to intimidate their children and partners by creating a confrontational scenario that is unpredictable, potentially humiliating for a child, and often dangerous. Despite a stay-away order, David M. asked his wife's permission to attend his daughter's karate tournament. The evaluator urged her to agree, which she did, but to set strict boundaries on contact, as a court order required. After the girl qualified for her belt, the husband left his new partner and approached mother and daughter in the stands, clearly inebriated. As she'd been advised, the mother rose, told him they were leaving, and proceeded to do so. The husband followed, blocked their exit from the gym, and then, in front of dozens of witnesses, threw the mother to the ground, leading her to call police. Both the evaluator and the law guardian agreed that the mother's action—and the daughter's subsequent report to the school of a physical injury caused by her father—were "overreactions" and recommended he get primary physical custody, which the judge gave him, limiting the mother's now supervised visits to one day weekly. In this case, as in the New York Case involving the *Nicholson* mothers, the evaluator, law guardian, and family court extended the father's coercive control of the children. All of these missteps would have been avoided had all of the actions and reactions—including the daughter's call to police—been put in the context of the ongoing coercive control.

In many of my cases, children have been forced to watch as their mothers are hurt, inspected, degraded, or made to confess to "affairs" they have never had or to other transgressions. False confessions of sexual liaisons in front of children was an important element in a recent case in which the husband was the target of coercive control by his wife. In this scenario, the child's "witnessing" is a tactical maneuver designed to intimidate the child and the other. Children can also intrude on abuse scenarios or stage a "witness" as a means of giving their mother support.

When women break free, abusers use the children as "blackmail." A millionaire who worked in real estate, Mr. A. had insisted his wife leave her profession as a corporate lawyer in New York when they married, and move to Connecticut full-time to care for him and his step-sons (who were only in his custody on weekends). For years after, their biological son, Richard, recalled his father's "continual" shouting and belittling of his mother during meals and after for "not working," being a "terrible mom," and, after she won a local election for the school board, for "never being around." He described an incident when his older siblings were away and his father took him to a movie because his mother was having a small party with other members of the school board. When they returned at 9:30 pm before the party had ended, "dad completely "freaked out" at "John," a man he believed she was sleeping with, "swearing, yelling . . . , threw a punch at John." Richard thinks a woman who was sitting on the stairs "hustled me to my room. I stayed awake all night . . . couldn't sleep . . . saw cop cars." The next morning "they were still fighting" and his father came into his room, yelled at him, and told him if he knew what was good for him not to say anything about what he'd seen, which he didn't.

Isolation

The purpose of isolating children is to frighten them, prevent disclosure, instill dependence and loyalty, and create a divide between mother and child that women can cross only by negotiating the nature and degree of their compliance with their partner's demands. Abusers isolate children in three ways primarily: from their peers and other potential sources of support in order to keep the secret and monopolize their time and services; from their mothers, in order to intimidate them and reduce their resilience; and from resources and opportunities needed to resist, escape, and thrive. The isolation of children causes their social, emotional, and cognitive development to atrophy.

Isolating tactics include proscribed or greatly restricted contact of children with their immediate and extended family, neighbors, friends, merchants, schoolmates, teachers, police, strangers, and health and social service personnel. Children may be physically isolated through confinement; denied access to significant social settings such as school, work, sports, or neighbor's homes; psychologically isolated within social settings though shaming, ostracism, and rules governing their behavior; and isolated as they move through social space by terroristic "silencing." The development of social media affords children a range of opportunities on their own to sustain relationships, report harms, seek outside assistance and attain information on their predicament unavailable anywhere else. Social media are always contested terrain, however, as batterers seek to shrink, eviscerate, or distort the child's presence in electronic space or to exploit children's facility to track, access, or control their mother. This dynamic reflects a larger reality, that isolation is never a fixed externality, but always involves a struggle by children to open and secure zones of safety and autonomy while batterers seek to find and close these spaces. Thus, isolation is experienced as a process of expanding and contracting personal space. The overwhelming effect of isolating children is increased dependence and a failure to thrive, particularly in young children, and low self-esteem, because of the lack of nurturing and positive reinforcement. Isolation can make a child feel abandoned, unloved and without mooring.

Isolation played the central role in the coercive control of the children in the homeschooling case discussed next.

Samuel W.

We will recall Samuel W., the evangelical contractor who periodically "cleansed" his home by burning his children's toys in the front yard, acts that terrified his five boys (ages nine to seventeen), and demonstrated his omnipotence. Martha and the boys had three sources of social support, friends in their church, her parents and grandparents in New Jersey, and the home-schooling network in which she was a leader. In addition to pulling his family out of the church because of his visitation, he had prohibited their interaction with the "homosexual" congregants (almost all of whom were in heterosexual marriages). Martha's parents had opposed the marriage, believing the religious group she had joined was a "cult" and that her independent will had been "drained out of her" (as her father told me) by Samuel. In response, at Samuel's insistence, the couple eloped, stealing money and her father's shotgun when they left. Martha had patched things up with her parents over the years. But though he allowed her to visit her family, the children were not permitted to visit or talk with the grandparents. Samuel had followed the two visits by her family in Pennsylvania with his "cleansing" rituals as well as by escalating other abuse. Although Martha "accepted" these destructive acts as punishment for herself, the older boys shared Samuel's view that Martha's attachment to her parents was to blame. Samuel had removed all pictures of her family from their home and prohibited her from taking the children to their grandfather's funeral, insisting "they never knew him." After the family received memorabilia from her grandfather's estate, Samuel "donated" these to Goodwill.

Martha's decision to homeschool the boys was based on religious conviction and the poor quality of education in the area. She worked part-time as a swimming coach at a local college. But she devoted much of her life at home to the children's education, well over fifty hours weekly, which Samuel deeply resented. She also acknowledged an ulterior motive, to have a sphere with the children at home which she controlled. Samuel Jr. had a learning disability requiring a good deal of individual attention. The house was sharply divided, with one room—devoted to Martha, the children, and the schooling—a shambles, in which the children took all their meals, and the rest of the house pristine and off limits except for sleep. Martha also helped to coordinate the state homeschool network and to facilitate a range of educational and cultural events with other families, including trips to museums and concerts in Philadelphia and New York City. The two older boys had done well on their SATs, and only Samuel Jr. was somewhat below grade level, remarkable considering his limits. Participation in the network was at the center of Samuel's struggle to totally dominate Martha's life and he would threaten to send the children to public schools whenever she questioned his demands. She feared "losing" the boys in this way even more than his physical or sexual assaults, she told me. One of his demands was that she quit her leadership position in the homeschool network, which she did. The family did not believe in divorce. I became involved after the court decided to award primary physical custody of the three older boys to the father and of the two youngsters to Martha. The children spent weekends with their noncustodial parent.

No sooner had the older boys moved to their father's new home in a rural suburb than he moved to monopolize their perceptions and beliefs. He replaced the homeschooling with cyber-schooling, immediately isolating them from their live social contact outside the home. While the oldest son had a driver's license, he was not allowed to "party" or drive with anyone but his brothers in the car. The children were cut off from the outside world, though they communicated nightly with their younger sibs. From this point on, Samuel wore the boys down with nightly "services" in which love for Jesus was equated with removing the Satanic influence of their mother from their lives. They were being "brainwashed."

Prior to my testimony, an "expert" opined about the mother's "failures" to adequately address the children's educational needs, particularly the son with disabilities. Next, a social worker described the family home as a "shambles," with stuffing visibly coming out of the couch and chairs that smelled of cat. This seemed to impress the judge, particularly given the family income and the fact that the wife was a stay-at-home mom. The mother was "shocked" when their law guardian told the court that the three younger boys described their mother as a "harsh disciplinarian" and preferred to live with their dad. Then the older boys testified. Using almost identical words, Luke (age sixteen) and John (age seventeen) explained that their father was "THE TRUTH" and that when they approached their mother's home for visits, the evil spirit of Jezebel came out of her, up through the chimney, and into them, making them unruly and disrespectful. The judge made the temporary arrangements for physical custody permanent, transferred legal custody of all the children to the dad and ended the required visits by the two oldest boys.

A court's response in cases like this can seem to confound common sense, especially from the vantage of a larger picture. In any given case, the judicial finder-of-fact can seem short-sighted, biased against women, or unfit to sit on the bench. But the fact remains that the chaos of circumstances that led this Pennsylvania court so completely astray forms a coherent narrative of coercive control once the facts are identified with a malevolent will.

Samuel used isolation and intimidation of the children as the primary means to control Martha, drain her assets, and take her children. The family was susceptible to social isolation because of its adherence to a Christian faith that favored homeschooling, opposed divorce, and deferred to the father's authority on family matters. But while these value commitments may have provided the ideological context for a certain insularity, Samuel structurally isolated his wife and children within the house by cutting them off from their church and their grandparents, constraining his wife and children to a single living space in the house that was kept in shambles (in contrast to his luxurious "home office"), and demanding that Martha complete all parenting, education, housework, and domestic responsibilities before he returned in evening so this time could be devoted solely to him. These constraints undercut her educational instincts, particularly in relation to the boy with learning disabilities, giving the impression that she was a "disciplinarian." The isolation was enforced by terroristic rituals by which Martha and the children were regularly "cleansed" of dangerous toys and books with bonfires in the backyard. Despite the coercive control, Martha preserved a "safety zone" within which she and the children retained some autonomy. In negotiating a working relationship in the homeschooling network and taking a leadership role, Martha had found a compromise between her fundamentalist commitments and her identity as an independent woman and college professor. This infuriated Samuel. After the couple separated, Samuel further isolated the older boys by pulling them out of their school network and into cyber-schooling, which he controlled. He also prohibited their socializing and insisted on rigid obedience to his prayer schedule. The result was that Samuel's control was transported "through social space" and emerged as "Jezebel" coming out of the chimney and threatening to corrupt the boys, as their father said she would. Samuel's coercive control over the children included the isolation and psychological abuse of the older boys and their "weaponization," with the collusion of the family court, to gain control of his wife, her assets, and the three younger children.

Aspects of Samuel's behavior—such as his allegations that his follow congregants were "homosexuals"—suggest a distortion of mind and appear to exaggerate patriarchal beliefs about the proper role of women and children that are shared by many of his coreligionists. Nevertheless, the impoverishment of his wife, the level of sensory deprivation, isolation, and psychological abuse of the two older boys in particular, and his steadfast pursuit of financial and other supports from his wife during the separation suggest an intent to monopolize the rights and resources available through the household for his personal disposal that is consistent with coercive control. Religious conservatisim is the context for the coercive control of the children in this case, not its cause.

Isolation of children to keep the secret is a particularly important tactical element in cases where children are also being sexually abused. Conversely, as the Hughes case illustrated in the last chapter, sexual abuse is a common means deployed to isolate children from their abused mothers as well as from friends and siblings. As an isolation tactic, however, sexual abuse of a child is a gambit fraught with risk because of the complicated mix of fear, recognition, denial, relief, and rage it elicits on the part of both adult and child victims. If the abuser's intent is to use sexual abuse to divide mother and daughter, so too do both victimized parties deploy the defense mechanisms of repression and denial to protect their bond against the common enemy, fearing that "facing reality" will make them more vulnerable. These dynamics were illustrated in the Hughes case.

Brianne and Tiffany Hughes

Although Keith beat, threatened, and screamed at Brianne when she was an infant and toddler, by the time she was a preteen, she had become his "favorite" and he punished her only sporadically, mainly when she "betrayed him," as in the incident when he destroyed her toys or, later, when she reported his assaults on Aiden to child welfare. Keith treated Brianne as a junior wife and personal servant, exploiting her willingness to assume the role of homemaker starting when she was twelve, a dynamic which I emphasize in the section on control. Though both Jeanette and Brianne derived secondary benefits from this role reversal, Keith compared Brianne's facility as a "wife" to her mother's "complete incompetence." Keith never sexually assaulted Brianne. But his efforts to isolate her appeared to stem from the same petulant jealousy about her time and attention he displayed toward Jeanette rather than an attempt to separate mother and daughter. He kept her from seeing friends or sabotaged her relationships. She recalled going out with friends as a teen only twice and being screamed at when she returned on both occasions. Meanwhile, because her father was "always in a rage," Brianne rarely had friends at the house unless she was babysitting Aiden. Even these attempts could backfire. She described an evening when her parents returned early from the only office party Keith allowed Jeanette to attend in over fifteen years of her employment as a dental assistant. She had apparently not been sufficiently attentive to him. With Brianne and her friend Brian in the room, Keith strangled and beat Jeanette, horrifying the youngster, who never returned. Brianne seems aware that this display of rage was as much for her benefit as it was punishment for Jeanette. Brianne told a poignant story to illustrate how Keith sabotaged her relationships. She had made special brownies for friends and clearly marked them "Please Don't Eat." Her father told her, "I don't care," and ate them. He repeatedly told Brianne that her mother had not wanted to have her, but that he had insisted. Of course, he did not add that Jeanette's hesitation was due to his mistreatment of Tiffany.

Adapting to coercive control has costs. As we saw in the previous chapter, Jeanette adapted to her fear of Keith by disbelieving Tiffany's plea for help after he sexually assaulted her, leading Tiffany to move out, isolating Jeanette and making her more vulnerable. Jeanette's ultimate response, killing Keith, resulted in her imprisonment. The way in which children adapt to coercion may also increase their vulnerability to being isolated and controlled later on.

Marissa G.

Marissa G. was a client in s custody dispute involving allegations of coercive control. In Marissa's case, I was able to follow the role of isolation as a control and adaptive tactic across two generations. Marissa G. had learned to cope with her father's coercive control by hiding in her room and steeling her body through rote repetition to withstand pain. The "skill" she garnered in endurance supported her success as a long-distance runner.

Marissa's mother, Sonya G., had been an accountant on her grandfather's plantation in Cuba before migrating to Miami as part of the Freedom Rides program. The family moved to Boston, where Sonya met and married Roberto G., a fellow Cuban who worked alongside her in a factory. The couple moved to Chelsea, a largely white working-class suburb, where Marissa attended schools in which she was one of the only Latina. Although Marissa never saw her father hit her mother, she described him as a "womanizer" and "alcoholic" who used his "constant jealousy" as a way to control every element of her mother's life: her money; whom she saw or talked to; how she dressed, cleaned, and cooked; and even what she could say during meals. She remembers him calling her mother "whore" and "slut," and repeatedly claiming that Marissa was not really his child. Her mother explained that her father's behavior was part of the culture of "machismo" in which a wife is the husband's property. But this explanation provided little comfort when her father extended the name-calling and rules imposed on her mother to Marissa, forbade her going out socially, limited all of her activities outside the home, and threatened to expel her from the family on the few occasions when she challenged him about seeing friends. Like so many abusive men, Roberto's jealous rages were projections of his own proclivities and views of women, since his wife rarely left the house except to shop and work. Marissa was popular at school and captain of the cheerleading squad. But she was not allowed to attend her junior or senior proms, had no close male or female friends until she was in college, and was not allowed to use the computer or visit or speak to others when she was home. Because her father's rages were unpredictable, she spent almost all of her time in her small bedroom at home, which he invaded periodically, on one occasion smashing her radio because she was listening to "the wrong music" while practicing cheerleading. As a ritual that made her feel safe, Marissa began to run circles in her room, sometimes for hours, and often until she was sure her father was out of the house or had gone to bed. In her junior year of high school, a gym teacher saw her run and wrote a letter home, and her mother convinced her father to let her join the track team. Marissa helped her college team win an NCAA championship in distance running and completed a graduate psychology degree at Harvard.

I met Marissa in her early career as a psychologist, in a custody dispute over two girls, ages two and seven, with man who sounded like an Ivy League version of her father, smoother around the edges but violent and controlling down to the everyday details of her dress, sexual performance, social calendar, recreation, eating habits, and health regimens. The court saw little prospect for shared decision-making. The seven-year-old had expressed her preference to live with the father, and a court-appointed guardian for the two-year-old recommended she also live with the father. The guardian's recommendation was largely based on reports, at least one confirmed by a hospital record, that the baby had been burned in a scalding bath on at least three occasions, though the person responsible was not identified.

The key to the case was that the adaptive strategy Marissa G. had developed to cope with her father's abuse of she and her mother as a girl, to isolate herself and to function normally from inside a psychological shell that shut out the noise of the outside world, was now protecting her from her husband's coercive control by keeping her from gleaning information about his mistreatment of their child that was vital to the girl's survival. The older girl's choice of the father was an example of "identification with the aggressor," an adaptation to coercive control I discuss in chapter 7. Reframing the dynamics in this family holistically, in terms of coercive control, helped lay the basis for a settlement that was not only equitable, but protective for the children.

Jonathan D.

Attempts to isolate children and/or alienate them from their mother rarely end with separation and divorce. To the contrary, when they no longer have direct access to their partners, abusive men frequently isolate their children as primary means to extend control over partners, particularly if they are primary custodians.

This is what happened to Jonathan D., the boy whom the court found had been "alienated" from his father by his mother after she'd joined the Clinton administration. No sooner had he moved into his new home with his father and step-mother than he was confined to his room for days on end. His mother told me Jonathan felt like a hostage, that he'd cut a cross in his arm to symbolize his being a "sacrifice" and that he'd run away secretly hoping he'd be sent to the residential program in Oklahoma with which his father had threatened him, where he felt he'd be safer than "at home." I explained to the Court that the boy's isolation at home was an extension of the father's behavior on the phone when the boy was with his mother, and intended to make him feel "cut off" at the knees for his disloyalty as well as to punish his mother. The psychiatric expert at the original trial had testified that the mother was guilty of "parental alienation," the argument the Court accepted. The father had had custody of the boy for four years, plenty of time to counter whatever "alienation" the mother caused, I opined. The Court should now consider other causes for the boy's distrust and hatred of his father, including the father's actual behavior and the boy's grievances. The court did extend the mother's visitation time slightly and removed her "supervision." But it refused to let Jonathan see either the pediatrician who had seen him prior to the original custody order or his previous psychotherapist, a social worker who had correctly diagnosed the boy's fear of his father as the source of his "alienation." The court ignored most of what I said, insisting that the partner abuse was long over, due to cessation of any violence. The case did not end well.

A child's felt sense of isolation can arise from being accessible to the abuser at any time and place despite ostensible "safety." Allison: "cause he'll be in the shop when mum wants to go in, and she wouldn't want to go in, so she'll have to wait and get her bits . . . and then there'll be snide comments . . . ."

Stalking, stalking-by-proxy, and cyber-stalking are means by which partner and ex-partners who had coercively controlled their wives made dozens of physical, photographic, and electronic contacts daily with their children, often leaving hostile and threatening messages, with the pretext of "checking up," passing on vital information (such as seeing the mother at a store or gas station or "just wanting to talk" to their children.). Children in my practice have been physically and, electronically stalked, visually monitored, tracked by hired professionals and surrogates, and stalked in their homes, bedrooms, front yards, schoolyards, classrooms, sports fields, on dates, and at the homes of friends. Stalking is an intimidation tactic because it is designed to instill fear, but its major effect is structural isolation and spatial ennui, because by interposing a threatening presence, the stalker makes every encounter fraught and conveys a sense that no place is beyond the scope of control. Among the most chilling accounts involve routine invasions of children' privacy in their everyday lives. The stalking that tends to surface in family cases usually involve social media. Abusive fathers in my caseload have texted their children guilt-inducing requests or messages throughout the day ("luv me?" or "missing u"); sent inappropriate photos or photos of their mother taken surreptitiously; and required a response from their children within a fixed time to sustain certain "privileges," like attending an after-school event. Even when there is a "no contact" order in place, police and courts tend to ignore the harassing and isolating effects of these calls, often out of sympathy for these men, even though the repeated violation of personal boundaries may indicate an obsessive offender who is potentially homicidal. Of course, any person can feel deeply pained or wronged if they are denied contact with their child. It is not always an easy call to distinguish child-centered anguish from venom born of possessiveness and jealousy at a former partner for which the child has become a vehicle. But this is the line we must draw to protect children. One way to draw the line is to note the child's discomfort at being used as a pawn. While it is always possible a child is trying to manipulate the court, once evidence of coercive control is on the table, the odds are high that the child is the covictim, not the person doing the manipulation.

In an era when even preteens are nimble in cyberspace, the isolation of children to affect coercive control is often hard to achieve. Abusive men routinely smash, confiscate, hack, burn, hide, and discontinue their children's mobile devices. But mobile devices and access to information on the web are too widely available for coercively controlling men to completely contain even a preteen's contact with a noncustodial parent or their sibs or to send photos or texts when the child, his mother, and sibs are being threatened. Moreover, coercively-controlling men depend on their children having access to phones, cameras, and the Internet both to track their children, including tracking their contact with their mother, and to use them for surveillance. In a recent case in a Connecticut Valley town, the judge gave temporary, sole custody to an abusive dad with a criminal record, including convictions for assault and domestic violence. The man had confiscated the son's phone and the judge had prohibited the mother from communicating with her son except in supervised sessions when the boy was too fearful to reveal what was happening to him at home. Terrified of the boy's isolation, the mother hid a phone in the bushes near the school. She told another parent to let the boy know, but the supposed friend told the school principal and the mother was arrested for violating the court order. Charges were dropped only because no communication had actually occurred. While the Connecticut case could be dispiriting, it highlights how transparent coercive control can be when we know how to recognize it.

Control

At the heart of the coercive control of children is an array of abusive tactics designed to keep them subordinate and dependent in three ways predominantly: depriving them of the means and resources needed for independence, arbitrarily regulating their behavior, and exploiting their capacities and resources. Control can be effective with children because they are thought to be naturally dependent, in need of "outside" structure and "appropriate" persons to exploit. Much of what children experience as control over their everyday behavior is learned by watching their mother operating under regimentation. Men learn many of the techniques they use to control children from their socialization in school, sports, religion, and work, as often from sibs, friends, and mothers as their fathers.

In the first edition of *Coercive Control*, I reprint "The List" of rules that Laura's husband, Nicky, applied to micromanage her every behavior during the day, effectively eviscerating her decisional autonomy in daily life. Incorporated as ritual behaviors into her routines and presented de novo outside the context of coercive control, Laura's activity appeared "obsessive," almost certainly the byproduct of a mental illness rather than of gender oppression. Rarely are the rules for living as detailed or explicit as they were in that case. But the rules laid down to govern children's behavior are often as intricate and as unrelated to any purpose other than obedience and shame as the rules used to govern women in personal life.

Brianne reported that Keith would constantly criticize how Jeanette cleaned, telling her that having her clean was a "waste of time" and yelling at for leaving hair on the floor. She reported that he would show her how it should be done by following her around with a dust rag and continually berating her for doing it "wrong." As a way to placate her father and protect her mother from his criticism, she told me, Brianne watched cooking shows on TV and by age twelve was doing all the yard work and cooking the meals and had major responsibility for cleaning. She would also do most of the food shopping. She would make up a list for the week, and Keith would drive her to store. While Brianne reported she enjoyed the sense of responsibility to start, she soon realized Keith treated her like a "maid" and that Jeanette was too frightened to do anything. Although Keith usually blamed Jeanette for the lack of money in the house—at some points he was spending thousands on drugs—he also blamed Brianne.

From the outside, this arrangement looks like classic instrumental "parentification," a reversal of familial roles wherein an adolescent or teen takes over an adult function usually due to parental incapacity. Here, however, the role reversal is structured to exploit both parties, with the mother's forced idleness establishing her shame and the teen's performance marking her estrangement from Jeanette because of her implied collusion in her mother's degradation.

The control tactics to which one child is party can disable a mother's relation to another child who is out of the loop. Importantly, Keith staged his commands at least in part with the audience of Brianne in mind, as he did his "explosions" about the utility bills. Jeanette and Brianne remember that Keith blew up about the cost of heat and electricity. In response, she told me, Jeanette tried to save money by leaving the heat off in the winter and keeping most of the lights off, even in the evening. Tiffany, who was not a party to any of the struggles over housework or utilities, thought her mother was too stingy to turn the heat on in winter, and stayed in her room with the door closed.

For some children, the rules are quite specific. Jess said, "If you touched the newspaper before he read it, that was it, you were grounded." For other children, control is diffuse and all pervasive. According to Dylan, "because things would just get escalated . . . like if he knew what she was doing all the time, he could control like, everything, he would try to like, do stuff to scare us and I, I dunno, but I dunno what he would do, it's just he wants to know like what's going on so he just knows like . . . ."[5]

In the Connecticut case in which my client killed her husband to stop him from getting his gun from his truck, the control was terroristic and isomorphic, affecting the mother and her children in almost identical ways. Although there had been minimal physical violence, she and the children were terrified. He controlled their domestic life in every detail from dawn, when she awoke to use the shortwave to plot his best route to work (she was denied dinner if he ran into delays), to dusk, when he finished "seconds" before she and the children were allowed to eat. If she or the children spent more than three minutes in the bathroom, an alarm they had to set would sound and all would be punished. So frightened were the boys (ages seven, nine, and thirteen), that they went to the bathroom in the yard, even in the dead of winter.

At the other end of the control continuum, abusers "weaponize" children, primarily to extend their capacity for surveillance and intimidation. Jeanette told me she felt humiliated when Brianne assumed her place with respect to shopping, cooking, and cleaning, although her fatigue was chronic and she would normally have welcomed her daughter's contribution.

A common figure in the family court is the "narcissist" of any sex or profession who will go to extreme lengths during a divorce to polarize their children's loyalties. One of the most persistent stereotypes about women's credibility in describing their experience of abuse is that of the manipulative woman motivated to make false allegations to seek advantage in a child custody dispute.[6] In fact, while women, as well as men, make false allegations of child abuse, when the Canadian Incidence Study of Reported Child Abuse and Neglect tracked child maltreatment investigations over two decades, it found that, of the small proportion of allegations found to be false (just 4%), 21.3 percent of these (over 1 in 5) involved fathers making false allegations against mothers, whereas just 1.3 percent of mothers made false allegations of child abuse against fathers.[7] The same study reported that only 4 percent of all cases were considered to be intentionally fabricated, with this rate being three times higher (12%) in cases that involved a custody or access dispute. By contrast, 36 percent of the women in an English study and 44 percent of 207 battered women in a US study reported that their partners threatened to hurt the children or to report them for abuse.[8] Significantly, this pattern, threats by male partners and allegations of child abuse by women, arise most commonly during a separation or divorce process amid a long-standing pattern of coercive control. Continued interference with a woman's parenting will typically continue post-separation unless an enforceable Court order is in place for the behavior to desist.[9] Endless litigation in family cases would be eliminated—as would associated lawyer fees and court costs—with early identification and intervention to stem coercive control.

7

Children's Strategies

Identification with the Aggressor

Thus far, our discussion has emphasized the deployment of parallel means of coercive control to oppress women and children and the parallel effects. Central to my discussion is that the harms inflicted on children by coercive control, like the harms inflicted on women, should be considered violations of "liberty" rights to their autonomy, dignity, and equality, on a par with the physical, sexual, or psychological harms inflicted on children. Moreover, the liberty and physical harms are inseparable. Recognizing that most nonaccidental child fatality and serious child injury is a form of "secondary victimization" intended primarily to dominate mothers elevates the significance of a global justice response that sanctions crimes against women and children equally as elements of a single course of torturous conduct. This creates a dilemma for those who shy away from sex equity in favor children's justice, since the reality of coercive control means that children can thrive only where women are safe, equal, and free.

But can we still treat children's victimization equally to women's when the children of victimized mothers align with the abusive father either by directly participating in the coercive control of the mother or by siding with the abusive dad in a custody dispute? This configuration, where the child is a surrogate, "weapon," or collaborator in abusing their mother is commonplace in my forensic caseload, and highlights a key element of coercive control that is unique to the oppression of children and their co-optation as partners and/ or participants in dominance. This chapter examines this dynamic though a close analysis of two children, Mariah Knock and Anna Covlin, who were aligned in family disputes with fathers who had abused them and their mothers. In *Knock v. Knock*, my client was Ona Knock, the abused mother. In the *Covlin* case, the abused mother had been murdered, almost certainly by the father, and my clients were the mother's sister and brother-in-law (the Danishefskys, hereafter the Ds), seeking guardianship of Anna. My special interest in the case was a recent policy directive from New York that "lawyers

Children of Coercive Control. Evan Stark, Oxford University Press. © Oxford University Press 2023.
DOI: 10.1093/oso/9780197587096.003.0008

for children" were obligated to represent the "child's wishes" rather than their "best interests." Anna wanted to live with the man against whom she would be a star witness.

The previous two chapters described the five major technologies of power associated with coercive control—violence, sexual abuse, isolation, intimidation, and control. In the abuse dynamic considered here, "child abuse as tangential spouse abuse," children are the subjects as well as the objects of coercive control, whose interest in "identification with the aggressor" may be material and emotional as well as reactive or defensive. With the sort of conflicting interests that surfaced in the *Knock* and *Covlin* cases—with their loyalty to their mothers tested by her fealty/dependence on their father, the probable killer of her mother, in Anna's case—we enter the realm of psychology in which the social scientist has only limited insight.[1]

The aim of coercive control is a monopoly over all resources available through a family space. Although a partner is usually the primary target, coercive control is a spectrum offense that seeks to disable all family members to a greater or lesser extent, including the children. In criminal proceedings this means that the victimization of the mother and children must be considered as part of a piece, even where the victimized mother has also harmed the child, a dynamic illustrated by the cases in the last section of the book. In family court, once coercive control has surfaced, the harms to the mother and child must be heard together because their liberty to act independently has been suppressed as a part of a single strategy. Even if violence has ended, inequities persist, noone negotiates freely, and hearing their cases separately with coercive control on the table puts them at a legal disadvantage and at great personal risk. With the aid of counsel, advocacy, and the protection of the court, the abused adult can represent the preconditions for restoring "free speech" for herself and the children. These preconditions normally involve temporary orders restricting access to the parties, freeing up savings and assets, protecting pensions, and assuring safe housing and transit, continued health benefits, school payments, and the like. Although evidence of coercive control is often sufficient to establish the abused woman as the custodial parent, once the court has ensured the woman's autonomy, it can make a forum available where the child's experiences can be shared, including any residual ambivalence they may have about their mother's capacity to provide safety. Putting powerful safeguards in place establishes a more equal playing field, where there was none. But it is only the beginning of the case for the child.

Nothing so confounds this process of creating an equal playing field as when a child's interest in a case is defined in direct opposition to the mother's claim of coercive control at the start. In *Knock v. Knock*, the daughter who accompanied her mother to our shelter expressed a preference to live with the father and testified no physical abuse had occurred, though I had ample written record it had. In the *Covlin* case, which I examine at great length, Anna found her mother's dead body in their New York apartment on New Year's morning, shortly after her father had moved out, after years when he had abused Anna; her brother, Myles; and their mother. Anna opposed a petition for guardianship from her aunt and uncle, the Ds, insisting she preferred her father's custody, a position the "lawyer for the children" supported because it comported with girl's wishes. Anna was a principal witness in New York's impending criminal case against Covlin. I was retained by the aunt and uncle to respond to the lawyer for the children.

What was I to do in these cases? In instructing lawyers for children to represent "the child's wishes," the judiciary was intent on replacing the myriad proxies that had simulated children's "interests" over decades with "children's voices." But it had not considered the boundary problem created by coercive control or similar constraints, when a child is not free to express their wishes. Furthermore, the girls' "wishes" compounded an injustice in both instances, the husband's power relative to his spouse, clearly not the judicial or legislative intent. How could I, also a critic of the "best interest" standard, override the child's expressed wish to live with their father while "listening to children voices?"

A coercive control framework allows us to reconcile this dilemma by interpolating the girls' wishes as a direct expression of coercive control. Both Mariah Knock and Anna Covlin's selection of their father was a rational adaptation to their father's abuse of their mother and the extension of the tactics to them. The operating principle for the court here is that, even if there is no violence, in the presence of coercive control, bifurcating the interests of mother and child while they are still being victimized considerably weakens both. Is there a concomitant risk that encouraging a "protective" bond between mother and child will increase dependence and retard the child's normal development? To the contrary, Emma Katz tells us, girls are strengthened by the experience of supporting their "mums" through a breach caused by abuse.[2] I suspect the evidence will shows boys respond in a similar way.

Domestic violence is an issue for children in as many as half of all divorces where custody is disputed.[3] This translates into approximately 50,000 cases annually in the United States, affecting well over 100,000 children a year. The vast majority of disputed custody cases where domestic violence is an issue involve coercive control. This is true outside the United States as well. A recent study reported that 78 percent of a large sample of Italian women followed for fifteen months after separating experienced high levels of violence, threats, manipulation, and control against themselves and involving their children, most of which occurred during father–child contact.[4]

With domestic violence, it is difficult to press a case without supporting police or medical evidence. But in my experience, the absence of police reports or medical records is no barrier to garnering evidence of coercive control affecting children. Children as well as adults leave long electronic trails that often include multiple threads relating to a single incident. Paper trails are also "hidden in plain sight." A California court was so worried about protecting a woman's safety, that it arranged visitation out of state at a heavily guarded facility. My client flew from New York City to a courthouse in Austin, Texas, where their daughter's visits with her father (who flew in from California) were supervised by local Rangers. The ex was nonetheless able to hide threatening notes to his wife in the baby's diaper, which she would discover on the flight home. The note was crucial evidence. Transactional evidence is consistent with the global nature of coercive control.

Among the thousands of disputed abuse cases annually in which some form of expert advice is offered, even a strong case of woman abuse is likely to be viewed skeptically if the children affected by the supposed "chaos" claim to be unaware or unaffected or take the stand in opposition to their mother's claims. With the woman and child's interest set in conflict, the family court will find the children's best interest is served by living and/or visitation arrangements that leave the adult victim at risk because she must "share" custody, "allow" visits at her home, drop off the children at a site to which her ex has access, or comply with "supervision" arrangements that can be easily subverted.

A majority of children in disputed family cases support the victimized parent, usually the mother. I find most of these children credible. But not always. I was hired by the lawyer for the children in one case in Baltimore. A Maryland mother alleged physical abuse of herself and sexual abuse of her daughters, age five and eight. Frightened he was stalking her, Mary took the girls to a shelter in California. A bench warrant was issued for her flight, and the FBI seized the family and returned them to Maryland. The charges were dropped because she hadn't been notified about the no travel order, and the custody case proceeded to trial. The children's attorney asked me to review two videotapes given to her by the mother in which they detailed how he had undressed and molested them. I viewed the tapes several times, compared them to other accounts I had of similar experiences and computer searched the word patterns. Although I could not identify an alternative source for the girls' difficulties, I didn't find the tapes persuasive. By contrast, the mother's account of her own experience had all the signs of authenticity lacking in the accounts from her daughters. I reported my findings to the children's lawyer and explained why I opposed separating the cases in principle. I asked for a meeting with the mother and her attorney and told them what I had found. "Let me tell you why I think you did this" I said to the mother, who was now in tears. "It's because you don't think your own abuse is serious enough to convince the court." I felt the woman's attorney also lacked sufficient perspective on her client's abuse. In a pattern I've come across repeatedly, her husband John had admitted to several serious assaults, once when he strangled her in bed and another when he threw her down a flight of stairs. But he claimed these were "one-time" incidents in a ten-year marriage and both times excited by jokes about his mother's cancer. John was also an alcoholic. Because he made his own beer, however, he had no credit card receipts from bars. In any case, we were able to flush out the more complete story once Mary recounted the history of coercive control, including almost nightly assaults, his sexual abuse, his tight financial control, his telephonic surveillance while she was at work, the circulation of bottles in and out of the house, and the numerous instructional messages he sent the girls. He insisted his wife was the major obstacle to his relationship to his daughters, but in a response that lost him the children's attorney for good, he failed to remember either what grade level his older daughter attended or name one of the many presents he gave the children on their birthday. Whether another evaluator would have taken the videotapes as they were represented, I cannot say. But the division of the children from their mother was clearly part of the coercive control strategy and offered John his only hope of success. John had not sexually or physically assaulted his daughters, as his wife originally claimed. But he had most definitely controlled their behavior so as not to interfere with his exploitation of Mary. She was granted full, sole custody of the girls.

In a small number of my cases, children appear to support an abusive parent out of a narrow self-interest and a belief that they are better off in his care, regardless of how he has treated their mother or them in the past. My impression is that some or all of the children oppose the claims of the victimized parent and support the continued involvement of the abusive parent in their lives post-separation in a significant minority of abuse cases, even if they are shown to be a target of abuse as well as their mother. The sources of children's opposition to a victimized parent range from coerced collusion and frank Stockholm syndrome to the child's belief that s/he can magically protect the victimized parent by placating an abusive father, perhaps in response to his threats to hurt himself if he loses custody or his plaints about abandonment. As an extension of this self-presentation, children sometimes portray their abusive fathers as the weaker of two parents and as requiring their support, a characterization to which lawyers for children are not immune. In the two cases I examine in this chapter, the children presented testimony that was hostile to the battered woman involved, who was their mother. In the first case, my client was Mrs. Ona Knock, a Connecticut aircraft worker involved in a divorce and dispute with her husband for custody over eleven-year-old Mariah. Mrs. Knock provided a five-volume diary (in Chinese) describing years of coercive control and physical abuse. In the second case, which I examine at length, my clients were the aunt and uncle of Anna Covlin, a nine-year-old girl who found her mother's dead body in a bathtub one New Year's morning. In these instances, the children's statements were transparently counterfactual. They insisted they had neither witnessed any abuse of their mother nor experienced any abuse from their father. I was asked to opine because someone suspected the falsehoods were an adaptation to coercive control. If they were right, what sort of adaptation was involved?

Of course, coercive control is not the sole source of a child's hostility toward their mother, even in an abuse case. Nor, even if a child is also being abused, can we assume they will identify with an abused mother or recognize her as an ally.[5] Peers, older sibs, extended family members, or grandparents often convince abused children to support the offending parent in a marital dispute. Even so, once coercive control is acknowledged, the influence of "domination" must be considered on every decision children make. So, in the *Covlin* case, our first order of business was to map the terrain of power that shaped Anna's open hostility to her aunt and uncle's position.

In the *Covlin* case, the forensic challenge posed by Anna's wish to live with her father was matched by a crisis in confidence on the part of my client. As is typically the case, I was hired to assess the abused woman. This means that in *Covlin*, I faced two adversarial attorneys, the husband's and the child's.

Given the rear-flank assault on my client by the husband through the child, it was incredibly difficult to keep the court's attention on the abusive spouse. Even under optimal conditions, with a sympathetic children's attorney on board who has met the child and shown a reasonable concern for their well-being, it can be dispiriting for a woman to experience a structural separation in court that mirrors the alienation from the child the abuser sought at home. And yet, even in *Covlin*, where there was no hope we would win over the child's attorney, my fiduciary obligation to my client cannot blind me to the secondary victimization of the child unfolding in the court room. Although I am charged with discrediting the child's testimony, I am ethically obliged to do so without further discrediting the child. My adult client is not likely to sympathize. Already disadvantaged because of the abuse and sham democracy in the relationship, abused women experience deference to children's rights in court as a betrayal that further diminishes their own rights. In this circumstance, some clients have abandoned their claims, feeling they have been failed by attorneys and experts alike. In *Covlin*, the abused mother was deceased, but I had assumed her interest by proxy through the aunt.

In cases of coercive control, children's stories are examined both as a source of evidence about abuse in the household and for signs of "duress." This is because, no matter how vehemently a child may deny involvement and evaluators dismiss their involvement, abusers almost always identify children as an obstacle to their attempts to control the family space and eventually extend their tactics to the children. The disparity in access to the child between a victimized mother, an abusive parent, and a conceivable evaluative or investigative function is simply too great and the risk of minimizing the child's danger too high not to assume every child where coercive control is deployed is under duress and be proved wrong. If an abusive parent is at large—and perhaps even if he is in custody—every child who is interviewed about coercive control in the household must be considered in danger.

In no instance is an assessment of coercive control more important than where a child stakes a position that is not only contrary to what the mother hopes and expects the child to take, but which she and her attorney interpret as hostile to her interests or worse, as strengthening the control being exercised over her by the abusive partner.

* * *

Mariah Knock and Anna Covlin testified that they had no knowledge that their father had abused their mother when there was considerable evidence to the contrary. Currently, abused mothers and their attorneys have three primary responses when children testify for or otherwise defend abusive dads. The most common approach is to discredit the child who seems to be "betraying" their mother. I had ample documentary evidence of the father's abusive behavior to convince me that both girls in these cases were "lying." In the *Knock* case, I had the mother's diaries. In the *Covlin* case, the father who was ultimately convicted of killing the mother had been assaulting and terrorizing her for years with the children present. There was also a considerable trail of court and police records. Mrs. Knock and the Ds saw the girls' testimony as a "betrayal. But I rejected this approach out of ethical concerns for the children. Nor did I feel it was wise to go after the girls' testimony in court. Critical cross-examination of a child is not likely to elicit much sympathy from the bench.

A legal tactic often used by abusers is to allege that the child's mind was "poisoned" by the other parent, in this instance the father, an instance of "parental alienation" (PA).[6] Compelling children to lie on their behalf and terrorizing or manipulating them into taking sides in custody disputes are consistent with the coercive control of children. Children I have interviewed as well as adults who were involved as children with the divorce of an abusive father have acknowledged lying in court and/or colluding with their father against a victimized mother. The forensic challenge here is no different than it is where any false testimony is compelled by abuse of power. I address the limited utility of "parental alienation syndrome" (PAS) later in the chapter.

A more subtle explanation for the apparent complicity of a child with an abusive adult is the "traumatic bond" that is illustrated in chapter 8 of this book. The mother in that case, Magdalena Luczak, was so traumatized by Mariusz Krezolek's violence to herself and Daniel Pelka that she took over his rules for living as if they were her own. She said or did what Krezolek told her, pretty much as he commanded. In a Pennsylvania case I described previously I found that teen boys who recited the litany of dad's religious visions as their own were operating in a fear/command economy of drastic deprivation. The image of the sexually abused child coming to the aid of his tormenter when police arrive comes to mind. In the *Covlin* case, the lawyer representing the relatives of the deceased wanted me to highlight a traumatic bond. The problem was that, except for a few police reports, I had no direct source of information on the abuse history of the deceased woman or of the children. The incidents of violence described lacked sufficient detail for me to conclude anything about the degree of exposure or impact. Moreover, the clinical picture of the children offered only a few of the affective clues consistent with what can be an almost fugue-like state associated with trauma. Mariah Knock was well spoken and a straight-A student. Anna's distress suggested a high degree of ego investment, not the absence of self associated with PTSD, for instance. The children of interest in this chapter appear to have declared loyalty to abusive fathers proactively, that is with a minimum of outright duress, and to an extent that confounded any obvious account strictly based on the malevolence of their father.

* * *

I offer an alternative approach. I analyze Anna's and Mariah's "betrayal" of their mother in these cases as examples of "identification with the aggressor," a psychological defense strategy some children adapt to accommodate coercive control when abusers extend it to a child in what we have termed "child abuse as tangential spouse abuse." As with traumatic bonding, the child seeks safety from uncertain danger by adopting the point of view of the abuser. But, in doing so, the child turns collusion to their advantage, managing to retain a modicum of selfhood amid a state of siege, "control in the context of no control." In shifting the emphasis slightly from a psychological adaptation to a defensive strategy, I hope to inject a volitional element into children's collusive actions that restores a modicum of their voice. In taking this approach, I am assuming children are victimized alongside the women who are also their mothers in these cases.

Children's victimization is mainly *secondary* to the victimization of their mother. In the *Knock* case, though the father had a flirtatious interest in Mariah, his efforts to control her were almost always in relation to controlling Ona Knock. Aside from the sexual assaults in their bedroom, the most common setting for his assaults on his wife were at and around the dinner table, where Mariah was forced to remain seated to witness his physical and verbal assaults on his wife and provide a receptive audience for his degrading comments about her. If Mariah cried or begged her father to stop, she too was slapped. But apart from that, Mr. Knock did nothing to hurt her, so far as we knew. The *Covlin* case was different because, after Shele's murder, Rod made Anna the major target of his coercive control, in large part to ensure she would give friendly testimony at his trial. But even here, his primary goal was to gain access to the millions in marital assets he had controlled while Shele was alive.

The distinction between "primary" and "secondary" victimization refers to which of the targeted parties possesses the resources the abuser seeks to appropriate, not necessarily to who suffers most or is hurt most severely. The distinction helps us recognize that the explanation for a given pattern of child maltreatment that appears to have nothing to do with a child's behavior for instance, may lie with the effect it has on the mother (the primary victim). Additionally, identifying a target as "primary" signifies the optimal point for intervention. Given the "secondary" role of her abuse, for instance, removing Mariah Knock from the home would have done nothing to reduce the coercive control in the home.[7] The secondary role of child harm in a man's overall strategy of coercive control tells us nothing about the seriousness or emergent nature of the danger he poses to a particular child. The fact that the child's abuse is "tangential" spouse abuse does not mean it is less important. Indeed, as we've already seen, it is frequently the children in these cases who are the first to be seen as "disposable."

Knock v. Knock

Knock v. Knock (621 A.2d 267, 272–73 [Conn. 1993]) set an important precedent in Connecticut family law because, in response to an appeal of a Superior Court decision in a case dissolving a marriage and awarding custody of a minor child, the Connecticut Supreme Court ruled that the trial court did not abuse its discretion in deciding the child's wish to live with one parent was not in her best interests. The Supreme Court ruled on the relevant section of the State Constitution: "Section 46b–56(b) requires only that the court take the child's wishes into consideration" (*Knock v. Knock*, 224 Conn. 776, 788–9 [1993]). Although a child's preference is one factor the court considers, it is not the only or the determinative one. It was my expert testimony in the case, which the Supreme Court also upheld, that convinced the trial judge that the child's wishes had been coerced.

Ona Knock, A machinist at Sikorsky Aircraft in Stratford, Connecticut, left the marital home in Stratford, with their daughter Mariah, age eleven, and took refuge at a battered woman's shelter. Throughout the three-week stay, Mariah Knock expressed open hostility toward her mother. Though the shelter workers dutifully recorded the mother's detailed history of abuse, the daughter told the child worker she had never witnessed her father's insults or assaults and wanted to live with him. Mariah was a straight-A student, well groomed and well spoken, and showed no outward signs of psychological distress.

Ona Knock testified that abuse began during the couples' courtship, shortly after they met at a Boeing Aircraft Plant in Seattle, where they both worked. After a brief separation, they had reconciled, moved to Connecticut, found employment at Sikorsky (the husband at a desk job), and bought a home, and Ona had given birth to Mariah. Within days of returning from the hospital, Ona testified, her husband had to "control everything." He "wanted every-thing to be perfect" and "treated me like a servant," she told the court. And when he wasn't happy with things, which was often she said, he'd "punished me." She described beatings, frequent instances when he would force her into a corner and then demand she stand or lie there through the night. He sexu-ally assaulted her and forced her to submit to anal sex. She said he garnished her wages and required her to present a weekly itemized budget for food shopping or other household necessities. She had no bank account or credit card. But "the worst" thing, she said, were the nightly interrogations around the dinner table. He and "his daughter" would be served first and then, when they were done and their places cleared, she would serve herself what was left and sit. He would then question her about her day, silly questions, such as "Why did you take your break at 10:15 am instead of 10:30? Who were you meeting?" Or questions about their life or the house and "didn't she care." Mostly he would insult her about her weight, how she had become "too tired" to do good sexual things. She was "too stupid" for anything other than "a ma-chine." After these interrogations, he would frequently beat her.

The husband's lawyer was a prominent divorce attorney. He insisted Ona's account was a complete fabrication, "a web of lies" spun out of "venom, malice and spite" with no proof. He put his client on the stand to deny he had ever struck or denigrated his wife, admitting only to "minor arguments" over the years to "the usual things couples argue about," such as the color of the draperies or whether she needed a new car. He presented several char-acter witnesses from Sikorsky who testified that they had seen the couple often at company parties together and never saw any trouble between them. Both employees appeared to have good work histories with few unexcused absences and positive work reviews. The lawyer claimed Ona Knock drank to excess and that her drinking frequently caused her to neglect her household responsibilities, about which Mr. Knock sometimes complained. The hus-band also had a record of involvement in the community and school which caused him to be often absent in the evenings. This explained why Ona Knock did the vast proportion of childcare. This would change after divorce, when he would be home more. The wife, meanwhile, had recently been transferred to second shift, which made it impossible to put Mariah to bed.

The lawyer for the children called Mariah Knock to the stand. She testified she had once heard her mother say something in Chinese she thought was a curse about her dad, but had never heard him raise his voice. She had never seen him strike her. She described their evening meals as "dull" and the "usual." When asked if she had to choose a parent to live with, she told the court she preferred to be with her dad because her mom was "too pushy" and "always wants to see my homework" and because he "always lets me do my own work" and "cares about my friends." "My mother doesn't relate very well to children," she told the Court. She described her father's new apartment as very clean, and "loved" "Chen," the new dog he'd bought her.

The lawyer for the children called a psychologist who testified that, according to the MMPI and several other tests, the father had no propensity for violence.

I was asked to recount what was known about "battering and its effects." I did my outline of knowledge in the field, starting with a summary of the Yale Trauma Studies Anne Flitcraft and I had directed at Yale, and placing an emphasis on the links to children. Hoping to impress the attorney for the child, I described myths and realities about abuse in such a way as to make the long, lurid history Mrs. Knock had given the Court seem credible. I was just beginning the work on coercive control at the time. The judge, the wife of the former head of Connecticut's AFL-CIO Labor Council, was known for her intellectual curiosity. I dropped some hints that these cases were often not what they seemed.

I mentioned a diary I had been shown by Ona Knock, five volumes in which she had memorialized twelve years of physical abuse, sexual assaults, and degrading quiz games he made her play, and including dates on which he had garnished her wages and the amounts returned for "necessities." An invaluable resource because contemporaneous. The problem was I hadn't actually read the diaries; I had her read excerpts to me. The diaries were in Chinese.

"You don't read Chinese, do you doctor?" The lawyer for the children snipped.

I did not.

"And you don't know, do you, standing here, whether what she was reading to you was from those books or made up or whether the books you were shown were diaries at all, do you?"

I did not. The cost of translating the entire notebooks was prohibitive.

We had one other potentially corroborative source, the written logs and records from the battered woman's shelter. Advised not to turn over confidential records without a court order, we asked the Court to subpoena the record, which she did. As we hoped, the story was recorded as Ona had told it in court, proof positive only of consistency—not veracity, of course, but something.

Alas.

Something in the record was visibly missing. At least two pages had been torn out from "The Children's Section," where the interview with Mariah had been.

The shelter record was incomplete, hence deemed inadmissible.

The judge was inclined to side with the law guardian and award the father sole custody.

The lawyer for the children objected to any testimony I might give specific to whether or not Ona Knock was a "battered woman." She argued that I was a sociologist, not a clinically trained professional and was therefore not qualified to diagnose "battered woman syndrome." The judge denied the motion and my testimony that the history I taken from Ona Knock was consistent with her being a victim of battering was upheld.

Then, on a hunch, I asked our legal aid attorney to call the child worker from the shelter to the stand. There was something she didn't want us to see. Else why tear out the page? She had torn the pages out of the log book she admitted, when she learned it was going to be read in court. She was frightened that what she had written would hurt their client. Even now, she felt it could violate client confidentiality to reveal it. After some badgering and quiet assurances from the judge, she admitted that during a sit-down meal with residents and staff, Mariah Knock had a sudden outburst. Standing, she pointed to her mother and screamed, "I hope you die! I hope you die!" These were the words the child worker repeated to the court now.

The courtroom fell silent. I knew we had won.

I could pretend the testimony was planned. It was not. But nor was I completely surprised. As if to fulfill the child worker's fear, no sooner had the witness left the stand than the attorney for the children rose to her feet. She recalled me to the stand. Previously, she had tried to limit my testimony as a "sociologist" to the general nature of abuse. But now, I was her witness and she had to allow me to answer fully whatever she asked.

"Doctor," now you've heard what they didn't want you to hear. Isn't that all you need to know about the girl's true attitude towards her mother?"

The door was open. I explained how children's fear may sometimes be masked by a pattern of "identification with the aggressor." I opined that these comments, "I hope you die," were what her father said repeatedly to her mother at meal times while Mariah was forced to sit and bear witness. If she had demurred or walked away, her father had slapped her. She had identified with him, I explained, because she needed to feel safe and believed (a) he was the stronger parent; and (b) her mother could not protect her from her father's abuse. In speaking in his voice to her mother, she simultaneously took sides against her mother, evoking guilt and sadness, and took control over the unpredictable outcome—her mother's death—that made her so anxious. Bringing him with her to the shelter gave her a certain power over the mother. Ona told me that an odd feeling came over her when she heard these words coming from her daughter: surrounded by women many of whom she knew withstood similar insults, she was able to steel herself rather than curl into a ball as she did at the dinner table, feel indignant, then rage, then sadness at what her capitulation had made her little girl do.

I said more, of course, getting in as much as I could of the evidence I had garnered of other instances of Mrs. Knock's abuse for which Mariah had been her father's audience. Mariah's fear was not the byproduct of her "witnessing," I told the court, not an "accident" because the couple had a fight at the dinner table. Mariah's presence was a critical component of the nightly drama Mr. Knock staged at dinner time. This was why she was not allowed to cry, look away, or get up and leave. Mariah's "experience" was designed as much to show Ona how her submission to him undermined her daughter's confidence in her and herself as to hurt Ona directly. Mariah was her father's "witness," first at home, during his abuse, and now here in Court.

The Court let me talk, apparently glad to hear information about the child's situation that the other attorneys wanted kept under wraps.

"But Dr. if a girl had experienced anything like what you described, someone else would have known. It would have shown up in her school work? Her attendance? Her general demeanor?"

This too was a question I was prepared to answer. At home, in her father's presence, Mariah lacked the space to feel anything but a dull emptiness borne of repression. In the shelter, there was no such censure of feelings. Mariah felt safe enough in the shelter to let her anger and anxiety surface, including her rage at her mother's failure to protect them both from her father's abuse. Absent a shelter stay, the mask the Court entertained would have been all it saw. When she shouted, "I hope you die," at her mother, she stopped being "daddy's good little girl."[8] She had taken on that role, I explained, both to defuse her father's anger at her mother (for which she blamed herself) and to keep herself safe by magically replacing her mother in his affections, the competitive side of being perfect. She was saying daddy's words. But her anger at her mother was real, as Ona realized. Mariah's "alienation" from her mother was her father's doing, the result of his coercive control. The last thing the Court wanted to do was replicate this alienation with its Orders.

The court found in our favor and the decision was upheld on appeal to the Connecticut Supreme Court (*Knock vs. Knock*, 224 Conn. 776, 783–86 [1993]).

* * *

The *Covlin* case came to court just after New York State had instructed lawyers appointed for the children to represent their "wishes" rather than their "best interests." The "best interest" standard was strongly supported by adoptive parents and many social workers. But psychologists, the early childcare movement, and advocates for abused women generally prefer that children be heard directly. This reflects a belief, founded in long experience, that regardless of whether one of the disputants in a custody case is an *abusive* father, a court-appointed attorney views the reconciliation of the couple as the child's ultimate aim, implicitly making the father's interest paramount for the child, if not out of a naïve belief that he is the more "reasonable" parent, than as the result of sheer bullying by the abusive father and his attorneys. Fathers' allegations of "parental alienation" by the mother had been used successfully in New York and many other states to discredit children who resisted coparenting or custodial arrangements that included unsupervised residence with an abusive dad. *Covlin* was a boundary case for the new standard: to heed the child's wishes meant opposing what the woman wanted. Was there an alternative way to *listen to children* in these instances that was compatible with women's integrity?

Identification with the Aggressor

In chapter 8, I examine Magdalena Luczak's apparent endorsement of the murder of Daniel Pelka by Mariusz Krezolek as an example of a "traumatic bond,"[9] a psychological concept widely used in the domestic violence field to explain how victims may become attached to and invested in abusive partners. Developed specifically to apply to children, Anna Freud's theory of "identification with the aggressor" is similar in some respects to the traumatic bond theory but allows for a dialectical reading of children's apparent collusion with abusive fathers that is more transactional than the traumatic bond theory and recognizes individuation as an enduring aim, which traumatic bonding theory does not. Anna Freud recognized that the child "identifies with the aggressor" *both* to ward off threats and danger *and* to serve individuation. Through the identification process, the child "co-opts" external authority as a form of self-discipline, incorporates it in part through introjection into the superego, and then draws on it again to guide the self (ego) toward independence. Anna Freud's work asks us to anticipate from Anna Covlin and Mariah Knock that their capitulation to aggressors would conceal and evoke a contradictory striving for independence, that collusion would be a means of defining and finding their self-hood, proving their mettle, so to speak.

Three features of the Freudian concept of "identification with the aggressor" apply to work with children involved with coercive control. First, to a greater or lesser extent, "identification with the aggressor" is an expected adaptive process among all children. Here, I am speaking about the oft-noted propensity for some children not only to model an abusive parent's behavior (imitation) but also to use the psychological tools of projection and introjection.[10] We must avoid the temptation to pathologize children who use this defensive maneuver or to approach them as enemies in the courtroom even if they or their attorneys denigrate our client. In the Pennsylvania case of the strict religionist I described earlier (chapter 6), Samuel W. told their two older sons that their mother was in league with the Devil. One boy testified that as he approached their mother's cottage, he *saw* "Jezebel" coming out of the smoke of her kitchen chimney. However preposterous, rather than dispute these claims, I described the boys' restrictive homeschooling, the father's withdrawal of the family from the fundamentalist congregation, his personal visitations with Jesus, and his promise that any lapse in their support for him would be met by their being sent to public school, where the children faced certain ostracism. By helping the court recognize the positive role identification with the aggressor played in helping this boy manage his inner conflicts and external threats, I was able to show that the mother's concern for the boys was caring and therapeutic and not vindictive, as the husband insisted. But nothing I said impugned the integrity of the boy's vision of Jezebel. Particularly important is showing the child's ego investment in the process of alignment with the abuser and its possible distorting effects (in our case on justice outcomes). The boy remained convinced his mother was Jezebel. But the judge helped him recognize his obligation to tutor his younger brothers in her home regardless.

The second useful element of the Freudian concept is that it conceives of the mobilization of defenses by children as strategic (my word—ES) maneuvers that are oriented both to developmentally specific tasks (such as the stabilization of superego or self-differentiation) and specific interpersonal goals such as "safety" or "autonomy." While focusing on Anna Covlin's personal goals was of no help in our initial motion for custody, which we lost, it was critical to her ultimate decision to provide state evidence (though even then, she asked that her father be shown leniency.)

Third, the Freudian theory offers an account of agency acting under siege that is more consistent with how children respond to coercive control than traumatic bonding.

When I entered the *Covlin* case, the plaintiff attorney and his clients made a strong argument that I should portray Anna's predicament as a traumatic bond. This made sense if for no other reason than to bookmark an instance in New York where the old guideline of a child's "best interest" would have produced a better outcome than the current standard, "listening to the child's wishes." But what would we learn from children if we only listen when they say what we want to hear? In this instance, had I focused on Anna's "traumatic bond" as the explanation for her dependence/collusion, I could not have emphasized her father's coercive control, her role as an intermediary, or the strategic function her identification with her father played in remaining true to her mother. I would have explained Anna's collusion, but not its strategic function in fending off her father's coercive control. Anna Freud gives us a lens through which to see these aspects of the case. For her "identification" is an assertion of agency as well as a defense.

Trauma theory remains part of our analysis. Finding her mother's body in the tub undoubtedly was traumatic for Anna. But "trauma" does not exhaust how she experienced and responded to events. Mariah Knock was made to sit silent at dinner while her father cursed and threatened her mother. Both young women would have benefited from trauma-sensitive intervention. "Trauma" is an excellent description of the general outcome when our capacity to integrate experience is overwhelmed; coercive control refers to the contours and effects of male domination in personal life quite specifically. Forensically speaking, a trauma framework is more useful in cases of stranger rape, whose sudden, violent, unexpected nature is almost synonymous with a traumatic experience. Analogous to a bombshell, the sexual assault is felt to be nonnegotiable, inaccessible to choice or compromise. In that response, the subject, "I" or "ego" plays little role, by definition. But subjectivity is at the center of how these girls responded to their aggressors; their coercive control was temporally diffuse, spatially dispersed, titrated, differentiated, mediated, and interactive, even as its effects over time were cumulative. Even the sexual assaults in coercive control are more likely to be experienced as diffuse, systematic, and terroristic rather than as sudden or traumatic, what I call "rape as routine." We are humbled in the face of a traumatic bond, sometimes horrified to the point of rescue. The child or woman with Stockholm syndrome clings to their abuser because they feel compelled to do so. We don't feel betrayed by their action. Betrayal implies choice, albeit in the context of constraint. Betrayal implies accountability. These children appeared to betray us because they appear to have chosen sides.

In its original formulation, Anna Freud (1946) described "identification with the aggressor" as a complex maneuver whereby a child deployed various psychological mechanisms to manage perceived threats to normal sexual development, mainly by anticipating and assuming the subjective stance of an external "aggressor."[11] In Freud's view, the principal source of the child's fear was its emerging libidinal attachment to the mother and the presumptive condemnation of this attachment and punishment by the father. For Freud, the "aggressor" is a psychobiological metaphor for the child's experience of the Authority (such as a Father) to whom s/he must reconcile its sexual urges. Interestingly, whereas Anna Freud views "identification with the aggressor" as a sign of ego strength because it allows children to ward off a threat or fear of attack by identifying with it, the more classic psychoanalytic interpretation of the mechanism was first offered by Ferenczi, who linked it to literal sexual abuse, physical abuse, and the terrorism by "chronically ill" parents against their children.[12] In other words. whereas Anna Freud described a "normal" identification process in which the child's ego develops defensively by identifying with a jealous or critical father, an imaginary "Aggressor," Ferenczi projects a child confronted by an abusive parent, a real "Aggressor," who reinforces the child's fears by flooding their brain with nonnegotiable standards for rigid obedience. Both models can be applied to explain Anna's behavior, the Ferenczi model to explain Rod Covlin's behavior and Anna's psychological adaptation, and Anna Freud's view to shed light on the extent to which her collusion with her father was *both* a behavioral manifestation of his abuse and a strategy for surviving his coercive control.

In this case analysis, "the aggressor" is synonymous with the abusive male who is claiming an effective monopoly over the means of coercion and control within the child's environs. In a court setting, this man appears in literal alignment with a child the woman thought she knew.

The use of terminology from psychology should not mystify the experience I'm describing. Although the psychological mechanisms involved can be subtle, everyday life affords numerous opportunities for children to observe and practice "identifying with the aggressor" at home, at school, and elsewhere in between. I suspect the games our grandson plays on his iPhone zapping starships have much in common with the games imitating the Golem my grandparents played in the shtetl. The success of video games is predicated on identifying with an aggressor, often a violent male superhero, fusing with his violence through game play and loosely situating the resulting onslaught through projection in a narrative of redemption or salvation enacted on screen. These and other popular media are exploiting the same basic psychological mechanisms of imitation, projection, and introjection that we see at work when children identify with abusive role models. Aggressive impulses and their mass mobilization for political or commercial purposes are universal phenomena. My point is simply that the coincidence of a medium for popular socialization with abusive parenting helps explain why many children initially normalize their experience of being parented by coercively controlling males. Watching an abusive father rant about money and conduct his round of daily inspections is not that different from the frenetic world encountered in gaming. The narrative of "redemption" that allows the displacement of aggression in the court setting is the alienation discourse of mother-blaming. What is different about the identification that occurs on the video screen and in the abusive home is that the former experience is selected and bounded whereas, in the latter exposure is ongoing and intrusive.

Is Parental Alienation a form of Coercive Control?

The attorney asked me to consider "parental alienation" (PA) as a possible angle on Rod Covlin's behavior toward Anna. In its generic sense, "alienation" describes a condition of "estrangement" without implying a value judgment.[13] In the family court context, however, when there is no solid physical evidence presented to justify it, a child's estrangement from a divorcing parent is assumed to have a negative connotation. Ambiguity in the phrase "parental alienation" has allowed it to be applied to describe children's estrangement from a parent regardless of whether the parent has actually tried to block communication to contact. In a New Jersey case in which I consulted, the court-appointed psychologist found "PAS" (and the judge followed her recommendation to place the boy with his father) though the mother was found to be *"fully supportive of father's involvement and visits."* The same psychologist made a similar recommendation in another New Jersey case. This time, the judge punished the nine-year-old boy who had refused to return to his father's home for visits by sentencing him to fifteen days of detention in a halfway house, where the boy was beaten. When the boy returned to Court, he agreed to "try again" at his father's house; the judge felt satisfied. In this case, the boy's "alienation" was based on his having been sexually molested by the ex-husband's step-daughter during his first visit. In the earlier New Jersey case, the boy had been locked out of the house for entire nights by his father—and on one occasion tied to a tree—as "punishment" for his mother's transgressions. For the Court, however, the principle operating in these two cases was not whether the child's decision to become "estranged" was reasonable or even "safe," but the apparently higher standard of whether the status of the evidence for the claim merited a challenge to men's rights to their children. When this standard has been applied, PAS has entered the lexicon of the family courts in the United States as a fabricated claim to counter a nonoffending parent when she raises abuse in a custody dispute. Not willing to suspend men's access to children because they have (only) abused their wives, but no longer finding it politically tenable to completely ignore abuse allegations either, the many family courts in the United States and the United Kingdom have entertained minimal evidence of abuse on one side and claims on the other side that the woman who makes the allegations is motivated by greed, revenge, or possessiveness to "spew her venom" at (i.e., to "alienate") the child. Given the arbitrary, archaic, and fragmented character of family law in the United States and the United Kingdom and the extent to which so much of coercive control remains beyond the scope of most conventional documentary sources, it is more wonder that evidence of abuse ever surfaces in custody disputes than that a cohort of psychologists has come forward to offer themselves as experts on "alienation."

Suffice it to say that whenever I come across a case of "PAS" where a child is estranged from a dad who is also alleged to be abusive, I suspect the child as well as the wife has been a victim of the man's coercive control and that the "alienation" claim is part of this strategy. As a general rule, for the sake of caution alone, I prefer to err on the side of "children's voices" rather than assume "manipulation" and favor a court-ordered compromise as in a child best interest.

The *Covlin* case raised a boundary issue for the principle of "listening to children's voices"—what to do when a child's is estranged from the abused mother, or her surrogates in this instance, and their expressed wish is to "support dad." Should we treat this as a special case of alienation perhaps? Rod Covlin was open and dogged in his attempts to denigrate the Ds and turn Anna and her brother, Myles, against them. Certainly, "alienation" from the in-laws was the effect of his behavior. But cutting the children off from their uncle and aunt was only an intermediary step in his control over them and particularly to his use of Myles to extend his control over Anna so as to ensure continued access to her and her loyalty throughout the trial.

At the time I agreed to assess Anna Covlin, it seemed highly likely that her father would be speedily charged and convicted of murdering her mother and that one of our major concerns—his continued tyranny over Anna as a witness to her mother's abuse and heir to her mother's inheritance—would be moot. As it turned out, Rod Covlin would not enter prison until 2020 and many changes would occur in family dynamics I did not foresee in 2009.

* * *

Coercive Control of Anna and Myles Covlin

The immediate cause of action in the case was a petition by the Ds for custody of their niece and nephew, Anna Covlin and Myles Covlin, against Roderick Covlin (Rod), the children's biological father, and his parents, David and Carol Covlin. Following the murder of Shele Covlin, their mother, the children were temporarily placed in their father's custody under the grandparents' guardianship. The guardians were to provide the children for regular visitations with the sister and brother-in-law of the deceased, Mr. and Mrs. D.

The court-appointed attorney for the children opposed petitioner's motion. Their petition was preceded by Anna resisting spending time with her relatives on court-ordered visits, or having Myles spend time with them without her. Anna was described in her documents as "anxious all during the stay" when Myles is visiting his aunt and uncle and as "hyperventilating" on these occasions. She told her aunt Peggy she "hated" her and never wanted to see her, has threatened to cut her aunt with a knife, has threatened to "cut herself" if Myles went on visitation again without her, and has said she feared what her uncle and aunt would do to her or to Myles if he went to visit them without her there to protect him. At one point, Myles also refused to go on visitations, became "agitated," hid when they came to get him, and then acknowledged that it was because Anna had told him not to go.

The attorney for the children argued that resistance to visitation was a reflection of the children's lack of any sort of close relationship with Shele's Covlin's family prior to her death. She believed that Anna's resistance to such visits was a normal consequence of and reaction to the sequence of traumas to which the children were subjected. Based in part on the wishes of Anna, she filed an application to terminate the uncle and aunt's access to the children. Her assessment of Anna's experience was summed up in her recitation of this eloquent and moving observation by the child: "First, mommy died. Then, they take my father away and now they are trying to take my brother." In this interpretation, Anna's fear related to becoming isolated from the most significant others in her life.

The attorneys for the uncle and aunt wanted me to respond to the attorney for the children. They asked me to consider whether Anna's resistance to visitation was related to Rod's domestic violence against their mother. There was no mention of domestic violence in the petition from the children's attorney. But my clients claimed Anna had been exposed to months of her father's abuse of her mom. At the time of the killing, Anna knew Shele had a protective order denying Rod access to their apartment, but he was living across the hall and, regardless of the order, had periodically intruded to threaten them. When Anna found the body on New Year's morning, it must have crossed her mind her father had carried out his threat.

After Shele's murder, the lawyers for the relatives told me, Rod isolated the children from everyone that they loved and were close to including their

Nanny, Rose, who helped raise them since their birth and Anna's therapist, Dr. S., who treated Anna for nine months prior to Shele's death and who was fully aware of the domestic violence perpetrated by the father. He also isolated the children from Shele's family, with whom they shared a loving and close relationship, spending Shabbat weekends, holiday dinners, and other occasions together.

It would be difficult to conceive of a more dramatic illustration of children's "exposure" to domestic violence than this experience of a mother's death. An "exposure" of this gravity can stir a regression in young children to infant-like dependence and servility. A surviving parent is a natural nesting spot for such dependence and could certainly sway a child's custodial preference in this circumstance. How fearful was Anna of her father? Was she so fearful that she could not even entertain the thought that he had killed her mother, as he'd threatened to do? Or, did she imagine he might do the same to her and Myles?

A forensic report my clients had solicited attributed Anna's reluctance to visit her aunt and uncle to a distortion of perception and cognition caused from her having been in a "high conflict environment" where she witnessed and experienced domestic violence from Rod. I was not shown this report and was not allowed to question the children. The petitioning relatives felt a need to supplement the report because, if taken alone, the emphasis it placed on Anna's psychological adaptation to past abuse and trauma might leave the mistaken impression that they were less concerned about the current threat Rod posed to Anna. The Court could acknowledge that Anna's attachment to her father was a byproduct of his inappropriate behavior in the marriage and still honor her wishes because the current predicament made her dependent on her father now. Too much emphasis on Anna's psychological reaction also masked another important vector shaping her behavior—Rod's motive for wanting to cut her off from her aunt and uncle. Until the murder, Anna had expressed a preference that her mother be the prime custodial parent and stood in strong opposition to her father. Indeed her stance, so important for throwing light on her subsequent change, had been a focal point of her father's anger both at her and Shele. If Anna was "identifying" with Rod now, it was because she had "adapted" to the new situation. How much of this adaptation was reflexive, how much voluntary, and how much coerced? My challenge was to frame this adaptation as consistent with Anna's psychological vulnerability, the constraints in evidence and the values, options, and choices that were in play. The equity issue in the case was the extent to which the constraints to which Anna had to fit her choices were the inevitable by-product of her predicament or imposed as an extension of Rod's murderous strategy toward his former wife.

Shele was dead. But Rod was not done with her. Apart from any emotional baggage he still carried for his former wife, his own fate at trial still rested heavily on evidence presented by his children, his in-laws, and his parents, the major persons capable of putting the seemingly anonymous act in the context of his abuse. To this extent, Rod's current manipulation of Anna and Myles was only secondarily about the children, in whom he had shown little interest when his wife was alive, but about the extent to which he could control them. The Ds were a link to their mother; cutting the children off from the Ds had the effect of isolating them from their mother's surrogates and therefore increasing their vulnerability. Shifting the guardianship to his parents had a similar goal, since he believed he controlled them already. If the children were with them full-time, they would effectively depend on him for validation and emotional support, a condition of dependence and vulnerability they were unlikely to risk by going against him at trial. His long-game plan with respect to Anna was to access $5 million plus in assets his wife had transferred to her daughter shortly before her murder.

Relevant Background

Rod and Shele met in 1998 and married six to eight months later. They had two children, Anna, born October 12, 2000, and Myles, born September 26, 2006. At the time of the assessment, the children were in the custody of Rod's parents, and Rod had supervised visits with them. The mother, Shele Covlin, was murdered on January 1, 2010, while the children were in the apartment, apparently in the early morning hours of New Year's Day. At the time of the report, Rod was the prime suspect in a murder investigation of Shele's death, which commenced following the exhumation of Shele's body and a finding by the Medical Examiner that the cause of her death was homicide and "neck compression."

There was little regarding marital history in the documents reviewed.[14] Rod, Shele, and their children resided in an apartment in Manhattan. Rod moved out of the marital residence in March of 2009, to an apartment in the same building, across the hall from the marital apartment. He forced her to cosign the lease for his apartment. He used the proximity to go back and forth between the apartments, intimidating her and the children, and at the same time having other women in his apartment. Shele initially simply hoped to reach an agreement to divorce and move on. But when Rod realized the economic impact of divorce on him, he tried to move back in, began to harass her, and became so erratic and violent that she felt it was unsafe for her and the children to have him in the home. In May 2009, Shele filed for divorce, exclusive use of apartment, and for an order of protection. In December, she was killed.

The divorce affidavit offers the following history:

> After Myles was born, Rod became more irritable and volatile. Despite being very intelligent, he was unable to sustain a job—with performance problems and interpersonal issues resulting in long periods of unemployment. Rod always blamed external circumstances for his job difficulties. At first, Shele believed him. This changed after she discovered Rod was using marital money to gamble and spending his time on the computer, at Backgammon tournaments, and day-trading, where he lost money. Rod eventually became so obsessed with Backgammon, he withdrew from household and childcare responsibilities. Shele became increasingly frustrated with having to do everything herself and a nanny. Rod came to depend on financial support from Shele, so much so that she paid for his MBA. Rod had begun to see other women, and on the night of their 10th anniversary (9/08), said he wanted an "open" marriage.

Coercive Control

Coercive control is often evident early in a relationship, but often doesn't become identified as a problem until the unmet needs of one or the other in a couple are thrown into focus by a watershed event such as a death in the family, job loss, or the birth of a child. The elements and dynamics of coercive control are not likely to surface unless they are addressed by specific questions to each member of the family. In this case, there were no police or medical records to mine for information or to help identify when various control issues emerged. The family "speaks" about abuse only as outside resources are used to mediate disputes. From this evidence, I got the impression that coercive control began early on, consisted mainly of threats by Rod Covlin against his wife and children, financial exploitation and control of Shele Covlin, treating the other family members as his servants, and taunting and humiliation. These abusive behaviors escalated in the spring and summer before the murder, when Rod repeatedly exited, then forcibly re-entered the household, and Shele acquired then withdrew an order of protection. About to enter divorce proceedings, Rod killed his wife because his regime of coercive control was being challenged. At that point, he hoped to continue his dominance of family resources by taking control of the children. What records there are, such as the divorce petitions, treat the family history as a downward spiral set off by Rod's increasingly erratic behavior, mental instability, sexually acting out, bad temper, and lack of employability. What is really happening is that Rod is living off Shele's income, gambling, building up debt, spending hours gaming online, having numerous extramarital affairs, exploiting two servants (his wife and Rose) while contributing nothing and extracting fawning obedience from two children. What appears to the outside world as scattershot, and may even feel chaotic to Rod, is experienced as terroristic to those living within his penumbra of unpredictability and fear. In any setting other than a marriage, the sheer level of suffering endured by everyone but Rod would make it apparent the lines of power creating havoc in this family stemmed from a central source of power and control and were being manipulated according to a criminal logic that served to benefit him personally.

Shele told her divorce attorney that Rod was always "very dominating" throughout the marriage toward her and the children. She also claimed that he had been verbally abusive throughout the marriage and had only become physically abusive in the last year, particularly after they separated. Up until year ago, she claimed, he had mainly just "shook" and "grabbed" the children.

Things came to a head when Rod moved across the hall in March. From the evidence available, it seems that his purpose in moving was to secure his control in the apartment while opening a new front ("across the hall") where he could continue to have other sexual relationships without losing touch with a wife he called his "meal ticket." As the children's expressions of anxiety made clear, Rod use of physical distance to increase the unpredictable and terroristic effects of his violence had a particular effect on Anna and Myles. Having come to depend on his proximity for cues to his dramatic mood swings into rage, their anxiety now became chronic, a mood shift that was observed by others in Anna. Nor could the children rely any longer on Shele as an intermediary to anticipate and protect them from Rod's outbursts. Anna felt less secure when Rod was absent than when he'd been at home because his break-ins were unpredictable. In coercive control, a sep-aration often occasions heightened tension and anxiety in children, in part because their mother's discomfort and fear appears to have no source other than them and because the new tactics are often less predictable and less sus-ceptible than the old ones to the sense of sound, smell, touch, or sight attuned to danger. The heightened anxiety in victims occasioned by a separation sig-nals that the abuser has adapted the means of coercion and control to "cross social space."

After he moved into the apartment across the hall. Shele reported, Rod's behavior became more "erratic, uncontrollable and violent." At that time, "Rod became more and more abusive at home, yelled at her and the chil-dren and at her in front of the children." Possibly, as Shele told the divorce attorney, Rod re-engaged the family because he realized what divorce would cost him economically. But it also appears that a lack of proximity caused Rod to panic that he was losing control. This feeling was aggravated when Shele not only accepted his pronounced separation but told him *she* was thinking about divorce, which jeopardized his basis of financial support. He responded dramatically, showing her that no barrier could prevent him from accessing her and the children when and how he wanted, not the physical barrier of a locked door nor presumably the legal barrier of a divorce. He burst in whenever he choose, assaulted her, destroyed her property, harassed her, chased her around the apartment, banged at the door at night, punched holes in the walls, threw their things off the shelves, and called throughout the night, depriving her and the children of sleep. When he was in the apart-ment, he followed her around with the children watching, calling her names. Anna, in particular, was an active audience for his intrusions.

On April 20, 2009, Rod broke in, became "enraged," and "threw Shele to the ground" in the view of the children and their nanny. This incident is re-ported in the divorce affidavit and in the interview with Rose.

On April 25, 2009, Rod came into Shele's apartment. She had packed his things that remained in the apartment and left them in a bag. Rod screamed, yelled, and cursed at Shele in the presence of the children, and then entered Shele's bedroom and destroyed her closets and threw all of her clothing on the floor. He then did the same in the bathroom and kitchen in a fit of rage in front of the children.

The tangible benefits of living apart did not assuage Rod's sense that his power and control over his family was waning. He saw his children aligned with Shele and projected that it was *she* and not *he* who was turning them against him. He was determined to show that they could not protect one another from him—breaking into the apartment at will, assaulting Shele despite their plaints, blaming the nonexistent order of protection (OSC) for not seeing them, threatening suicide in front of Anna. Things came to a head on Mother's Day, which threatened his narcissism because it focused attention on Shele and the children (and steeled their courage) instead of himself.

On May 10, 2009, Rod was at Shele's apartment. When she mentioned divorce, he became increasingly irate, and told Anna that Shele was divorcing him and was going to try to keep him away from her. Anna was very upset. Then, he left and returned and began moving all his belongings *back* into Shele's apartment against her will. Shele told him he did not live there anymore. Rod cursed at her in the presence of the children, called her a bitch and a cunt. After this, Anna asked Shele why Rod had to move back into the apartment.

At this point, the cumulative effect of Rod's coercive control of Shele was destabilizing—she felt unable to control her immediate environment, particularly with respect to her own physical or sexual safety or the safety of her children. Myles increasingly looked to cues from Anna for his safety, and she, although still strongly aligned with Shele, recognized that she and Myles were on their own.

Five days later, May 15, 2009, Shele filed for a stay-away order against Rod that was uncontested, and for sole custody. After testifying before the court, she was granted a full stay-away OSC for herself and the children by Judge Kaplan. The order had no provisions for immediate safety and no real enforcement mechanism. As such it was more provocative than protective. Too little, too late.

After Rod was served with the OSC, he called Shele's company, UBS, and spoke with her superior to falsely accuse Shele of being an unstable drug addict. Shele had to have a series of meetings at UBS to assure the company that the allegations were false.

On May 20, 2009, the Return date, she withdrew the OSC and entered into so-ordered stipulation. Shele was being harassed by Rod and feared his violence would escalate with further involvement of the Court. She hoped the divorce would end things. Continuing harassment was a violation of the order, but there was no proactive enforcement.

Within a week, Rod was again coming and going to her apartment as he pleased. He screamed constantly at her and the children, ostensibly for no reason. At the time of the divorce action, Shele claimed, "Rod is now attempting to move back in."

Each element of Rod's behavior toward Shele and the children was designed to close off their options to his control. If she tried to break free by filing for divorce or custody, for example, he threatened to harm her, to convince the children "there was no God," that he would "make things ugly," that he would make accusations that would "ruin her," that he would call the IRS regarding Shele's family members to report fraud; and that he would call the police about a friend of Shele's and tell them he was a drug dealer. In an email to her previous attorney, Shele described being made fearful because, when he learned of the divorce, Rod would bang on the door; call her during the night, and call her cunt and bitch in front of the children. Rod also told Shele that if she divorced him he would take the case to trial and fight for sole custody even though he knew he would not win but would force her to use all of her money on legal fees. There is one documented threat when Rod threatened to kill Shele by shoving a knife down Shele's throat. In July, Rod broke into Shele's cell phone account on the Internet and changed her passwords. He also posted on Facebook that Shele had taken the children from him.

The Coercive Control of the Children

Even in the absence of supportive police, medical, or social service records, there is ample testimonial evidence that Rod Covlin deployed coercive control against his wife and children while they shared an apartment and after they were living separately; that his coercive control contained the major tactics associated with the pattern, most notably violence, intimidation, stalking, isolation, degradation, regulation, exploitation, and control; and that the coercive control had a range of harmful physical and psychological effects on all family members, severely restricted their autonomy liberty and dignity, and almost certainly culminated in Shele's death. In addition to exploiting Shele financially and treating her like his servant, Rod targeted her protective function as a mother: by repeatedly forcing his way into the apartment after he had been excluded and in direct contradiction of his wife's expressed wishes, he demonstrated to the children that she had little power to protect them against his anger and little authority over her own household.

Had Shele been charged in the death of her husband, I would also highlight the resourcefulness she displayed to get him out of their lives and the persistence with which Rod transgressed each and every boundary she set, limiting her options. I have no way to know whether Rod was motivated by a narrow self-interest to keep from losing support due to divorce or had suffered a narcissistic wound to his self-esteem because Shele was breaking free.

Absent the homicide, New York Family Court would probably have awarded custody to Shele, even had Rod disputed custody as he threatened. Given Rod's persistent disregard of boundaries, the postdivorce level of risk to Shele and the children would have remained high regardless of the settlement terms. In my experience, however, New York Family Court orders rarely anticipate the continuation of abuse beyond a divorce. So it is doubtful that extraordinary protections would have been put in place regardless of the evidence presented. Anna's loyalty to her mother would have remained unwavering under these circumstances.

The attorney for the children had an interesting set of facts. Anna told her she "hates" her Aunt Peggy, had threatened her with a knife, became physically ill when Myles goes to her Aunt's without her to protect him, and threatened to cut herself if he does so again. It was "this "resistance" (*sic!*) that she assessed was a "normal" reaction to "the sequence of traumas" surrounding the mother's death. In this interpretation, Anna's most prominent fear related to her becoming isolated from the most significant others in her life. In the default scenario, guardianship of the children would remain with Mr. Covlin's parents, with whom the children now resided.

The particulars of Anna's behavior are troublesome. But in what context? Anna's behavior fits the attorney for the children's interpretation only if we assume that the threat she faced from Rod Covlin ended once he killed her mother. In this scenario, Anna's suffering is ascribed to a series of "traumas" secondary to her mother's experience of violence, presumably including though not necessarily limited to "witnessing" her dead body. Even if we assume Anna had not seen her father kill her mother, the attorney for the children finesses the fact that the father from whom she now presumably fears separation is the key source of Anna's exposure to threats and violence against she, her brother and her mother in the first place. In fact, Anna has had to steel herself against her father's coercive control at least since 2006, when Myles was born, and had to defend her family alone for much of this time because Shele was too psychologically damaged to do so. By killing her mother, Rod has not only removed a primary line of physical, psychological, and economic defense for Anna but also exposed the utter vulnerability of her and Myles to Rod's predations. For her, physical separation from Myles is now as intolerable as living outside the visible sphere of Rod's presence.

Rod too finds himself in a new position with his wife gone. In the past, Rod selected his abusive tactics with the children for their effect on Shele. In July, he had taken Myles to a hospital emergency room to have him accuse Shele of sexually and physically abusing him. Rod took both children to New York Presbyterian Hospital and told the doctors that Myles claimed Shele hurt him in his anus and penis. Rod showed the doctors a scratch on Myles's thigh in support of his allegations. No injuries were found. After a series of desperate attempts to locate the children, Shele filed a report with New Rochelle Police. Then Shele received an early morning call form an ACS worker that the children were safe at New York Presbyterian Hospital. She told Shele about Rod's report of sexual abuse to Myles, questioned Shele, and returned the children (at 5:30 am). The ACS worker reported that when Rod asked Myles if Myles wanted to live with Rod, Myles said yes—Anna confirmed this. As a result of this, Myles suddenly became attached to a blanket, which he had not done before. Myles's response was almost certainly elicited under duress.

In response to this incident, Shele changed the terms of her will, making the children the beneficiaries of the $5 million at her death, not Rob, which made him furious. The murder and placing the children with his parents as guardians (whom he thought he controlled) appear to be in direct retaliation to Shele's taking away his money and nesting it with the kids and are consistent with his coercive control, including "child abuse as tangential spouse abuse." Rod manipulated Myles to indict Shele regarding sexual abuse. Rod's attempt to "weaponize" his son failed because Shele mobilized police and ACS on her behalf and because Anna, on whom ACS relied, denied ever having seen her mother hit or otherwise abuse Myles. The ACS report also reveals another dimension of Rod's duplicity. Rod told ACS he was "divorced," though he was not; says he took the present apartment "to be near the children after the divorce," when his obvious purpose was surveillance within the marriage; and represents himself as "employed," though he was not at the time. Manipulating a child to make a false report of sexual abuse is a criminal offense in New York. But ACS chose not to pursue it. With Shele gone, Rod's access to the money depends on his control of Anna. After Shele's death, Rod exploited Anna to indict her aunt.

The changed circumstances since Shele's murder are telling. A hole is opened in the lives of these children that will never be wholly filled. But the mother's death also was the penultimate incident in the tortuous ordeal to which they had been subjected along with their mother, since Anna was six and through all of Myles's life. The children were almost always awake and present when Rob was in their apartment as well as during those incidents when he cursed, yelled at, threatened, and assaulted Shele. Shele reported that Rod was physically abusive to the children, that he had thrown things in the presence of the children, that he had taken Anna out of the shower and shaken her violently, and, on one occasion, had thrown Myles into the shower, naked and crying, simply because Rod perceived that Myles (who was then only two-years-old) had "misbehaved." He had also insulted and demeaned Anna on several of these occasions. The mediator in these incidents was Shele; she was, in all probability, also the intended audience. As a result of these experiences, Shele reported in her divorce petition, both Anna and Myles had expressed a fear of being alone with Rod and had undergone a number of mood changes.

For Anna and Myles, being left with their father was potentially as traumatic as losing their mother. Even before she lost the protection of her mother, Rod targeted Anna for special treatment. Rod's behavior toward Anna was seductive, passive-aggressive, and showed no respect for boundaries. Rod spoke to Anna about his girlfriends, spoke openly to Shele in the presence of Anna about his girlfriends, and brought his girlfriends to his new apartment across the hall when he knew his family was home and aware of what was going on. Rod repeatedly told Anna that Shele's purpose in divorcing him was to keep her and Myles from him. He told her he could not see her because there an OSC forbidding it, when there was none. Rod told Anna that Shele was going to make things up so Shele could get an OSC. Rod told Anna that Shele had him thrown out of his home and now he had to move away. Rod told Anna that he wanted to make up with Shele, but that Shele and her lawyers wanted to fight with him and that she should not discuss things he talks about with her because he will get in trouble. During the long period when he was unemployed, Rod also threatened suicide on numerous occasions with Anna present, stating he was going to "step off a curb in front of a car" because he was "depressed."

Rod involved Anna in discussions about the divorce and pressured Anna to take his side. Shele claimed this caused Anna to have "mood changes" and "acting out behavior," for which she got a referral to a therapist. On another occasion Rod would not let Shele say hello to the children when she tried to go up to them and hug them, yelling and screaming about the order of protection.

According to a psychologist who evaluated Anna, the shock of her mother's loss caused her dramatic shift from opposition to her father to his loyal supporter in the weeks after her mother's death, substituting one dependency for another.[15] This assessment minimizes the courage, strategic prowess, and resilience exhibited by a nine-year-old girl who had withstood her father's abuse, insults, rages, and transgressive behavior both at her mother's side and then, when her mother could no longer protect her, as her brother's source of resistance.

The outside psychologist apparently identified the defensive nature of Anna's dependence on Rob, highlighted by coming upon her mother with her father trying to resuscitate her. But two other emotional facets of her attachment are equally important. Anna is furious at her father for abusing them all, taking their liberty, and killing her mom. She is also terrified of him because she was so angry and had reason to fear the consequences if her anger at Rod surfaced. It is likely that the knife assault on her aunt and uncle—against whom she had no previous animosity—was prompted by the rage she feels toward her father displaced by fear of what her father would do to her if saw her feelings. The language she used for the aunt and uncle— "They 'hate' me; "I hate them"—that was Rod's language for them, as it had been also his language for Shele. Anna's choice of the knife was his weapon of choice. "I will push a knife down your throat," Rod had told Shele in Anna's presence. Even Anna's threat of self-harm if she doesn't get her way—echoes to a word what Rod said to her mother in front of her, what he said to her about himself, and what he said to her and about her aunt. In this way, Anna Covlin managed her rage against her father by integrating it with her fear of him, then displacing it into its opposite, loyalty toward her father and hatred toward her aunt. By attacking her aunt (a safe target) and ingesting the remaining anger as a gesture of self-harm, she kept herself safe, hoped to protect Myles, and survived to act another day. Properly interpreted as a response to current danger as well as a recent loss, Anna's "collusion" appears "strategic," an example of "control in the context of no control." She has "identified with the aggressor" in an attempt to survive and escape his coercive control.

Postscript 2022

My clients were unsuccessful in the *Covlin* case, but the children were cared for. The original Court orders were kept in place, and Rod's parents remained the legal guardians of Myles and Anna Covlin, honoring "the children's wishes," as the lawyer for the children argued they should.

Although a great deal of circumstantial evidence pointed to Rod Covlin's responsibility for Shele's death, he was not formally charged with her murder until 2019, ten years after she was killed, when he was convicted and sentenced to twenty-five years in prison, which he began serving in 2020. Rod's parents, whom he believed he controlled, broke decisively with their son over the children's inheritance and no longer supported him at his criminal trial.

I have no information on the children during the period they were in Rod's care, roughly until 2014. But by the time Rod came to trial in 2019, the children had been living with their grandparents for almost five years; he had been arrested twice for trying to have his parents killed (so as to get access to the children); and he had been implicated in a plot to marry Anna to a man in Mexico to get her money. Through all this, he persisted in his coercive control of Anna, including a plot to frame his daughter for her mother's murder by writing a note, posing as her, which read, "All of these years I have been so incredibly afraid and guilty about the night my mom died. I lied. She didn't just slip. That day we got into a fight about her dating. . . . I got mad so I pushed her, but it couldn't have been that hard! I didn't mean to hurt her!"

Historically, when family courts have been guided in cases involving allegations of domestic violence by "the best interests of the children," they often based findings on misconceptions about the nature of abuse (such as abuse isn't serious if violence isn't severe), the scope of abuse (such as abuse ends when the relationship ends), and the exposure of children (such as a man who abuses his wife will not harm the children) and have made arrangements that left children and their abused mothers at extremely high risk for abuse to continue. The new understanding of coercive control greatly broadens the family court's understanding of the nature, scope, and intent of abuse as well as the extent to which children become secondary victims even when they are not direct targets of physical assault. The substitution of the "child's wishes" for the child's "best interest" as a standard for custodial assignment in cases involving allegations of abuse takes a critical step forward because it acknowledges that even very young children may have critical rights at stake in families that merit an independent voicing when subjugation is in the room. The *Covlin* case presents a boundary example because here, the child "wishes" were formed strategically to manage coercion and control, not to maximize the well-being of the child. Given Rod

Covlin's continued presence in the community, his stealth, access to money, and general propensity to exploit those around him, there was probably no safer alternative available to the family court than the one it chose, though the positive outcome appears to have been fortuitous.

Though things may turn out relatively well, considering one of their parents is killed and the other is in prison, we must still ask whose voice we are hearing when Anna tells us she wants to live with her father. Is Anna's voice the voice of coercive control? It is true that everything Anna says and does—her threats against the aunt and uncle, her fear of losing Myles, her suicidality, her support for a man she had fought for two years to keep from encroaching on their lives—is shaped to the contours of coercive control. To this extent, Anna's "collusion" with Rod's is in no sense a byproduct of her will, at least in the sense that we ordinarily identify as "free." But Anna's "collusion" is also her defense against Rod's coercive control. It is her only way to maintain a self in survival while under siege, her way to maintain what I call "control in the context of being controlled." By "identification with the aggressor" Anna accommodates Rod's wishes; incorporates parts of his anger as her own (threatening to use a "knife"); and adapts his mode of resistance to protect Myles (threatening suicide if they are separated). All of these are both "aggressive" (toward the outside world) and means to keep herself safe. Through this multiform defensive armor, Anna owns and manages her rage, guilt, and sense of loss through a variety of defensive psychological maneuvers that create a space into which the Court can move. Only if an option is created that offers actual safety from Rod as one component, is it possible for Anna to let down her guard sufficiently to hear a voice that is even partially her own. For Anna to speak in her own voice, her father has to get his foot off her neck. This presumably is the function of the long jail sentence.

PART III
CHILDREN OF COERCIVE CONTROL

8

The Coercive Control of Magdalena and Daniel Pelka

A Case of Tangential Spouse Abuse

This chapter illustrates the forensic analysis of child abuse as tangential spouse abuse, when a partner's primary purpose in coercively controlling a child is to subordinate his adult victim. I assume the perspective of Daniel Pelka, the child who was killed. The weaponization of the child is a unique element that distinguishes the coercive control of children from other forms of coercive control. Children in these cases are considered "secondary" victims because the coercive control of the adult partner usually antecedes the child abuse, the tactics used to harm the child(ren) are chosen for their effect on the adult victim primarily, risk to each is assessed by the cumulative danger to both, and ending the coercive control of the adult victim usually ends the risk to the child, often by pursuing criminal charges against the primary perpetrator. Cases like the coercive control of Daniel Pelka challenge straightforward forensics because adult victims are often a focus of criminal charges or other legal attention, as the mother was here, often regardless of whether they directly harmed the child or caused a death. The charges usually stem from the degree to which the adult victim is said to have "colluded" in the child's abuse, "failed to protect" the child from harm, or actively abused the child in ways that appear to be unrelated to whatever domestic violence may have occurred. My role is to exculpate the mother by identifying the sole responsibility of the primary perpetrator, delineating the mother's protective response within the constraints imposed by her own abuse, and articulating the role of the child as a medium for the father's abuse and the mother's attempts at self-defense and safety. An important facet of my work is listening to "the voice of the child." In this case, this meant deciphering the physical, behavioral, and oral signals sent by Daniel about the coercive control to himself; his

Children of Coercive Control. Evan Stark, Oxford University Press. © Oxford University Press 2023.
DOI: 10.1093/oso/9780197587096.003.0009

mother; his sister, Anna; and his abuser, Mariusz Krezolek, as well as to a range of "helpers," including teachers, police, and the pediatrician.

The substance of my analysis is the highly publicized case of Daniel Pelka, a four-year-old who was starved and beaten to death in Coventry, England, in 2012, and the 2013 trial and conviction of the mother, Luczak, and her live-in boyfriend, for directly causing the boy's death.[1]

Background: The Killing of Daniel Pelka
by Mariusz Krezolek

In 2012, The British Home Office adapted "coercive control" as the best framework for a new "cross-governmental response" to women and children through its health and social service systems.[2] In contrast to the previous emphasis on discrete assaults, the new "working definition" (WD) defined coercive control to include "Any incident or pattern of incidents of controlling, coercive or threatening behaviour, violence or abuse between those aged 16 or over who are or have been intimate partners or family members regardless of gender or sexuality." Controlling behavior was defined as "making a person subordinate and/or dependent by isolating them from sources of support, exploiting their resources and capacities for personal gain, depriving them of the means needed for independence, resistance and escape and regulating their everyday lives." From 2012 to 2014, the new WD replaced more than twenty conflicting definitions that guided the funding and delivery of services to abuse victims throughout Britain. Over the next few years, coercive control became a serious new criminal offense in England, Scotland, Ireland, and Taiwan, and in California, Connecticut, Hawaii, Washington and several other US states.

The trial of Krezolek and Luczak for the murder of Daniel was one of the last to be carried out under the old framework. The failure to prevent Daniel's death and the opacity of the SCR carried out by the British Government to identify the causes for this failure dramatize the need for a new approach. In this analysis, I show how a coercive control framework could have been applied to save two lives by mental health practitioners, social workers, pediatricians, police, judges, and nurses.

Case Background

There never was any doubt that Krezolek delivered the fatal blows meriting his thirty-year prison term. But Luczak was also charged with murder, and the couple was tried, convicted, and sentenced together. The Crown acknowledged Luczak may have been abused by her boyfriend. But even if this was so, it contended, this had little bearing on her behavior. Throughout the trial, the Crown insisted there was little difference between their involvements.

Luczak admitted failing to prevent Krezolek from killing Daniel. But there was no allegation that she struck or otherwise abused her son. She insisted she had not done so and claimed to have been too frightened to oppose Krezolek because of his abuse.

During their trial, unflattering photos and other negative portrayals of Luczak were as pervasive in the English tabloids as had been the images in the United States of OJ Simpson handcuffed, unshaven, and head down after his arrest for killing Nicole Brown and Ronald Goldman in 1994. Typical of the media representation was a photo identifying her as "The evil mother who put love of drugs, alcohol and vile boyfriend before Daniel's basic needs." The motion for separate trials was rejected. So their stories, like their fate, became inseparable.

Much of the media reported Magdalena's claims that Mariusz had beaten, raped, and repeatedly threatened to kill her. But neither the legally required SCR completed by a host of service professionals under expert guidance before the trial nor any of the commentators in the press connected this "admission" of abuse to Daniel's murder, let alone suggested that Magdalena's victimization might reduce her culpability for Daniel's death.

The Crown Prosecutor (CPS) presented a photo of Magdalena to the jury, describing her appearance as "expressionless" and as "cold indifference" to the boy's suffering as he died. I suspected it was more likely that the young immigrant woman with little English at her defense during the trial had been rendered near insensate to the events around her by the terror in which she lived. Mariusz's presence in the house had been unbearable. His presence in the courtroom extended this terror into a defining moment in her life.

A year after she went to prison, Magdalena hanged herself in her cell on Daniel's birthday. Magdalena had not stopped Mariusz from beating and starving her son. But was she merely a bystander? Using Magdalena's "sin of omission" as the starting point, the Crown built a case for her legal guilt for Daniel's death by highlighting critical junctures during his deterioration when she actively concealed the realities at home, deceived outsiders, and encouraged behaviors that hastened the boy's decline. In his sentencing, the judge pointed to two such instances he considered particularly heinous. Though she was aware Daniel was so hungry that he would take food from a school dumpster, Magdalena told his teachers to limit Daniel's food intake at school to the cheese and bread she provided for his lunch. Magdalena failed to tell his caregivers about his abuse and instead gave accounts of his injuries she knew to be untrue. A week before his murder, when she had taken Daniel for a pediatric exam, Magdalena had kept from the clinician the vital and potentially life-saving information that abuse by her live-in boyfriend was the source of Daniel enigmatic medical and physical problems, including his extensive bruising and his dramatic weight loss. Even at this very late juncture, intervention would have saved Daniel's life. Seemingly perplexed by the case, the pediatrician resorted to blood workups for obscure metabolic disorders, provided vitamins, and made a referral for another opinion.

Before adopting the Crown's viewpoint, I ask readers to take on faith that when refracted through the prism of the victimization of mother and son, Magdalena's ostensible "collusion" will reappear as behavior designed to resist, refuse, and expose Mariusz's coercive control, while minimizing harms to herself and Daniel. These are examples of what I call "control in the context of no control." I identify Daniel's ostensibly self-incriminating behavior such as his theft of food at school and his confession of the theft, as similarly intentional and strategic in relation to his own safety rather than as "provocations" that led to his tragic demise. The respective struggles for survival by Magdalena and Daniel illustrate the parallel dilemmas posed for battered mothers and their children when coercive control takes the form of "child abuse as tangential spouse abuse."

The Serious Case Review

The family in focus was well known and highly visible in every sector statutorily responsible for the problems at issue. A conservative estimate is that during the period when these events occurred, Magdalena and Daniel were seen, questioned, interviewed, tested, and assessed by over four dozen separate home visitors, visiting nurses, home nurses, school nurses, nurse midwives, pediatricians, teachers, assistant teachers, police, and social workers. A number of these professionals had received specialized training to work with abused or neglected children and a number are licensed to do so. Dozens of these encounters took place in a critical time period for Daniel when opening a window a crack could have been life-saving. The information that should have prompted early intervention was readily available both in written records and from participants. Mariusz, too, was often seen by police, midwives, home visitors, and the pediatrician. In my experience, this level of prior knowledge and professional involvement is common when children are killed in a domestic abuse scenario and may even be typical. Failure here arose from the absence of a framework to properly recognize the dynamics of coercive control, not from shortcomings in training, professional commitment, or practice.

The SCR report in the Pelka case is a seventy-six-page, single-spaced document with three appendices reviewing the known facts of the case; describing and assessing each recorded encounter between an affected family member and provider professionals in the home, school, pediatric clinic, and other points of service; enumerating conclusions about the overall quality of the services received; and recommending improved practices. I critique the overall approach to child protection assumed by all the professionals involved in the Pelka investigation and reflected in the overview adapted by the SCR. Coercive control of Magdalena was the source of Pelka's risk. For me, the spatial intersections between Magdalena and Daniel (the "when?," "why?," "how?," and "what?" of those interactions) are functions of the increasingly constrained field of action defined by Mariusz's coercive control. The exclusion of Mariusz from the purview of the professionals involved in this case, whether conscious or not, created a blinder that deflected all of their efforts from achieving the only meaningful objective, namely removing the immediate threat to the family. This ensured that all subsequent efforts would be ineffective. The SCR concluded that the events that led to Daniel's death were largely out of sight. But this observation merely heightens the tragedy of the case, since for the purposes of inflicting his will, Mariusz. was in plain sight. As it turns out, he was also physically present at key moments when his presence went either deliberately ignored (as in the pediatrician's office) or elicited no response (as when he forcibly removed Magdalena from her hospital bed). So when the SCR concludes that tragic events were "out of sight," this is a professional euphemism for the ideological blinders that made the abusive man in the room invisible. These were times when key personnel responsible for health and safety simply decided to "look away."

Despite his having no official presence, the pervasive influence of Mariusz on the SCR as a specter is felt by his distorting effects on everyone in the case. His abuse is documented as well, both reflectively, in the parallel physical deterioration of Magdalena and Daniel, and in notes made by police, a home visitor, a nurse, and a teacher. However, the abuse is treated not as a problem with an identifiable cause about which something decisive might have been done early on. Nor is it linked to any events in the case, let alone offered to explain why Magdalena or Daniel behave as they do, why they remain silent one moment or say what they do in the next, for instance. Instead, the abuse takes its place alongside other "facts" about Magdalena's condition (she is "an abused woman") and is woven so tightly into a tapestry with the other facets of her life such as her poor facility in English, problems in her earlier marriage, her alcohol use, her immigration status, and her insufficient income. In this manner, the abuse ceases to have an alien existence as a hostile act susceptible to remediation and reappears as a byproduct of who she is, as a mother and woman. It is as if any victimization she suffered at the hands of Mariusz was an inherited deficit she brought to the table rather than the primary cause of their son "starving" and growing increasingly "malnourished." I call this process "overcontextualization." It describes a common type of sociological analysis in which so many contributing factors (facets) of an experience (abuse) are identified that the object/person being assessed loses their specificity and appears to be a thing (is "reified"), in this instance, to be something she is (an "abused woman") rather than a person with a lived history. When applied to casework, overcontextualization has the unintended consequence of justifying institutional inaction (by child welfare, police, and the school, in this instance) while paralyzing the victim with an overwhelming array of contradictory expectations and demands. There is no greater opening for analysis, forensically, than uncovering, documenting, and then revealing the numerous opportunities when key professional actors encountered men engaging in coercive control and took no notice.

Rather than parse her problems into those for which she is responsible, remediable problems associated with the existential condition (such as poor housing), and those (such as abuse) caused by bad actors for which she needs to take concerted action on behalf of herself or her children, these are collapsed into a single profile of her relative risks. She is an "abused" mother. In the eyes of her providers, an "abused mother" is a not a type of abuse victim with responsibility for a child, but a subtype of mother whose peculiar deficit predisposes her to poor housing and poor parenting, thereby depriving her of the assumptions of deference due to other types of mothers. An abused mother is a woman who is disqualified because of her poor choices from the deference accorded to motherhood.

Each tragic dimension of the family's ecosystem had its counterpart in professional service providers who ran in tandem with these social factors, making errors inevitable. The irony is that, in the final analysis, the professionals in the Pelka case were able to ignore the ill-effects of their interventions because their malfeasance affected Magdalena and Daniel much in the same way as Mariusz's did; it isolated and silenced them, rendering them increasingly unable to respond to them as well as to him.

The Child's Voice

Retrieving children's voices poses a major challenge to forensic assessment in coercive control cases. Prohibitions, limits, and directed speech are common means of suppressing children's autonomy in coercive control, dividing their loyalties and enlisting them as allies. All children have visual, aural, emotional, and verbal responses to coercive control. Accessing these responses can take patience and imagination, and interviewers must resist the temptation to view children's reticence, claims of development delays, or even "trauma" as impugning the utility of a child witness, even among very young children. Another major obstacle to hearing children's voices is the temptation to identify with their fear of the abuser and so to miss echoes of resistance. Many practitioners so completely empathize with children's' fear and utter vulnerability that they miss the ego strengths shielded behind these feelings, the calm in the face of the storm, the courage in the face of adversity, and their kernel of rage.

Among the hundreds of professional encounters with the family, I saw no evidence that anyone had a conversation with Daniel. But if Daniel's silence is deafening, this is not, as the SCR claims, because he had poor language skills or lacked confidence. Daniel was reticent, but vocal in school and in all his interactions with his sister, Anna. As could easily have been discerned if the possibility had been imagined, Daniel does not talk about what is happening to him at home because he and his mother have been shown what will happen to them if they do so. Daniel's silence is the direct result of his being silenced by Mariusz, the agent who manages to remain off stage while the play is being analyzed. Only if we first posit Daniel as normal developmentally, can we then imagine his "failure" to articulate his predicament in words as a "refusal" to do so, as a rational adaptation to "coercive control." The vectors of power in coercive control extend "through social space" like the strings on a marionette, limiting the person's capacity for current attention by continually reminding them of their commitments to the "rules of engagement" or else. Mariusz is not invisible; he simply remains "unseen."

The persistence of acts whose author commands anonymity creates dilemmas for those who observe these acts and must respond. It is by explicating these dilemmas and drawing attention to the forcefields around them that we substantiate the presence we seek. Mariusz is not often observed directly, but his acts are well-known, albeit indirectly, through their effects on Daniel and on Magdalena. The first appearance of these effects seems alien to their nature and leaves the appearance of paradox: a boy who is well-liked by other children goes "silent"; a boy who comes to school neatly dressed loses thirty pounds; a mother who presents her children well-groomed each day instructs the teachers to restrict her son's food intake to the lunches she provides. Without recognizing Mariusz's malignant tyranny as the explanation, observers reconcile these paradoxes by attributing their cause to heretofore unrecognized deficits in the targets— Daniel is "silent" because he "lacks confidence" and "language skills"; Magdalena's collusion reflects her underlying "ambivalence" about the abusive relationship. Why do the professionals involved employ such apparent distortions? They fear Krezolek; they fear getting "involved," and becoming "overwhelmed" by the scope of the problem. Some of the professionals involved used denial and projection to manage their fear by first ignoring what they knew about the source of the effects they observed on Daniel and then making it appear that the effects emanated from Daniel himself, much like the "force of nature" to which the pediatrician alluded when he asked for the metabolic workup for a rare blood disorder. To this extent, Daniel became a "totem" for the teachers and the pediatrician. Like a totem, to whom a premodern people might turn to manage fears of the unknown, is how the various professionals in Daniel's orbit attempted to manage the fearsome power of Mariusz through its effects on the boy. A similar analysis applies to Magdalena, so long as her voice was taken out of the context in which it was submissive, plaintive, and protective, it was misinterpreted as hostile and defensive of concealment.

Reconstructing the Pelka Case

Because the primary sources in this case are deceased or otherwise inaccessible, I relied on the SCR case review, the trial record, and news reports. This was problematic because both official records were constructed to highlight Magdalena's coresponsibility and refer to her abuse largely to diminish its importance. Thus, the record on which I rely is part of the case for prosecution.

Our first challenge was to put Mariusz back into events from which he was removed.[3] In Daniel's condition of deterioration, no prompting from the school or the pediatrician nor even further x-rays or other testing should have been necessary to reveal the most prominent risk factors Henry Kempe identified with child abuse in 1962—dramatic weight loss due to no known medical cause accompanied by scattered muscle-skeletal bruising in various states of healing, withdrawal, regressive symptoms, etc.[4] So transparent was this diagnosis that even the normally gun-shy SCR questioned the pediatrician's "professionalism" for turning for the differential to a blood workup for a rare metabolic disorder, let alone dispensing vitamins for the thirty-pound weight loss.

But in emphasizing a professional lapse, the SCR begged the question: what would prompt a reasonably intelligent physician to search for a "force of nature" that had brought this child to the brink of starvation? The mystery was resolved at the trial, where the pediatrician acknowledged that "mother's boyfriend" (Krezolek) was in the room during the last visit, a fact he had conveniently omitted putting on his own medical record of the encounter. Mariusz was smirking and making "threatening gestures" toward them both throughout the visit. Now, we had three pertinent facts in the pediatrician's decision matrix—the boy's presentation of risk profile, the mother's account of the boy's deterioration at home, and the threatening presence of "mother's boyfriend." It is hard to see, under the circumstances, what more Magdalena and Daniel could be expected to do.

What were the physician's options? The pediatrician could have asked Mariusz to step out for a moment, so he could be alone with the mother and boy, introducing emergency rescue as an option. Or he could just have talked to Daniel about what was making him afraid. Whatever the specifics, it was the physical threat posed by Mariusz's presence in the room, and nothing Magdalena did or did not do, that sent the pediatrician scurrying to find an obscure cause for Daniel's deterioration.

Once we properly situate Mariusz as the source of illegitimate authority in the case, the vectors of all family transactions, statements, and behaviors in the house, market, school, doctor's office, or elsewhere can be repositioned with reference to Mariusz, starting with how they meet their primary needs for safety (defensive) and autonomy (assertive). As is the case in any regime of terror, in a family regulated by coercive control, normative guidelines for daily living become command rituals of subservience and degradation punctuated by outbursts of benevolence directed at "favorites" whose docility or fawning yields quickly to resurgent terror. Behaviors by dependent women and children that appear "self-serving," collusive, irrational, or passive to outsiders are forensically reframed as "strategies of endurance, resistance, and survival" in relation to a decipherable calculus of ethics and risks, including the behaviors of minor children. The initial purpose of this contextualization process is to demonstrate a client's normative capacity even under extreme duress, not necessarily to defend the substance of their decision-making. Identifying a strategic logic behind Magdalena's action illustrates her capacity for purposeful, ethical or value-laden action that some have thought inconsistent with high levels of victimization.[5] The caveat here is that the choices she is given are already contingent on her operating within a universe where the most desired options, those involving autonomy, safety, liberty, or dignity for herself and the child, for instance, may have been foreclosed by a malevolent other. This is no academic turn of phrase. In many of the narratives they have provided, women and children have often identified an actual moment in time in their struggle with coercive control when they recognized that the free air had gone out of the room, that the degree of unfreedom in their lives was intolerable and incompatible with continuing to live *as if* they were freely choosing their daily routines. Within the context of coercive control, the "choice to choose" is always fraught and all choices made by women and children are assessed as context-contingent, as bounded by the perceived availability of options (what is put on the table may not be relevant); the perceived consequences of choosing "wrong" ("the 'all-else' proviso"); and the decreasing likelihood that any choice will make a difference in the outcome. In the last instance, which is illustrated in these case chapters, the victim may simply " 'refuse' to choose (by withdrawing from an embezzlement scheme or child abuse scenario, for example) or may choose a path they perceive is a lesser evil, the option I refer to as "control in the context of no control." Refusing to choose in situations of enormous perceived constraint is also an option. What the philosopher Herbert Marcuse dubbed "the Great Refusal" qualifies forensically as an important tactic in resistance/ self-preservation, particularly with children, who may have fewer illusions than adults about the futility of "choosing anything."[6] To reiterate, my account contrasts to an account which holds that victimization entails a total relegation of purposeful action and a second which holds that victimization is a temporary incapacitation related to what is on the table or perceived to be available as an option at a given time.[7] In the context of coercive control, victimization is neither a state-of-being (as is implied by terms like "the battered woman" or "the rape trauma victim") nor an "event," but an unfolding process of incapacitation and resistance in which the power to shape self and other is being appropriated.

I depict Magdalena for the Court as a person whose choices are value laden by the requisites of autonomy, such as dignity, liberty, security, and physical integrity. I describe the power valence (coercive control) that is constraining the available choices; and track the degree to which modes of adapting to these constraints (resistance, escape, refusal, collusion, etc.) are consistent with the original values, albeit in diminished form. This is what is meant by, "control in the context of no control." By behaving strategically with respect to survival for herself and the boy (hoping to elicit attention and support without inciting retaliation/escalation from Mariusz), Magdalena merits recognition as the covictim of this crime not as its perpetrator. She continues to defend autonomous personhood, though she has none. Her actions, though unsuccessful, remove her responsibility for the failure to protect.

Reframing Magdalena's Experiences of Abuse

Prior Abuse

Between 2005 and 2009, when she met Mariusz, Magdalena was primarily involved with Mr. P., Daniel's father, and Mr. A., a man to whom Magdalena turned initially for protection from Mr. P. These relationships, like her relationship with Mariusz, were violent, in all three Magdalena's use of alcohol to cope confounded her predicament, and elements of coercive control deployed by Mr. A. extended to the children. For my purposes, however, the remarkable feature of these earlier relationships is Magdalena's resiliency, the range of coping strategies she used to protect herself and the children, and her success in extricating herself from the abuse, despite the failure to help of the multiple service providers through whose portals she passed.

The record of the relationship to Mr. P. consisted of classic domestic violence, documented by a half-dozen incidents of police involvement, all involving physical altercations or "fights," all occurring in their shared home and with Magdalena and Mr. P. both reported to be drinking or drunk. Though police calls represent only a small proportion of actual instances of abuse, I saw nothing in the record indicating coercive control. In the context of ongoing abuse, Magdalena's intoxication indicates her vulnerability, both because is unable to properly defend herself if drunk, and historically, because alcohol abuse is a mode of adaptation that minimizes but not does nothing to end the pain. Importantly, drinking also disqualified Magdalena as a worthy client for police. Thus, when she reported a sexual assault by Mr. P., police failed to investigate, because "she had been drinking." In the context of ongoing domestic violence from Mr. P. and repeated frustrated police visits, Magdalena took an "overdose" of tablets and alcohol in two suicide attempts and, in a third attempt, she threw herself in front of an approaching ambulance, gestures consistent with the "pleas for help" our research team identified among abused patients at Yale.[8] In September 2008, the hospital referred the children for services to assess the impact of Magdalena's suicide attempt, but there was no follow-up, no mention of domestic violence as the cause or context of the suicide attempt, and no "safety audit" to determine whether it "was safe at home" for Magdalena or the children to return. The hospital made a referral to the local abuse service and arrangements were made to "contact mother," but nothing more was done.

Instead, after her second stay, Magdalena left the hospital with an "unidentified male." She was twelve weeks pregnant. A visiting midwife also noted she had "no money." The same midwife also noted "a history of abuse" but made no referral. She saw this as a past concern.

Between November 2009, when Magdalena left the hospital with an "unidentified male," probably Mr. A, and January 2010, when she had her own flat, she moved back and forth between Mr. P. and Mr. A. Mr. A. was arrested in several assaultive incidents, once when police found Magdalena holding Daniel protectively when they arrived, and once when he tried to force his way into her flat with a knife, and he was tried and convicted on the weapons possession and given a community order of 120 hours of unpaid work. Over the next year, police, the health visitor, probation, the children, and community services mobilized the full arsenal of their resources to respond to this relationship. On various occasions, police arrested Mr. A. (for possession of the knife); arrested both parties; removed Magdalena and the children to her sister's for "safety"; "took no action" (because she was drunk); and assessed Mr. A.'s risk as "moderate," then changed it to high, and finally resentenced Mr. A. (suspending his community sentence) and imposed a thirteen-week nightly curfew, which he promptly violated. Two things are notable about this service response. Despite repeated admonitions from the press, the CPS, the SCR, and the trial judge, that Magdalena was "doing nothing" about her abuse or the risk to the children at this point in her life, Magdalena was calling for help and talking to anyone and everyone about her predicament. Equally important is that it would be hard to conjure a more "service rich" domestic violence response. Far from being invisible to the community as they would become later on, Magdalena and her children were "well known" to the police, health, and the refuge communities as victims of abuse. It was not from want of trying that the response system failed to prevent Daniel and Magdalena's deaths. The police response was abstracted from the inter-personal context in which the crimes took shape and the punishment meted out, "community" sentences and "curfews," were administered without re-gard to their effect on that context. Punishing Mr. A. by confining him to the home/community ensured his continued proximity to Magdalena, for ex-ample, virtually guaranteeing that either his coercive control would continue to Magdalena and the children or they would have to seek additional refuge. Even the breach for which Mr. A. was eventually convicted involved the knife, not the stalking, the break-in, or the assault. Her experience was that police and justice intervention made her space-for-action more constricted.

In the SCR account, Magdalena's abuse history with her prior partners set the stage for the tragic narrative that followed, wherein Daniel's deteri-oration was made the more inevitable by his unfortunate caretaker, an alco-holic, immature immigrant who is involved in drunken brawls with a series of boyfriends who abused her. The Crown's narrative is less subtle. But the moral logic at trial was essentially the same. The prosecution argued that throughout these ordeals Magdalena selfishly chose her own immediate gratification via sex or alcohol over her own or her children's well-being, failing to seek appropriate support, concealing the realities of abuse at home, all the while actively confounding assistance. Both the accounts painted the fatal outcome as the result of tragedy—the one social, the other moral—for which the systems presumably on the watch to protect women and children from abuse bear no responsibility.

The SCR was right about this much. Magdalena was already extremely am-bivalent about outside intervention of any kind for herself and the children before she met Mariusz. As we've seen, however, her skepticism was reality-based, not a failure of nerve. Nothing had worked. Repeated solicitations for help led nowhere, promised support was withheld, the men whom she'd had arrested were returned to the home and community to hurt her again, and her basic needs for money, employment, and housing had gone unmet. Given this experience, she adopted a utilitarian approach: Although police might be some use in emergencies, calling police did nothing to enhance long-term security. Both calling police and refusing further intervention when the situation calmed were consistent with her experience of how policing worked. Note, her response placed no objective limit on what police could have done. The further requirement that a victim press a complaint against her assailant is neither a legal prerequisite for arrest nor desirable when the offender is a partner. The Court's disinterest in Magdalena's well-being was not lost on Mr. A., the abuser who returned. But instead of pursuing the assailant based on this evidence, they took Magdalena and the children to stay with her sister and referred the case to child protection. Again, she "would not cooperate" and no charges were filed. Even so, as their triage suggested, police were well aware that Magdalena was faced ongoing danger and that her "paralysis of will" was a reflection of danger she faced even across social space—police now raised the risk status of the case to "high." Today, this could have prompted an investigation and arrest for coercive control. At the time, however, the police response signaled a warning to Magdalena that nothing would be done.

Death reviews in domestic violence or child abuse cases almost always include long, complicated histories of involvement with police, battered women's programs, and multiple other health, family, children, and social services agencies. Not only are the offenders or victims in such cases almost always "known" at various points of service. The records of these encounters can be mined for information that is vital to every dimension of a case, including narrative portions where more informal, personal observations may be recorded. Resources promised, delivered, or withheld critically shape what options are perceived, selected, or rejected. Even if only one or two incidents in a record contain a positive identification of a partner assault, there are usually enough "probable" or "suspicious" events surrounding these incidents to form a scatter diagram of the duration of any domestic violence that occurred as well as other forms of physical or sexual abuse. Aligning police reports, medical records, child protective service reports, school reports, court records, and other records of contemporaneous encounters usually adds substantial insight into the breadth of the abuse, whether sexual coercion or stalking was involved, for example, the extent of drug or alcohol abuse, and how children may be affected. Narrative portions of these records are likely to provide invaluable complementary information. Arraying women and children's records historically allows me to appreciate the window that can be opened by seemingly routine service encounters. If abuse does not directly prompt an encounter, if it provides the context, I assume it is "in the room" and that the reason why it fails to surface may reflect a constraint in the presenter's life or on the receiving context. This was the expectation that led me to suspect the something or someone had caused Daniel's pediatrician to "fail" to probe abuse as the cause of his injuries in their last encounter. I discovered the handwritten notation on the medical record that "mother's boyfriend is in the room" serendipitously. But I was alerted to look for "hidden" or "unofficial transcripts" in all encounters when domination is in the room, including those involving physicians.[9]

In the Pelka case, based on the SCR, the myriad service professionals were running blind. Was this an instance of normal professional insularity? Or was there a spectral influence at work? To clinicians individually, each episode of domestic violence was as if de nuevo rather than part of an ongoing pattern of coercive control. Although these episodes collected in individual records, these data were never aggregated. A family was seem, once separately, then huddled together in fear, but thought to be merely "overwrought" because the clinicians had no way to gauge the historical depth or the scope of the oppression occasioning their fears. By dropping a net over these aggregate episodes, the coercive control perspective shifts the terms for evaluation from situational dynamics to their historical and political contexts. Conversely, instead of assessing each service encounter as more or less professional in terms of the facts presented, we look at the service response as a whole over time on a continuum articulated with the problem set articulated by the child/family's presentations over time. This enables us to gauge the progress of coercive control in relation to the changing institutional response, from Daniel's shifting presentations at his school, for example, or Magdalena's timid interventions, or his visit to the pediatrician, to the school and pediatric referrals.

The assessment of coercive control Is "global," because the victims transit through multiple sites and because control strategies extend to these sites as well, both aggressively, to compete for attention/resources victims may dispense at the site, and defensively, to prevent victims from accruing support.

This is the significance of assessing how coercive control affects Daniel at school or at the pediatric visit. The corollary principle is that children best thrive in families or family-like relationships when the competent adults responsible for their care can follow their children across the spectrum of their activities to advocate in their interest as free and self-determining persons. Coercive control adds a burden of "safety" and "protective" work to maternal responsibilities that keeps mothers chronically too exhausted to attend to their own needs. Thus, though Magdalena is technically "with" Daniel at school and in the pediatrician's office, her capacity to negotiate on his behalf has been severely compromised by Mariusz, forcing her to communicate through physical signs, gestures, and simple linguistic pleas that require a certain awareness of oppression to interpret. Daniel's appearance and behavior at school signaled his distress, but nothing about the mother's stoic accompaniment suggested the global nature of the oppression they both faced and that defined the child's immediate risk. For this insight, these professionals would have had to plumb their own records historically to retrieve Mariusz from their dead files. So long as Magdalena appears to cope, whatever the effort expended in so doing, the children are considered her problem. When her capacity demonstrably breaks down, will they move in. By then, in this case, it was too late.

I would change the balance of responsibility in favor of police/social work intervention to stem coercive control early on, before Mariusz designated Magdalena as Daniel's "capo."

Domestic Violence or Coercive Control?

Early in her relationship with Mariusz, Magdalena and Daniel were treated for injuries that should have raised suspicion with trained healthcare professionals. However, instead, Magdalena was diagnosed as "depressed," prescribed antidepressants, and given no follow-up. Soon thereafter, Mariusz strangled Magdalena, a high lethality episode, which caused a loss of consciousness (at the least, as some women experience brain damage).[10] He also cut her with a knife. She also reported numerous rapes. The children were present, and he was arrested but not charged and returned home. The professional services in England that Magdalena encountered in 2010 (when domestic violence was officially considered a public problem for which offenders were responsible) were widely available. Every health and social worker in England received professional education on how to identify the problem, and abuse offenses were widely publicized and often resulted in prosecution and jail. Readers should know this fact to appreciate how retrograde was both the professional response in this case and the response by the SCR, starting with the absence of domestic violence expertise from the SCR. This was almost certainly because the domestic abuse was seen as irrelevant to the child's murder. In its summary, the SCR described domestic abuse as a "major pattern of this family's lifestyle" and attributed the fact that she was abused by three partners not to any failure in the protective response, let alone to the criminality of the men involved, but to Magdalena's inability "to detect abusive relationships" and not "learn" from "previous experiences" so that "her own behaviors" (e.g., her violence) helped "fuel altercations." By contrast with this assessment, the record indicates that the "altercations" were almost always assaults, beating, and rapes; that far from simply "detecting the abuse," Magdalena called police numerous times for help, and frankly discussed abuse with home visitors, her GP, visiting nurses, and probably anyone else who cared to listen. If she and her children became ready targets for abusive men, it was because those to whom she turned for help never took her ongoing freedom and safety as their primary concern. Be clear. I am talking here not from the perspective of my expertise on coercive control, but from the perspective of what the Government held to be best practice at the time. I remain agnostic as to whether the failure was endemic to social care in Britain or the result of myopia imposed by the narrow child-saving paradigm in hand.

Many of our cases end in this period with one party, most often the woman but sometimes the abusive man, being killed. Had Magdalena refused to be oppressed and killed Mariusz, in either self-defense or proactively, in our case our approach would emphasize how she had exercised optimal strategic intelligence within the constraints he had imposed, "control within the context of no control." If the killing had not been in response to an immediate assault, we would accept the challenge of showing the many other ways Magdalena had tried (and failed) to lift the yoke of oppression off her back. In this instance, I would document Magdalena's response whenever she felt she was being terrorized or entrapped, even if no violence was involved. At every moment, I would want to know: What did you fear might happen? What options did she have? What did she do? Did it help? So, for example, Magdalena's decisions *not* to call police or to deny abuse appear to make tactical sense when in the context of what happened when she had had Mariusz arrested.

He was returned and hurt her even more severely. Women who blame them-selves for "bad choices" when things do not work are often taking responsi-bility for making a choice within the narrow range of options where none are good—"control in the context of no control." Magdalena had a friend staying at the house for several nights. But Mariusz was persistent, unpredictable, and dangerous, and this tactic did not afford long-term protection. In these circumstances, safety planning entails expanding the ground over which women and children can walk.

During the next year, both Magdalena and Daniel were seen for injuries whose providence should have raised alarms, but did not. As Mariusz's control over the family escalated, an assessment concluded abuse was no longer an issue because the couple had stopped drinking, ostensibly because Magdalena was pregnant. Pregnancy is the highest risk point for physical vi-olence and control in abusive relationships both because many narcissistic abusers interpret the impending birth as a competitor for the woman's at-tention and because pregnant women are physically more dependent and vulnerable, a condition which abusive men exploit. Instead, the assessment "considered that all of the domestic abuse in the past had been closely related to alcohol misuse."[11] The case was closed.

There was never any evidence the abuse was alcohol related. Magdalena undoubtedly drank in excess, as police reports made clear. But our early re-search at Yale and case studies show that battered women typically "abuse" alcohol to supplement their normal drinking to medicate the alternating currents of chronic and unpredictable stress associated with coercive con-trol.[12] If providers believed alcoholism was an underlying issue, why was rehabilitation never prescribed or even recommended? More likely, health providers and social work, like police, viewed "alcohol on breath" as yet another stigmata that disqualified Magdalena from being treated as a full person. With a coercive control perspective, the "ongoing" nature of the vio-lence would have signaled a heightened level of entrapment and risk of hom-icide for all family members. Even if the violence had temporarily ended, an assessor would suspect a shift to other means of coercion and control.

In a visit to the antenatal clinic, Magdalena told the midwife and the con-sultant obstetrician that her partner was pressuring her to get a termination. Forced abortions, like unwanted pregnancies, are common forms of repro-ductive coercion that accompany coercive control.[13] In addition, because a female partner may be more physically vulnerable or dependent during a pregnancy, abusers often shift to nonphysical forms of control. Magdalena explained the change in her partner's tactics to the clinicians as best she could, but they misinterpreted her account as an attempt to minimize the violence. She recounted an implied threat that included the fetus. But again, they shared concerns only for her own physical safety. But, in the context of ongoing coercive control, it should have set off alarms about the safety of all current and future family members.

Soon thereafter, Magdalena developed a kidney infection requiring hospitalization. Mariusz came to the hospital, pulled out her IV, and insisted on her discharge against medical advice. Here was a transparent enactment of coercive control of the woman and fetus, the only such act in the case history. Pleas for help were everywhere. By forcibly kidnapping her from her hospital bed on their watch, Mariusz resolved any ambiguity about his demand for her services. The hospital attack is a criminal assault. The midwife for safeguarding did her job or appeared to until she ran into a wall. It is hard to contemplate the cynicism needed to turn away at this point: A hospital visit is a rare escape opportunity from coercive control, but Magdalena's time was limited, she was desperate and before they could respond, Mariusz was there, snatching her back.

The hospital grab was a critical juncture. Magdalena and the children were invisible to the community over the next few months. Since there was no open case, they were not missed.

Not only had Magdalena not concealed the abuse. By this time, as case notes indicate, Mariusz's abusive behavior was well known to the range of providers involved with the family, even if he was never identified for assessment, interdiction, or management. After the kidnapping in front of hospital staff so she could be home to care for the children, there could be no issue of deception with respect to what he was capable of. Or even frankly of the ways her abuse related to the children. In fact, Magdalena now saw her abuse in relationship to the pregnancy and the children. She called the community midwife to report that Mariusz strangled her (again) and pulled her hair and requested help finding safe accommodations. She said the relationship was over. Not having a safe place for the children was now a barrier to leaving. Nothing was done.

The fetus is an animus of intense jealousy and competition in coercive control as well as an object through which to control the pregnant woman. By contrast, a baby's birth often precipitates a crisis in relationships characterized by coercive control if only because the unpredictable demands of maternal caretaking wreak havoc on authoritarian regimes of time regulation and exclusive possessiveness. Mariusz had demanded Magdalena terminate the pregnancy in April and had strangled her in July, in her last trimester, when she reached out for help to leave him. Baby Adam's birth and the arrival of Mariusz's mother from Poland presented the ideal time for a global assessment of the safety situation in the home. In a global assessment, the well-being (safety, but not only) of all members of the family is assumed to be a function of the absolute level of violence and coercive control in the home, regardless of whether each person has been separately targeted. Had this occurred, all three children would be safe and Magdalena Luczak would not be dead.

Coercive Control of Magdalena and Daniel by Mariusz Krezolek

On May 2, 2010, Magdalena made the first call to police for trouble with her new partner, Mr. Krezolek. The call included sounds of the children crying. Police observed she had a fractured finger. Mariusz was arrested for assault, but released because Magdalena refused to make a statement. She told emergency department (ED) personnel the injury was caused by a "door slamming." The next day, when she went to the ED alone, Magdalena identified the source of the injury as the door slammed by Mr. Krezolek. But by now, this woman was "well known" from her record even if she had never encountered these specific personnel. A story was accumulating of what was happening to Magdalena at this ED and throughout the infrastructure, but not as background for intervention.

On July 5, Magdalena explained to a health visitor in the home that a suspicious bruise observed on the left side of Daniel's head was caused when he "fell over." On July 20, the health visitor completed Daniel's three-year assessment. There was no record Mariusz was present. "Domestic abuse" was "discussed," by whom is unclear, though both women would have been aware that Mariusz's absence from the home was the critical safety factor for everyone in the family.

The medical record includes dozens of visits for abuse-related injuries, including at least strangulation, in which Magdalena lost consciousness, an attack with a knife, and numerous sexual assaults as well as visits in which Daniel as well as his mother were treated for abuse-related injuries. Children were identified as present at all of these incidents. Mariusz was arrested on one occasion, but not charged and returned home. Magdalena was diagnosed as "depressed," prescribed antidepressants, and given no follow-up. Most of this record was established between 2005 and 2010, when "domestic violence" was considered a high priority for police and health services in England, services for abused women were widely available, every health and social worker in England received professional education on how to identify the problem, and abuse offenses were widely publicized and often resulted in prosecution and imprisonment. The failed response I have documented both by providers and the SCR in the Pelka case was not, therefore, due to a lack of commitment to domestic violence intervention or a lack of empathy for abused women and their children. To the contrary, both the clinicians and the SCR saw Mariusz's abuse as an individual and family problem with no direct bearing on the global deterioration they observed in Magdalena and the children.

In its summary, the SCR described domestic abuse as a "major pattern of this family's lifestyle," and attributed the fact that she was abused by three partners not to any failure in the protective response, let alone to the criminality of the men involved, but to Magdalena's inability "to detect abusive relationships" and not "learn" from previous experiences," so that "her own behaviors" (e.g., her violence) helped "fuel "altercations." Trained to see domestic violence through a lens of individual and family problems, the numerous assaults, rapes, and strangulations she reported became "altercations." Whereas the record indicates Magdalena called police numerous times, frankly discussed abuse with home visitors, her GP, visiting nurses and probably anyone else who cared to listen, the apparent continuation of abuse was identified with her failure to "detect abusive relationships." By separately cataloging the elements of a single criminal course of conduct—assault, rape, strangulation, stalking, and child abuse—as minor crimes or personal or family troubles, the elaborate apparatus established to protect women and their children from domestic violence had effectively downsized coercive control to better suit social service administration than the justice or equalities agenda.

On July 21, Magdalena told her GP she was having a "domestic problem" with her boyfriend. She was diagnosed as "depressed," prescribed antidepressants and given no follow-up. On August 8, in what is described by police as an "altercation," Mariusz strangled Magdalena so that she lost consciousness, and cut her with a knife, causing a "small cut." Mariusz was drunk, and the children were present. He was arrested, not charged, and returned to the house. Magdalena said he had agreed to stay with a friend.

Magdalena also told police Mariusz had raped her "many times." These allegations were not pursued. The Crown and the trial judge could not have had this encounter in mind when they claimed Magdalena did nothing to expose Mariusz's propensity for violence.

There were also clues that abuse went far beyond physical and sexual assaults on Magdalena. Magdalena told police Mariusz was "using child pornography." The computer was examined and the images were of children who were fully clothed. So the police decided to do nothing. In the context of his campaign of terrorism, an obsession even with clothed children is an implied threat to extend abuse "or else." When Magdalena broached Mariusz's behavior toward the children, he reacted defensively and described her increasing use of amphetamines and cannabis to stay awake, a clue to his campaign to keep her up at night with threats and awaken her at all hours with sexual assaults.

In August 2011, Mariusz was put out of the house. But after three police checkups on August 10, 14, and 18, Magdalena agreed to let him return and "didn't want any more help from police." This did not mean she felt safe, however, but that she felt in as much danger when he was living separately, when he stalked her, as when he was living there. Over the next few months there is scant evidence from the household, indicating that Mariusz held them as virtual hostages at home.

Violence was continuing. On November 14, 2010, Magdalena was seen at the ED because she was "cut by broken glass falling on her." Now, abuse extended to the children. For the first time, Anna is enlisted to help protect Mariusz from disclosure. Police responded to a neighbor's complaint on December 27 and noted the children were present. No referrals were made. On January 6, 2011, Mariusz and Magdalena brought Daniel to the ED with a spinal fracture on his left arm. He had multiple additional bruises on the arm and an additional bruise on his shoulder, which Magdalena attributed to his falling from his bike. The medical examination suggested "twisting" had occurred and that the swelling and pain would not have been delayed, contrary to what the parents claimed. A referral to CLYP failed to turn up any evidence of abuse. When Anna was interviewed, with the friend of Magdalena translating, she confirmed Magdalena's apparently fabricated story. This is first indication of Anna's presence as a witness, covictim of coercion by Mariusz and/or participant in the abuse.

Even as coercive control escalated, police and the social services withdraw. A core assessment in February 2011 concluded abuse was no longer an issue because the couple had stopped drinking, ostensibly because Magdalena was pregnant. Pregnancy is the highest risk point for physical violence and control in abusive relationships both because many narcissistic abusers interpret the impending birth as a competitor for the woman's attention and because she is physically more dependent and vulnerable, a condition which abusive men exploit. So immense is the problem of abuse during pregnancy, that a separate monograph is needed to do it justice.[14] Instead, the Assessment "considered that all of the domestic abuse in the past had been closely related to alcohol misuse." The case was closed by the CLYP in May 2011.

The complex role of alcohol and substance abuse in coercive control is beyond our scope. Suffice it to say, no evidence exists that Magdalena's drinking played an important role. Alcohol and drugs are no more likely to be implicated in coercive control than any number of other social and family problems. Mariusz abused Magdalena when he was sober as well as drunk, and whether Magdalena was drinking or not. Our early research at Yale and case studies show that battered women typically "abuse" alcohol when they supplement their normal drinking in an attempt to medicate the alternating currents of chronic and unpredictable stress associated with coercive control.[15] Meanwhile, while Magdalena undoubtedly drank in excess, as police reports made clear, if providers believed alcoholism was an underlying issue, why was rehabilitation never prescribed or even recommended? More likely, police, health providers, and social work used Magdalena's drinking as another stigmata that disqualified her from having legitimate justice claims. In fact, despite the CLYP conclusion, that drinking had stopped, throughout this period, Mariusz was still drinking heavily, though he was apparently rationing Magdalena's access to alcohol, almost certainly because she fought him when she was "drunk." This was a variation on the CLYP view, that Magdalena's drinking had caused the violence.

The new health visitor for the child received notifications of three previous domestic violence incidents (November 6, 2009; August 8, 2010; December 29, 2010). But because she saw these as "old incidents" in a case that was now closed, they raised no current concerns. An assessor would suspect a shift to other means of coercion and control even if violence stopped.

In an April 4 visit to the antenatal clinic, Magdalena told the midwife and the consultant obstetrician that her partner was pressuring her to get a termination. She denied physical violence and was told what to do if she felt threatened. A letter was sent alerting the GP and the child protection midwife to "social issues" in the case. Forced abortions, like unwanted pregnancies, are common forms of reproductive coercion that accompany coercive control. In addition, because a female partner may be more physically vulnerable or dependent during a pregnancy, abusers often shift to nonphysical forms of control. Magdalena explained the change in her partner's tactics to the clinicians as best she could, even recounting an implied threat that included the fetus. But again, they shared concerns only for her own physical safety and misinterpreted her emphasis on her partner's intimidation and control tactics as "minimization of violence." I commend the GP whose letter in the file calls attention to "social malaise." But our patient and her pregnancy are at imminent risk.

Anna was being kept home from school. Four days after the clinic visits, on April 8, the school wrote Magdalena about her attendance. In itself, this was not remarkable. But read in the context of the history of violence, Magdalena's report of "pressure" and a possible extension of Mariusz's control to the children, Anna's attendance problem merited investigation of the situation at home.

On April 26, 2011, Magdalena was diagnosed at the ED with a severe urinary tract infection and hospital admission was urged to stay. She refused admission, told them she had "no money and no job" and "[had] to be home" because of her partner's job. Offers to call the partner's job and provide child care assistance were refused. The midwife for safeguarding contacted police, reviewed the history of abuse, including Daniel's recent suspicious injury, but when she discovered CLYP had closed the case concluded, "there were no child protection concerns." Here, another opportunity was lost, possibly because the midwife for safeguarding decided not to confront child protection with what was, from my vantage, the first global assessment of the child's risk. Less than two weeks later, on May 5, Magdalena was admitted to the hospital with kidney stones and developed a further infection. On May 10, Mariusz came into the hospital ward, demanded Magdalena be discharged, and pulled the drip out of her arm. No police were called, and Magdalena was allowed "to take her own discharge" later that day against medical advice. In the context of coercive control, Mariusz's intervention amounted to "kidnapping."

Even if our index of suspicion was not raised until now, here was a transparent enactment of coercive control of the woman and fetus, the only such act in the case history. Pleas for help are everywhere: an immigrant woman who is compliant to a fault refuses a hospital admission, insists no one but her can be home (to protect the children) and reveals the material basis for her dependence ("no money, no job"). Her refusal of assistance is also transparent (she has pleaded for help with child care in the past): her problem is not "child care" but Mariusz's insistence that *she* care for the children as he demands. By forcibly kidnapping her from her hospital bed on their watch, he resolves any ambiguity about his demand for her services. The hospital attack is arguably a criminal assault. The midwife for safeguarding sees the big picture, but backs off what she hits a wall. Still, it's hard to contemplate the cynicism needed to turn away at this point: a hospital visit is a rare escape opportunity from coercive control, but Magdalena's time is limited, she is desperate ("no money, no job") and before they can respond, he is there, snatching her back. Window was opened. Now shut. So is the case. "There are no child protection concerns."

After the hospital grab, the family becomes invisible for the next few months and, because the case has been "closed," is not missed. In cases where coercive control has been ongoing, periods of "no contact" should raise the highest concern that a regime of isolation is being installed, and contact initiated. Magdalena missed all of the prenatal visits arranged for at a new hospital. New appointments were made. But nothing was done to initiate contact.

In July, Magdalena was briefly admitted to the hospital because of possible preterm labor. But she again discharged herself and again denied any physical abuse.

During June and July, Anna was injured on four occasions while at school, three of them to the head, by falling over. Although harmless in themselves, in the context of an ongoing coercive control at home, a cluster of "accidents" such as these would be deemed "highly suspicious of being abuse related."

Whether or not readers still question Magdalena's protestations at trial, three facts seem incontrovertible, that she had reported dozens of violent incidents in the past involving all three partners and would do so again (see July 13 report); that these reports and coincident statements to police and health providers were sufficient to establish the presence of violence (and now coercive control) in the home; and that Magdalena's reports as well as independent evidence confirmed that Daniel, and probably Anna as well, were also targets of abuse. There were also instances when she had denied abuse, during a maternity visit, for example, because she feared Krezolek would beat her and the children or throw them into the street if she talked or she feared police would do nothing, as they had in the past, and things would get worse. Regardless of whether Magdalena's reports were consistent, by the time Daniel was ready for school, Mariusz's abuse of Magdalena and her children was well known to the range of providers involved with the family, even if he was never identified for assessment, interdiction, or management. Nor was his identity, his motives, or his capacity for violence ever in doubt after he kidnapped Magdalena by force in front of hospital staff so she could be home to care for the children.

On July 18, Magdalena reported that Krezolek was "very controlling." Nothing was asked and no follow up suggested. His mother was staying until September from Poland. Baby Adam was born in August 2011. The midwife had a long discussion with the CLYP duty officers prior to discharge about the wisdom of sending Magdalena home with no referral. Since the previous case was closed and no new information had been added, it was decided, a referral would not be helpful. So none was made.

The fetus is an animus of intense jealousy and competition in coercive control as well as an object through which to control the pregnant woman. By contrast a baby's birth is often precipitates a crisis in relationships characterized by coercive control if for no other reason than the unpredictable demands of maternal caretaking wreak havoc on authoritarian regimes of time regulation and exclusive possessiveness. Mariusz had demanded Magdalena terminate the pregnancy in April and had strangled Magdalena in July, in her last trimester, when she reached out to police for help to leave him. Baby Adam's birth and the arrival of Mariusz' mother from Poland presented the ideal time to for a global assessment of the safety situation in the home, including a full work up of Magdalena, Anna and Daniel for coercive control. In a global assessment, the well-being the safety, well-being and self-sufficiency of all members of the family is assumed to be a function of the absolute level of violence and coercive control in the home, regardless of whether each person has been separately targeted. Although Daniel may not have as yet been harmed by Mariusz, for instance, his enhanced risk is implied by the threats to the newborn, intimidation of Anna, the disablement of Magdalena and control over her function as caretaker. At this point, today in England, Scotland and many other countries and some U.S. States, Mariusz Krezolek could have been charged with the serious crime of coercive control and removed from the home and community. Had Krezolek been appropriately arrested and charged, Daniel and Magdalena would be alive.

Daniel Pelka: Child Abuse as Tangential Spouse Abuse

Daniel started school on September 14, 2011. Within the first week, Anna had two more injuries associated with accidental falls at school.

When Daniel entered school, at age four, the end game began. From then on, Daniel was visible to the community on a daily basis and Mariusz's only hope of concealing his abuse was to extend his coercive control of Daniel to his behavior at school. Since it was inevitable that Daniel would be "seen" at school, it was essential to Mariusz that he not be "heard" and that Magdalena manage any concerns about his appearance without revealing her own predicament. Mariusz now supplemented nutritional restriction with daily interrogations and indoctrination sessions designed to instill strict adherence about what could or could not be said. Daniel was beaten, tied to a chair, left alone for long periods of time in a room with only a mattress, and denied access to toileting. Mariusz also escalated his control over Magdalena, micromanaging her relationship to Daniel while using a combination of shouted curses, physical abuse and sexual assaults in ways that made her numb. Magdalena was to clean Daniel up, dress him for school, get his biscuit for breakfast and pack his hunk of bread and piece of cheese for lunch. After dinner, Mariusz questioned Daniel about whom he talked to during the day; Daniel's "success" at the evening interrogation determined what would happen to Magdalena as well as to Daniel, whether she'd be allowed to sleep lying down, for example, or raped or beaten or starved. This was way too much for Daniel and he became so emotionally confounded that speech itself became fraught. When Daniel couldn't participate in the interrogation, Mariusz became furious and blamed Magdalena. At this point, an emergency rescue would have prevented Daniel's death. But there was not enough time to prepare or investigate a charge of coercive control against Mariusz. I will briefly replay the end of the story, primarily to provide closure. But a forensics of coercive control is designed to provide access to an abuse dynamic before it has encompassed children, by recognizing the implied threat posed by the range of liberty harms to adults when they first take hold in the insults, injuries, and indignities of personal life. Because coercive control is an ongoing offense that involves multiple elements and crosses social space, it is not easy to "crime" and more closely resembles a complex financial scam than a simple assault or burglary. But once it is ended, most of its effects can be reversed or remedied.

Up until the time Mariusz stepped up his abuse of Magdalena and enlisted her as his surrogate in controlling Daniel at school, the new coercive control laws could have protected the mother and children. The catalog of acts constituting the crime included dozens of physical assaults, sexual assaults, and incidents of stalking; destruction of property threats, including threats to kill; and instances of isolation, stalking, psychological terrorism, financial manipulation, and psychological abuse affecting Magdalens and the children and extending to all areas of their lives and gleaned from the parties, neighbors, witnesses, family members, and service professionals. The information needed to charge Mariusz was readily available through medical, police, and child service records, eye-witness accounts (as in the kidnapping), victim and witness statements, and from Mariusz's own statements. Even if available information provided only a small sample of what was truly going on in the family, little more than a willingness to entertain the possibility would be needed to recognize a comprehensive form of enslavement in our midst. Even a modest prison sentence for Mariusz would have kept Daniel and Anna safe when they set foot in the schoolyard. Framed as a single course of malevolent conduct, the same events that shared into fragments during the years when the Pelka/Luczak/Krezolek family was being "served" fall seamlessly into place along a continuum of coercion and control that marks a clear pathway for child saving and woman saving.

La Fin: From Tangential Spouse Abuse to Homicide of a Child

Day after day, a mother would present a cleanly dressed, well-groomed child at school in an ever more desperate state of physical and emotional disrepair. And what about the mother? However much Magdalena prepared for the day, she was increasingly wan, depressed, and unresponsive. Did everyone at the school really think it possible this "immature, self-involved and semi-literate woman" was simply too naive to appreciate how being identified as the mother of such a child would make her appear? The woman was desperate, not naive, and extremely brave to be pleading for help in the face of tyrannous odds, albeit through silent witness. Presenting her son as living contradiction of her making took guts. This is another example of a phenomenon we find repeatedly with the children of coercive control, that they are "invisible in plain sight."

As the anxiety created by risking discovery by having to separate from Daniel each day mounted, Mariusz intensified his surveillance of their behavior at home, fearful that even the smallest unchecked impulse would explode the entire façade of his control. Nightly interrogations were followed by crackdowns on "betrayals" by Magdalena: she was no longer allowed to sneak Daniel "illegal" foods, or to remove him off schedule from the "cold bath" or feed him in the tub. Whereas before, he could threaten or punish Daniel to hurt Magdalena, now, Mariusz depended on her to control Daniel during a time and in a space where he had no direct control over her and where betrayal was a constant threat. Tightening the reins on her at home—depriving Magdalena of food alongside Daniel, using rape as a weapon—merely made the morning contradiction more glaring, when, under his screaming gaze, she applied concealing creams to herself and Daniel to hide the bruises. Where his primary objective had been to control Magdalena, now Mariusz stepped in to exert direct control over the boy's physical and psychological being, making him the "primary victim" of his coercive control. Ironically, this choice made Mariusz more vulnerable to detection and interdiction. Daniel no longer saw Magdalena as an intermediary, but a fellow captor.

The experience of victimization was mutual. Magdalena initially colluded in Daniel's suffering, primarily to minimize her own. She had rationalized her behavior when she did so by assuming Mariusz would only make things worse if she did nothing. Pushing the boundaries of Mariusz's regulation of Danial also allowed her to test her mettle against the limits of his authority in ways she was terrified to do where his rules concerning her behavior applied. Magdalena's transgressions went only so far, however, and she was aware that Daniel's deterioration had been only slowed by the little extra food she got him and the few blows she prevented, not stalled, and that his overall downward trajectory would be transparent.

It was from the perspective of prisoners on work release that Magdalena and Daniel approached the school. No surveillance was in place. But the nightly interrogation sessions made Magdalena feel that Mariusz might as well have been listening in. The gambit she chose was to plead by rote imitation. When Magdalena told the teachers not to give the obviously hungry boy anything more than the lunch she provided, she transferred the agonizing dilemma she felt at home to them. This was as much resistance as she had the courage to muster, to show them the impossible choice she faced. Now, they too would have to choose between what was "safe" for them (and please "the mother") and what was best for the child. The teachers chose not to be distracted from their primary charge and saw the mother as capricious rather than strategic. Since the scars of healing often appeared hours after the morning cream was applied, simply taking Daniel to school as she was told was an act of rebellion against Mariusz that could expose him. It should have done so. I am certain that the teachers "knew." Whether they understood what they knew without a coercive control framework, I cannot say.

Entering school was also a crossroads for Daniel. Now, if he needed more food, he had to secure it himself, by borrowing or stealing from other students or "dumpster diving." These activities were strictly forbidden at home, where Mariusz interrogated Daniel nightly; and when Daniel naively confessed, he administered nightly punishment. The consequence of severely limiting Daniel's diet was to set off a downward spiral of begging, stealing, interrogation, punishment, and further deterioration. When Mariusz realized that Daniel was losing his grasp, he told the boy to remain silent at school. The result was the "voicelessness" that Daniel's teachers and assessors mistook for the diffidence of an immigrant child. But if he was not speaking directly about what was being done to him at home, Daniel was talking loudly in other ways; he was begging others for food; even his stealing, which was observed by teachers, was a form of talking. Then there were the visible bruises for which he was as guileless as guiltless. These were observed, recorded by the young teaching assistants in the classroom, and the information was conveyed to the Head. The school was the penultimate point of rescue. The pediatric visit was the last.

* * *

Starting with a child's death, a forensic analysis based on coercive control reframed this case of child abuse as an expression of the tyranny exerted over the woman in this family (i.e., "tangential spouse abuse") and of the struggle of all victimized family members against this tyranny. However insane or impulse-ridden his behavior may have been, once Mariusz usurped command over Magdalena's life, his strategy evolved logically in response to challenges or dilemma she posed to his singular interest in "dominance" as well as to challenges posed by Daniel and Anna. Thus, Mariusz attempted to manage the threat of exposure when Daniel entered school by escalating his coercive control of both parties, taking Daniel and Magdalena as direct targets of binding, isolation, starvation, and physical abuse rather than playing them off against each other as he'd done in the past.

But what if the tragic consequence was not yet "known?" I have entered the case at various points to illustrate how the model could have been used to decipher the logic of coercive control and elicit a vocabulary of motives consistent with early intervention. The utility of the model as a heuristic ended when it became clear that two options that would have prevented the tragedies had been effectively foreclosed, Mariusz's arrest and incarceration and Magdalena's escape with the children. From then on, we are in forensic mode: I interpret Magdalena's action and Daniel's actions dialectically, as simultaneously expressing diminished autonomy and the struggle to resist diminishment, an example of "control in the context of no control." They do not collude in their own demise. Although Anna is not nearly so constrained as her younger brother, we are also obliged to consider that at its most apparently "collusive" (when she lies about the source of her brother's injuries, e.g.), that her behavior may also include an element of rebellion, resistance, and alliance with Daniel. This conjecture about Anna's motive is not a conclusion, but a hypothetical construction laid out as a way to listen, watch, and learn what questions to ask. Such conjectures are invaluable to identify moments of resistance amid apparent compliance with evil, to defend women and children whose inaction implies passivity, and to restore the sense of agency and pride among survivors. Even in hindsight, to seriously consider the sort of reframing process I propose here requires we imagine our subjects as fully entitled persons to start, as citizen children and future adults, who have equal claims to rights and liberties whether they are young, female or immigrant, however they are raced or sexed, old or native born. No one should be relegated to naught on a state registry. Why so many good people did so many bad things in the Pelka case is puzzling. But the facts are not unique. Nor will having a coercive control model in hand automatically thwart the urge of many otherwise well-intentioned professionals to retreat from their principles and best instincts in the face of terroristic threats to others. "What I will tell my Guarda?" the Irish Police Captain asked when he was instructed to place a priority on coercive control. "Do I say, 'Let that man go who has just stolen a woman's I-Phone and computer and respond to the 'Domestic?'" I sat silent. Then the Deputy Chief rose. A slight, gray-haired woman who looked to be in her early sixties, she spoke in a thick brogue. "Young man, you tell your officer she's bringing Liberty through the door." So, I hope, by giving fear the name and face of coercive control, we can help our professionals find the courage they need to know what they already know.

Had Magdalena and her children been recognized as victims of coercive control early on and appropriate intervention pursued, two lives and countless hours of human suffering would have been spared and thousands of hours of service time could have been put to a useful purpose. As a heuristic, the coercive control framework supports decisive, early intervention such as an arrest or a protective order based on relatively limited information (three or four reported incidents and the application of a straightforward assessment tool) and follow-up planning for even more decisive action (e.g., imprisonment) based on predictions about the future if other elements of coercive control are manifest. In both court and community contexts, the paradigm is most helpful where the early presentations of a case draw attention to a variety of sources that confound clear assessment. For example I suspect coercive control whenever a client's report reflects a discrepancy between the level of fear/dependency experienced and the violence/threats used to elicit it. In the community setting, in the past, coercive control cases had been experienced reflexively as an accumulation of "nuisance" calls that frustrated front-line responders who often responded passively (by "withdrawal"), aggressively (labeling the victim as "well known") or passive-aggressively ("everyone is going to jail"). In the Pelka case, the prevailing practice was to keep the disparate records of the numerous encounters with Mariusz and Magdalena at distal service points, so many police calls with police, home visits with social work, midwife visits with the health service, and so forth, and then, usually in response to an incident considered emergent, to "coordinate" a best response by scanning the various fragment summaries. In the new approach, the additive weight of repeat calls signals a coercive control investigation through the multiple sites of a family's life-cycle seeking a single vector explanation. In this case, providers had almost a two-year window on Mariusz's abuse between the time he was identified as a repeat domestic violence offender and when he first targeted Daniel. During that time, evidence was accumulating through several hundred encounters he and Magdalena had with dozens of police, health visitors, social workers, teachers, midwives, and others. Had the system been able to take the cumulative effect of Mariusz's oppression into account, Mariusz would have arrested and charged with "kidnapping" or a similarly serious charge when he forcefully removed Magdalena from the birthing clinic. Instead, the CLYP had closed the case, leaving front-line responders without backup in the wake of a resurgence of incidents requiring a forceful response. Instead of heading downstream to rescue those who can be saved from drowning, the coercive control framework refocuses attention at the source of the problem upstream by organizing the initial morass of seemingly trivial events (drownings) into an intelligible pattern of dominance.

I return to the most controversial claim in the book in the Conclusion, to move from a forensic of coercive control to new criminal and family law that recognizes the secondary victimization of children to monopolize the rights and privileges in a household as a serious criminal offense. Suffice it to say here that I foresee a major shift in our concern for children from their basic physical health and safety to their well-being as fully entitled rights-bearing persons. It is against this principle of children as equal persons that I reframe their right to be free of all forms of "coercion" and "control," both those imposed secondary to the abuse of their mother, and those in which children are "weaponized" to subordinate their mother.

9

A Modern Media

Rachel and Her Children

I entered the Pelka case after the child was killed and the mother had committed suicide. When I met Rachel and her children, they were still at risk.

The "facts" were stacked against the mother. Rachel was charged with a felony, "creating a risk of injury" to her five children, and faced a long prison sentence despite having suffered horrendous physical and sexual abuse along with hostage-like levels of control from her live-in boyfriend, Roberto Sabastian. Rachel's five children were in foster care, including the newborn, whose father was Roberto.

The newspaper's story was headlined "Modern-Day Medea." I reviewed the grizzly photos of the children's injuries, then searched medical records, police reports, witness interviews, and DCF files, hoping to find references to domestic violence. What I did learn was that each of the five children had been fathered by a different man, the four youngest by illegal immigrants from Mexico. An earlier apartment had been left in complete shambles. When the water was turned off, according to a neighbor, Rachel had stolen water.

Roberto had been returned to Mexico after a short sentence. Unlike Magdalena Luczak, who denied abusing her son, Rachel insisted she was the only one who had hurt the children. Her oldest son Marc, confirmed she'd hit him. The State's attorney offered a deal.

Rachel had confessed. Her son testified she had hit him, and there was strong circumstantial evidence supporting the charges. But I recommended they reject a deal. Rachel and the children convinced me that their basic rights and liberties had been abrogated. We convinced the Court that Rachel should not be held criminally liable for the children's injuries, and they were returned to her. To achieve this outcome, I framed the interactions between Rachel and her children as the response to the predicament they all faced due to Roberto's coercive control.

Children of Coercive Control. Evan Stark, Oxford University Press. © Oxford University Press 2023.
DOI: 10.1093/oso/9780197587096.003.0010

Here, as in most of the previous cases, the abuse of the children was "tangential" to the spouse abuse. But in this instance, Rachel also hurt the children, not only Roberto. As it turned out, her actions were constrained by Roberto's implication that if she didn't hurt the children, "I would do worse." But this fact alone does not explain the choices she made. Nor does it explain her inaction when Roberto placed Marc's hand on the stove burner to "teach him a lesson." Or Maria's belt marks. Or why Claudia was left in the basement. The children's claims for justice from Rachel are more straightforward than Daniel's claims on Magdalena.

Our defense in this case rests on the systemic nature of coercive control rather than the constraints Rachel faced at each misstep. I argue that once Rachel's capacities to protect herself and the children were disabled by coercive control, her only choices involved varying degrees of oppression and unfreedom for herself and the children. Once the minimum conditions for free and safe choice are off the table, Rachel bears no legal responsibility for her "bad choices." But what about the children's independent claims to safety and autonomy? Do they share Rachel's perspective that hers were among the best possible among a small range of bad options? What do the children of coercive control say when they are invited to speak?

Rachel was physically injured more seriously than Magdalena Luczak. However, their predicaments were similar. Both women were forced to negotiate for their own and their children's safety within the context of their partner's total control, "control in the context of no control." Things turned out relatively well for Rachel, all things considered. Nevertheless, until Rachel's acquittal, she and her children were no less victims of the justice and welfare systems than Magdalena.

Background

On September 11, 2014, based on injuries observed on the hands of seven-year-old Marc, the principal of the Orange, New Jersey, school reported a case of suspected child abuse to the Newark department and the New Jersey Department of Children and Families (NJ DCF). Further investigation revealed numerous bruises on the boy's back, buttocks, legs, and arms. Marc told police that he had been struck recently with a belt and slapped by his mother, Rachel, and her life-in boyfriend, Roberto, after he was found playing with a BB gun.

When Marc failed to return home as usual, Rachel called the school and was told he had missed the bus. Shortly afterward, the police arrived at the house, accompanied by a caseworker from DCF. Rachel's four other children were taken into custody, including a newborn, and she and Roberto were placed in the back of a police car and taken to the station for questioning.

A week earlier, the same DCF investigator had visited the home and found the baby in the basement washroom. Her report of the scene had the poignancy of a Dickens' novel.

> The baby, Claudia, age 1 year, was lying on the mattress with a bottle in her mouth. She had a variety of blankets around her. She was noticeably dirty, has a smell about her. Diaper (cloth) soaked completely. A small bowl with bits of food on it lay on the mattress next to her. She cried a bit. Advised mother that child can't be left alone down here. . . . Mother said "Ok, I respect your opinion, if that's what you think, I'll take her out." When the mother didn't move. . . . I moved aside the bed frame and mattress and lifted the baby out.

Importantly, the cellar could only be accessed from an outside bulkhead. The caseworker accompanied Rachel around the house and into the first floor. Dickens redux:

> In the one bedroom, door closed, 3 year old Maria was playing in closet. She appeared fairly clean and dressed. The room was dark, with dirty smell, dirty sheets and bunk beds. Smelled of feces, although none were visible. Mother acknowledged she could not provide for Claudia's needs.

No action or services were recommended.

At the Robert Wood Johnson Hospital, an examination of the children revealed numerous bruises on the three- and four-year-old girls, almost certainly due to physical abuse. Of particular note were the marks on the back and legs of the three-year-old girl, Maria.

During questioning by detectives, Rachel admitted hitting Marc with a belt in the BB gun incident. She was the only one to "discipline" her children she insisted, defending her actions as "how I was treated when I was a girl." Roberto also admitted hitting the children and using a belt on Maria. The couple was charged with four counts of risk of injury to a minor, offenses related to the alleged abuse of Marc, Stephanie, and Maria and the neglect of Claudia.

By the time the public defender got approval for my services, Rachel had made bail and was staying at a battered woman's shelter. The pictures in my mind were not pretty. What scenario could justify the harms these children had suffered? I tried "anticipatory empathy," a technique of relating we'd learned in social work school. I thought of Hedda Nussbaum, whom we met in chapter 2. Hedda had been widely condemned by the feminist community for failing to protect Lisa Steinberg even though, at the time of her death, Joel Steinberg's abuse had rendered Hedda barely recognizable.

But Hedda had never abused her child, and Steinberg's abuse of Hedda was well documented, even if he was never charged with assaulting her. Apart from one police note, there was nothing in any official documents to support the public defender's hope that Rachel could benefit from a battered woman's defense. Roberto's short arrest sheet consisted only of public nuisance offenses such as "drunk and disorderly," and "leaving the scene of an accident" that supported the State's case that the children were hurt amid a chaotic and disorganized family.

If the medical findings for the children, Rachel's confession, and Marc's statements to police held up, a plea bargain offered the best chance.

Rachel

My preconceptions of Rachel left me unprepared for the tall, striking, impeccably dressed, and articulate twenty-seven-year-old woman who met me at the Women's Center in the working class town of Jersey City, New Jersey. Rachel shared negative expectations of our encounter.

R: My therapist holds you in very high esteem. To be honest, I thought "another psycho guy." I had a really bad outlook after dealing with Dr. J.

During her court-ordered evaluation at the Child Study Center at NYU Lagonne Hospital in Hackensack, the psychiatrist had refused to interview Rachel without Roberto in the room.

R: He said Roberto would be handcuffed to the chair. I said "I don't care if he's handcuffed to the wall." And I told him that I didn't even want to be in the same building with this man. It was already court-ordered that it be separate. I made him call my attorney. . . . I spoke to him on the phone . . . and he told him "they are to meet separately." So, the psychiatrist changed his tone.

Rachel was capable of anger, when it involved standing up for herself. She was anxious that Roberto would return illegally from Mexico (which he did) and furious that DCF had taken her children. But, when we met, she showed no signs of depression, inappropriate affect, hypervigilance, or other signs of PTSD or another psychiatric disorder. If Rachel was not suffering the effects of trauma, why had this strong-willed twenty-seven-year-old woman stolen water from her neighbors, abused Maria, beaten Marc with a belt, or left her one-year-old in a basement to which there was no access from the house?

Family Background

The youngest of three children, Rachel no longer saw her father, an alcoholic. She remembers him telling her, "I had my son and daughter. I didn't need you." Her mother still lives in the area, but their relationship is also tense. Rachel moved in with her boyfriend's family at fourteen, after her parents moved "yet again," so she could finish high school. The boyfriend sexually assaulted her repeatedly. Fearing she would be forced to move out before graduating, she never told the family, with whom she still remains close.

At eighteen, Rachel met Joe, Marc's father. She was living independently in a condo, had a car, was working at a bank in the affluent town of Princeton, New Jersey, earning $400 a week, and caring for her sister's daughter. The couple discussed marriage and Joe put a deposit on a ring. Then, he walked out. Although she was using birth control, Rachel became pregnant, was laid off, and moved back home. She decided to have the baby. As she explained:

R: Religion was part of it. That and I thought if I don't have Joe, at least I have a part of Joe. And when I told Joe, he said well that's your problem. And I said I wasn't asking anything of you. I just wanted you to know you're going to be a father whether you're happy with it or not.

Rachel suffered from toxemia, and Marc was born two months premature.

In the evenings, Rachel often brought Marc to the diner where her mother and sister worked. A number of undocumented Mexican men lived at an adjacent boarding house. Thousands of miles from their families, the young men gravitated naturally to the already bilingual mother. Stephanie was born two years after Marc, in 1987, the child of an immigrant Rachel met at the diner. Stephanie was also premature and suffered from colic and a milk allergy that made her difficult to train and moody. Stephanie's father helped care for her until he returned to Mexico when she was three.

When Rachel became pregnant yet again, this time with a younger man, his older brother immediately ordered him to return to Mexico, which he did. He returned shortly after his daughter's birth and gave her some financial support. The girl was named Katalina.

When Rachel met David, Claudia's father, her own father had moved out and she and her children were living with her mother (who worked nights). Rachel and David dated for some time, lived together, discussed marriage, and planned to have a baby. Based on her prior experience, Rachel insisted that David inform her in advance if he had to return home. However, shortly after Rachel became pregnant, in February 2005, David left suddenly for Mexico. Rachel later learned that he had gone home to break a prior engagement which he had kept from her. When he left, however, she felt abandoned and angry.

Given what Roberto did to Rachel and the seeming disregard of her children with which she was charged, it may seem ironic that Rachel traced her attraction to the immigrant men to their gentleness and their "family orientation."

STARK: So when you say "family," what do you have in mind?
R: I guess the family I was trying to create. . . . And that's the first thing that started me talking to most of these people is they started talking to my children and doing things for the children.

Rachel was also rebelling against her father, who was openly contemptuous of Hispanics and blacks. A child of an alcoholic, she had an overreliance on external cues for signs of love.

Sexual abuse as a teen and parental rejection scarred Rachel's self-esteem and added to the self-doubts evoked by approaching potential partners with a premade family. Rachel defended against these "hidden injuries" by developing the capacity for self-care evident in her determination to finish school as well as for a certain detachment from physical and psychological pain.[1] Although these traits may have increased her vulnerability to abuse, Rachel chose boyfriends whom she could dominate, at least emotionally and intellectually, an obvious contrast to her tumultuous relationship with her father. But the impermanence of her male partners largely reflected men's well-known problems with emotional commitment and the divided and inevitably transitory loyalties of immigrant workers, who may be called home or forced to move at any moment. As Rachel put it, "unfortunately, the only man who stuck around was the one I wanted to get rid of."

Rachel had never been struck by a man before meeting Roberto. She used the same physical discipline with her own children she had witnessed growing up in an extended Italian family network, including spanking and an occasional slap. She wishes she had learned alternatives and admitted "overreacting" by yelling a good deal while trying to toilet train Stephanie, unaware of the physical problems created by her allergy. But I saw no evidence of child abuse or neglect prior to her meeting Roberto. Apart from a report by Marc that he was once slapped by David—an incident Rachel cannot confirm—none of the other men she dated hit or otherwise mistreated the children. To the contrary, the men in her life treated the children more kindly than they did her.

The Relationship with Roberto

Before David left for Mexico, he introduced Rachel to his cousin, Roberto, who began working at the diner. David asked Rachel to teach Roberto English, and they met almost daily. When David left, Roberto spent time with the children, attended birthing classes, and gave Rachel general support in a difficult time. She was attracted to Roberto. When David returned in April 2005, she kept her distance, not wanting to be hurt again. David began "harassing" Rachel, making threatening phone calls and warning he would come for his baby after she was born. Roberto offered to move into Rachel's mother's house to "protect" her, treated her with "respect," and initially slept on the living room couch. He was, she reports, "my knight in shining armor." Shortly afterward, her "knight" moved into her bedroom.

Note, Roberto established a relation of dominance prior to physically assaulting Rachel, and early in the relationship, his violence was sporadic and could easily have been misinterpreted as impulsive. The following description divides the relationship into three phases, each characterized by a specific constellation of coercion and control and corresponding "arenas of resistance and compliance" where Rachel could weigh her options and "breathe the air of a free woman." As I've indicated, these arenas are made up both of literal "safety zones" like physical spaces, tangible objects, persons, websites, and the like, and psychological strategies for defending against, escaping, or minimizing abuse such as "forgetting." Children adapt to coercive control is similar ways, devising strategies, carving out places, fixing on objects, relationships, choosing magic words or phrases, focusing on a point in space or on the wallpaper, real or imaginary, on which to displace, defuse, disperse, or attach a portion of their emotive attention at the height of stress. These behavioral adaptations are both a defensive response to intrusions on autonomy and assertive of an alterity that remains beyond the grasp of the aggressor. Throughout the relationship, as quickly as Rachel forged them, Roberto sought to search out and close these zones of safety and autonomy, to "get your full attention," he would say, increasingly restricting Rachel's mobility as well as her decisional autonomy. In the third phase I describe, which culminated in the arrests and the children's removal, Roberto's control over Rachel's everyday life became comprehensive. In defense, Rachel withdrew emotionally, showing less and less reaction to Roberto's physical assaults. Only then, when she denied him direct access, did Roberto turn to the children, hoping to exact the desired response from Rachel by hurting them or having her hurt them, the pattern we now can recognize as "child abuse as tangential spouse abuse."

During the approximately two years they were together, Roberto assaulted Rachel several hundred times, a pattern in violence that is best described as "ongoing" or "continuous" rather than as repeated, for instance, particularly when we appreciate the range of tactics he used. At the time of her arrest, Rachel was entrapped much in the way a hostage or prisoner-of-war might be, and her capacity to resist or escape his abuse had been largely disabled, though not completely, as we will see.

The Onset of Abuse: February–September 2013

Roberto was initially "respectful" of Rachel's feelings.

RACHEL: Actually I think I had an instant attraction to him. Because he did something for me right off. I met him when he first came into the country. It was my birthday and I was upset at David because David wasn't going to spend my birthday with me. And here we were at the checkout. Roberto, who I knew didn't have anything to speak of, when he found out it was my birthday, he bought me a rose. Because that's out of custom, because one man doesn't buy another's man's woman a gift.

At first, Rachel interpreted Roberto's numerous suggestions for how she should live as concern for her family's well-being.

RACHEL: David was hassling me and Roberto made suggestions about how to handle it. "You shouldn't really hang around the dinner, it doesn't look good for you and your kids, you should keep them at home. . . . Better to have cooked meals at home, than out at the diner. You'll feel better about yourself if you take care of the house . . . and your kids."
STARK: So he had a real idea of what a traditional woman was like?
RACHEL: Yeah.
STARK: And alot of those things did make sense?
RACHEL: Yeah. And I did feel better. Because the kids and I would be home.

Shortly after they began living together, Roberto suggested that Rachel rename her daughter Maria after his grandmother. Although the change was opposed by her family, she felt "it made us more like a family." Under the guise of romantic love, Roberto had established a pattern of deferential behavior with expectations for obedience whose substance extended to general subordination. Rachel asserted herself against his control, broke things off, resisted, and negotiated. Roberto resorted to violence to disregard the limits she set. Rachel threw him out.

The first assault occurred several months later. Rachel had asked Roberto not to drink around her, and he had agreed to do his drinking at the boarding house where David and the other Mexican men lived. One evening, when Rachel went to pick Roberto up at the boarding house, David also came down and tried to talk to her. She asked Roberto's permission, and he replied, "you do what you think is right." Rachel was six months pregnant at the time with David's baby. An argument ensued during which Roberto told David, "she's mine, she does what I tell her," and ordered Rachel into the car. Then, Roberto told David, "I can do anything to her and she's still mine." He told her to relax and stop crying, then suddenly slapped her across the mouth. Rachel was shocked. Then, he told Rachel to kiss him, which she did. On the way home, he broke both the dashboard and the windshield with his fist. Roberto passed out when they arrived home. But the next day Roberto apologized and blamed his behavior on the alcohol. She told him if he hit her again, they were through.

Two weeks later, David called. Although Rachel did not talk to him, Roberto began to cry, then became furious, slapped Rachel and then hit her with the back of his hand until she bled. Rachel called a cab and threw Roberto out of the house.

After only two weeks, Roberto was calling every day, crying, telling her he "made a mistake" and promising not to drink. Unlike her father, both her brother and uncle were violent when drunk, making Roberto's interpretation of his "loss of control" credible. Believing he really wanted her, she allowed him to return. His violence now became routinized. It seemed impossible for her to get him out. Within days of his return, Roberto was pushing, shoving, and slapping Rachel almost every day. Sometimes because he'd been "hassled" at work by David or other Mexicans because of his relationship with Rachel. He was constantly correcting her behavior and the behavior of the children, explaining after beatings that, "if your father had disciplined you and raised you to be a decent woman, you wouldn't be where you are in life today. Somebody has to do it."

Roberto was violent several times a week, but he only hit Rachel when her mother was out of the house or when she and the children were in bed. Roberto treated her like his servant. She was not going out "at all" any longer and spent her days cleaning the house and cooking for Roberto. She was treating him "like a king" and "giving him what he wanted before he wanted it," following an exact schedule that he required. She would cash her check, turn the money over to Roberto, and he would give her money for food or clothes, as he thought appropriate. She had to account for every penny and was not permitted to go to the store alone. If he couldn't go with her, her mother would do the shopping for her. She was learning to be a "Senora."[2]

Her regime was definitely patriarchal, but Rachel felt her life was generally "calm" and "family-like." Despite restrictions on her own femininity, she felt minimally restricted in her parenting, and all ostensible signs suggest she was an exemplary mother. Marc and Stephanie were in Head Start and Rachel had only Maria with her during the day. Rachel and the children were now on AFDC. Roberto played no role in disciplining the children and never hit them. Nevertheless, Marc and Stephanie were aware of the fights.

The Escalation of Violence and Control:
September 2013–January 2014

Roberto wanted sex at least once a day, often two or three times. One night after intercourse, when Rachel was 7.5 months pregnant with Claudia, she began to bleed. The doctor proscribed sex until after the birth. But several weeks later, Roberto returned from work, demanded sex, and, when Rachel told him "I can't," he raped her, telling her he didn't care what happened to "David's baby." Immediately following the assault, Rachel experienced contractions and bleeding. Roberto accompanied her to the hospital, staying with her "even to the bathroom," and attended the birth. This showed, she felt, that "he loved me more than anybody ever had." But, when the doctor handed him a girl "who looks just like his father," he hissed, "I'd like to throw her right in the garbage because that's what she is, just like you."

There were still "good times." When Roberto and Rachel went away for a weekend, they planned to move to Mexico, buy a house, and create a "real family," a dream Rachel held dear.

Violence escalated one evening when Roberto came home, supposedly upset because someone had taunted him about Rachel at work. She was in the process of changing. She knew she would be hit because "his eyes were black." "When he's like that," she says, "once he gets started, he doesn't stop." Although she begged him to "just talk," he pushed her around the bedroom. He punched her and "backhanded" her. Then he did something he would do frequently in the future: he removed his belt and began snapping it in a taunting way. He started off by hitting her lightly with the belt. Then he hit her harder and harder. When she tried to get away, he kicked at her, hitting her in the face, blackening her eye. She fell to the floor and he began to kick her. When her nose starting bleeding, he stopped. This incident occurred just one month after Claudia's birth.

As a result of this beating, Rachel had problems with her ear. She saw a doctor who recognized the injury had resulted from a beating, but did not counsel her or otherwise intervene. Shortly after this assault, Rachel stopped responding when she was hit, neither crying nor begging Roberto to stop, both of which had "infuriated" him in the past. Although Roberto always blamed his drinking and promised to stop, Rachel insists he was abusive whether or not he was drunk. Then, one night, two weeks later, Roberto and his "best friend" returned home drunk and Rachel served them dinner. When his friend asked why Rachel had a black eye and was covered with bruises, pointing out that Roberto had everything a Mexican man could want ("she waits on you like a king"), Roberto brutally beat the man, "turning the house into 'a holocaust'" with blood and broken furniture everywhere. Rachel intervened to save the man's life and was herself struck. When Roberto realized what he'd done, they washed the man up and drove him home. They took him to a doctor several days later.

In November 2013, when Claudia was two months old, Rachel found out she was again pregnant, this time as the result of a rape by Roberto. That night, Roberto punched her repeatedly in the stomach, causing her to miscarry. He said the miscarriage was her fault because she aggravated him. He demanded sex immediately after the miscarriage.

Rachel was now completely isolated from her friends, whom Roberto believed were not good for her or else were jealous of what they had. For her birthday he had gotten her a car, which she taught him how to drive, and he occasionally drove himself to work. In general, however, she drove him to work, picked him up, and drove the children to school, but was not allowed to drive the car alone or for any other purpose. He carefully monitored what she and the children ate, where they went, how they dressed, insisting that Rachel wear only dresses, "never pants."

Roberto had started to spank and slap the children. At first they argued about whether this was right, Roberto insisting that since he was their father, he should discipline them. Rachel soon stopped protesting.

Concerned that Stephanie was not wearing appropriate clothes, the director of Head Start talked to Rachel about abuse and warned that it could "overflow" and affect the children. The discussion was couched in such vague terms, Rachel was not sure what she was talking about. In any case, her own abuse was not identified or her need for help was not addressed.

Rachel became increasingly depressed after Claudia's birth, sensing she was "trapped" with Roberto and that "there was no way out." One night, when he insisted she drink with him, he put a tattoo of his name on her arm, to show the world she was his "now and always." That night, she felt completely degraded and cut her wrist in a suicide attempt, stopping only when Claudia, who was in her room, began to cry. When Roberto saw what she had done, he grabbed for the knife, they struggled, and her hand was cut. He called her crazy and bandaged her up. Looking back, Rachel realizes that when she attempted to hurt herself, she was barely aware of the children.

On Christmas Day, 2013, Rachel had Roberto arrested. She had driven him to work, but he needed to take a cab home because the brakes on the car were not working. When he returned, she was leaving to go to her grandmother's house for Christmas dinner with her mother and brother. Her mother and Roberto fought, and Roberto threatened Rachel, who knew she would be beaten whether she stayed or left with her family. Then her mother put her in the car, as a way to protect her, she realizes now. Roberto tried to follow in her new car, but was drunk and wrecked it. He left the car, then called her to come home, said he had a knife, threatened suicide, and talked about them both dying. Terrified, she called the police and returned home, where the police were waiting. They arrested Roberto for "evading responsibility" for the accident. But the police also asked Rachel to accompany Roberto to jail and to court the next day to help translate for him. When he was released, Roberto sent the children to their rooms, turned up the radio, and told her ,"You said you were afraid—I'm going to teach you to be afraid now." He beat her severely, then acted "as if nothing had happened."

Shortly after Christmas, 2013, they moved out of her mother's into a house of their own. At this point, "fights" (pushing, slapping, etc.) were less common than "beatings" in which Roberto punched, kicked, and whipped Rachel to "discipline" her. Rachel's mother, Roberto's friends, and the children were aware of and repeatedly exposed to Roberto's abuse of Rachel.

By this time, Roberto's abuse of Rachel was "well known" to police, Head Start, and Rachel's friends and family. Note that each had tried to intervene in their own way by focusing on Rachel. Each intervention made things worse. Had the police opened the window afforded by Roberto's arrest and charged Roberto with the serious continual offense of coercive control against Rachel, no harm would have come to the children.

The Coercive Control Extends to the Children: January–September 2014

Getting their own place completed the process of isolating Rachel and her children from potential sources of support. In the new house, Roberto exercised total control over Rachel, and beatings with objects and threats with weapons alternated with physical abuse, including burning her with cigarettes. The birth of Roberto's son proved only a minor interlude in this escalating pattern of assault and intimidation. Meanwhile, Roberto extended his abuse to the children both directly, by slapping, beating, burning, and whipping them, and indirectly, by forcing Rachel to escalate her own disciplinary practices. Afraid that Rachel might leave or kill him, Roberto ensured that she was never with all the children alone. Meanwhile, Rachel became less and less able to function as an autonomous adult, neglecting basic household chores, losing state assistance, and living for a time without basic comforts. The focus of her life shifted to sheer survival: living like a virtual hostage, every element of her life was oriented toward placating or resisting Roberto, minimizing the hurt he could do to her and the children. Rachel reached out for help, investigating foster care for Claudia for example. She also began to save money to plan their escape.

The previous beating by Roberto when they returned from court convinced Rachel that Roberto could easily kill her. She was under his total control, even with respect to the children. She wrote:

> After that, I listened to his every command. . . . I shower the children at certain times. I shower when he allows. I go to the bathroom when he allows. I have my hair styled how he wants. I sleep when he wants. Get up when he wants.

Rachel and the children would occasionally visit neighbors when Roberto was at work. The neighbors reported her being frequently bruised.

Roberto increasingly used objects and/or weapons in his assaults. Roberto would throw knives at Rachel and threaten her with a knife. One evening, when he held a knife to her throat, she kneed him in the groin, the first time she had physically retaliated. Roberto doubled up and cut her throat with the knife. He dropped the knife, and she picked it up. He told her, "If you're going to use it, make sure I'm down for good."

Roberto put his cigarettes out on Rachel's hand or arm. He would touch her skin with cigarettes to taunt her because she was only allowed to smoke at his discretion. He hit her with bottles. The first few times he burned her with cigarettes she fought back. But then she realized that "if he doesn't get a reaction, he doesn't win." The scars from these assaults are still visible.

After she had threatened Roberto with the knife, he became fearful that she might kill him or poison him. He insisted that she taste all food first, something his father taught him. By this time, Roberto had destroyed or disposed of all possessions that in any way reminded him of Rachel's past.

Roberto became increasingly strict with the children, extending many of the control tactics to them he'd deployed with Rachel. In addition to dictating what they ate, when they slept, and that they took showers, he would occasionally hit Marc, Stephanie, and Maria with his belt. In addition, he instructed Rachel when and how to hit the children. She believed that if she did as she was told, the children would suffer less than if he hit the children. As it turned out, the children believed this as well. At this point, Rachel lived in fear for her life. But she was also afraid that he might kill her or her children if she left.

When Rachel was five months pregnant with his child, Roberto told her to report David to the police for making harassing phone calls. When Rachel was talking to the detective, she mentioned David's name. Because of this, when she hung up, Roberto beat her with a wooden board that had metal brackets attached. The scars from this assault remain.

Roberto played a game with Rachel's mind. He would wake her up whenever he pleased. Sometimes he would do this by initiating sex while she slept. On other occasions, he would place his hand over her face and mouth, so that she would awaken gasping for air. When she awoke, he would feign sleep, so that she would think she was sick or crazy. Or he would just slap her suddenly in her sleep. Eventually, she would only pretend to sleep. As a result, she was chronically fatigued.

When Rachel was seven months pregnant, in August, they moved again, Rachel doing almost all of the physical work. The house in which they had been living was a shambles. The family that rented the house described finding filth everywhere, faucets broken, walls with holes—this from a family whose mother had prided herself in her homemaking skills.

Shortly after they moved, Roberto beat Rachel so severely she went into labor, six and a half weeks early. At the hospital, they gave her medication to control the contractions. She was "covered with bruises," but no one said anything about them. Despite the contractions, he continued to push and hit her.

During the second week in August, Rachel called a DCF caseworker and asked about foster care, explaining that she wanted to report someone for abuse. Two weeks later, she called the caseworker again, this time saying she wanted to place Claudia in foster care because she needed medical help. The caseworker gave Rachel the number of a foster placement agency. No assistance was offered or further information solicited.

In the summer of 2014, Roberto worked nights. When Rachel drove him to work, he would insist that the children be left behind to assure she would return home. She knew Marc was too young to watch his sisters, and was terrified. But, she rationalized, it might be better for the children to stay home than watch her get beaten or be slapped and yelled at themselves in the car. This terrified Rachel. After Robertolito was born, Roberto would have him come with them when they were going to his work. Rachel believed this was because he was Roberto's son.

When Roberto came home from work in the morning, he wanted sex. So Rachel would lie down with him and the children would "nap" or play in their bedrooms. Then she would get up with the children and try to keep them quiet. Sometimes the children would play in the bedroom and he wouldn't mind. But at other times, if they made noise, he would yell at Rachel or punish her or the children. They would usually play outside.

Roberto would call frequently from work, sometimes several times an hour. Or he would come home suddenly to check on her.

Meals often sent Roberto into a rage. He frequently threw the food in Rachel's face. On other occasions, if a meal didn't satisfy him, he would put hot chili peppers and lots of salt on the food and force Rachel to eat it.

When Roberto was sleeping, the children would sometimes come down to the basement with Rachel and play when she was drying clothes. Roberto regarded Claudia as "David's child," and Rachel was particularly fearful he would hurt her, though she was far too young to be hit. So, if Roberto was home, even if he was sleeping, Rachel made sure that Claudia was always with her when she went to the basement.

When she was eight months pregnant, Roberto tied Rachel's hands together and raped her. He would have her shower the children two to three times a day. He insisted the house be spotless when he returned from work. Given Rachel's state of exhaustion, this was impossible. Rachel's attitude toward her abuse changed. She was no longer openly resisting. She was deeply depressed. She told Roberto, "I don't care what you do to me. Just get it over with." This infuriated him even more, she believes, because he wanted "reaction."

When contractions were four minutes apart, he demanded sex, she protested, and he raped her. When contractions were two to four minutes apart, Roberto refused to take her to the hospital, apparently wanting to make sure the children stayed with him. Rachel wanted the children to stay with her mother, but Roberto knew this might give her an opportunity to escape. He said, "Let them stay here. I'll know where they are. I'll know where you are." But she insisted.

Once again he accompanied her to the hospital and never let her out of his sight, even going to the bathroom with her. Rachel's extensive bruises, both recent and old, were obvious.

STARK: Let me ask you this. If when you were in the hospital, a nurse had said to you, "you shouldn't be taking this" or had asked you questions about what was going on at home, do you think you could have heard this?
RACHEL: I think I could have.
STARK: Because earlier . . .
RACHEL: At that point, I think I would have. If somebody had said, you know there's a way out, I would have.

There were no questions, however.

When Roberto told Rachel he wanted yet more children ("three boys and three girls"), she asked to be "fixed." Roberto had long since stopped apologizing to Rachel after he beat her. But he would apologize to the children after he beat them. Roberto's excitement about having a son was short-lived. When she came home from the hospital, Rachel realized something fundamental had changed in his attitude toward her and that her life was now in grave danger. The change was driven home when he beat her with the four-day-old baby in her arms. Something had also changed in the way he yelled at the children. She determined to get out, but felt Roberto could read her mind.

The children simply tried to stay out of Roberto's way. Maria was particularly fearful and spent hours alone in her bedroom. This was when Rachel laid the mattress in the basement for Claudia. At first, the idea was to provide a place for Claudia so she wouldn't crawl on the cement floor while she was doing a wash and the other children were down there with her. Later, however, Rachel began putting Claudia there when Roberto wanted her to, because he wanted her "out of his sight," for instance, or because he didn't want to be disturbed while he slept, and when she went to pick up Stephanie at the bus and Roberto was in the house. On one occasion, according to Marc, when Roberto had been playing with the children and Claudia started crying, "Poppy hit her with the belt." Rachel confronted Roberto, but he denied it, claiming, "you think I'm too rough with her because she's David's daughter." Nevertheless, Rachel believed Claudia was fearful of Roberto and tried to keep them apart.

Just days after Rachel returned from the hospital, she confronted Roberto about his treatment of the children. "They're not my kids," he told her. It was his day off. They had a fight, and Roberto beat Rachel. That day, because she was afraid, Rachel now realizes, Maria refused to come out of her room. Although Maria had been potty trained for over a year, she had a bowel movement in her pants. Roberto went into the room and yelled, "Your bedroom smells." Discovering the reason, he determined to "teach her a lesson," and told Rachel to undress Maria, clean her up, and put her in the shower. Then, he turned the cold water on. Rachel grabbed Maria out and screamed at Roberto "Are you crazy?" Roberto wouldn't allow Rachel to dress Maria and started snapping his belt, something he had only done with Rachel until that point. He hit Maria repeatedly with the belt, until you could see the bumps. Maria said nothing despite the beating and Roberto yelling at her to "say something." This was how Rachel had come to respond to Roberto's assaults. Finally, Rachel tried to intervene. At that point, Maria turned to her and said, "Mommy, please make him stop. Tell Pappy I'm sorry." Roberto apologized, Rachel and he argued, and he hit Rachel.

This fight prompted a neighbor's call to DCF, and a worker came to the house to investigate on September 4, 2014. The DCF report notes that Rachel is "overwhelmed," that the children appeared cared for and that she has a "very supportive ally in her boyfriend." Another DCF caseworker, who had visited earlier in the year, made a follow-up visit several days later, submitting the report excerpted at the beginning of the chapter. Rachel repeated that she felt overwhelmed and could not care properly for Claudia. To reiterate, the worker noted that Rachel had difficulty responding to her request to remove Claudia from the basement, that Claudia was wet and had a bottle with sour milk, and that Maria's bedroom had dirty sheets and smelled of feces. Despite the multiple bruises that were obvious to police later in the day, many of them long-standing, no questions were asked about abuse, no attempts were made to interview Rachel's "supportive ally," and no protective interventions were recommended for Rachel or Claudia.

On a previous occasion, Marc had taken some scissors out of a drawer and Roberto had beaten him with a belt. A neighbor observed bruises and marks on Marc's arms and legs and reported hearing the children "scream" at night. Marc had already been questioned by another neighbor, whom he told, "Roberto gets upset when people ask questions." Roberto had "accidentally" shot Marc with the BB gun in the rear when he had mistakenly crossed the line of fire. A few days later, on September 10, 2014, Roberto again caught Marc with the BB gun. He had been told not to touch it. Roberto was furious. Fearing that he would hit Marc the way he had beaten Maria, Rachel hit him twice in the back with a belt. Rachel simply wanted to make it to the weekend, hoping that her mother would give her the money to leave. Roberto took the belt from Rachel and told her he would show her "the proper way to discipline." He hit Marc repeatedly in the back of the legs. When Rachel protested and told Roberto to stop, Marc replied, "Its ok mommy, I deserve it." Roberto took Marc over near the stove. Then, he placed his hands on the electric burner.

It was the next day that Marc failed to return from school. Rachel was terrified. Several hours after she was told that Marc would be driven home by the principal, the police arrived with the DCF worker who had visited most recently. Rachel's first thought was that Marc had been in an accident. The social worker said they were taking her children and she would see them Monday. When the police entered the house, Roberto stuck fast to Rachel. While she was nursing the baby in the bedroom, with a police officer only yards away, Roberto grabbed her hair and told her she had better say all the right things or she'd have worse problems when she was released. The officer passed outside the open door during this incident, but said nothing. Although the officer observed the bruises on Rachel the police put her next to Roberto in the car. On the way to the station, Roberto reiterated his threats, telling her what to say and threatening her (in Spanish) if she did anything else.

When they arrived at the station, the detective showed Rachel pictures of the children's injuries, told her she was a terrible mother and that, unless she cooperated, she would never see her children again. One officer observed multiple bruises on Rachel, including bruises on her face, arms, legs, and thighs, and drew the logical conclusion. The children had already told police Roberto beat them. Instead of charging Roberto with these assaults, a detective pounded his fist on the desk and demanded that Rachel admit Roberto had battered her. The detective then stood, started pacing, and returned to the table and again pounded on the desk. Just before a beating, Roberto also would pound on a table and yell. Rachel became numb with terror. It was at this point that she admitted to beating the children, insisted she alone was responsible for their discipline, that Roberto was "supportive," and that she had sustained the bruises during childbirth.

Rachel's "confession" contradicted what the children had told the police, what Roberto had already told the police, and what was obvious to detectives who directly observed her physical condition. But she was arrested along with Roberto, and both were charged with risk of injury to the children. She was then placed in a cell next to Roberto for seventy-two hours. During this time, he instructed her on how to behave and what to say and threatened to hurt her again if she didn't do as she was told.

What about the Violence?

The extent, frequency, nature, and effects of physical violence in this case were extraordinary. But the overall pattern of physical and sexual violence is typical of cases in which children are involved. Had Rachel taken the opportunity afforded her to kill him when Roberto invited her to do so, I could have built a strong case for provocation or justifiable homicide. Based on her oral and written statements, sparse institutional records, and eye-witnesses to assaults or seeing her "covered with bruises," we could array Roberto's assaults along a continuum of increasing severity, from slaps to cigarette burns, kicking, stabbing, and beating with the board to the multiple rapes, attempted suffocation, and so on. Moreover, crime, interview, and survey data from the United States and around the globe strongly support the argument made in my book on *Coercive Control* (2006; 2022), and illustrated in this chapter, that in 45 to 75 percent of cases once thought to involve "domestic violence," physical and sexual assault are not merely "repeated," but "continual," "ongoing," so as to constitute the pattern of "serial" or "terroristic" abuse associated with the serious crime of coercive control and commonly associated with the coercive control of children. It will undoubtedly take the family and probate courts much longer than the police or the criminal courts to acknowledge this reality, though a number of countries and California, Connecticut, Hawaii, Massachusetts, Washington, and a number of other states have already broadened the definition of abuse they entertain in family matters, recognizing that a "course of conduct" is involved rather than a single act, and that the scope of oppressive means deployed is rarely confined to the female partner, marriage, or home.[3]

In Rachel's case, the Court allowed me to testify in detail about Roberto's frequent and often appalling assaults. I used the Campbell Dangerousness Assessment Scale (DAS) to classify the abusive incidents and show that

Rachel had suffered most of the factors that predicted risk for homicide, including serial violence, sexual assault, violence with objects, alcohol abuse, threats to kill, violence in public or against others, and violence during pregnancy.[4] These assaults extended from his initial assault on Rachel within months of their living together to the day the couple was arrested and included pushing, slapping, punching, choking, kicking, stomping, "beating her up," hitting her with bottles and a board, throwing food in her face, and force feeding her "hot" food, throwing knives, cutting her with a knife, whipping her with a belt, and burning her with cigarettes He also gagged her while she slept. I called particular attention to Roberto's assaults when Rachel was most vulnerable, while Rachel was eight months pregnant with Claudia, for example, and a similar episode that occurred just prior to the birth of Robertolito when he tied her hands behind her back with a belt. As a result of these assaults, Rachel believed his claim, "[I could]do with you what I want," a threat she knew meant that he could take her life. When she and Roberto were arrested, Rachel was suffering a slow death to which she might ultimately succumb.

But the story of Roberto's physical abuse took us only so far. To start, apart from a few minor incidents of physical abuse witnessed by David, the neighbors and in the presence of police, this credible history of physical abuse was based almost entirely on my interviews with Rachel and her children. There was no corroboration for the overall pattern. During her questioning by detectives, police berated Rachel for not naming Roberto as the source of the recent bruises they observed on her body. Neighbors, family members, police, DCF caseworkers, hospital staff, and the teacher at Head Start also observed the physical results of Roberto's assaults, including black eyes, bruises, abrasions, contusions, and burns. The miscarriage Rachel suffered shortly after Claudia's birth and the hospital visit for labor six and half weeks before Robertolito's birth both followed beatings. But Roberto was never charged or arrested for battering Rachel, domestic violence was mentioned only once in police reports (see below) and was completely absent from her medical records, and the children had not mentioned Roberto's violence when they were interviewed. In fact, apart from speculation by neighbors and several helping professionals about the source of Rachel's physical symptoms, there was no direct evidence whatsoever that Roberto ever laid a hand on Rachel. I could testify that Rachel's description of Roberto's frequent and varied assaults met the standards for both internal and external validity. Still, she had visited a doctor only after Roberto injured her ear by kicking her in the head and sought no medical treatment even after she cut her wrist in response to an attack.

Rachel's experience of violence also illustrates another potentially confounding feature of this case that can only be illuminated by coercive control, that Rachel could become Roberto's "punching bag" (and he could presumably extend abuse to the children) because he was already and simultaneously *subjugating and entrapping* her by other means of nonviolent coercion and control. Roberto had insinuated himself into her life the way any con man might, through false pretenses of caretaking and protection, and the violence began only after he was in her house and in her bed, had isolated her from family and friends, and had set out rules for everyday living about which there was a tactical consensus, around dress, eating, washing and toileting habits, and so forth. Against this backdrop, the appalling nature of Roberto's physical and sexual violence actually created a forensic predicament by raising the question of "why someone in Rachel's situation stuck around." Again, although emphasizing extreme violence might help us if Rachel had retaliated against Roberto, to the prosecutor, the simple fact that she stayed with Roberto in the face of so much violence made her complicit in the "failure to protect." In fact, from the standpoint of the children, Roberto's violence, which burst forth in rages of jealousy or in response to feelings of disrespect or disgust, is not pertinent to any significant extent. Even in terms of understanding the wrongs that Rachel suffered, the physical violence was secondary to the deprivation of autonomy. Unless we posit the aim of Roberto's abuse as coercive control, to subordinate Rachel and her children and appropriate the resources and privileges available through their exploitation for his personal benefit, the effect of that aim, the entrapment of the family and the pattern of erratic violence against Rachel, can seem irrational, the product of mental illness or dysregulation, and her "endurance" misguided or even masochistic.

Emphasizing Rachel's appalling physical ordeal was also a nonstarter because Rachel looked and sounded nothing like a victim when we got to Court. She was well-spoken, had a sharp sense of humor, was able to give as good as she got from the CPS and showed no psychological evidence of learned helplessness, PTSD, or another disorder secondary to violent traumatization. She described herself as having been depressed and had refrained from sharing her situation with the Head Start teacher, hospital staff, or police. But she was upbeat when I interviewed her and explained her failure to seek professional help as a reasoned assessment of the relative risks such a choice posed compared to the little good that accrued when she had sought help from police and DCF in the past. The court accepted that Roberto had beaten Rachel. But the relevance of his abuse of her for her mistreatment of the children was unclear. If she was in command of her rational faculties, how could we explain, mitigate, or excuse the bizarre series of events for which she was indicted?

The biggest problem with mounting a case based on the physical abuse Rachel suffered was that fear for her physical safety was not the primary source of the terror Rachel experienced. Rachel was afraid when she hurt the children, afraid for herself and them. But her decision-making was strategic, not reflexive.

Reframing the Failure to Protect

Rachel presented the same enigma as Hedda Nussbaum, Magdalena Luczak, Tondalo Hall, and the other women in my practice and thousands like them who face criminal charges related to abuse, neglect, failure to protect, or posing a "risk of injury" to their children in the context of a relationship in which they are being abused. Even if the violence has been long-standing and severe, as in these cases, it is rarely documented; and even if they suffered serious psychological harm, as Hedda Nussbaum had apparently, women like Rachel and Magdalena continue to make choices about parenting throughout the relationship, including in these cases, the choice to harm their children. Here is the paradox we have to manage forensically: reasonably intelligent and otherwise normal women in control of their faculties tolerate and/or confess to heinous crimes against children. The mystery is solved only by identifying the logic behind their choices as a response to the implications of coercive control for children, the dilemma created by having to exercise what I call "control in the context of no control."

The first challenge is to explain that coercive control constrained Rachel to remain with Roberto and not a predisposition, personality problem, or family history. Rachel lacked such commonly cited predisposing factors as witnessing or experiencing abuse as a child or a previous abusive relationship. Her personality profile is normal. To be sure, her dysfunctional family history nurtured a romantic ideal in which she played housewife, mother, and caretaker to a nuclear family with Roberto at the center. At the heart of many coercive control scenarios is a con artist who plays off this romantic ideal. He was Don Quixote, Don Juan, Mark of Zorro, and James Bond in one.

At first, Rachel writes, Roberto worked twelve hours a day and spent all of this free time with her and her children. She continued:

> by mid-May, he and I had a complete relationship, friendship, intimacy; he was helping me with my children, he started making suggestions that he felt were beneficial to us, I shouldn't hang around the diner, keep the house cleaner, the ways I fed the kids and what I fed them, the times they went to bed. (I promised no contact with David since he was no good for me and the kids and only upset me.). I had never felt so loved and cared for as I did then.

Roberto was already on a "con" in which Rachel's compromises were mere means to total domination. It is also undeniable, as Beth Richie astutely points out, that socialization to sexual inequality conditions women to forms of "gender entrapment" based on the equation of love with subordination.[5] Even so, Rachel's initial miscalculation reflected a strength rather than a weakness. She was reaching for trust in a world which offers very little, an application of an ameliorative feminine calculus in which a certain trade-off of selfhood is warranted in exchange for "friendship," "service," "intimacy," and care for children. Although Rachel was not "asking" that she and the children be diminished and demeaned, she recognized that a certain self-effacement and compromise are the costs of companionship, any companionship, not just with a man.

In hindsight, Rachel realizes that Roberto's "suggestions" were the initial steps in her entrapment. Still, she struggled to bring his behavior into conformity with the ideal companion he projected long after the abuse began. His jealousy, resentment of David (whom she also loved), and his difficulties with alcohol seemed plausible explanations for his "outbursts." Rachel's ideas of romance may have been distorted by the sexist dichotomies drawn for her as a girl (see the discussion below). But, she parsed each of the problems Roberto posed and responded in a rational and strategic way: demanding he drink only at the boarding house, promising not to see or talk to David, eliciting promises of reform, and forcing Roberto to leave when he broke his promise and assaulted her a second time. Rachel appreciated the dilemmas their relationship created for Roberto among his Mexican friends and hoped to compensate for the embarrassment her pregnancy with "David's baby" caused him by ending her questionable social behavior and providing other proofs of loyalty. When Roberto cried and begged for forgiveness, she was convinced he loved her. From the vantage of Rachel's experience with the "perfect Italian fiance," the role of the Mexican senora Roberto held out seemed attractive. Rachel's strategy of deference and accommodation made things easier for Roberto, but it was his criminal logic that led him to seize the reins of power, not her spirit of compromise.

Irrespective of why Rachel restricted her activities, she was already isolated from her social network when Roberto returned to her house after the second assault. Now, he substituted a regime of routine, but relatively minor physical assaults for "outbursts," pushing Rachel or shoving and grabbing her, for instance, supported by dramatic acts of intimidation. Roberto smashed the car windshield and dashboard, removed and snapped his belt as a warning, beat his friend "bloody," and called from work at all hours to check up on her. He also destroyed objects that had personal significance for Rachel. Since he often smashed things as a preamble to assault, when he broke her property, she was terrified, even when no physical attacks followed. This combination of chronic, low-level physical intimidation with "explosions" of seemingly irrational terrorism is typical of coercive control.

The experience of being physically and psychologically terrorized was compounded by the experiences of being entrapped and subjugated. Roberto's omnipresence was made possible by her prior isolation from her mother, sister, and friends at the diner, and his seeming omnipotence reflected his assumption of control over every facet of her life, from her means of survival and support through the microdynamics of everyday existence. He seemed omnipotent because he was everywhere and she felt alone.

Isolation

From the day he moved in, Roberto pressured Rachel to stay home, avoid the diner, cook at home, and stop seeing friends whom he felt were either no good for her or jealous of her good fortune. At first, his concern seemed to provide the organization the family lacked. But Rachel soon realized she was restricted to the house. Roberto used sexual terrorism to isolate her from her family. According to an anonymous call to police, Roberto molested Rachel's niece (for whom she was sitting), resulting in a break with her sister. To Roberto, the time Rachel spent with her mother or other family members was "disloyalty," an issue that came to a head on Christmas Day, 2013, when he wrecked his car following her to her grandmother's house, then threatened to kill himself (and her) if she didn't return immediately. A male neighbor reveals that Roberto forbade Rachel to talk with other men because this was not something Mexican women did. She was also forbidden to drive her car except to transport him to work or the children to school; she was forbidden to shop by herself; and she was expected to remain in the house all day, while Roberto was sleeping. Roberto was jealous of David and other Mexican men. But his basic motive for restraining her was to make her his personal property.

As Rachel's functioning deteriorated, she withdrew as much out of fear her predicament would be discovered as of Roberto. She no longer confused Roberto's possessiveness with caring, but realized that restricting her activity regardless of his presence provided the only security against his unpredictability. After Roberto beat his "best friend" bloody, Rachel was frightened of what he would do to family members or neighbors who intervened or to her, if she asked for help. These was why the neighbor and Head Start teacher who offered to help thought she seemed "anxious" and "reticent." She was too frightened to say anything to the neighbor in the evenings when the children played in her yard. She became less and less mobile, until she left the house only to get Stephanie at the bus or to drive Roberto to work. The second move made isolation complete. She now had a car—and there were often two or three at the house. But she was not allowed to drive by herself. When Rachel drove Roberto to work, he insisted she leave all the children home, except, later, Robertolito, ensuring she would immediately return. If DCF became involved, Roberto warned, they would find out she was "crazy" and take her children. This threat, which I have come across in many cases, was communicated to a neighbor by the children as an excuse for refusing to disclose the situation.

Helping professionals also contributed to the isolation of Rachel and her children. The fact that the neighbors heard screams or observed bruises increased Rachel's anxiety about what would happen if Roberto's behavior was disclosed. As a formerly battered woman herself, Mrs. Sontoro comforted Rachel and the children without demanding that they discuss the abuse. By contrast, police, the Head Start teacher, the nurses at the hospital, and others to whom the abuse was transparent believed her reticence signaled Rachel's complicity in the situation and either did nothing or actively exacerbated her isolation by insisting she admit to the abuse. After Roberto beat Rachel for the first time with a belt, he kicked her in the head, injuring her ear. The physician recognized the signs of assault, but did nothing to indicate concern. On the one occasion when Rachel might have escaped, when she was with her family and had Roberto arrested, the police used her as an interpreter, leading to a rape and beating. Rachel had abrasions and bruises on her face, arms, back, trunk, legs, and thighs when she came to the hospital in premature labor and when she was admitted to deliver Robertolito. Again, there were neither inquiries about abuse nor referrals. On September 11, 2014, police investigating allegations of child abuse and neglect observed Roberto pushing Rachel and pulling her hair and using coercive language and saw her multiple bruises. Officer Kehoe's report details the bruises he observed and concludes "R. was being abused (beaten) by her boyfriend Roberto." Although this evidence constituted probable cause that a domestic violence crime had been committed and should have resulted in an arrest under Connecticut's policy of "mandatory arrest," no charges were filed. Instead, police placed Rachel and Roberto together in the back seat of the cruiser and in adjacent cells (where he continued to intimidate her in Spanish), badgered her to implicate Roberto in her injuries, and then, when this failed, told her she was a "bad mother" who would never see her children again. Finally, there was the response of DCF. Caseworkers with the Department of Children and Families are given directives requiring them to assess for domestic violence in cases of suspected child abuse or neglect. Moreover, Rachel had requested help with Claudia. During two investigative visits to the house, however, the caseworker ignored physical and circumstantial evidence of woman battering and offered no assistance. Instead, Rachel was chided for inappropriate parenting and Roberto was described as "supportive." By denying the abuse, minimizing its significance and then focusing blame for both the children's problems and her own on Rachel, professionals involved in this case reinforced Roberto's strategy of isolation, compounded her sense that he could do what he wanted to her without sanction or other consequence, and reinforced his warning that if the battering was exposed, she would be blamed, not him.

Control

Building on the substructure of isolation and fear, Roberto used control over such basic resources as money, food, and clothing for personal support and to impoverish Rachel and the children and increase their dependence. Rachel was receiving AFDC when she met Roberto, getting a small supplement from Maria's father, and sharing household expenses with her mother. Since Roberto knew "best" how to reorganize her life, he took her monthly check and dispensed only what he thought she needed. Like many other women in my caseload, Rachel was regularly questioned about all expenditures, never allowed to go shopping alone, and hit if Roberto thought she spent money frivolously. When they moved out of her family home, Rachel also stopped receiving state assistance and the couple survived on Roberto's meager wages, reduced substantially by his expenditures for alcohol. A letter from the new tenants at Hickory Street reveals there was no running water in the bathroom, no heat, broken windows, and little electric. Illustrative of their desperate state is a neighbor's accusation that they were stealing bottled water and the alarm at Head Start over the children's clothes. Note, at this point, Rachel and children are impoverished for the same reason hostages or prisoners of war are impoverished—because of imprisonment, exploitation, deprivation, and control.

Roberto's control over food and clothing was particularly significant, since these areas of decision-making were identified with her ideal role as a "Mexican" housewife. Roberto demanded she fix complete Mexican meals like a "Senora."[6] When he was dissatisfied with the food, he threw it on the floor, hit Rachel in the face with it, or else spiced it hot and forced her to eat it. When he became convinced Rachel was trying to poison him, he forced her to taste everything first. Roberto determined how Rachel and the children would dress, telling her what to put on when he was home. Because he disapproved of women wearing pants, she could only wear dresses. He also told Rachel how to wear her hair.

Roberto's control extended to Rachel's basic bodily functions, including eating, sleeping, sex, going to the bathroom, or moving about the house. In addition to the mental games he played while she slept, he regularly interrupted her sleep by calling her from work throughout the night, returning home suddenly, or awakening her on his days off or while they were napping by slapping her, putting his hand over mouth and nose ,or by initiating sex. Rachel became too fearful to sleep while Roberto was awake. As a result, she was chronically fatigued and depressed and regressed to an almost childlike state of dependence.

Roberto demanded sex even when Rachel was forbidden to have sex by the doctor, when she was four centimeters dilated, when she returned from the hospital having just given birth, and when she began spotting. Roberto demanded sex regardless of whether the babies were present. His demands that they take a "nap" when he came home from work in the morning meant the children too had to nap or remain unattended, making it extremely diffi-cult to properly prepare Marc or Stephanie for Head Start or, later, Marc for school. Roberto enforced his rule over when, where, and how the couple had sex through rape and beatings. Aside from Rachel's fear, the most significant consequences of Roberto's sexual assaults were two unwanted pregnancies and the loss of one baby. Sexual assault (rape) extended Rachel's sense of physical violation, undermined her will, and was part of the process of objec-tification that eventually led her to attempt suicide.

Roberto told Rachel when she should or could shower and insisted that the children take two or three baths or showers a day. By this time, Rachel asked permission to go to the bathroom. Control over children's hygiene is a fundamental facet of their coercive control.

Entrapment and the Abuse of the Children

The culmination of control was a hostage-like condition of entrapment in which Rachel felt her autonomy reduced to near zero. In combination with her extreme isolation from familial and social support as well as alternative interpretations of her reality, Rachel felt as if she were living in a prison cell—albeit a cell whose bars were invisible—and that the points on her moral compass were being reset in accord with the options Roberto defined as real, including those that defined what was good or safe for the children.

Rachel made Roberto's catalog of distorted emotion her own, not because she accepted or admired it, but because his narrow and obsessive frame set the boundaries within which it was safe for her to think about the children. So, for example, she came to define them as "bad" (or, at least, to conclude punishment was "for their own good") if they disturbed Roberto's sleep, ex-cited his ire by violating one of his many rules, or failed to comply with his beliefs about dress, food, or cleanliness. This provided little security, how-ever, because Roberto's rules were erratic, contradictory, and designed to calm his inner anxiety, gratify an obsession, or to create the appearance of a "family" that conformed to the rigid ideas he had internalized through his own abuse as a child. This was illustrated by the "rule" that the children shower and change their clothes several times a day. The sheer amount of attention to detail the rule required meant attempts at compliance quickly degenerated into desperate efforts at evasion and enforcement. What initially felt to Rachel like an attempt to create order in her household weakened any genuine authority she had had with her children, exposing her and the children to even tighter (and more irrational) controls by Roberto, even less related to the realities on the ground, increasing her own anxiety about the consequences of violation, and reducing her disciplinary repertoire to more extreme forms of punishment. Because Roberto's rules were irrational and contradictory, the more Rachel sought security for the children through adherence to the rules, the less able she became to manage their behavior with the normal tools of parental discipline. Moreover, the less the rules appeared to bear on any sentient reality, the more the children experienced Rachel's role as authoritarian rather than protective. This is the pattern I term "patriarchal mothering," where the maternal function becomes the means of allocating the authority of the abusive husband/father. Rachel faced a classic double-bind: running or directly rejecting the rules were unthinkable. But even if she wanted to enforce the rules, that was impossible because they were changing, contradictory, and unworkable.

Rachel felt "trapped" after Claudia's birth. But, it was only just before she entered the hospital with Robertolito (when she told Roberto, "I don't care what you do to me") and when she returned from the hospital after his birth that she fully realized he had no regard for her life and would eventually kill her if she didn't escape. Moreover, when Roberto beat Maria with the belt and she refused to cry, imitating Rachel's response, and burned Marc's hand on the stove, she realized his violence against the children was following the same path as his violence toward her. When she was arrested, Rachel was preparing to escape with money borrowed from her uncle.

Rachel's case illustrates how the "story" woven to prosecute battered women in child abuse cases is a peculiar mix of gender bias and compassion for children. As we saw in chapter 3, the child protection narrative is framed so as to exclude the male partner, thereby making the architects of physical abuse invisible, focusing only on "the mother." She, who is "the victim" of abuse, must now also be responsible for its effects, including its effects on children. Once the unifying source of power and subjugation is driven off stage, the compassion caseworkers feel for children is displaced as anger at the battered mother because she is the only one left standing to bear responsibility for harming the child. Family and probate courts have been all too willing to assume this scapegoating function from child welfare.

Without envisioning Roberto as the agent constraining Rachel's choices, the DCF workers drew a connection between the sorry state of the household (symbolized by the odor of feces in Maria's room), the pathetic condition in which Claudia was found in the basement, Rachel's psychological state, and her capacity to parent. To set the stage for outside intervention, the reporter invented a dialogue in which Rachel validates the classic vignette of the abusive mother as "depressed" and "overwhelmed." Referring to the basement, the caseworker wrote:

> Advised mother that child can't be left alone down here. . . . Mother said "ok, I respect your opinion. If that's what you think, then I'll take her out." When mother didn't move. . . . I moved aside the bed frame and mattress and lifted the baby out.

To the caseworker, Rachel's decision to keep Claudia in the basement was irrational and her reluctance to remove the child when advised to do so was a sign she was generally sluggish, overwhelmed, depressed, and unable to cope. In reality, Rachel was "frozen" not by depression but by the dilemma described above: should she follow the worker's dictate, take Claudia out and put her at risk of being seriously beaten or killed by Roberto, or should she refuse, try to protect Claudia from Roberto, and be defined as a "bad mother" by the worker? There was another facet as well to Rachel's dilemma at this moment, whether to reveal Roberto's abuse—and risk both his rage and the caseworker's punitive response—or to appear "crazy." Remember: Rachel had tried the disclosure gambit before without results. Rachel could not protect Claudia unless she was protected herself. But if she asked for protection for herself, her child would probably be removed and she—or the children—might be badly hurt. In the matrix of power in which she found herself, Rachel chose a dangerous gambit: she sought aid by drawing attention to her problems with Claudia although given the range of problems in her life at the moment (including the probability she would be killed), these were not the most significant. By projecting an image of herself as "unable to cope," she hoped to accommodate the preconceptions of child protection and so, indirectly, to garner the supports needed to protect herself and her children. Rachel strategically used her depression to seek resources for her daughter, an example of what the literary critic Kenneth Burke called a "comic corrective," turning an apparent deficit into an asset.[7]

The police posed an identical dilemma to Rachel when they demanded she accuse the terrorist boyfriend they had put next to her in the squad car and in an adjacent cell, telling her she was a "bad mother" and that "you will never see your children again."[8] When she refused to comply with this untenable request, they became abusive and threatening.

As we saw in the response by New York City to the *Nicholson* mothers, the agencies designed to provide protection and support often reinforce the battered mother's dilemma by placing women like Rachel in what psychiatrists call a "double bind."[9] In the classic case, a parent makes their love contingent on the young child assuming a distorted sense of reality. To avoid the pain of separation implied by the withdrawal of love, the child adapts a "false self" in accord with this distortion. Since implicating Roberto evoked an unbearable sense of existential risk, Rachel assumed the "false self" of "bad mother" that was projected onto her by the police and DCF. As we saw earlier, once she was safely away from Roberto, her anxiety dissipated rapidly, and she was able to refuse the face-to-face meeting with Roberto proposed by the Yale psychiatrist. Starting in the 1970s, the psychiatric literature identified communication that puts children in a double-bind with the so-called schizophrenogenic mother.[10] In Rachel's case, the pathology that infected communication derived from the gendered frame within which she was perceived and the children's abuse was interpreted. With the major source of external constraint, Roberto's coercive control, obscured, the scope of plausible interpretations of why the children had been harmed was considerably narrowed. A third alternative, asking for help, had ended disastrously, confirming Roberto's warnings about what would happen if she "talked." Thus, when Rachel was arrested, the power of CPS and the police converged with Roberto's coercive control to narrow the cognitive frame through which she was perceived by the world and through which she perceived herself and the world around her, including her children. To this extent, the institutional response became part of her entrapment.

Closing the Safety Zone

In a pioneering study, psychiatrist Elaine (Carmen) Hilberman identified a "homicidal rage" in many of her battered mental health clients.[11] Ideally, we would like a battered parent to separate their commitment to nurture a dependent child from the mounting rage they feel as their needs for autonomy, personal power, empathy, and social connection are denied or suppressed by a malevolent other. Family attorneys and judges despair of clients who use the courtroom to "spew their venom" at one another. But this is clearly preferable to taking the anger out on the children, an all too common alternative, or somaticizing it in depression or other psychiatric symptoms.

Next to anger at being hurt, exploited, and oppressed, fear is the victims' primary emotion. Both fear and anger are continually elicited and must be continually managed by victims of abuse to minimize harm to themselves and others. With coercive control, which targets autonomy and dignity as well as physical integrity, women and children devise "safety zones," facets of their lives where they can temporarily nest, feelings (such as fear and rage) that are too dangerous or too uncomfortable to express, or parts of themselves they hope to keep in abeyance for later use. I examine the use of safety zones as a strategy of resistance and survival at length in my book *Coercive Control*. Suffice it to say here that one way to describe the dynamics in abusive relationships, particularly when children are involved, is by the efforts for victims to create, conceal, and defend spaces in their lives where they feel relatively free of constraints and for abusers to locate and close or destroy these spaces.[12]

After she stopped going to the diner and Roberto had destroyed the personal objects she had in the house, Rachel sought to meet her need for a world apart in the relationship with the children and by maintaining her household as the "real family" she hoped for. As Roberto undermined any sense of self derived from household work, Rachel's attempts to maintain autonomy became increasingly limited to and confused (or fused) with her childcare. Gradually, her relations with the children became the only safe place to express a range of needs and feelings denied expression by Roberto, including her anger. Rachel continued to care for her children. But her caring was increasingly filtered through the dynamics of Roberto's abuse until it too became a function of his coercion and control, an example of what I have called "patriarchal mothering." In Rachel's case, this pattern was quite literal, as when, behind threats and intimidation, Roberto commanded her to discipline the children in specific ways. But patriarchal mothering also occurred indirectly, as when Rachel hit the children or took other inappropriate measures (such as leaving Claudia in the basement) to "protect" them from more severe punishment threatened by Roberto. Here, the patriarchal specter set limits on how and where Rachel could exercise her ethical judgment with David's child. There were also times when Rachel took out the fear and anger evoked by the battering on the children. Ironically, contrary to the belief that she had abandoned her interest in parenting, in these instances, she had defined motherhood as the only viable arena for self-expression. That Rachel's efforts to protect Claudia from Roberto took on the perverse form of "neglect" was a function of objective constraints over which she had no control.

Child Abuse as "Tangential" Spouse Abuse

Earlier, we reviewed the difficulty of countering "risk of injury" or "failure to protect" charges by arguing that severe, long-lasting physical abuse alone caused a mother to lose her capacity for protective action or decision-making. Even had we presented evidence Rachel had been severely injured and psychologically damaged by Roberto, the ingrained normative assumptions about mothering and the extent of child abuse before the court make the evidentiary standard employed to assess her battering very difficult to satisfy. The challenge I met in her case was to provide the court with a conceptual framework that mitigated Rachel's culpability. In the previous chapter, justice would have been served if Krezolek had been convicted and sentenced for the murder of Daniel Pelka and the coercive control of Magdalena Luczak. Justice for Rachel was never on the table, and justice for her and the children would have entailed the unconscionable burden of retaining Roberto for trial in the United States. In the last case, a mother accepted a plea of responsibility for the death of a child as the direct consequence of coercive control. Unless her case is reopened, she will not get justice. We will continue to testify in Court case after case, seeking to eke out what justice can be had for women subjected to coercive control and the children who are harmed or die on their watch.

The premise of this book is that courts will continue to treat abused mothers no differently than any other mother who fails to protect their children, withholds medical care, or willingly exposes them to the untoward influences of violence, drugs, or alcohol, unless and until they appreciate the extent to which children are being abused and killed as secondary victims of coercive control.

To reiterate, the defense narrative built from coercive control shifts the focus of legal attention in failure to protect cases to decision-making under the conditions of extreme duress created by coercive control. In particular, the scope of coercive control is expanded to recognize child abuse as "tangential" spouse abuse, where children are "weaponized" to undermine a partner's authority in all areas bearing on family maintenance, including but not limited to parenting. Children are "secondary" victims in this process because their treatment, including whether they are physically or sexually abused, and even by whom, is a function of whether and how this abuse disables resistance to and/or facilitates control over the resources and privileges available through the household. Although children may be mistreated before their mother is abused, the dynamic illustrated in Rachel's case is more typical, where the abuser extends his coercion and control tactics to the children in response to a woman's independence, refusal or resistance to demands, threats to leave, or other signs that direct forms of control are no longer effective in subordinating her will. The abuser neither hurts the child or causes the child to be hurt because of any ill-will toward the children—he may feel none. His sole purpose in using or hurting the children is to effect his mastery over their mother and the resources and privileges to which he believes she controls access. Conversely, the abuse of the child may have a tangential effect on the spouse without actually harming the child.

The risk to children in relationships characterized by coercive control is function of the absolute level of coercive control at work, regardless of whether violence is a prominent element of the abuse and regardless of whether a child has already been injured or otherwise targeted for specific abuse. Since children are almost always targeted when they are present in homes where coercive control is deployed, their continued safety depends on the degree of freedom for all parties to make protective decisions, sibs, grandparents, and mothers included. This can be established only if an assessment maps how resources are acquired, distributed, and applied globally in the family space as a whole. Simply put, if the range of choices available to a mother are significantly enhanced, the children's prospects improve considerably.

Children may be weaponized at any time in a relationship, though, because many women derive a portion of their self-worth from the experience of childbearing and parenting, pregnancy, giving birth, and bonding with infants are common targets of the abuser's coercion and control. Common themes in this period are the batterer's obsession with his partner's loyalty and his jealousy of alternative attachments, including those she feels toward her fetus, children, and future children during pregnancy. Violence during pregnancy illustrates child abuse as tangential spouse abuse. Tangential spouse abuse, like battering generally, can be conceived of as a staged experience that unfolds in tandem with the strategies used against the mother.

In the early phase of their relationship, Roberto showed little interest in the children's discipline. Instead, he used the children's care as a pretext to isolate and control Rachel and to support her transformation into a traditional "senora." Roberto suggested Rachel not take the children to the diner, the major source of her social connections, and, at home, managed how she dressed, fed, and cleaned them. This illustrates an early phase of "patriarchal mothering," where the wife is managed as an unpaid governess, but the lines of discipline and authority remain hierarchal, with the mother exercising reasonable autonomy on how the father's rules are implemented. The second phase of tangential spouse abuse involves tightening the reins on the children's behavior by dictating discipline to the mother, holding the mother accountable for the children's behavior, and/or assuming the children's discipline directly. In the homeschool case summarized earlier in the book, the father delegated responsibility to the older boys to hold their mother responsible for disciplining the younger boys. Because the abuser has little interest in the actual content of the mother's interaction with the children, his demands are at increasing odds with their capacity. Meanwhile, when the abused mother attempts to install her partner's demands, her emotional availability to the children atrophies and they experience her increasingly as alien, tensions mount, and an "explosion" often ensues during which abusive violence may escalate or the abuser may enter deus ex machina to take over the "education" of the children. This dynamic was critical in the murder of the thirteen-year-old girl discussed in the next chapter.

Rachel initially adapted Roberto's suggestions because she believed they showed he cared about them as a "family." In Roberto's mind, compliance signified Rachel's consent to "rules" that had the force of domestic law. The transition to the second stage occurred when Roberto wanted Katalina's name changed to Maria, his grandmother's name. A secondary function of the name change was to further isolate Rachel from her mother, who refused to call her granddaughter anything but Katalina. The first assault occurred shortly afterward. Now, Roberto directly oversaw Rachel's enforcement of "rules" for how the children should dress, behave, eat, and wash; what they should say; and to whom they should talk. The disciplinary arrangement—father makes the rules and mother oversees compliance—formally resembles how authority is distributed in many classes and cultures, as well as in Roberto's native Mexico. The resemblance was real, but superficial. Roberto would yell at the children occasionally or order them about. But when they failed to meet the standards he set, Rachel was the primary target of his anger, not the children. Rachel, in turn, attempted to regiment the children's behavior according to Roberto's rules, adapting new means of discipline that conformed to a new level of required domestic order which she initially thought reasonable. Importantly, however, it was the effect of his control of the children on Rachel that concerned him, not the children. Since Roberto's expectations and rules were constantly changing, consistent enforcement was impossible and discipline futile, the opposite of the effect sought in the traditional family. The result of arbitrary rules, inconsistent enforcement, and chaotic punishment is the same in families as in other organizational settings with these characteristics, authority is experienced as pervasive but unknowable, leading to a pervasive hopelessness and unresponsiveness in the ranks. Rachel's "failure" to control the children quickly became an occasion for Roberto to further intimidate and isolate her. To the extent that there were real and serious consequences for Rachel if children violated Roberto's rules (e.g., made noise while he slept), she had a profound self-interest in assuming his disciplinary project as her own. In fact, Roberto's coercive behavior had little to do with how the children behaved. As this became clearer to Rachel, her discipline became less rather than more flexible because "anything might set him off."

The third phase of tangential spouse abuse is characterized by two concurrent and contradictory themes, pressure on the mother to escalate her discipline of the children and use of the children to intimidate the mother. If the mother separates or shows other signs of independence, the children may be enlisted in the mother's intimidation or isolation through "spying," may be held "hostage" either literally or indirectly, or may be intimidated and isolated directly. In the latter cases, the batterer may initiate physical abuse of the children or may even kill them.

Shortly after the birth of Claudia ("David's child"), Rachel stopped reacting to Roberto's assaults and even fought back on several occasions. In response, Roberto escalated the rules she was to enforce with the children—requiring that they wash three times daily for instance. He also demanded that Rachel discipline the children more harshly, leading on one occasion to Rachel hitting Marc on the back with a belt. In addition, Roberto used the children against Rachel, asked them about her whereabouts, presented them with "proof" that she was crazy, and restricted her access to them unless he was present. Each of these maneuvers further undermined Rachel's authority, making it necessary, for her own safety, to escalate discipline. While some of the earlier forms of discipline orchestrated by Roberto seemed merely pointless, the choices now confronting Rachel involved steps she viewed as wrong, even dangerous, though not obeying Roberto could be even more so. Roberto insisted that Marc (who was seven at the time) was old enough to watch Claudia, Stephanie, and Maria while Rachel took the baby and drove him to work. Rachel knew this was "crazy," but she acquiesced, rationalizing that it was better than if the children saw her assaulted in the car or were hit themselves. She had few alternatives, since Roberto demanded being driven and wanted to separate her from the children so she would not try to escape. Marc claims Roberto also hit Claudia during this period, though this was never confirmed.

In the final stage of tangential spouse abuse, the abuser extends the full force of coercive control to the children to enforce their loyalty and obedience. This may include escalating or serial physical abuse, frequent threats, the micromanagement of their everyday lives, including their relationships to friends and family, their sexuality, and deprivation of vital resources, including food, clothing, sleep, or money. He may now define mother and children as a single unit in opposition to himself and interpret signs of independence (from children or their mother) as disloyalty or "betrayal," including displays of mutual affection between mother and children. If the mother succeeds in separating, the batterer may respond with a dramatic act of violence that includes the children (burning the house, e.g.) or, as often, an attempt to alienate the children from their mother, often with the court's assistance.

After Robertolito's birth, Roberto reenacted with the children the same cycle of violence and apology that initially typified his abuse of Rachel. His assault on Maria has already been described. Importantly, the hospital stay served as a safety zone for Rachel, giving her space to think about her life. Not only was she able to get the hysterectomy Roberto opposed but, when she returned home with four-day-old Robertolito in her arms, she confronted Roberto about his mistreatment of the children and he beat her, terrifying Maria. Still, when Roberto turned on the cold water in the shower, Rachel pulled Maria out and again confronted him. Roberto now saw Maria and Rachel as part of a joint resistance and so turned the anger at Maria he had only shown to Rachel until now, snapping and using his belt. Maria too sensed the affinity with her mother and, like Rachel, refused to cry or say she was sorry. It was only after Rachel intervened and Roberto turned to hurt her that Maria conceded, telling her mother to "tell Pappy I'm sorry." This interplay between Maria and Rachel in the face of Roberto's abuse is typical of the collective prowess women and even very young children exhibit in the fact of global oppression.

By his own admission, Roberto had beaten Marc with the belt on a previous occasion for taking some scissors out of a drawer. A neighbor observed bruises and marks on Marc's arms and legs and reported hearing the children "scream" at night. These "fights" were often provoked when the children resisted Roberto's rule that they shower three or more times daily. Roberto also admitted "accidentally" shooting Marc in the rear with the BB gun when the boy had mistakenly crossed "the line of fire."

Rachel's loss of control over the children and basic household maintenance was certainly aggravated by her depression and exhaustion. But it was the sheer number and absurdity of Roberto's rules that ultimately made it impossible for her to devise a general code of behavior for the children, even a very strict one. The complexity and contradictory nature of the rules constrained Rachel and the children, not their psychological incapacity to cope. Roberto's assessment of whether his rules were working for the children was based on how their adherence affected Rachel's behavior, an indicator over which they had no control. Nor could Rachel predict Roberto's response to the children based on their behavior. To ensure her own and the children's safety, therefore, Rachel implemented a regime of global authority, focusing her discipline on obedience for its own sake, no matter how irrational the dictate, and tried to micromanage the children's every move in anticipation that it could elicit a punitive response. This challenge would have exhausted her even without a newborn in the house and Roberto not demanding continual servicing. The result was chaos: Rachel's generalized authority was increasingly ineffective, she let the children do as they pleased, fulfilling Roberto's accusation that she was a bad mother, and only intervened when the children's behavior was extreme or Roberto threatened to intervene himself. In these situations, hitting seemed appropriate either to protect the children from Roberto's even harsher punishments or because, unable to control Roberto, she struck out at the only other source of chaos she could safely blame, hoping to "keep the lid on" until she had the money to escape. A third motive, to protect herself from being hurt, remained beneath the surface. Both Marc and Maria told me they understood that, when their mother hit them, this had little to do with their behavior and that the alternatives were worse.

Fearing that Roberto would beat Marc the way he had beaten Maria, Rachel hit him in the back twice with the belt. Roberto was not satisfied. He took the belt from Rachel, said he would show her "the proper way to discipline," then hit Marc repeatedly in the back of the legs. When Rachel protested and told Roberto to stop, Marc replied, hoping to protect his mother in the only way he knew how. "It's ok mommy," he said. "I deserve it." Roberto then took Marc to the stove and placed his hands on the electric burner.

Conclusion

I have described this scenario at length because, so far as I know, it is the first narrative account of the coercive control of children outside fiction. The children of coercive control are being subjected to the criminal elements I describe in millions of homes without recognition or redress.

In assessing the children of coercive control, our working assumption is that every abused woman possesses the "average level of parental competence" needed to care for and protect her children, but that this competence, expressed until now only indirectly in the poor choices she is forced to make under duress, fully emerges only when she is protected from coercion. With caveats for age and developmental vulnerabilities, I also assume that children possess the "average level of competence" needed for self-protection, albeit in the context of their interdependence. From these assumptions, two things follow.

First, unless proved otherwise, where coercive control is present, children will be harmed ("abused" and "neglected") as the direct result of violence, intimidation, and control tactics of the abuser, irrespective of whether the mother or the children has been their primary focus and regardless of whether the abuser or the victim mother harms/constrains the child. Ranging from the relatively minor instance when she left Marc home to care for his younger sibs to hitting Maria with the belt to leaving Claudia on the fetid mattress in the basement, there are numerous instances in this case where Rachel's treatment of the children could be considered abusive or neglectful. Note, unlike some lines of defense, we are *not* arguing that Rachel was forced to make the specific choices she made. Nor are we insisting the choices she made were safe choices for her children or even the best possible choices at the time. They were not safe choices, and I have no way to know what other options might have been at her disposal. Our forensic argument is that the constraints on liberty at the heart of coercive control limit the target's decision-making field to options that are *all unsafe*. Coercive control is a crime because it denies free people the resources, capacities, and rights to do what they want and need to do. Rachel is not responsible for hurting her children because, under the conditions of her oppression, she could not do otherwise.

The child here is a victim, but s/he is the secondary victim of the constraints on the mother, a child victim of coercive control. When Rachel left Marc home to care for his younger sibs, this was not her choice, but Roberto's, to ensure she would return home promptly after dropping him at work. Rachel hit Maria to prevent Roberto from doing worse; she brought Claudia to the basement because she was "David's child." Claudia was safer in the basement than she would have been elsewhere. In each instance, Rachel made a global calculation that reflected the overarching structure of tyranny in her life as well as a tactical decision about how best to respond to the existential dilemma. Were there better tactical decisions available that Rachel might have chosen? Perhaps. My first-year social work students probably memorized a dozen coping strategies that were more appropriate than those Rachel adapted. But Rachel was living in a world where there no good options, not a social work class. In any case, accountability for harming the children falls squarely with the abuser and is "shared" only if there is a history of child abuse by the primary victim prior to the onset of coercive control.[13]

Second, courts should consider a woman's actions in the context of the range of realistic choices afforded in the abusive situation and apply the assumption of "average maternal competence" to reframe behaviors that appear dysfunctional (or malevolent) as protective of self and child. Instead of concluding that a mother is "bad" because she puts her child in a damp basement that is inaccessible from the house, the Court should wonder what possible constraints could lead a reasonably competent mother to take such an action. A related principle—the logic of maternal resistance—also applies to the set of apparently self-destructive or pathological behaviors sometimes presented by abused mothers, homelessness, substance abuse, or attempted suicide, for example.[14] In the context of coercive control, these behaviors, like those that may harm children, are often strategies to minimize, diffuse, or avoid harm by "owning it," what I call "control in the context of no control." In Rachel's case, the decision to take Claudia to a basement room that was inaccessible from the house while Roberto was home appeared to the DCF worker as clear evidence of "neglect." But within a context governed by

Roberto's jealous rages, the may have been the best way Rachel could imagine to protect "David's child." That Claudia's health might have been jeopardized in the damp cellar was preferable to exposing her to Roberto's revenge. That resistance here is couched in attempts to control a facet of the environment that is off-radar or not yet targeted for micromanagement and is a signal to intervention of where empowerment of a mother can begin.

The thrust of my forensic narrative is accountability, the same major aim as criminal law. Nothing I have said relieves Rachel of responsibility for hurting her children, though they may forgive her, as Marc told me he had done when we sat down briefly when he was home from a tour of duty in Afghanistan, or she may forgive herself. Many battered mothers lack adequate parenting skills, are mentally ill, or become addicted to substances for reasons that have nothing to do with coercion or control. Many of Rachel's inappropriate acts cannot be reframed as rational, even within the context of control. Her growing subordination to Roberto clearly had a psychological dimension, for example, which distorted her sense of judgment, damaged her self-esteem, and caused her to regress to a time when the approval or disapproval of significant adults was a primary basis for her self-worth. She idealized the role of the Senora, for example, and emulated forms of self-abnegation that were alien to her ebullient personality, wit, and intelligence. For this I blame coercive control by her Italian American father, whose racialist hatred and physical abuse of her and her mother drove her to see the extended, multigenerational open family life in the Mexican American community as nirvana. This dynamic contributed to her capacity to rationalize levels of violence and neglect of the children—her own and Roberto's—that were incompatible with her basic sense of responsibility, let alone her notions of right and wrong. She attempted to manage her growing rage at Roberto in the safest way she could, by directing it against herself, and attempted to control it through passive-aggressive means, a suicide attempt, also an example of "control in the context of no control." But even her suicide attempt appears to have been a direct response to Roberto's tattooing his name on her body, an example of a rational adaptation rather than of underlying psychiatric disease. Nevertheless, her mode of reacting reinforced her increasing immobility in the face of harm, her chronic fatigue, and a certain resignation to her fate, endangering the children.

Rachel's suicide attempt was an active attempt to control her fate compared to the hopelessness that overtook her after Claudia's birth. External evidence of this feeling comes from the Hickory Street house where garbage accumulated, basic conveniences were absent, and the couple stole drinking water from neighbors. Unable or afraid to openly resist Roberto or show her anger, Rachel adapted passive modes of resistance, pretending to sleep, refusing to react to Roberto's assaults, and, finally, telling Roberto, "you can do anything you want, just get it over with." Even elements of this reaction were functional, since crying or begging Roberto for mercy made him more violent, not less, a lesson not lost on Maria. Rachel's physical state during the relationship should be kept in mind: during almost two years of serial assault, Rachel had given birth twice and had one miscarriage. In other words, she was pregnant during all but one or two of the months the couple was together.

A coercive control analysis does not mean we are insensitive to psychological nuances of women and children's lives or naive to the reality that most of life is led in the interstices of the power grid set by male domination rather than on its fault lines.

The point remains. Once coercive control is established, the burden should pass to the State to prove that sufficient free agency is available to establish culpability or, for that matter, to distinguish clinical symptoms or moral deficits from protective, survival-oriented adaptations to abuse. For instance, Rachel adapted to the violence, and particularly to the multiple rapes, by distancing herself from her physical self, stepping outside her body and functioning through significant phases of the two year ordeal as if none of this was truly happening to her or her family. This adaptation reduced her capacity to evaluate what was happening to the children, But attend also to this. Rachel's propensity to minimize also had protective effects, keeping her from exposing the abuse and so risking almost certain and even more severe harm to herself and the children. Unlike Rachel, Magdalena Luczak brought their son's abuse to the attention of his school and pediatrician. That did not end well. Distancing also allowed Rachel to keep cool at moments when a more "normal" mother would have lost it, such as when Roberto beat Maria with the belt, and might have provoked even more serious and perhaps lethal violence. That Rachel was in at least partial denial is evident from reports that she concentrated on "the good times" and that, "apart from the beatings, everything was going smoothly." However fantastic it may seem, the positive attitude that results from a kind of psychic splitting is a common survival mechanism employed by childhood victims of sexual abuse, hostages or prisoners-of-war.[15] Rachel's positive attitude toward even the most devastating moments in her life helps explain why Roberto's terrorism did not damage her children even more fundamentally.

Both Maria and Claudia—both of whose Quinceaneras I've attended—reported using "splitting" quite effectively to survive abusive relationships.

Rachel unquestionably internalized a good deal of the world as Roberto presented it, a world in which the assaults were provoked by her own failures as mother, housekeeper, money manager, cook, and sexual partner. Ironically, however, as with so many other battered mothers in this book, Rachel actually gained a sense of control through the process of internalizing blame: if her shortcomings caused Roberto's violence, then by altering her behavior she might prevent it. By contrast, as it became clear that nothing she did affected Roberto and that her limited attempts to present her problems to others were similarly ineffectual, she withdrew into herself, losing touch with some basic protective instincts. Through this process, Rachel became a dysfunctional caretaker, a fact that she denied because she felt an overwhelming guilt about failing in her maternal responsibilities.

The coercive control model neither minimizes the psychological effects of physical abuse on women and children nor the personal responsibility women like Rachel must bear for behaving shamefully with those they love. Its claim, to reiterate, is that, absent a detailed working knowledge of the dynamics of an abusive situation, it is often impossible to demarcate where behavioral adaptations to external constraint end and psychopathology or moral culpability begins. Given this, the most parsimonious assumption, and the only rational or ethical assumption on which protective or justice services can precede, is that the child's safety and the mother's capacity to protect the child are compromised by the same source, the strategies of coercive control employed by the man who sets out to dominate them.

10

Carmen Barahona

My client in this case was Carmen Barahona. In 2020, Carmen, then age sixty-nine, accepted a plea deal by which she would avoid a death sentence in Florida in exchange for testifying against her husband Jorge, pleading guilty to conspiring with him in the murder of their adapted teen daughter, Nubia, and accepting a long prison sentence. I was asked to assess whether and how Carmen's history of abuse contributed to Nubia's death and to her behavior with respect to the child's murder and/ or complicity in the death.

A week before Nubia is presumed to have been murdered, Jorge removed her from the home she shared with Carmen and four siblings, ostensibly to stay with a relative. Based on evidence they collected at the apartment, from Jorge's van, and what they were told by the four surviving adopted children, at Nubia's school, and from Carmen's coworkers, police concluded that Jorge had kidnapped and killed Nubia as the culmination of a course of conduct during which he and Carmen had beaten, bound, and starved the twins (Victor and Nubia) and subjected them to torturous physical and mental ordeals over many months. Jorge browbeat and slapped Nubia and Victor into "confessing" various plots to poison the family and kill him; left the twins naked and bound in the bathtub for hours at a time; and tied them to chairs, forcing them to sleep on the floor and to eat scraps while bound and isolated in a room. Carmen described times when Jorge forced her to watch him bind, slap, or otherwise mistreat the twins. But she also acknowledged bringing them food while they were bound in the tub or confined on chairs, on the floor or in a backroom and binding their hands. She pointed to the twins' admissions of guilt to support Jorge's delusions about these plots as the pretext for binding them. The children supported Carmen's claim to have been abused by Jorge. But they also identified her as playing a key role in their mistreatment. Nothing in what Carmen or the children recounted explained why she failed to respond to Jorge's escalating mistreatment of Nubia or to the child's sudden "disappearance" from their home. Had Carmen reached out for help of any sort, the child's murder could have

Children of Coercive Control. Evan Stark, Oxford University Press. © Oxford University Press 2023.
DOI: 10.1093/oso/9780197587096.003.0011

been prevented. Instead, she acknowledged, "I felt relieved he was taking care of the problem."

I close the book with a defense of Carmen Barahona because no other case in my practice has so tested the limits of the paradigm to address the predicament coercive control poses for women and abused children or so thoroughly convinced me of its utility to frame early intervention with children to prevent tragedy. Carmen was less severely physically abused than either Magdalena or Rachel, and she participated in harming the children to a far greater extent. Moreover, whereas the men in the previous two cases lorded over their partners as would a traditional tyrant, Jorge was economically and emotionally dependent on Carmen to an inordinate extent. Yet, I sympathize with Carmen's plight because under the duress of coercive control, she suffered a corruption of her moral capacity at the very core of a humanity which we widely share such that each of her decisions, calculated to minimize the children's immediate suffering, seemed too banal to portend the profound evil that was becoming ever more inevitable in the world she inhabited. I have tried to capture Carmen's perspective, albeit framed by her experience of coercive control. Readers are urged to enter the matrix of her decision-making sufficiently to ask whether, seeing the world as she did, facing the same constraints, they might have behaved similarly.

The complex of medical, behavioral, and psychiatric problems that motivated Jorge's increasingly obsessive efforts to isolate, disable, and control Carmen and the children are beyond my scope. Suffice it to say that Jorge appeared relatively stable during the early months of his relationship with Carmen, almost certainly because he'd been in prison, where his medications and addictions were controlled, but he had significantly deteriorated before the children came into the home. Through most of the period covered in this review, Carmen did everything: she went to work and managed his business, cooked and did the housework, and supervised the children' activities and schooling. Apart from completing most of his exterminator appointments, Jorge watched TV, stayed in bed, or micromanaged the children. By all appearances, Jorge was dependent on Carmen physically, financially, and psychologically, and appears to have been helpless without her guidance for a significant period before and during the months when the twins were tortured and one killed. Ironically, Jorge's illness appears to have made his coercive control tactics more explicit, but not less effective or devastating. As we shall see, even from within the context of his dependence, Jorge controlled every facet of Carmen's and the children's existence, including her behavior at work and their behavior at school and work. I call this dynamic "coercive control from below," because terroristic control over women and children emanates from a man who may look powerless on standard meas-ures of family function and be all but invisible to outsiders, but who none-theless operates, much like a vacuum pump, by sucking the air of life out of a household so that it implodes.[1]

Jorge initially pressed himself on Carmen based on self-denial, def-erence, idealization, and "respecto," not on defamation; he asserted his self-interest largely by its abnegation. She was his pin-up girl. Jorge's self-presentation was "I am nothing." You, a "Senora," are "everything." There is no confusing the destructive content of the power dynamics in play shortly after they married. But before then, Carmen experienced a euphoria akin to romantic love. The contrast between Jorge's idealization and the combi-nation of disdain and indifference she had felt as a child and in her marriage was stark. Carmen was abused the entire time the twins were in the home. But it was only after the twins were legally adopted that Jorge exercised a level of coercive control over the family space that took the opportunities for support and survival off the table. At that point, Carmen's will and con-sciousness were no longer her own.

Carmen and the children were Jorge's victims, and he was convicted of the child's murder. But, whether he is legally responsible is another matter. It seems clear to me from his prison history, the case records, and the history provided by Carmen, that Jorge Barahona deteriorated during the course of their relationship as the direct result of a serious psychosis aggravated by the habitual use of alcohol and drugs to medicate anxiety and paranoia. When he kidnapped Nubia, Jorge was in a fugue-like state; by the time Jorge took the child's life, he was responding to demons beyond his ken. Had the coercive control been identified as the root of Nubia's or Carmen's problems, Jorge could have been arrested, medicated, and/or charged and stopped. The child would not have been killed, the other children would not have suffered, and Carmen's life would not be spent in prison. Carmen does not believe Jorge had evil intentions toward her when they became involved and insists to this day she does not understand why Jorge did the things he did. Although the prosecutor in her case could not explain Jorge's behavior, he saw Carmen's confusion as "denial and minimization" and as part of her guilt. On whether Carmen is legally accountable, I remain agnostic. In my view, a major onus falls on the State of Florida and its various school, health, and child serv-ices in this case for missing the myriad warning signs that the Barahonas posed an extreme risk to their children. Our challenge is to decipher the manifestations of coercive control before the situation becomes emergent, not to fix blame, so we can get it right the next time.

After reviewing Carmen's complicity in the children's abuse, readers may concur in the Court's condemnation of her inaction. For me, the very ambiguity of her position, the corruptibility of this otherwise well-intentioned, principled woman is dramatic reinforcement for my underlying message, that had the coercive control linking Nubia's problems to Jorge's control of Carmen and the children been recognized, Nubia would be alive and Carmen and her children would be thriving. Whatever forces drove Jorge, he targeted Nubia for special treatment and hurt the twins in the way that he did to consolidate his control over Carmen and the household.

Can we completely disregard Carmen's child abuse? I emphasize two facets of the situation that significantly diminish her responsibility, how Jorge established "coercive control from below" over his more technically adept, economically independent, and emotionally responsive wife, and how Carmen negotiated a "harms reduction strategy" for herself and the children within the thicket of Jorge's coercive control. Rachel (chapter 9) and Magdalena Luczak (chapter 8) hit their children to keep them from being hurt more seriously. Carmen's harm-reduction strategy is more circumspect and includes "scapegoating" a precocious sexually conflicted teenage girl to displace harm from more vulnerable children. But in all three cases, the argument for "complicity" is mitigated by showing how the impulse to protect was constrained and redirected against its aim, to control, what I term "control in the context of no control." Before accepting this argument, I consider Carmen's behavior from Nubia's vantage, particularly as the child calculates her own prospects in light of the protection needs of her more vulnerable twin. In the Pelka case, discussed in chapter 8, I interpreted Daniel's silence about his abuse at the pediatrician's as way to protect Magdalena from Mariusz, "the ogre in the room." Nubia's voice is far more equivocal. Yet this is an important test: Can the paradigm seek justice for women while recording the "voice of a child?"

In exchange for a plea of guilty and a probable life in prison, Carmen Barahona was spared a trial and a possible sentence of death, a pyrrhic victory you may feel when you read what she endured. As I write, her case is still on appeal in Florida. There was never a good outcome possible in this case. But if readers can engage the fact here, the predicaments faced by most children of coercive control will seem like light lifting.

The Barahona Case: Family Background—A Child of Coercive Control

Carmen migrated to the United States from Cuba, with her parents in 1952, at age two, and lived in Miami since 1959. Both her parents died while Carmen was incarcerated on the pending charges. Until her death, Carmen said, she and her mother talked on the phone "every day." She never mentioned being abused to her mother either in her first marriage or her second.

Carmen is a survivor of coercive control in her family of origin as well as a victim in her marriage. Carmen initially described her childhood as idyllic and her parents as "awesome." In fact, Carmen feels deeply unappreciated by her mother and was frightened of her father. Carmen blames herself for not becoming a "star" like her older brother and younger sisters. But an insidious family selection process was at work. She told me

> I was just there for them. My brother he was the boy and he played base-
> ball and my father would go to all the practices and my sister, she was the
> brainy one . . . and I was taking care of my sister when they were out with
> my brother . . . and then my sister she had the career. I didn't have a career,
> I didn't go to college, I didn't make anything of myself.

The sex-race stereotyping played off physiognomy. Her sibs are fair, with blond hair and blue eyes resembling her mother; she is dark and broadly built, like her father. She recalled a family photo where "My mom is sitting with my brother and sister and I'm standing over here. . . . I'm in the picture but I'm not in the picture . . . look like an 'outsider.'" The family hierarchy mirrors the intermarriage strategies useful to survive the Cuban Revolution (1958). To keep from going "down," the upper-class mother married Carmen's father, an uneducated dirt-farmer from rural Camaquey Province with good work habits but no social or cultural accoutrements. Some furnishings and a few heirlooms followed the family to the United States. Without the requisite so-cial position, Carmen's father sustained the traditional Catholic patriarchy over a high-status wife by doing so directly, working doggedly to live above his means, and using his raw personal power to intimidate and maintain "face."

From early in her childhood, Carmen's father established his authority through a regime of coercive control over his family; he regulated every aspect of the daily lives of his wife and children according to principles of order assigned arbitrarily and without reference to the religious and cultural institutions that gave male authority the aura of legitimacy in Cuba.

Carmen told me apologetically that her father was "rough around the edges," exhibiting a propensity to minimize that would become manifest in her relationship to Jorge. She acknowledged her father allowed neither her mother nor her to have unauthorized conversations ("I couldn't talk to anyone," she told me). She had strong role models of working women on her mother's side of the family. But the values promulgated by her father centered on rigid sex roles, which she and her mother were helpless to resist. As a preteen, she and her mother were "terrified" of her father: "If we saw him drive up, each of us would run to our room." "I spent a lot of time in my room," she admitted, "I felt safer there. Shut off from the rest of the world." She says she never saw her father hit her mother. But she acknowledged he controlled her and her mother in many other ways. She recalls several occasions on which he made her cry. Shutting things out felt safer than confronting whatever was going on, particularly with the ogre in the room, setting the stage for how she would accommodate her abuse later. Carmen considered herself and her mother "close." But this "closeness" rested on an unspoken pact not to reveal how deeply afraid each felt of the man in the house.

Carmen would resurrect this early adaptation to coercive control in her relationship to her mother later on when she talked to her daily without mentioning that Jorge was starving the children. In her relationship with Jorge, she also adapted another facet of her mother's life-strategy, to exhaust her self-development to bolster a male ego within the confines of a rigidly imposed authoritarian regime.

Carmen's isolation was so severe that she spoke no English when she entered first grade at age six and was only allowed to speak to her mother in Spanish, a means used to isolate her mother as well. Carmen had no social life. In junior high school, she "couldn't stay after school with other kids; there was no dates, no going to movies with friends . . . they [her parents] wouldn't let me go to the beach with friends; I always had to have an adult chaperone with me." "I had no close friend," she told me.

Carmen was caught in a psychological "double-bind" of being on her own and powerless that became a core theme in her entrapment as an adult. "According to my parents, you're going to be protected." At the same, she was on her own. Her father told her "never let anyone abuse you. Always stand up." But she was never offered any means to do this. Instead, her father insisted her mother be her constant chaperone, even to the prom. So she was led to believe she was on her own, but lacked the means to stand up for herself. So when Ray started "showing up at the house" and just "sitting there with mom, I just assumed 'this is how it's going to be.'" "You're going to marry him," my father told me. The idea that Ray would extend her father's protection was tragic-comic. Carmen has carried the message that she is only someone so long she is ensconced in the penumbra of male authority.

The Marriage to Ray

The marriage to Ray was her escape from home: it was loveless, abusive, and controlling. She used the marriage to form a sense of herself as worthy person and a mother capable of fiercely loving children.

Carmen met Rene (Ray) A., when she was fourteen and he was eighteen. Marriage to Ray was an exit plan both parents supported, in no small part because Ray endorsed their views. In an earlier generation, she might have entered the Church. Carmen had college plans, but she abandoned them because Ray told her he was against her going to college, her parents supported Ray's decision because "you had to work weekends, and that was it."

Ray was loyal, lazy, and self-involved as well as abusive and unaffectionate. Nevertheless, Carmen used what she acknowledges was a loveless marriage as a context to mature and establish a modicum of independence. Carmen told me that it was with Ray she learned she had needs of her own, including a need for children.

There was even more regimentation with Ray than in her family home; she was responsible for servicing all of Ray's and their domestic needs. She told me,

> I couldn't wear pants, no tee shirts, "your breasts are showing" . . . : wanted to get out of that . . . no toe polish, nail polish, no ankle bracelets cause "only boys wore ankle bracelets." I couldn't dye my hair. . . . With Ray, I couldn't be myself . . . dye my hair in my 30s. . . . I couldn't wear certain earrings cause they were too wide.

She shared, "one day I bought dishwashing liquid, Dawn, and he said it was no good, he threw it away, he brought Palmolive instead, and I never again used Dawn." If she disagreed, he demeaned her and second-guessed every decision she made. Ray's controlling behavior was familiar to Carmen because of her father. But she didn't choose Ray because he was controlling or abusive.

Everything changed for Carmen when her children were born (Ray Jr. in 1972 and Jennifer in 1980) and she suddenly felt she had "something that was mine," a cherished responsibility from which she could derive a sense of pride, self-fulfillment as a "mother" she did not feel as a daughter or wife. Carmen's experience of mothering is seminal to understanding Carmen's decision to foster—even when Jorge was in no shape to do so—her attachment to the children and her fierce defense of this attachment even as the pillars of her physical and mental realities were being shorn. Importantly, the most dramatic acts of self-assertion she described with Ray involved standing up to the school and her in-laws when her children's interests were at stake, refusing to visit Ray's family, for example. Later, when Carmen intervenes on Nubia's behalf after the sex-shaming incidents at the school, she will again redirect anger from her own mistreatment outward.

Carmen met Jorge Barahona at Sears, when she was picking up a delivery for her husband. When Carmen met Jorge, her relationship with Ray was in freefall. Still, she had more independence than at any point in her life, she had a job, with increasing supervisory responsibility and the children, which made life with Ray tolerable. Without Jorge entering her life, I don't think she would just have walked away.

Carmen Barahona is about to encounter her third regime of coercive control, an experience of exchanging one authoritarian family setting for another, I suspect may not be unusual. Case histories like this open a window to a the larger trajectory on which coercive control unfolds that can rarely be gleaned am empirical study or clinical assessment.

The Relationship to Jorge Barahona

Carmen's role in Jorge's murder of Nubia was the endpoint of a downward spiral that can usefully be described in three phases. The abuse of Carmen Barahona was manifest in Phase I and had extended to the twins by the time they entered public school in Phase II. But the implementation of a full regime of coercive control in Phase III was not inevitable. The fatality could have been prevented. Three things concern us here: Jorge was relatively stable when he met Carmen; Carmen witnessed the downward trajectory of Jorge's illness over which neither she nor presumably Jorge had much control; and the effects of Jorge's illness on Carmen and the family were articulated in a pattern of coercive control they all assumed as a torrent of blame for failing to keep him from failure and suffering.

The couple met when Jorge was on the cusp of a recovery. He was just out of prison, was well medicated, and had stopped drinking almost entirely. During the relationship, Jorge underwent a lengthy but progressive decompensation into severe psychosis with manifest symptoms of paranoia, hallucinations, and hypomania only partially masked by chronic pill and alcohol use. The complex etiology of Jorge's disorder is beyond our scope, though it included the horrendous abuse he had suffered as a child. For Carmen, the most dramatic effect of being caught up in the coercive control was a state cognitive dissonance known as "perspecticide" where a victim is unable "know what she knows," in this instance, what Jorge was doing to their daughter.

Phase I. Courtship, Marriage, and the Decision to Foster

At the outset, Jorge's relation to Carmen and Jorge was characterized by mutual commitment to a relationship based on a strict hierarchical division of labor in which Carmen provided the mainstay of support. Based on her demonstrated capacity as a parent and homemaker and the reasonable circumstances in which she lived, there was a sound basis for selecting the couple as foster parents. The placement of the twins was probably ill-advised from the agency's vantage, but the mother was well intentioned.

Carmen chose to partner with Jorge. When Jorge met Carmen, he honestly believed she had come to him from another world. Carmen sensed this and welcomed the attention, even the self-centered imago he conjured of her. He was far more emotionally attached and dependent on her than Ray ever was. Jorge was living at home with his mother and brother. He seemed devoted to Carmen's every wish when he was with her. She willingly acceded to his demands for attention, since the rest of her life was full with work, the children, and serving Ray. Later, after Carmen divorced and she and Jorge moved in together, she endeavored to live within the idea he projected of a proper senora. Jorge was no less "patriarchal" in his expectations that she be subordinate than was Ray. Unlike Ray, however, who kept Carmen subordinate with cruelty, Jorge held her on a pedestal with adoration and self-denigration. It was when Carmen attempted to renegotiate their unequal distribution of responsibilities that Jorge's expectations for obedience were manifest.

Shortly after they met, Jorge identified Carmen and her children as his mark. Deception and withholding seemed credible stratagems to adopt, given his psychological status, low level of education and employment, and serious behavioral deficits. He disclosed nothing of himself and deflected everything back on her, so she alone was in the spotlight. Her needs and wants were paramount. As if she were talking to a recording device, Carmen became exposed, talking frankly about her sexual dissatisfaction with Ray, her jealousy of her sibs, and the absence of love in her life. Jorge remained concealed. Carmen was dimly aware of some significant deterioration in Jorge's life. But he convinced her this was "no problem now" and "in the past." Jorge exhibited classic borderline traits as well as the traits of a con man, insinuating himself into every possible space in Carmen's life while deflecting attention from his own impoverished sense of self by doing it "for her." Carmen was being conned and exploited. But unlike the typical con man, Jorge's aim was not to take what was hers, but to make his dependence on her invisible and irrefutable, so he could live in and through the image of her he now possessed.

Why did Carmen choose to live in Jorge's ideal "family?" Her own dependency issues were in play when she took Jorge's rehabilitation on as a project. Having been "on her own" with Ray, she welcomed someone who came in to "take over" her life for her, even if it meant she did the heavy lifting. Jorge's fantasy also resembled the "show" family her mother longed for back in Cuba. Their decision to foster the children was consistent with their family's developmental trajectory and, she admitted, she wanted to give Jorge the family he lacked in his home. Meanwhile, there was nothing Carmen did for Jorge she had not done for Ray, including the bills. The relationship with Jorge was sexually satisfying, at least initially, the one with Ray was not; Jorge was worshipful, Ray treated her like "dirt." The third difference was most important: Ray had little commitment and would disappear for long periods. Jorge could not bear to be separated from Carmen.

Carmen complained about her neglect by Ray. Jorge made her and her needs the center of his life. He began calling her work, first occasionally, then several times a day, soon even more frequently, asking "What did I want? What did I need?" "When I met Jorge," she explained, "everything revolved around me. I never felt anything like that with Ray." "He would complement me. I wasn't used to that." Jorge waited during the months it took for Ray to move out of the house once Carmen asked him to leave. Jorge defined himself in and through Carmen. She became the person for him he was not.

Shortly after they began dating, Carmen began to experience some aspects of the relationship with Jorge as suffocating. When she wasn't at work, he was always at her side, seeming to attend to her needs. "If I had to go grocery shopping, he would go with me . . . if I went to get gas, he would have to pump it. I like to go look at things, but he would be right there with me." She didn't see the encroachment as a prelude to total possession. Ray "hadn't even offered me an aspirin," she remembered. But Jorge was always concerned about what she wanted to eat; he didn't want to see her cry. In fact, the only feelings he wanted her to display were those he could manage with professions of love, bravado, or promises based on lies. The emotions he recognized in her were those that elicited comments he learned from the soaps, in prison, and on the street.

Carmen was hooked. This was the attention she craved as a child, what she needed, her "knight in shining armor." Unlike Ray, Jorge put Carmen before his own mother. He insisted his brothers respect her. With Ray, "I mowed the lawn, cooked, washed, cleaned; He'd watch TV. . . . He was king of the castle . . . and when I came in from mowing the lawn, he'd need something to eat or drink." But Jorge told my daughter, "you need to help your mom (because) she works hard." "Jorge never let me mow that lawn again." With Ray, Carmen was treated as little more than a servant. The services she had performed on command for Ray—the cooking, cleaning, money management, e.g., she now did voluntarily, this time from the vantage of a pedestal on which she received unrelenting attention down to the smallest detail of her activity. The powerlessness of being kept on a pedestal felt different from the feeling of being ground underfoot. I call the process "coercive control from below."

To Jorge, Carmen's family was also "perfect." Before long, Carmen was providing not only the usual round of domestic services for Jorge but also those of a nurse, personal servant, secretary, office manager, and job counselor.

The arrangement wasn't perfect. While Carmen was constantly involved in servicing Jorge and then the children, she was allowed to do nothing for herself. She told me she felt increasingly like she was a ghost in her home, going through the motions of days that seemed to have less and less to do with her. Jorge had stopped drinking. But he had done nothing to address the underlying rage that he had used alcohol to medicate while he was living at home. The fears that he felt, the self-loathing awakened by the memories of his sexual abuse as a child, had been displaced into an ideal of a family made up of Carmen and the children. He slowly began to regress to a childhood dependency when all his basic needs were met. Now, when he awoke, his clothes had to be laid out neatly at the foot for him to dress, his breakfast served, his orders and equipment at the ready.

Pathology is in the room. Jorge's psychiatric condition made him prone to paranoia, delusions, and bouts of mania, depression, and rage. Carmen exhibited symptoms of a "dependent personality disorder." Even so, both Jorge's support and caring for Carmen and the children and Carmen's desire for attention and the appreciation she felt at being cared for were genuine. Jorge was good to them all early on, taking them all to Disneyworld because her daughter Jennie wanted to go there, "We got along really good." She explained, "I felt I really had someone I could lean on. He was very protective . . . he'd make sure I was safe and not hurt, no matter what the context." Carmen had not seen Jorge "before" as he would soon become in the last phase of the relationship. Although he was drinking heavily, chain smoking, in chronic conflict with his mother and brothers, and in terrible physical shape when they met, she learned this only later from his mother. No sooner had he declared his love, than he "threw away" the bottle, gave up cigarettes, reconciled with his family, and embarked on a new business, the exterminator business, in which he had regular responsibilities. These positive changes, which his mother confirms, showed the sacrifices he was making "just to please me." The narcissistic features of Jorge's disorder make it possible for him to be incredibly charming and appear well-balanced for periods of time, even for months. So when we envision Carmen amid the squalor of the last few months of Nubia's life, we have to appreciate what a shocking contrast her life was for her too, much like going from living with Dr. Jekyll to Mr. Hyde in the novel. The fact that the "new" Jorge was the main man she had known and that both Carmen (and Jorge) believed this man was the byproduct of their "love" helps explain why she mistook his regression back to the condition in which he had suffered most of his life as a slippage from which he (they) could quickly recover rather than regression to the mean.

Viewed through the prism of its outcome, the two principals seemed doomed to their fate. But there was a period in this relationship of shared affection when both parties drew a meaningful sense of self-worth and purposiveness out of it, Jorge because he was managing his demons and caring for others and Carmen because she had found a man who treated she and her children like persons rather than as objects. This is the context in which

Carmen decided to continue the relationship with Jorge and in which she agreed to foster.

Phase II. Fostering the Children and Jorge's Deterioration, 1999–2009

During this phase of the relationship, Jorge and Carmen built a successful exterminator business and fostered five children, four of whom they adopted. The division of labor in their household was highly skewed, where Jorge went to work and distracted the children during nap or bath time and Carmen did everything else. Sometime during 2007, Jorge's psychological condition deteriorated significantly and Carmen found herself increasingly responsible for the logistics as well as the accounts of the business, the childcare, home maintenance, and Jorge's personal, physical, and psychological support. However unfair, this arrangement was not unjust.

Hopefulness that they would now have the family they craved motivated the decision to foster and ultimately adopt the four children they had fostered, Jorgie Jr., Jennie, Victor, and Nubia. In addition to Jorge's desire to become a parent, Carmen's decision to adopt was based on rational calculation: they had available space, the older daughter was interested, and there is a perceived need for adoptive parents.

The fact that Jorge was not assessed when the children were placed is not surprising. As we saw in chapter 4 on *Nicholson*, the "fathers" in foster families are rarely assessed as part of safety assessments, let alone screened for a history of physical or sexual abuse, despite the high rates of child abuse and homicide in adoptive homes associated with domestic violence, the reduced visibility of children once adoption has been achieved, and the formidable legal obstacles to rescuing children once adoption is completed. Placement based on a single competent parent is particularly unwise when special needs children are involved, each of whom by definition requires an extraordinary degree of individual attention. Moreover, since the risk with special needs children is likely to be cumulative, staggering the placements changes little. Even so, Florida is located in reality, not social-work land; placement is a largely unsupervised system of child farming, and even the small core of experienced, well-intentioned staff are eventually burned out and made cynical by the absence of community resources to support children. Deaths in care are dreaded. But as we saw in chapter 2 in New York City, fatalities have an become essential driver of expanded budgets. It is a miracle we have as few tragedies in care that we do.

The downward trajectory that culminated in Nubia's death had its onset in 2008, when the twins, Nubia and Victor, had already been in the care of the Barahonas for almost four years. During the previous decade, starting in 1999, when baby Jorgie Jr., a child with a diagnosis of autism, came to live with them when he was 4–5 days old, through the 2008 incident, the Barahonas fostered three special needs children, two of whom they adopted, Jorgie Jr. (2001) and Jennie (2007). There is nothing in the records to suggest that care of the foster children other than the twins was remiss. To the contrary, the record suggests that Carmen Barahona not only exhibited extraordinary competence in caring for her foster and adopted children, including a special needs child, but that she did so alone, virtually unaided by her husband, and while effectively serving as Jorge's secretary, route planner, and business manager. Jorge played no role in the children's feeding, bathing, transport, or other care. But nor did he harm them in any way.

This background on the Barahonas experience is important because it suggests that a critical change in circumstance led to the tragedy, not a failure in either parenting or the initial placement decision.

Over time, the scope of Carmen's responsibilities increased to include not only home maintenance and care for the children but also the maintenance and conduct of Jorge's exterminator business and his personal maintenance as well. With respect to the household and schooling, for example, Carmen deferred to Jorge as a man and a Mexican. Carmen explained, "when it came to school things, he doesn't speak English too well, he was more afraid to say something wrong . . . he never graduated high school . . . he never offered to help (with school activities and events), and I never asked (him to) . . . he'd stay with the other two (children) while I was taking the others (to school) . . . he never washed dishes, never swept floors or mopped." He also believed household and childcare tasks were "women's work." With respect to the business, meanwhile, Jorge was increasingly unable to make appointment, track addresses, record services, bill, or complete other rudimentary activities needed to make his business function. She stated, "In the morning, I got his schedule ready (for the day), and all he had to do was take his folder, get dressed, and go. When he came home, he gave me the folder, I took care of all the scheduling . . . the books . . . I did everything." Once, when she stopped doing his work because she felt overwhelmed, Jorge "fell apart, failed to keep appointments, complaints poured in and the business was on the verge of collapse."

His disability extended to his clothing. Describing her routine, Carmen stated, "At night before bed, I would line up all the kids' clothes and get his uniform ready, so when they get up they had everything ready." She would wash his uniforms with the children's and set them out together. She also answered his business calls "because he wanted to show he had a secretary and his English was not that good." Jorge's dependencies are not unique. Among my professional clients as well as among faculty colleagues, I have encountered similar dependent profiles that extended to wives who ensured their husbands had showered, put on a clean shirt, and brushed their teeth before leaving the house. But both Jorge's history of sexual abuse and alcoholism and the rapid decline of autonomy suggest a clinical etiology.

Some of Jorge's most dysfunctional work behaviors were hidden from them both because Carmen sought to redress gaps in service and assume tasks almost as soon as they surfaced. Missed appointments were rescheduled; unscheduled visits were billed after-the-fact; lost bills retyped; lost payments were covered; invoices were retrieved from heaps or garbage. One result of this catch-up activity was that Carmen experienced Jorge's collapse piecemeal, as a series of missteps or learning deficits that could be remedied. But filling in the holes took a toll. Within a few months, Jorge's inability to focus was matched by Carmen's hypervigilance. If he was off the clock, she was on. The particular deficiencies evoked a general panic. Carmen's driving fear was that "If I didn't do everything, we would lose the business." Pretty soon, Jorge, "didn't do much of anything." Apart from Carmen's frenetic efforts, the family was a shambles and all the children were at risk. Jorge was completely dependent on a person whom he controlled with his whims. But his control was generic, rooted in disability, not in terrorism. This dynamic of "coercive control from below" is common among older couples, particularly where the abusive husband has become physically disabled and a son or daughter is caring for an older, abusive parent.

Explaining why she was overfunctioning while Jorge was underfunctioning, Carmen pointed to innate ability. She stated, "Part of it is I think he wasn't competent enough to keep up with it, keep it on schedule. He didn't know how to do it, couldn't wrap his mind around it." I asked her if she considered that her husband was suffering from a disabling psychological condition. She did not. Lacking experience with mental health, Carmen approaches psychological stress, including her own, largely through a moral grammar of motives related to relative self-efficacy. Thus, instead of sticking to standards of basic competence—such as a capacity to dress or wash oneself—or recognizing a limit to how much work she could tolerate, she continued to assume more and more of the total workload in the family, only dimly aware that her overfunctioning in this way made her incapable of rational choice or judgment. But she felt that there would be a time and place for everything.

Were it not for the presence of the children, Carmen's acclimation to the deterioration of her husband might resemble the adaptations millions of women and men make in families in which one party has Alzheimer's or a similar degenerative physical or psychiatric condition and the other party holds on through a combination of denial, exhausting physical labor, and sheer grit. Carmen had propped up Jorge's life in part because she felt sorry for him and in part because it supported the illusion that she could create a solid foundation for both of them. He had no car. So she bought him a truck, got him his license, tutored him through the exams, set up his appointments, and organized his billings. How many mothers have done this for a son or daughter hobbled by drugs or alcohol? What appears like futility and overcompensation to an outsider initially felt like self-sacrifice to Carmen. Children had no business being a party to this ritual. But the same illusions that drove Carmen to bolster Jorge long past the time when he could be helped outside of an institution sustain millions of households at high levels of dysfunction because the alternatives seem frankly inconceivable. Most families in the world have no access to alternatives to self-maintenance. There is nothing in this story that made tragedy inevitable. But once the family opened itself for inspection, the factors combining to move events in this direction were easy to discern.

The fault line was the children. By 2009, when trouble with the twins became acute at school, the two pillars of Carmen's life, her husband and the business, were collapsing. In the midst of this, Carmen was still talking to her mother "ten times a day" painting a rosy picture, the habit they had set in her childhood of gamely talking about everything but the ogre in the room. The evidence suggests that as things deteriorated at home, Carmen adapted as she had done all her life: she "split" psychologically, functioning robotically day-to-day at her job and with Jorge as if things were normal while denying the dangers in front of her with the children, stuffing deep inside herself the foreboding that something terrible might happen at home. Feeding the children and getting them to bed was a check box, like making sure the truck had gas. Reflecting this attitude, she commented, "I had everything in a system . . . he knew I had it that way . . . his calls, the scheduling, the paperwork, and follow ups (with his clients)." Carmen shared, "as long as I did my routine, it was the only way I could get it done. The children were part of this schedule, "I had to have them fed and bathed, before I could start his calls for next day scheduling, and I can't call people late . . . if I was busy bathing one, he'd keep any eye on the others . . . he would put on a video for them." In the past, even when they were in her rear view mirror, watching TV with Jorge while she was giving Nubia a bath for instance, she had an eye on them. Then, not so much.

Phase III. The Crises Converge and a Child Is Killed (2009–2011)

Everything was set for their demise before the children entered. The coercive control of children is rarely about the specific children. The child who is killed is rarely meant to die.

To keep their household intact, Carmen compensated for Jorge's psychological deterioration by assuming global responsibilities for managing the home, business, and the children. This adaptation strategy afforded a modicum of stability. But tragedy became unavoidable once Carmen consented to adopt Nubia and Victor. She made this decision under pressure from Jorge, thereby reifying his image of an "ideal family," which bore no relation to the resources in their home. The implosion of the ideal stemmed from the coincidence of two crises: Nubia's inconsolable need for recognition and support, and Jorge's use of coercive control to disable Carmen. Nubia's struggles to be free of gender shaming at school caught the attention of DCF, which threw Jorge into a panic. Jorge attempted to manage the situation by isolating the twins from public view. He found Carmen's alliance with the twins at home equally threatening and determined to sever their relationship. To accomplish this, he had to disable Carmen's protective function, the same capacity with which she kept him functional. Without Carmen's support, Jorge decompensated rapidly, deploying stepped up violence, threats to kill her and her family, cruelty to the children, and a broad spectrum of coercive and controlling tactics that turned Carmen into his "capo," a guard and functionary in the virtual concentration camp he constructed for the twins. Humiliated and degraded, Carmen tried to find her ground as the sand slid out from under her, and was only able to contribute in small, but woefully inadequate ways to the children's well-being in Nubia's final days.

This final phase of the case poses two forensic challenges, to clearly de-marcate how the lines of power emanating from Jorge's coercive control constrained *all* of the relevant actors in the Barahona family, and to identify how Carmen and Nubia responded to their respective constraints. Until now, I have been somewhat equivocal in identifying Carmen as a "victim" of coer-cive control, in part because, however ill-suited her choices turned out, they followed a certain feminine logic rooted in Cuban culture, escape from an abusive father and husband, and an attempt to maintain a relationship with a man who idealized her. Up to that point, Carmen was arguably a hapless victim of her own actions and bad choices, including her choice of partner. But once Jorge turned on Carmen and the twins, the context shifted to one in which there were only bad choices and safety was not an option.

The Controversy over Adopting the Twins

The twins, Nubia and Victor, were taken from their biological parents when they were 3½ years old because they'd been repeatedly beaten, molested, and sexually abused; they were placed for foster care with the Barahonas. As a result of their mistreatment, including "having them do things together," the children suffered severe psychiatric and cognitive problems, including PTSD in the case of Nubia and in Victor's case, a developmental delay that caused him to be almost labile and deferential to his sister like a much younger kin.

Nubia had been born with ambiguous genitalia, which resulted in the girls at school calling her names.[2] Nubia's condition required constant monitoring and should have been managed in a medically licensed foster home—presumably the Florida Department of Social Services wanted to keep the twins together—and explains much of the "disheveled state, hunger and body odor" reported by the school and attributed to improper care by the Barahonas. Although the problem was eventually addressed surgically, in 2009, it was a continual source of annoyance, bullying, and embarrass-ment for Nubia. Carmen told the teacher Nubia was "uncomfortable" around the other girls at school, but never revealed the source of her discomfort, claiming that Nubia's physiology was "private." In fact, Carmen had never been educated about Nubia's condition during the placement, adoption, or medical intervention process. The school lacked the information to provide the appropriate protection and supportive response, let alone help elicit Nubia's voice in her gender assignment.

The final DCF investigation before the twins were adopted made clear she required specialist support. It found that Nubia had an insatiable appetite; was stealing money and food; was losing weight and hair, and had missed two weeks of school due to heavy bleeding (not further specified). At a minimum, even if the social workers believed all of these problems were due to Nubia's "condition" rather than her home situation, the mother clearly "needed support." But DCF was concerned only with whether Nubia's problems were related to improper foster care, not whether the Barahonas could manage the level of complexity required to safely raise these special needs children. DCF ascertained only that Nubia had "survived," not whether she could thrive in this home. Few questions were asked about Victor because his mode of adaptation was passive, regressed, and withdrawn. In some ways, the placement with the Barahonas was even less appropriate for him than for Nubia. His passivity may have saved his life. But it is unlikely to have done so for long without his sister's care and protection. The decision to allow the Barahonas to adopt these children was professionally unsound and put them both at the highest possible risk.

Meanwhile, at home, both through the ritual enactments they'd brought from the earlier placement and the soap opera melodrama in which Carmen and Jorge imagined them playing, the twins were assigned roles and speaking parts to which they were held accountable. Nubia was a "seductress," "thief," and "master of deception"; Victor was her "hapless dupe" and "coconspirator." Carmen's descriptions barely conceal her competitive feelings toward Nubia. She described how the twins "acted out" at home where Nubia played Jorge's "little princess" "to play us off against each other" and competed with Carmen to "mother Victor," feeding and showering with him, for instance. According to Carmen, if Nubia "told him to jump, he would say 'how high?'," an authority with her brother that Carmen sorely lacked. Carmen also acknowledged feeling jealousy when Jorge treated Nubia more leniently than Victor or the others. The point remains. Because they lacked training to manage children with special needs, the Barahonas interpreted these expressions of illness in Machiavellian terms, as malevolence, and responded as they might have to a normal teen exhibiting similar behavior.

To her credit, Carmen vehemently opposed adoption, largely because of the problems she had managing the twins' behavior, Nubia's increasing difficulties at school, and particularly what both she and Jorge read as their competitive hostility toward the younger sibs. Carmen reported, "I wanted to give them back before their adoption. I kept telling him if they're capable of this now, what do you expect when they're teenagers?" The arguments became physical, and Jorge beat Carmen. Jorge declared "NO, those were my kids." Again and again, he declared he could handle it, "he would change them." I asked Carmen, "Was this realistic?" She now acknowledges it was not. I asked her if she went along with the adoption because she was afraid of him? She said, "Yes, I was afraid of what he might do to me. But I felt sorry for him too." The transition from fostering to adoption was uneventful so far as Florida's Department of Children was concerned. It sealed Nubia's fate.

Nubia and Victor Are Withdrawn from School

During the period between the adoption of the children in 2008, Nubia's corrective surgery in July 2009, and the removal of Victor and Nubia from their school sometime in September 2009, the family and its individual members were seen by myriad professionals, including several dozen teachers, social workers, doctors, and nurses with some specialized training in abuse detection.[3] Had any assessment of coercive control been made of any member of the family, the extreme danger to the twins could have been identified and tragedy averted. By October 2009, there was little anyone could have done to save the child.

Carmen's involvement with the exterminator business tempered Jorge's physical abuse in the period surrounding the adoption of the twins. This situation had changed by the summer of 2009. In Carmen's account, Jorge's abuse of her and the children in this period tracks the downward trajectory of his physical and mental health, starting with extremely paranoid behavior with his business. He refused to return to finish work he'd started because the homeowner told him to come in through the back instead of the front door; refused payment from customers he thought suspected him of stealing, and "fired" a customer who asked him to remove his shoes before entering. Over the next year, Carmen watched him lose pride in the work he did, the business he'd built fall apart, his competency wane, and then realized that his mental condition made it impossible for him to hold a job. Because this was the condition he was in when they first met, she experienced his failure as also her own.

Toward the fall of 2009, Jorge also isolated Carmen by refusing to go on family vacations or attend any family holidays like Thanksgiving or Christmas. When she visited home, Carmen felt like a puppet on a string. In 2010, he extended the tactic to the children, refusing to allow the twins to go on holidays to his in-laws.

I asked Carmen why she hadn't shared the abuse with her family during the holiday visit. She was afraid of what her older son might do, she confessed. But she also demurred, she said, because so much of it wasn't dramatic—"he broke my lip" pushed me against the wall" and because she didn't have the words for the invisible forms of abuse she was experiencing. And because it would confirm what they thought of her, that she could do nothing for herself.

I asked her, "if someone had knocked on the door before all of this stuff happened and offered to tale Nubia and Victor to a boarding school or a home where they could get one on one care, what would you have said?"

She replied, "If anyone knocked on the door, he wouldn't let me go to the door. If anyone had to come out to the house, he took care of it. I wasn't allowed to engage with anyone." By the summer of 2009, Carmen was already considering options within an arena of choices in which there were no safe choices.

For a time after the adoption, Carmen drew closer to Nubia and they bonded around doing her hair and buying puzzles at the dollar store and making them. But after an incident in which the Barahonas believed the twins tried to drown Jorgie Jr., and Victor urinated on Jorgie Jr.'s clothes, Jorge announced he was "going to handle it."

The division of caretaking did not become complete until October or November 2009, when Jorge took over full responsibility for homeschooling the twins. Months earlier, he had already demarcated homeschooling as the domain to keep the twins separated from Jorgie and Jennie, and in which to ensure their obedience to all rules. Arguments centered less on whether separation was appropriate—Carmen also believed Nubia and Victor were sexually molesting Jennie in her bed at night and wanted them separated—but on whether Jorge was capable of caring properly for the twins on his own, the issue which became the focus of assaults a few months later.

The separation of the children for management holds the key to what happened next. So we must consider whether Carmen's apparent acquiescence in this decision can be accepted at face value. When I put this decision in the context of what is happening to Carmen's performance at work, Jorge's physical abuse, the tactics he's using to control her and the children, and his rapid deterioration psychologically, I believe Carmen primarily withdrew from the twins in response to terroristic threats and only subsequently rationalized the shame she felt at doing so by citing the twins' misbehavior. I believe Carmen knew at the time—she certainly knows now—that nothing the twins did or said or did not do justified any of the punishments meted out. Ironically, she is more ashamed to admit she has let down her father—by allowing a man to abuse her—than to acknowledge she played a role in a child's death.

There was an extraordinary level of coercion and control being used to prevent Carmen from rescuing Nubia. Jorge had hit Carmen early in their relationship. After 2008 and by the fall of 2009, his assaults were occurring several times a week and more. They usually began with jealous accusations almost as soon as she returned from work, and continued until it was time to bathe the children. She recounted instances adding to over 100 assaults, many attacks including numerous types. These assaults included throwing something at her; pushing/shoving/grabbing; kicking/hitting; wrestling her; punching her in the back, head, and upper arms; beating her up; dragging her by the hair (on three occasions); and attempting to strangle her (twice). He also threatened her with a knife and said he could kill her and her parents numerous times. These assaults occurred over hours and included multiple elements, and sometimes lasted several days. As an immediate result of these assaults, Carmen reported sustaining minor bruises, lost hair (due to hair pulling); a sprained back; broken ribs (one occasion); and headaches from being punched in the head and being dragged by the hair. She described an incident in which she was thrown on the floor, resulting in a hairline fracture that required her to wear a brace. On this occasion, the one instance she required medical care, Carmen told the physician she was injured in a fall.

With the exception of the incident with the knife, none of these assaults was life-threatening, and Carmen told me she did not think Jorge intended to kill her, though she took more seriously his threats against her family. The significance of the assaults lay not in the injurious effect of a particular attack, the broken ribs for instance, but in their cumulative effect, a sense of terroristic fear that felt hostage-like. Moreover, from the summer of 2009 on, the assaults were "continuous" "when he really started to lose it—he went downhill." Carmen insists she does not know if Jorge was also hitting the twins as often or as hard during the days when he was alone at home with them. But she told me, after the couple divided childcare and decided which of them was responsible for whom: "the kids got worse after that and they were constantly fighting with him." The fact that no report was filed or notice taken for so much violence is not surprising at this point in the book. Remember, when a level of terroristic fear is established, the criminologic calculation of the "time to violence" in which we expect a victim to report a crime does not apply. This is because the "abuser is always on." The opportunity to report in a situation like this is a fiction constructed by those who have not walked in the shoes of our victims. There is no time when someone is "free" of fear.

Carmen saw Jorge's violence as symptomatic of his psychological state. She remarked, "he had never done that before, he never would have laid a hand on me, but by then he was not working . . . he wouldn't work, he'd just be in front of computer, looking at dead people." Eventually, according to Carmen, Jorge stopped working entirely because, "he didn't want to be around people." When he quit, she knew he was sick. "He . . . loved his job, like a doctor." And she had tried to keep him at work, as if simply sending his body to the job could recreate the feeling of self-respect. An outside observer might have seen a deranged derelict. But for Carmen, the derangement was a temporary aberration in an uneducated artisan workman.

Before 2009 Carmen had retained relative autonomy in the domestic arena, where she had always had sole responsibility for housework, meals, planning entertainment, organizing Jorge's job, and bathing and bedding the children. It was these activities which Jorge now sought to micromanage, targeting how, what, and when she cooked, for example, which magazine article she read, and detailing every aspect of cleaning, including stores, products, and size containers. The shows she could watch on TV were controlled. ("I couldn't even watch *Golden Girls* because he thought they were raunchy and man crazy"). If she chose sporting events, Jorge would accuse her of just wanting to "see men in tight pants," and "you like this because you like black men, that's what you want." His jealousy extended to aspects of self-soothing, such as her music. She reported, "If I sang a song or listened to a song, he'd say it was because it reminded me of someone . . . so I stopped listening."

These two events—Jorge's psychological deterioration and escalation of his abuse of Carmen and the children—came to a head when Nubia's problems at school prompted new DCF concerns with the Barahonas in 2010. Nubia, who had been a good student, was suddenly having behavioral and academic problems at school as well as the ongoing experience of being shamed for being a "he/she." Carmen recalled Nubia "crying every morning before school," leading Carmen to "let her stay home," sometimes with Jorge, on many occasions. No one involved with her education considered that Nubia's distress at school reflected her home situation and the failure to address the gender shaming. School was a safe place for Nubia to "act out"—precisely because it might attract the attention of DCF as Jorge feared—a cry to help with the situation at home which Jorge interpreted as a sign that she needed to be withdrawn. Carmen's acquiescence in Nubia's withdrawal is more ambiguous, possibly a disguised plea for help.

In June 2010, DCF visited the house because of Nubia's extended absence, and Carmen finally wrote a letter to the School Board about her condition and the upcoming surgery to address it. The July surgery did not satisfy Nubia, however, and fearing Nubia might attract additional attention from DCF, Jorge adamantly refused to let her return to school, telling Carmen, "you're not sending her back to school, she will start all this stuff again . . . they will be sending DCF to the house." Carmen prevailed, Nubia did return for the start of school, and she again reported being bullied. A referral to DCF seemed likely. Jorge was furious. Carmen said, "He punished me. He said, 'You have Jorgie Jr. and Jennie, these are my kids [referring to the twins– ES], you have nothing to do with them.' I cook for them, wash them and that's it. He never left them alone with me. They weren't allowed to talk to me or be near me." Carmen knew leaving the twins at home was a bad idea. She looked for options. She considered sending Nubia to boarding school, but they have to be past the fourth grade and she was in third grade, "and they [boarding schools] were expensive, very expensive—Not an option for us."

Carmen tried to make the transition successful. She purchased books and workbooks for the twins to use in their homeschooling. But Jorge refused to allow her to check on their work or provide them with constructive feedback. And he was unable to do the work himself. He had already decided, "I had no right to check what he was doing . . . you don't want to do it, you can't check up on me." According to Carmen, by the end of September, Jorge had cut her completely off from the twins.

By October 2010, things had escalated at home. Jorge was so dysfunctional he was no longer able to work and the twins were supposedly being "homeschooled" by him during the day. The isomorphism of his management of the twins and his micromanagement of Carmen was perfect but not visible to anyone outside. Carmen's income barely met expenses and they fell behind in the mortgage. Carmen reports "relief" that Jorge was managing the twins, who posed a real risk to their younger sibs. But she was also aware that Jorge was enraged at Nubia, was lecturing the twins for hours about

Jesus, and putting them in the bathroom for punishment. Carmen worked days and so was not fully cognizant of what Jorge was doing to the twins in the daytime. But on more than one occasion, she told me, she had to remove them from the tub before she bathed the younger children.

The isolation of the children in an abusive home was a sign of the highest risk. Carmen recognizes the signs now. With the twins out of school and the adoption complete, agency involvement ceased. At the point when the adoption agency should have stepped in, it withdrew. In the winter of 2010, Carmen was only dimly aware something "bad" was happening to the twins. Though she was "in" the house every morning and evening, Jorge kept much of his most harmful behavior "off stage" while presenting the twins in various states of disarray and contrition. Carmen experienced "perspecticide," she did not "know what she knew," and functioned throughout this period in a fugue-like state frozen by terror of her circumstances. Her workmates confirm that her demeanor during this period suggests someone who is paralyzed by the competing terrors of what will happen if she discloses—that Jorge will harm her and she will lose the children—and if she does not—that Jorge will harm the children and she will lose them. I don't think her fear of Jorge leaving entered into the picture. Indeed, she says she offered to get him a place and pay him to leave.

The evidence from Carmen's work is critical to assessing the global nature of her disability. The rapid deterioration of a female employee who has been functional is a common expression of being subjected to coercive control. Carmen was like a corpse on furlough. She reported, "At work I wouldn't talk to anyone. They'd ask what was wrong. I didn't want to think, just focus on my work, watching the clock, and then I have to go home, I have to go home, I didn't want to go home. . . . I'd start to shake when it's time to go home. I didn't confide in anyone. . . . I felt like a robot, not thinking, not feeling, just existing. . . . I wanted to die, I just gave up, I couldn't take anymore, I surrendered." Work had been a safety zone where she could shut out what was happening at home. Now, the means she constructed to shield her at home was with her always. She says I was "living in a bubble" "not knowing how I got to work or to school . . . behaving entirely on autopilot, without thought." Jorge's constant calls kept bringing her back. She was no longer able to go out for lunch while at work, because she had to be by her desk to pick up her phone in case Jorge called. She was required to check in with Jorge once she dropped off the children at school, and again once she arrived at her job. This is an example of how "coercive control crosses social space." With cellular and video technology, the abuser is always on. When he became anxious or jealous, he had Victor or Nubia call, often with aimless queries about what she was doing or dinner.

Because of the continued intrusions at work, Carmen arrived home at the peak of terror. Simply drawing near the house could paralyze her with fear because, "I knew what was coming. If I walked in and smiled, [Jorge would think] I had done someone out there [had sex with another man], but if I was not smiling, he would say, 'why are you not smiling?' . . . If I talked, he would say, 'why are you talking,' but if I was not talking, he would say, 'what are you planning? what are you hiding?'" and he would threaten her by saying things like, "Just remember, I can do a lot . . . you'd be dead before you can call someone." The scripts implanted by serial conflict ran nonstop in her head. The tension in these moments felt worse than the beatings that followed.

By mid-2010, Carmen's domestic problems had become manifest physically to those who knew her, "I couldn't eat," she told me, "I was losing my hair, patches of hair missing, friends thought I had cancer." She never told her mother about the abuse. But her mother told her she was afraid for her. "'I know something is happening. You're losing weight, hair falling out.' My mother also thought I had cancer." She told friends she was on a diet. Jorge was no longer working and was convinced he could "cure" the twins by preaching to them," along with isolating and beating them. By the summer of 2010, Jorge had begun "confining them, sometimes separately, or together in a closet, the laundry room or bathroom." The twins would be required to stay on the floor by his bed or in the bathtub. Having started by locking them in the bathroom only during the day, he came to believe that the only way everyone else in the household could sleep safely at night was if they were bound (at night too). Carmen reported coming home from work on several occasions to find the twins in a large recycling bin in the yard.

DCF visited the home after Nubia's two-month absence. No relevant questions were asked or information shared. At this critical juncture, a single questions about coercive control could have saved Nubia's life.

Carmen was the only potential buffer to Jorge's complete control of the children. Her leaving the house each day for work and to take the children to school created a risk of exposure he found increasingly intolerable. At the same time that he feared her betrayal, his complete dependence on her in every other way elicited a morbid phobia that she secretly wanted to betray and destroy him. From at least November 2010 until the removal of Nubia from her home, Jorge extended his micromanagement directly to Carmen and she became no less his primary victim than Nubia and Victor. Like them, she was forced to devise her options from an ever narrower range of choices, all of them bad.

During the last months of Nubia's life, Carmen presented the major threat to Jorge's hegemony over the household, not the twins, who were bound for most of the time he wasn't with them. Carmen constantly attempted to intervene and badgered Jorge with passive-aggressive "questions" that made him "nuts." "I was dealing with him, "she said, "he was beating me, he's telling me I was cheating on him and everything just happened one thing after the other, he'd sit on the couch and just stare at me." He threatened he'd do something to her parents, to her, to the kids. He wanted to hurt her. Given his propensity for paranoid thoughts, I'm sure Jorge was convinced she wanted to hurt him. Carmen hid in their bedroom afraid to come out. In January, Jorge moved out to the family room. He would just come and go in the bedroom when he needed to sleep.

Carmen maintains that from September 2010 through February 2011, "the kids [Nubia and Victor] were with him wherever he went." She told me that during September the twins remained at home, but that "he wasn't putting them in the bathtub" at that point. "However, later on, the twins, "never really did their lessons . . . and he forced them to stay in the bathtub, at first without restraint, but later he needed to 'secure' them because there were 'getting into things in the bathroom.'" Carmen admits that Nubia and Victor were made to spend extended periods in the bathtub, and that by December, they spent so much time being bound, there were ligature marks on their wrists and ankles and the marks from the beatings were noticeable." She believed that Jorge kept the twins isolated and bound in the bathtub "almost permanently, in order to keep others from seeing the marks."

During November and December, with the little kids out of school for vacation, Jorge called and demanded Carmen return from work and help Jennie and Jorgie Jr. with their homework on the computer. She told me, "I would come home, go to the kids [Victor and Nubia], Jorge would have them in dining room till dinner. . . . Jorge would take them back to the bedroom with him, and I would help Jorgie Jr. or Jennie with homework and showers. If I came home and they were in the tub, then I'd bring them out, and Jorge would sit with them out there [in the dining room]."

Carmen was aware that Victor and Nubia were being segregated, put in the bathroom, and being bound in the tub as early as October. She may not have recognized the extent of the children's plight that early, since they were restrained mainly during the day when she was working. But she recalls some occasions when she would untie them after she returned from work and bring them into the living area. She also recalls occasions when Jorge would punish the twins by sending them to the tub from the dinner table. In these and related activities, she functioned in the role of capo, the concentration camp prisoners who policed other prisoners: she served meals to the twins in captivity, replaced their bonds, or moved them from room to room. She operated with the mentality of a guard, easing the plight of the children on her watch while being careful not to overstep the rules. Jennifer Lopez (daughter) testified that Carmen sometimes snuck food to Nubia when Jorge was sleeping. But I have no reason to believe this happened frequently.

At the other extreme, there were times when Jorge forced Carmen to watch him bind, slap, or otherwise mistreat the twins or to isolate them in a room or bind them herself because he knew how degraded she felt by this display of her helplessness and because "complicity" in their maltreatment could be used to keep her from calling law enforcement, DCF, medical personnel, or anyone else in a position of authority. Statements by Carmen confirmed by Jennie and others suggests there were times when Carmen slapped Nubia and tied one or both of the children up.

Apart from serving as a guard, keeper, and accomplice under duress, Carmen provided a passive witness as Jorge browbeat and slapped Nubia and Victor into "confessing" various plots to poison the family and kill her husband. She may even have bought into Jorge's delusions about these plots to some extent and thereby given his views added legitimacy in the eyes of the younger children, specifically, after the twins admitted to these plots. Whether or not there was actual "evidence" that the twins' fantasies extended to plotting is irrelevant to the immorality of the punitive response and in no way justifies its tolerance by Carmen. One can acknowledge that "shitting on Jesus" was an "act of aggression" by the twins, for instance, and still insist it revealed their utter powerlessness and vulnerability in the face of the Golgotha, not their culpability. That Carmen, even momentarily, embraced Jorge's wildly distorted imago of the children as monsters speaks to how diminished in moral stature she became in Jorge's hands. By Christmas, the twins were no longer visible to the community, a frequent prequel to child homicide. Carmen stated that Victor and Nubia were not allowed to attend any holiday or family events, because "by then they weren't my kids anymore. I had to make excuses to my family, making dumb excuses."

By January 2011, Carmen maintains that Victor and Nubia were still kept at home with Jorge, and that there were, "a lot of arguments with him and Nubia." By this time, Carmen was numb to her own fear and Jorge was popping so many pills he was in a constant state of frenzied wakefulness, much like an amphetamine high. Carmen could have been watching a horror film on Netflix. She repeated Jorge's ruminations as he insulted and tormented the children. "He wouldn't let me get involved. . . . He'd say this is this way and they wouldn't listen, they're pushing his buttons . . . they know how to push them, like poop on the prayer, or poop all over the walls and medicine cabinet . . . and that was making him angrier and angrier." Again, she is staring at the children with both horror (at the fate they are inviting) and envy at their willingness to do what she is not capable of doing. "They were just getting back at him for what he was doing . . . that's what I thought it was." She acknowledged that Victor and Nubia were being abused, stating, "yes, I told him so, but who wants to be screamed at?" After all, she too was being abused.

The contradiction Carmen felt when Jorge interpreted her defense of the children as a slight to him and hurt them worse came to a head in December, when "things got to a point I couldn't even talk to him . . . he'd come at me if I even opened my mouth, and he'd be worse. He'd say I was against him," referring to Victor as "your papoose," because "I would defend the kids [Nubia and Victor]."

Since her attempts to challenge his mistreatment of the children were met with "you don't care if they disrespect me," followed by a torrent of verbal and physical abuse, Carmen found it easier to avoid him by taking care of Jorgie Jr. and Jennie together whenever she could, making sure they took baths, had clean clothes, and ate cooked meals, things Jorge did not do. She loaded them up with bread with milk and sugar in the morning ("poor man's French toast") in case he sent them off with no lunch and cans of spaghetti and sandwiches if he allowed them to take lunch. There were also other little ways, too numerous to recount, in which she eased the suffering of Victor and Nubia by generalizing not what *should* be done, but what Jorge would have done in his best moments, loosening the children's bonds, sitting them up in the tub, moving them from the floor to the bed, and so on. The idea was to fill in enough of the blanks left in the children's lives that they would survive and Jorge wouldn't notice.

In January, when Victor and Nubia ended all open resistance to Jorge, he concentrated his anger at his wife as the only possible threat left to his exposure. He broke Carmen's cell phone ("because you are trying to share my business") and smashed it on her head. On at least two occasions, he grabbed her by the neck, pulled her across the room and choked her so she couldn't breathe. She reported "you feel like your whole life is just leaving you. I would wake up on the floor, he'd be kicking me in the back, punishing me so I would wake up—everything was on me then."

Shortly after this beating, Carmen saw Nubia alive for the last time. The tragic undertone comes in retrospect because she now knows what happened. Superficially, the facts tell us little. Carmen returned home from work midafternoon to find Nubia had thrown up. She cleaned up. Jorge beat Nubia while Carmen cooked spaghetti in the kitchen. Carmen served Nubia dinner in her bed, fed the rest of the family, bathed the little children, put them to bed, did the laundry, and retired. In the morning, she set breakfast for the twins on their dresser and left for work.

Here is Carmen's account. Read it with what we already know about how she copes with the terroristic violence in her life, how she tries to find moments of autonomy for herself and the children in the niches of their lives where spaces still exist. Jorge was still asleep when she left. He would kill Nubia later in the day, disappear the body, and then return home to start removing the living room rug, a chore Carmen had asked him to do two years earlier.

Carmen's Account

> Jorge was upset because Nubia forced herself to vomit to annoy him. He told her to stop vomiting," accusing Nubia of "doing this on purpose . . . he ordered me to clean it up. He took her into the room. I could hear him yelling at he . . . beating her, she was crying, saying "No Papa, No Papa!" . . . it was a Wednesday—I came home because Wednesday I would do some mid-week grocery shopping.

Not wanting to bear witness to what she thought would be a terrible beating, Ms. Barahona stated that she went to kitchen and heated up Spaghetti O's. She recalled, The account continues

> She [Nubia] was sitting on his side of the bed. She was leaning up against the nightstand. . . . I came in with dinner, she didn't want to eat, she was

not hungry. I thought she was just upset . . . she seemed OK, so I didn't stress dose [her medication]. I didn't force her to eat. She just wanted juice, so I gave her that, and brought Victor in. Jorge was on the bed, watching TV, Victor was eating. I went out, finished laundry, cleaning, and feeding the other two [Jennie and Jorgie] who were doing homework in the family room. He [Jorge] was in the room [bedroom] with Nubia and Victor. I bathed the two kids [Jennie and Jorgie], put them to bed, went back, and did all the uniforms, and put everything out—the things I do every night. I went back into the room [the master bedroom], and the kids [Victor and Nubia] were laying on the side of the bed asleep and Jorge was in bed half asleep. I went to bed and then got up next morning. The kids [Nubia and Victor] were still asleep. . . . I got up like always, showered and dressed. The kids [Jorgie and Jennie] got up and ready. I made breakfast, brought in two bowls of cereal for Nubia and Victor, and put them on my dresser next to where they were laying down. I said goodbye and I left.

Conclusion

Rachel, Magdalena Luczak, and Carmen Barahona were ashamed they harmed their children, and Magdalena and Carmen were devastated not to have prevented their children's death, like Adrianna Oyola and other mothers whose children were killed by abusive partners. Magdalena took her life. After years of reflection, Rachel and Carmen have come to appreciate the incredible obstacles they faced. Carmen now recognizes that the symptoms of withdrawal and denial she exhibited were "normal" responses to the unbearable burden of trauma she was asked to carry. Because of COVID mainly, I haven't visited Rachel or her extended family in several years, though we talk every few months. When we last talked and she asked me to conceal her identity, she told me she is now ready to sit down with her daughter (now also a mother) and share their experience. Carmen has read my chapter, but we have not discussed it.

At the end of our interview, Carmen told me she is perplexed by how the children responded to Jorge. Specifically, she was both amazed and frightened by the twins' "resistance" to Jorge's authority and their apparent willingness to risk his violent overreactions—"setting him off," so to speak—by what she regarded as minor willfulness. Carmen knows that Jorge needed no pretext to discharge: he abused her when the water was too cold and not cold enough and for "no reason." So, nothing the children did or did not continue do would have led to a different outcome. But if the twins knew this, she wondered, why, unlike her, didn't they perform a charade of acting contrite in front of Jorge or admit their behavior was responsible for his abuse as she did? Carmen told me that watching Nubia stand up to Jorge made her realize that she had *chosen* to reinforce his delusional behavior as part of her transactional relationship to Jorge. To this extent, she realizes, she had "chosen" the relationship with Jorge over the children, albeit to preserve her life, possibly even betraying them. She feels guilt about this, though I don't confuse this with legal responsibility in Nubia's death. The script felt familiar. When Carmen was a child, her mother had supported her father's pretexts at rationality when he had arbitrarily curtailed her femininity. From her mother, she'd learned that soothing the male ego was one price you paid for safety in marriage. As a girl, she felt betrayed by her mother, left alone when she needed recognition, much as I imagine Tiffany Hughes felt when she disclosed Keith's sexual assault and her mother chose to believe Keith's denial. As Marc might have felt when he told his mother it was "alright" for Roberto to beat him bloody for taking a scissors out of the drawer. From the vantage of her own experience, Carmen now understood the double-bind her mother experienced because of her husband's coercive control. But Nubia, she dimly understood, was now enacting the script she, Carmen, had been too fearful to voice as a girl. From the vantage of imagining Nubia's voice—"shitting on Jesus"—Carmen saw through her own complicity with Jorge's tyranny and recognized that when she endorsed the view of Nubia as a devil child or bound the twins' legs or helped them sit up while leaving them to eat in the tub, she was a Judas in league with a monster. In this realization, she felt her mother's predicament as never before. Or perhaps for the first time. She also recognized the courage in the twins' resistance. And the martyrdom. She wishes now she had dropped the illusion of safety she gave her mother, disclosed her abuse by Jorge, and received some response.

I don't know whether the children's various acts of defilement took courage or just reflected a profound desensitization to social cues. Carmen blames the children for pissing Jorge off, in part because he beat her when he got angry, not them. But she also secretly admires how they took the worst he handed out and literally "shit" on his endless prayer services or his music lessons, an example of what the German political philosopher Herbert Marcuse called "the Great Refusal" to choose between equally horrendous evils, submission to mindless, religious prattle or sordid degradation, beatings, and death. To

Carmen's eyes at least, the children demonstrated a third alternative, a level of resiliency rooted in consanguinity, because they had one another, which Carmen lacked. Daniel Pelka's link to his sister, Anna; Marc's to Adullah and his other sisters; and the twins' loyalty to one another, and, of course, the precarious bonds each of the children in our cases maintained with their mothers—here lies the stuff that the future will be made from if we put justice at their backs.

Carmen's own assessment is that "I did not stop him." She is touching a much deeper sense of obligation to her children than the State has the right to demand. What is remarkable to me was that she sustained a response of any kind, let alone one that ameliorated the effects on the twins. Her responses were tactical rather than strategic, drawn from a broader repertoire than the children's and complicated by Jorge's continual scrutiny. Jorge told police he punched his wife when she tried to call for help and "If she tried to tell me, I just avoid it" and call her "a joke." Once he punched her so hard, for falling asleep in the van, that it caused a migraine. Direct confrontations resulted in the severest beatings. Once, she recalled, "Jorge was leading the twins to the bedroom and I heard screaming. Nubia was on the ground, bleeding from the head. Jorge said she was talking back to him, so he pushed her into a wall. "I stopped him and confronted him." In response, he threatened Carmen with a knife and choked her till she passed out. That was the second time he'd choked her till she lost consciousness. On the day before she last saw Nubia, Carmen reported, "Victor came home with a badly cut upper lip, and Jorge said Victor fell," and Victor corroborated the story. Carmen told Jorge she did not believe the story and warned Jorge that he "couldn't keep abusing kids." In response, "he turned and hit me. I was bruised, but not bleeding . . . then he threatened to kill my parents by setting off a chemical bomb at their house." Carmen's resistance might not have been very effective, or as robust or as all-encompassing as one would have liked. But it was sufficient to make Jorge aware that the children were contested terrain and amounted to as much as most people would probably muster in the same circumstances.

When Carmen returned home from work on Thursday, Jorge told her he had brought Nubia to Laura's (Jorge's sister), which Victor confirmed. The following day, Jorge told her to get Nubia's things so that he could bring them to Nubia at Laura's house—a fiction she allowed herself to believe. Nubia had already been killed. Carmen had three other foster children she had helped to live.

Conclusion

The Children of Coercive Control reframes the global agenda for child protection in the context of the safety and empowerment of women. It provides the basis for a new approach designed to replace segmented "abuse" agendas with an emphasis on early intervention to create stable, egalitarian families.

I first identified the coercive control framework in my book *Coercive Control* (2006; 2022) primarily as it affects women and other adult victims. In *Children of Coercive Control*, I applied the framework to families with children. The most serious cases of child abuse, child sexual abuse, and nonaccidental child fatality occur in the context of coercive control of the mother. I describe how to identify the children of coercive control and advocate removal of the perpetrators so children can remain safe at home and thrive.

The subjects of this book are the millions of children worldwide whose futures are jeopardized when their father or another person deploys a combination of violent and nonviolent tactics to monopolize the resources and opportunities to which they are entitled in a family space. Currently, when these children are injured or thought to be "exposed to domestic violence," they are identified as "abused" by the child welfare system. After their families receive services, the children are likely to be removed, languish in foster care, be murdered by an abusive parent, or disappear from the system. This is the downward spiral I would end. Part I demonstrated that the current approach to protecting children affected by domestic violence has not helped children and has increased both their risk and their mother's risk of ongoing and possibly fatal abuse. Part II described the coercive control of children in the context of their mother's abuse and provided dramatic case examples of their subjugation in this context. Part III provided a nuanced look in real time at how women and children struggle to survive the constraints of coercive control. If coercive control is properly identified and victims are protected by the removal of the abusive adult, the children of coercive control can develop normally. Moving the agenda for child protection from child abuse to the coercive control of children would provide a huge increment in equity

Children of Coercive Control. Evan Stark, Oxford University Press. © Oxford University Press 2023.
DOI: 10.1093/oso/9780197587096.003.0012

and justice for women and children, significantly reduce nonaccidental child death and injury, and enhance family stability across a broad swath of humanity.

This Conclusion reiterates the core arguments in the book and the implications of *Children of Coercive Control* for policy and practice. I close with a note of humility.

Part I: The Context for Coercive Control

All persons subjected to coercive control experience a sense of entrapment akin to enslavement, including children. This book has demonstrated the significance of coercive control as a context for child maltreatment, described the elements of coercive control when it is applied to children, including the use of children as proxies and as weapons—"child abuse as tangential spouse abuse"—and demonstrated, using illustrations from my forensic practice, how the children of coercive control struggle to survive its devastating effects. Until now, the prevailing wisdom in services to protect children globally has been that child "abuse" and "neglect" are separate problems that overlap because of a similar etiology in maternal immaturity/ malfunction. In this view, the death and serious injury of children in families is the tragic but often foreseeable consequence when a downward spiral of intersecting constitutional, medical, psychological, behavioral, and environmental factors erode a woman's capacity to provide and protect. The mother's capacity to protect is allegedly compromised when she "engages in" domestic violence. In this approach, the aim of community surveillance of domestic violence by pediatric, child guidance, and child welfare personnel is to detect the early signs of the downward spiral in maternal functioning and intervene when domestic violence becomes a persistent issue, primarily to prevent its effects on children. The first line of prevention involves services and support to end the domestic violence, with temporary placement of the children if necessary. Where services are "refused" or a situation is deemed intractable, as it often is, the mother may be charged criminally and/or have her parental rights abrogated. This is what happened to the *Nicholson* mothers, whose challenge to removal because of their experience of domestic violence is described in chapter 4. In *Nicholson*, the practice of punitive removal was ruled unconstitutional in a US District Court. Unfortunately, without a clear policy alternative, child welfare systems in the United States and elsewhere continued the practice of punitive removals.[1]

The Children of Coercive Control challenges the prevalent assumptions behind services to children by implicating coercive control, a discernible criminal pattern in the etiology of "child abuse." Like the African proverb, I prefer to stop the man who is throwing babies into the river, than to try and rescue as many children as possible before they drown.

Part I set the political stage on which a new approach was needed to women and children experiencing "domestic violence," and introduced two ideological blinders that kept service providers from seeing coercive control, their unwillingness to acknowledge abusive men at the center of the harm they were recording ("the invisible man") and the belief that a person cannot be both an abuse victim and a good mother at the same time. Chapter 2 extended the discussion of the blind spots that kept the Courts from seeing "the abused mother" as the living embodiment of coercive control. Among other real-world scenarios, I recounted the case of Hedda Nussbaum, who was excoriated by the press as well as several prominent feminists, for failing to save Lisa Steinberg, her adapted daughter, though she herself had been beaten, raped, and held prisoner by the father. I illustrated the "invisible man" theme with two cases. The first involved the drowning of baby Aedan Moreno, the son of Adrianna Oyola, in Connecticut during supervised visitation by a father who had never hurt the child and carried his picture in his wallet. Because he had not breached an order of protection and "only" stalked and threatened his wife but did not assault her, the judge considered his abuse had ended. In the second case, a mother was charged with failing to protect two teenage daughters whom the husband admitted he had kidnapped and beaten. In the Oyola case, had the judge worked with a coercive control framework, the woman's statements, police reports, and the man's texts would have provided sufficient evidence that he intended to use the child to hurt and punish the mother for resisting his control. The killing of Aedan Moreno also introduced "child abuse as tangential spouse abuse," a form of secondary victimization where hurting or killing the child is designed to hurt and control the wife, and the offender need show no animosity toward the child. In the case of the Vietnam veteran, who made no effort to conceal his responsibility for hurting his daughters, child welfare and the courts simply lacked the means to hold a man accountable for controlling his children and the tools to respond to a woman who could have protected the girls if justice resources were at her disposal. Coercive control is the relevant tool to have in hand. Coercive control brings the "invisible man" out of the wings to center stage and shows that the "abused mother" is a construction that results when criminal constraints are imposed on women's developing relationship to her child rather than used to protect that relationship.

The Yale study summarized in chapter 3 found that the vast majority of children who had been physically abused were hurt in the context of violence against their mother, that violence against a mother and child was longstanding in most cases ,and that in cases where oral reports were available, the same man was abusing mother and child. In no case, however, was the man responsible for abusing the women and children identified or held accountable for his abuse. Instead, the children who were "darted" at Yale were referred to child welfare. The Yale studies identified the blind spot coercive control was designed to illuminate. Under a coercive control law, the abused mothers and children would be identified as covictims at an early visit and the father or surrogate responsible for the abuse identified and administratively managed.

In the years between the Yale studies (1988) and the *Nicholson* case (2004), mounting evidence, including our own, that "domestic violence" against mothers was a major context for child abuse, led child welfare systems in New York and numerous other cities, counties, and countries to apply domestic violence assessments to all intakes of families. The dissemination of these protocols did not greatly improve services for women and children, however, at least not with respect to the huge problem of domestic violence, but instead led to the draconian response illustrated by the *Nicholson* case. Once children were inappropriately labeled ("darted") as "exposed to domestic violence," a process began that punished the mothers for being victimized, harmed the children, and entrapped the families in ways that limited their capacity to elude further abuse. Chapter 4 described this process in real time and included thumbnail sketches of how the *Nicholson* mothers and their children were coercively controlled by police, lawyers, social workers, and supervisors from the Administration for Children's Services (ACS) in New York City. Services were offered to the *Nicholson* families in exchange for their children being returned. But the trauma caused to the children by placement and the strictures on family functioning associated with compliance continued to undermine family health and safety. *Nicholson* laid the groundwork for coercive control because it showed the prevailing institutional response to children exposed to domestic violence is untenable.

The lacuna in child welfare is not hard to pinpoint. The social allocation of childcare responsibilities primarily to mothers and other women explains the administrative focus of child welfare on "women and children." But this political reality, and the subsequent restriction of the child welfare purview to women and children, leads to a serious blind spot in the capacity for child welfare to protect children from domestic violence. Because the men involved with these families are administratively irrelevant to child welfare, the fathers or mother's boyfriends are not "clients," and their abusive behavior is seen only indirectly through its effects on the behavior of women and children, who then become the objects of management. Because men are not the clients of child welfare, the service system does not recognize either "violence against women" or "child abuse" as the consequence of "woman battering," let alone of "coercive control," but only identifies mothers who "engage in domestic violence," cause their children to be "exposed," and are thus guilty of "abuse" and "neglect." Instead of empowering women and children and increasing their capability to move freely and develop their capacities in personal and social space, the "rules" imposed by child welfare to manage domestic violence victims and their children, including rules for contact, reinforce their dependence.

Where coercive control becomes law and policy, the types of cases that surfaced in *Nicholson* would be redirected where they can be resolved in the interests of health, safety, justice, and accountability of all victimized parties. Since violence against women is almost always embedded in patterns of coercion and control that extend over time and include stalking and other strategies that "cross social space," the only effective means to protect women and children from ongoing abuse is interdiction with abusers or otherwise removing the source of coercive control. With abusive men removed from the community, the mother and child can be safely ensconced in their homes and empowered with community-based support and services.

I consider the role played by child welfare and the family court in the *Nicholson* case a form of "social entrapment," because no male abuser was involved in this coercive control of these mothers and children, whose harms extended from physical and sexual abuse in foster care to the deprivation of their rights and liberties. Thus, while the children of coercive control are victims of individual abusers, the inequalities perpetuated by abuse are reinforced by the institutions of social betterment charged with diffusing family conflict (the family court) and family breakdown (child welfare and the child guidance clinic). The coercive control of women and children by individual men, the entrapment of women and children by child welfare, and draconian custodial and visitation arrangements in which abusive men are allowed continued access to their children form a continuum of coercive control for millions of families. Replacing abuse by individual men with punitive social regulations that constrain women and children's development according to invidious gender, race, and class stereotypes is no antidote. Coercive control laws and policies will protect children only if accompanied by a radical devolution of child welfare and the family court and significant gains in the equity agenda affecting women's status and support for "mothers across the international social landscape."

Part II. The Coercive Control of Children: The New Model

The Yale research and the *Nicholson* case laid the empirical and political groundwork to reexamine children's experience of abuse in the context of new information about coercive control. Part II describes the major elements of the coercive control of children, both the similar tactics abusers deploy with women and children (chapters 5 and 6) and those tactics which are distinctive to how children are coercively controlled (chapter 7).

In 2018, Scotland became the first country to identify "child abuse" as an element of the serious crime of coercive control, anticipating the policies I advocated in this book. By this time, two things had become clear. Although the punitive response by child welfare systems to abused women and their children remained widespread, there was a growing consensus in policy circles that the approach critiqued in chapters 3 and 4, screening, the provision of services, and the removal of children if services failed, wasn't working. Not only had child abuse and fatality rates remained stubbornly high[2] but also, as women increasingly rose to prominence in government and social service administration, the abrogation of mother's rights in policies that were blatantly victim-blaming was increasingly deemed unconscionable and untenable. Important too was increasing pressure from "protective" parents and antiviolence and children's advocates on government services and the family court to hold perpetrators accountable for the effects of their abuse on the fabric of family life.

Part II introduced a model of the major tactics used to in coercive control of children. Chapter 5 and 6 described the major abusive tactics that are used in various configurations in the strategy to coercively control women and children—violence, sexual abuse, psychological abuse, intimidation, isolation, and control; identified a class of offenders as current and former male partners (as opposed to the mothers targeted by child welfare); and specified a motive for the abusive behaviors—to capture and monopolize the resources, capacities, and services available through a family space. Chapter 7 described the unique tactics used to coercively control children, when children are "scapegoated" or used as surrogate victims for their mother and when children are "weaponized" as a means to hurt and control, examples of what I term "child abuse as tangential spouse abuse."

Violence

Physical violence remains an important component of child abuse in the context of coercive control. What readers who are familiar with the child abuse and domestic violence literature may find surprising is that, when the goal is subjugation rather than infliction of pain, the violence tends to be low-level, frequent, even "routine," methodical, torturous, and terroristic rather than sudden or injurious. Meanwhile, in contrast with the delusional or depressed parent thought responsible for "battered babies," the abusive parent deploys the technology used in coercive control with meticulous care to detail, often in small targeted doses, seeking to confound the child's capacity to resist or disobey; he tends to "harass," tease, push, pinch, punch, and kick the child. Aedan Moreno (in chapter 2) became a target when her mother was no longer accessible and the fatal assault was also his father's first on him. More typical were the cases of Daniel Pelka (chapter 8) or Nubia Barahona (chapter 10), children who died as the result of an extended period of deprivation and punishment designed to hold their mother's attention and obedience. In none of the cases I review was the abuser who harmed the child "out of control." Like coercive violence against women, abusive violence against children in coercive control cannot be assessed by its level, means, or injurious effect, but by its frequency, duration, and cumulative effect on the child's autonomy. It is also distinctive because its aim is domination and the assumption of personal, economic, and sexual privilege, not the infliction of individual pain.

Sexual Abuse

The pattern of sexual abuse experienced by children subjected to coercive control is also generally distinctive because it is low level and diffuse rather than sudden, intense, or injurious. My caseload includes reports of sexual assaults by fathers on very young children where the sheer physical insult involved overwhelmed any other criminological dimensions. In general, however, the sexual abuse of children in coercive control encompasses a far broader spectrum of sexual insults than conventional pictures of incest or rape, largely because its function is not to hurt the child but to bring the adult victim to heel. Conversely, children's descriptions of being sexually abused in this context emphasize feelings of loathing, "feeling dirty" or "shame" or "disgust," for example, rather than feelings associated with trauma, such as fear, injury, or pain. While none of the children were sexually abused in the Barahona case (chapter 10), and the professional response was shaped by ignorance about the variety and fluidity of Nubia's sexual development rather than transphobia, the combined effect of Nubia's isolation at school, her withdrawal by Carmen, and the ostracism of the twins at home was a profound experience of gender shaming that enraged her. Within the context of their isolation and confinement, the only outlet for Nubia's rage was to provoke Jorge, by "shitting on Jesus," for example, behavior that also confounded Carmen.

In emphasizing the controlling function of the violence and sexual abuse, I am not suggesting that providers downplay the psychological trauma of being raped by a father or step-father, as Tiffany was in the Hughes case in chapter 7. Keith's sexual assaults elicited her drug use and had a devastating effect on her sense of self. But Tiffany explained that she also experienced the rape as her step-father intended it, as an assault on her sexual persona, as a fissure in her bond to her mother, and, as she told me, as an attack on her dignity and autonomy as the mother of Aiden. This insight into Keith's motive is pertinent because it indicates a political edge to the experience of victimization which is important in recovery. In the context of coercive control, sexual assault on a child is always a political act that signals the aim of domination, as well as a sexual crime. It also reminds us that, in a forensics of coercive control, offenders should be accountable for the particular ruptures their behavior causes in family systems, mother–child relationships, and systems of self, as well for the concrete losses and harms caused by their assaults.

Psychological Abuse

Psychological abuse is the third important element in the coercive control of children. I afford it less space in this book than it merits. All of the children to whom I've spoken as well as the adults who shared their experience as children recited a catalog of slights, put-downs, and indignities that would fill the check boxes on lists of psychological abuse, including the types identified by baseball legend Joe Torre.[3] I chose not to emphasize psychological abuse in the book for two related reasons. First, I minimize psychological abuse because it lacks the salience and structure of more concrete forms of harm, such as control, exploitation, isolation, and deprivation, for example, at least in the criminal justice setting. Courts simply are not prone to weight it as highly as more tangible forms of harm. A related and more important reason I de-emphasize psychological abuse is that I am unclear about the independent clinical or forensic status of demeaning comments, put-downs, name calling, berating, "gaslight" games, and the like outside a context where the target of the abuse is not already isolated or constrained in their response by other forms of coercion or control.[4] My clinical impression is that many (certainly not all) of the effects children (and women) attribute to psychological abuse are the result of prior and coexisting deprivations and constraints that impair their capacity to evade or defend against the insult. I know "words without weapons" can be devastating. The average trust with which children endow parents opens them up to be hurt deeply by a casual sarcasm or put-down, even when no coercion or diminishment is intended. The academic and professional worlds are replete with examples of hierarchies where vastly unequal exchanges are maintained by negative feedback loops akin to psychological abuse. I am concerned, however, that social workers, psychologists, and clinicians of all stripes who work with children not undervalue the importance of material, physical, and sexual threats to children's security and well-being and so the degree to which persons who present and appear as psychologically vulnerable are suffering under identifiable forms of concrete duress that can be removed.

Intimidation

Abusers intimidate children to get them to say or do something, to stop doing or saying something, or not to say or do something that provides support for their mother or otherwise undermines their control over the household. The intimidation tactics used with the children of coercive control run the gamut from a range of menacing physical confrontations, including stalking and "inspections," through the destruction of pets, toys, homework and other cherished possessions. Literal threats against children illustrated throughout this book include threats with weapons, exposure to the cold, slapping children at the table, holding a child out a window by his legs, and making the dog "disappear." Here, I want to underline three less transparent facets of intimidation tactics that are illustrated in the case chapters, "shaming," the terroristic nature of threats in coercive control, and the use of "witnessing" as an intimidation tactic.

Shaming is a specific tactic used to intimidate children in coercive control by continually devaluing a child to their self and in the opinion of significant others. Abusers can use child-shaming as a form of intimidation because the effect of making a child feel badly about their self is to inhibit their wishes, values, and interests, including their interest in opposing the abuser's continued control over the mother and resources in the household. Any aspect of the body, physical appearance, performance, speech, thoughts, identity, or behavior can be targeted for shaming. The emotion of shaming is self-hatred or loathing rather than fear, but the two feelings, fear and self-loathing, often combine to stifle a positive sense of self in a child.

In the Barahona case, there was a short period when the family functioned relatively well. The twins may initially have been separated from the other children to protect their younger sibs. Carmen made an unsuccessful effort to surgically address Nubia's "ambiguous sexuality." Despite these positive signs, the coercive control of Carmen Barahona posed a risk that the adopted children would be neglected, abused, and/or killed during the entire period they were engaged with the children's agencies. Once the twins were adopted, the risk was manifest in harm. The decision, means, duration, and nature of the twins' confinement in the bathroom and the combination of ridicule, denigration, and isolation (withdrawal from school) used to manage Nubia's struggles with sexual identity were designed with the specific aim of silencing them, erasing their identity, and rendering them immobile by denying them self-respect. The denigration of the twins constitutes an independent element of harm. We know less about how Daniel Pelka was shamed when he was forced to eat and toilet in his bedroom at home. Magdalena "cleaned him up" in preparation for school, where his teachers described him as well-kept and unassuming. But apart from his bruises and the emaciation observed in the pediatrician's office, I imagine that the boy was feeling shame as well as hunger when he stole food from dumpsters. A more straightforward example of shaming earlier in the book is where the father and two older sons by a previous marriage heckled, ridiculed and humiliated the woman's youngest son, until she fled from the table and ultimately from the house, seemingly abandoning her claims to custody as well as household assets. In that case, the shaming not only affected the mother but devastated and possibly alienated the boy from his mother, who told me he felt abandoned.

A second characteristic that bears reemphasis is that intimidation consists of threats or punishments so out of proportion to the source of the displeasure or rule infraction that the effect is paralyzing. The "terroristic" effect is achieved by the discrepancy between the threat and its object as illustrated by the trucker who threatened to make the dog "disappear" because his son left the lawn mower running to get a glass of water. In an Ontario, Canada, case in which my client, Theresa Craig, testified that the knife she was holding told her to stab her husband Jack, he had tied and gagged their nine-year-old son to teach him not to touch his guitar. Passive deprivations can be equally harsh, like the example of the father who stopped all oral communication with his wife and daughter because the teenager had failed to tell him about a canceled pickup at music school. The "silent treatment" for an equally minor infraction reported by another child lasted two years. It is hard to mistake the sudden escalation of an established pattern of "sulking" into a campaign of contempt and disdain for an "overreaction." Three things mark terroristic threats as "controlling behavior" rather than behavior that is "out of control"—that the threat is often made in a mood of studied calm, that the threat is usually made in the presence of the wife and/others as a warning and a proprietary claim, and that the threat comes from nowhere and has no emotional context or pretext. While the extreme deprivations Jorge Barahona imposed on the twins caused them to restrict their routine activities like eating, bathing, or using the toilet, his terrorism with the children was sufficient to make his wife his capo in containing the twins if they tried to escape his hold, so afraid was she of what he would do to her or them or the other children. Some children react to terroristic violence by becoming labile and overdependent on their mother; others, seek safety by "identification with the aggressor," like Mariah Knock, the girl who told her mother in the shelter "I hope you die," or Anna Colvin (chapter 7) who testified on behalf of the father who killed her mother. Other children carry their father's anger toward their mother into their relationship with her or into relationships with men or other women later in life.

Child witnessing is also a far more complex and nuanced experience than the current literature allows. On one side, "staged witnessing," where abusers post their children or pose their abuse so that the sights, sounds, and consequences are unavoidable to the children, is a third unique way in which abusers use the intimidation of children to control their mothers. Examples of "staged witnessing" in the book include the subjection of Mariah Knock to her mother's denigration, the trucker who lined up his children with the mother in the backyard and instructed them on where she would be buried ("next to the dog"); Keith Hughes driving away Brianne's boyfriend by causing him to witness his abuse of Jeanette; and the husband who attacked his wife at their child's karate tournament. Here, the aim is to confound the mother's shame by her awareness of the child's disgust as well to elicit that sort of defensive alignment that was illustrated in the *Knock* and *Covlin* cases. Child witnesses are often called in later confrontations to confirm "confessions" from earlier abuse episodes. On the other side, children often place themselves in positions to see, hear, or film abusive incidents as a means of giving their mother support or magically protecting her. Even lying awake during an episode of physical or sexual assault can give a child a sense of safety, both because s/he knows when the assailant is done and because his mother is "alive."

Isolation

The purpose of isolating children is to frighten them, prevent disclosure, instill dependence and loyalty, and create a divide between mother and child that women can cross only by negotiating about the nature and degree of their compliance with their partner's demands. Abusers isolate children in three ways primarily, from their peers and other potential sources of support, in order to keep the secret and monopolize their time and services; from their mothers, in order to intimidate them and reduce their resilience; and from resources and opportunities needed to resist, escape, and thrive. The isolation of children causes their social, emotional, and cognitive development to atrophy.

Isolating tactics include proscribed or greatly restricted contact of children with their immediate and extended family, neighbors, and friends, merchants, schoolmates, teachers, police, strangers, and health and social service personnel. Children may be physically isolated through confinement; denied access to significant social settings such as school, work, sports, or neighbors' homes; or psychologically isolated within social settings though shaming. The case of Samuel W. illustrated a common structural dimension of isolation, when the rundown section of the house to which the mother and boys were confined for their work and leisure contrasted markedly with the home office suite in which the father lived. By putting the older boys into "cyber-schooling," Samuel W. further isolated the older boys from their mother, causing the alienation projected in their experiencing "Satan coming out of the chimney" when they approached her house. As means of isolation, cell phones and social media are contested terrain. Abusers depend on children to carry cell phones and retain access to social media to track, access, and control them as well as to track and monitor their mother. They also seek to shrink, eviscerate, or distort the child's presence in electronic space. Meanwhile, the development of social media affords children unparalleled opportunity to evade isolation by sustaining relationships, reporting harms, seeking outside assistance, and attaining information on their predicament unavailable anywhere else. Isolation can make a child feel abandoned, unloved, and without mooring and result in "identification with the aggressor," as we saw with Anna Colvin. But children continually contest their isolation by seeking to open up their space for relationships and action, making their experience one of alternating constriction and release.

Isolating children as a control tactic is not without risks, in no small part because of the complicated mix of fear, recognition, denial, relief, and rage it elicits on the part of both adult and child victims. In the Hughes case, where Keith raped his step-daughter Tiffany in order to isolate her from Jeanette, when Tiffany moved out, Jeanette lost the primary buffer between herself and her husband. This increased her sense of vulnerability. Keith attacked her, and she killed him.

Some women use isolation as a tactic to adapt to coercive control. Marissa G. hid in her room and ran circles to steel herself from the fear elicited when she overheard her father beating her mother. While the "skill" helped her as a long-distance runner in college, the adaptation to fear of violence caused her to retreat into denial on three occasions when her husband put the baby in a scalding bath. Note, the strategy Marissa G. "learned" as a girl to cope with her father's abuse of her mother, to isolate herself and to function normally from inside a psychological shell that shut out the noise of the outside world, she applied to protect her from her husband's coercive control. That the strategy was "defensive" (hence the byproduct of an assault by her father/husband) rather than "adaptive" is indicated by its unintended effect, to keep her from gleaning information about his mistreatment of their child that was vital to the girl's survival. To the extent that coercive control by Marissa G.'s father makes her and the baby vulnerable to coercive control by her husband, coercive control extends across generations.

The case of Jonathan D. also illustrated the enduring effects of isolation, in that instance long after a separation and divorce. After a DC Family Court transferred sole custody to his father and step-mother, they confined the boy to his room for days on end completely cut off from his mother and friends. In response to his isolation, Jonathan told me he felt like a hostage. He had dropped from an "A" to an "F" student, cut a cross in his arm to symbolize being a "sacrifice" and said that he'd run away secretly hoping he'd be sent to the residential program in Oklahoma with which his father had threatened him, where he felt he'd be safer than "at home." Rather than recognize Jonathan's isolation as an extension of the father's coercive control over his ex-wife, the family judge reinforced it, by forbidding him to see either the pediatrician or the social worker who had correctly traced the boy's fear of his father to his earlier exposure to his abuse of his mother. After a lengthy court battle, Jonathan's mother gained increased access to her son and was better able to protect him.

With respect to stalking, I want to emphasize that physical, electronic, visual, and proxy stalking are universally adapted by abusers not only to intimidate the child but also to give children the feeling they are always alone, even when they are among friends or on dates, that all encounters are fraught and their every move is being watched for signs of betrayal. Although abusive men go to great length to confiscate, smash, sabotage, and monitor their children's social media, however, coercively controlling men also depend on their children having access to phones, cameras, and the Internet to an inordinate extent, both to track their children, including tracking their contact with their mother, and to use them for surveillance. Moreover, the universality, fluidity, and interchangeability of mobile and digital media gives children as young as eight an inordinate capacity to keep collective records of each other's experiences that is invaluable when restrictions are put in place. Safety planning with schoolage children involves electronic communication nets located in hyperspace parallel to those that are increasingly common among women in the refuge stream.

Control

The physical abuse of the twins in the Barahona case was appalling. But their physical torment was the result of their being trapped and their resistance effectively frozen by the micromanagement of their everyday lives, extending across the spectrum of their activities from eating, sleeping, bathing, and toileting through the hours they spent doing rote "homework" and listening to their adopted father's Jesus chants. Had the control tactics been identified and Jorge removed, the physical abuse would have been prevented. This level of exploitation was possible particularly after the twins had been withdrawn from public visibility and Carmen had capitulated to be Jorge's watchdog, almost certainly because she preferred a modicum of respite for the twins to beatings and sexual degradation from Jorge. This abuse could also have been the focus of police intervention. Jorge's behavior has no rational explanation. It is ordinarily possible to drop a plumb-line from the control tactics men deploy with women and children to a combination of rational calculus of gain and their socialization in school, sports, religion, work, or their families-of-origin. But I found no basis in Jorge Barahona's background or social world for the combination of terroristic threats, bible passages, and lessons in reading comprehension that formed the heart of his abuse. So I see no intervention short of interdiction that could have helped.

Identifying Carmen as a victim of abuse could be difficult because she was high functioning. I used the Barahona case to illustrate "coercive control from below" because, although Carmen was being beaten, sexually abused, bullied, monitored, and constricted in any number of ways, she was the only parent moving the children through social space and was doing so, moreover, seemingly in command of her field of action, with respect to the clinic and school, for example. Magdalena Luczak also presented her child to school outside the purview of the abusive partner. But in contrast to Carmen's apparent autonomy, Magdalena appeared to school authorities and the pediatrician only slightly less fragile than her son. So, if Carmen was like a "capo" to her son, Magdalena more closely resembled a Spanish "accompana," someone who escorts their children to social functions to ensure they attend and behave. Rachel's relationship to her children presents a third option: where Jorge took over parenting the twins, and Magdalena oversaw Daniel's compliance with Mariusz's rules, Rachel was the means by which Roberto disciplined the children. Despite these differences, all three women adapted the moral frame set up by their abusive partner in which it was safe to think about the children and which defined what was good and safe for the children; all three women, to a greater or lesser extent came to define them as "bad" (or, in Carmen's case) to conclude punishment was "for their own good") if they disturbed their partner (drinking in Jorge's case, Roberto's sleep, Mariusz's "peace"), excited his ire by violating one of his many rules, or failed to comply with his beliefs about dress, food, or cleanliness. At the other end of the spectrum are abusers who "weaponize" children and/or appropriate their sexuality or physical labor, sometimes transferring esteem to the target child, as the "real" cook, wife, or mother, basically to disempower and demean the mother. This dynamic was illustrated in the *Hughes* case when Jeanette's husband raped Tiffany and had Brianne assume her place with respect to shopping, cooking, and cleaning.

Child Abuse as Tangential Spouse Abuse

Chapter 7 highlighted three important ways in which the coercive control of children is distinctive, the use of children as surrogates for the adult victim, the "weaponization" of children as means to control a partner, and "identification with the aggressor," when a child assumes and internalizes the perspective of the abusive partner. Whether or not the child suffers the physical consequences of coercive control, sides with an abusive father in a custody dispute, or participates in physical or other abuse of a child, a minor child remains a "victim" so long as they function as an instrument of coercion and control of the mother/partner.

A unique dynamic in the coercive control of children involves the selection of a target child as a "scapegoat" or "whipping boy" who is punished as a surrogate for an adult victim, usually because the adult victim has a high profile job or a position of public visibility on whom the abuser depends. Earlier in the book, I described a New York City case in which the father had taken "early retirement" from his position as a bank president to "write his memoir" on a childhood in Pakistan. While his money was presumably "tied up" in overseas investments, the family lived off the mother's income on Wall Street. To enforce his control of the woman and her assets, but leave no marks that could raise suspicions at her work, he singled out their teenage son as the "whipping boy" to terrorize her, ridiculing and smacking the boy repeatedly while the husband cursed and demanded money and other concessions from his wife. The husband's first assault on his wife, a near fatal attack with a barbell, came years into the marriage, when she announced her attention to divorce. By then, both teenagers in the family were medicated for depression and anxiety and a school counselor had noted "trouble at home." But no one noticed that the children's restricted emotional vocabulary was the result of the general obliteration of liberty by the father in the home.

In other unique configurations in my caseload, the child becomes a surrogate for the abuser, is used as a "weapon," or collaborates in the mother's abuse seemingly as an equal partner. These scenarios make it extremely challenging to treat children's victimization equally to women's because the children are aligned with the abusive father and either directly participate in coercively controlling the mother or, side with the abusive dad in a custody dispute. Chapter 7 looks at child abuse as tangential spouse abuse through the lens of two teens who were aligned in family disputes with fathers who had abused them and their mothers. In *Knock v. Knock,* eleven-year-old Mariah Knock testified she had seen no violence and the only evidence I had that my client had been abused was a five-volume diary in Chinese. In *Covlin,* my clients wanted custody of twelve-year-old Anna, who said she preferred her father though she had found her mother's lifeless body in their apartment on New Year's morning shortly after he left and had witnessed many of his physical and sexual assaults on her. In *Knock,* in a note from their shelter stay I was allowed to put in evidence, Mariah had told her mother, "I hope you die, I hope you die," seemingly voicing sentiment she had witnessed her father express. My special challenge in the *Covlin* case, which we lost, was a recent policy directive from New York that "lawyers for children" were obligated to represent the "child's wishes" rather than what their "best interests." Anna wanted to live with the man against whom she would be a star witness.

In both *Knock* and *Covlin,* I showed how a coercive control framework reconciles the dilemma posed when a child denies the mother's victimization by interpolating the girls' wishes as a rational adaptation to the extension of the father's abuse of their mother to them. To explain the psychological mechanism involved, I draw on iterations of the psychological concept of "identification with the aggressor" by Anna Freud and Sandor Ferenczi. Both theories project a child whose ego develops defensively by identifying with a jealous, violent, or critical father. But whereas Ferenczi anticipates a real "aggressor' " who reinforces the child's fears by flooding their brain with non-negotiable standards for rigid obedience, Anna Freud's model describes a "normal" identification process in which the alignment with the father by the child serves the important developmental task of breaking the Oedipal dependence on the mother. For our purposes, the mechanism that is applicable to the two cases is "collusion" with the father as both a behavioral manifestation of his abuse and a strategy for surviving his coercive control. To the extent that I can frame the child's wishes as an adaptation to their being coercively controlled, I endorse the child's prowess rather than discredit it.

In chapter 7, I speculate that the case where an abused child defends an abusive parent illustrates a psychological process, "identification with the aggressor." A similar psychological dynamic is widely exploited for commercial purposes in violent video games, Netflix, and the other proviolence, prodominance narratives with which our cultures abound. In highlighting a common impulse that causes children to nest their sense of self with an abusive adult and to identify with violent role models in the media, I make two points. First, the frenetic, repetitive, intrusive, paranoid behavior of a coercively controlling father searching for a hidden object is familiar to children from the world of gaming. What children often do not recognize is the second point, that whereas the aim of gaming is to give a child the experience of confronting and managing the paranoid and delusional and then turning off the screen, exposure to coercive control is ongoing and intrusive. At home, there is usually no "off" button, until there is an arrest and removal.

This is not a book about bad parenting, demanding women, or "controlling men." Millions of us so-called good parents have spanked, ridiculed, threatened, blackmailed, bribed, or employed another of the coercive and controlling behaviors featured here with our children, at least occasionally, to punish them, induce behavior they are resisting, make them stop behavior felt to be undesirable, or just because we didn't know what else to do. Nor do I claim that physical punishment or *just* psychological abuse is harmless. It may not be. What I am describing is light years removed from bad parenting, and even from the alcohol aided family brawls in which our neighbors in the next apartment in the Bronx beat one another and their two children on Saturday nights when I was in elementary school. Nor am I talking about a parent, man or woman, who is obsessive in their habits, unforgiving in emotional exchange, and needing to "win" every exchange, no matter the cost in emotional sanity or family harmony. I don't condone the use of emotional blackmail or physical violence in any relationship, let alone the sort of demeaning commentary and sarcasm that hurt more deeply than any blows. But I recognize that most people, even in the so-called developed countries of the world, face social, economic, climactic, and demographic challenges to survival that test even the strongest family bonds. And I realize we make do with all sort of personality types and behavioral idiosyncrasies. What I am describing has nothing to do with rigid personality types, orthodox religionists set in their patriarchal ways, or narcissists who believe that what is real is only what is real for them. Coercive control is not a parenting strategy, a personality type, or the result of a misunderstanding of how to conduct relationships; nor does it result from ignorance about how to behave with respect and decency in relationships. Coercive control is born in a will to dominate, a self-interest in aggrandizement and the opportunities to exploit women and children (primarily, but not only) created at the juncture of women's newly developed capacities and the persistence inequalities that make those capacities vulnerable to capture and exploitation. Note, women are vulnerable not because they are weak, but because they are unequal; only because women can develop their capacities and resources so far, and no further, can men block and then co-opt that development process to themselves. Coercive control laws obstruct the co-optation and exploitation process. But only the free, full, and equal development of those capacities can end the peculiar vulnerability of women and children to coercive control.

What Now?

In policing, the technical step of replacing a misdemeanor offense of domestic violence with the serious new offense of coercive control that includes children seems relatively straightforward. When child abuse is subsumed as a bespoke element of coercive control, police are directed to evidence and charge the same acts ("assault," "intimidation," "isolation," "psychological abuse," control) committed against children as against adults. With policing, the main challenge arises because of the complexity of the new offense, the variety of elements that can be evidenced, the new forms of cyber, historical, witness, and testimonial evidence that come into play and the extent to which abusers pursue their victims—and so must be pursued, through physical, social, historical, and cyberspace. Although there is an important role for frontline policing in case identification, liaison with victims, witness contact, and pursuit, much of the case development involves specialization. The work with children is more likely to involve collaboration with schools, daycares, sports leagues, and other institutions of secondary socialization in the community, but is beyond our scope here.

With child welfare, however, the shift to a coercive control perspective is complicated by the mission-driven commitment to children's well-being and the long-honed skepticism of "mothers" at all levels of the welfare bureaucracy, not only in the field. The challenge, to reiterate, is that because the use of co-ercive control tactics with children—what I am identifying as child abuse—is mainly designed to reinforce the control over/submission of the mother, as a form of secondary victimization, the best intervention strategy is to "harden the primary target" through family-friendly woman empowerment approaches in liaison with investigative policing and law enforcement. In this sense, case-work with the children of coercive control is like working with a child whose mother is a slave of sex-traffickers. In any case, whether or not a child has been harmed, intimidated, isolated, or controlled, the risk that the abuser will kill, kidnap, or seriously harm the child is a function of the overall level of coer-cive control being deployed and the level of disempowerment already effected on the primary victim and/or others in the protective network. In the current assessment scheme, if an abusive father is seen as having a singular venom at his partner and has not abused his child, he is assessed as a low risk to the child by child welfare and in family court. But where coercive control is in play, the abuser is assumed to have a global interest in domination, much as con man or embezzler might in their marks, and is assessed at high risk to use the child as a pawn to gain control over his wife and her assets, like any other means. This was illustrated in Oyola case in chapter 2, when the man who drowned his son carried his picture in his wallet, doted on him and never struck him. Had his coercive control been identified by his earlier statements, abusive acts and breeches of orders, the judge could have extended the protective order in place, which the father had respected because he was afraid of the police. Remember, an abuser kills a child not because he has any animosity toward the child—he may or may not—but because he has access to the child and because disposing of the child is the best way he knows to affect his victim with the least risk he will be deterred.

Without the "tail" of child fatality and child abuse, which occur mainly in the context of coercive control, the legitimacy of a quasi-judicial bureauc-racy like the child welfare system seems in doubt. The vast majority of child welfare cases involve threats that children share to a greater or lesser extent with other family members and unrelated others in their community, sub-standard housing, homelessness, lack of variety in food, substance abuse, poisoned water, environmental hazards, lack of healthcare, lack of birth con-trol, unemployment, poor literacy, and so forth. The welfare function needs to be returned to the community. But in the twenty-first century, this almost certainly does not mean resurrecting the neighbor-based self-help networks that were so popular during the Great Depression, World War II, and the radical revivals of the 1960s and 1970s. When every newly arrived refugee from Iraq, the Ukraine, Sudan, or Venezuela has a cell phone and an IP address, the "safety nets" we build around women and children must encompass a dispersed social space through which women and children can freely transit to work, play, health, safety, and family life without fear of interception.

Some final words about my approach. My training as a social scientist prepared me to interpret and organize many types of social information, such as the quantitative evidence from medical records reported in chapter 3, primarily to illuminate how social organizations function. Strictly speaking, because my aim in examining the evidence of coercive control is to build a link to criminal activity, my application of "forensics" is not "science." In fact, the main social scientific finding in the field, including our own, that abuse harms children mainly because they "witness" or are otherwise "exposed" to domestic violence, is diametrically opposed to the conclusion reached in this book based on forensics, that the most significant manifestations of "child abuse" and "domestic violence" are secondary effects of coercive control. I propose "coercive control" not as a scientific proposition or a statement about the etiology of child abuse, but to show how nonaccidental child fatality, child abuse, and other forms of child maltreatment are linked temporally and spatially to various forms of women abuse such that interrupting the woman abuse would greatly diminish child fatality and child abuse. Unlike much social science, my forensic analysis is also proscriptive. I support incarceration solely as a justice antidote and have no illusions either about its effect on perpetrators, victims, or society-as-a-whole. I support any alternative that is as likely as imprisonment to ensure that women and children benefit from the rights, resources, and liberties that are restored when coercive control is undone. My support for interdiction is not unqualified. With a serious crime of coercive control on the books that extends to children (such as the Scotland Act of 2018), I see no reason to continue to police and enforce misdemeanor domestic violence offenses or, frankly, a host of nuisance and behavioral offenses that currently constitute the bulk of the misdemeanor caseload.

As opposed to the quantitative evidence used by much of social science, this book on children, like my earlier book *Coercive Control*, relies on the "thick," rich descriptions available through forensic cases. My case are summaries are compiled from audio and word files of about 150 women and children with whom I have been involved professionally in my capacity as a forensic evaluator. In the Pelka case (chapter 8), where I had no direct access to any family members, I had a trove of records, reports, and files compiled for the serious case review (SCR) as well as a transcript of the trial record. Complementing this trove of material are the life-stories dozens of women and children have shared with me over the years, accounts I receive weekly via email or other electronic communications, and perhaps, most tellingly, the feedback I receive from a range of advocates, health, justice, and social work professionals from around the globe who have found the new framework useful and, in some cases, even life-changing. Needless to say, only extensive experience on the ground will determine whether my model captures the major features of the widespread pattern of abuse.

I reiterate an earlier point. The recognition that coercive control is the most important context for child abuse and fatality is new. But the ground I covered was well prepared by several generations of advocates and researchers who laid down an empirical thicket of irrefutable evidence that "domestic violence" against women was the most common concomitant, context for, and cause of physical, sexual, and psychological trauma to children.[5] Federal initiatives in the United States, Great Britain, and elsewhere were themselves a response to grassroots advocacy movements. But state funding and policy initiatives in each of our countries were indispensable in setting a tone in which to we could go beyond harms reduction and broach the issue of "justice," "equality," "dignity," and "independence" for women and children. Although I am critical in retrospect of the ways in which the child welfare and family court systems downsized the issue in our respective countries, the fact that two systems historically tied to disciplining women to be wives and mothers assumed "domestic violence" as an issue at all was a step forward because it put a class of harms on public budgets that had been hidden "behind closed doors." Unfortunately, along with extending their dominant "maternalism," the fact that the child protection and child welfare kept the men who were destroying the lives and prospects of millions of their clients outside their administrative purview led to punitive interventions with children and derogatory labels for women that abusers used to weaponize children when women filed for protection orders or divorce in family courts. By 2010, when the grassroots shelter/refuge movement circled the globe, it was taken for granted within the advocacy movement and by a broad range of police, health, and social service providers in the government sectors that children had shared the experience of abuse with their mothers as they did the transit to safety. This insight, based in experience, was bound to clash with the expectations of the child welfare, child abuse prevention, and child-saving establishment.

I first identified the significance of domestic violence as an important context of child abuse and child fatality the 1980s and of coercive control is the most significant context for violence against women and children in 2006. In 2018, by unanimous vote, the Scottish Parliament adapted a serious criminal offense which identified "child abuse" as an element of coercive control. In March 2021, Canada saw the coming into force of Bill C-78 with amendments to the federal 1985 Divorce Act (The Divorce Act, RSC 1985, c 3 [2nd Supp]). The amendments, which specifically identified coercive control, require that family violence be considered when making best interest determinations for children. Prior to these amendments, the Divorce Act made no reference to family violence. In 2022, Emma Katz published *Coercive Control in Children's and Mothers' Lives*, the first ethnographic description of how coercive control affects family relationships. Although Emma Katz's research draws on an English sample, her eloquent plea that police, child welfare, and the family courts broaden their purview to include the coercive control of children has applicability to many other countries, including the United States. Momentum is building. Though the focus on children is new, over 1,000 monographs on coercive control have been published since 2006. In California, Connecticut, Hawaii, Massachusetts, New York, Washington, and other US states as well as in Australia, Canada, China, Denmark, England, Ireland, Taiwan, Turkey, Wales, and parts of Europe, Asia, and Africa, criminal justice and family court agendas are being altered to reflect the equity claims of abused women and children to redress from coercive control. In some of these areas as well, the "child protection" agenda is already undergoing a radical shift from an ameliorative "child abuse" child welfare approach to an approach that seeks prevention of harms to children through early intervention to protect women. The rapid dissemination of the new framework is illustrated by developments in Australia.

In August 2022, findings derived from a two-part risk assessment for coercive control were accepted by a judge in the Queensland District Court and by a judge in the Federal Circuit and Family Court of Australia. The risk assessment findings have also been accepted in a Queensland Court of Appeal case and in various Family Court cases in Australia. The judgment in the District Court of Queensland in March 2022 on appeal, found wholly in favor of the victim. The assessment was devised by investigative journalist and academic Dr. Amanda Gearing and is based on the framework in my book, *Coercive Control*, the UK Home Office legal guidance on coercive control, and the Homicide Timeline developed by Professor Jane Monckton Smith. Amanda Gearing is also the journalist who reported on the murders of Brisbane mother Hannah Clarke, thirty-one, and her three young children in February 2020. The mother and children were set on fire in the family car in a suburban street by Hannah's husband, who was the father of the children. In a popular news analysis, Gearing applied the coercive control model to the facts of the case and identified that if Hannah and her family and police had understood the earlier behaviors of the killer as being coercive and controlling, Hannah and her family and friends and police would have recognized the risk of serious harm or death much earlier, and potentially could have saved their lives. The parents of Hannah Clarke called for coercive control to be criminalized in Australia.

As I wrote this in September 2022, the attorney general of New South Wales (NSW) was preparing a draft crime bill on coercive control to introduce in the new Parliament. The train had left the station.

In the last two decades, a revolution has been underway in how societies address the predicaments women face in personal life because of their unequal status. In over a dozen countries and many US states, this revolution includes identfiying and interrupting coercive control. But the revolution will not succeed if children are left behind. The revolution to extend the right to be free of tyranny to children is as radical as the revolution to treat women's right to be free of abuse—a matter of equality, liberty, and justice as of respect and common decency.

Despite international conventions protecting children's rights, in most countries and in most of life, children are regarded as less than full persons.[6] One consequence of the relatively low status accorded to children is that their nonphysical suffering is rarely attended to and that violations of their rights and liberties are rarely noticed, no matter how egregious. *Children of Coercive Control* is predicated on the belief that we have reached a level of development at which the rights and capacities of children merit respect, support, and nurturance as full persons alongside those of all other persons. The coercive control of children will take its place among the most serious offenses only when children are afforded status as full persons. At present, we acknowledge the suffering of childhood late in life, when it is given eloquent expression in film, fiction, or memoir by its survivors. It is time to recognize

the right of persons to live their childhoods free of deliberately inflicted torturous suffering as they are experiencing it.

A Final Note of Caution

My book on children is based on legal cases from my forensic practice
supplemented by examples from the news, fiction, memoirs, Netflix, and
film. Can a model of criminal behavior based on these sources be reli-
able, particularly in an era when any memory can be virtually installed or
photoshopped? The best I can do is paraphrase a district attorney friend
who, when I asked why he was depending on the testimony of "Izzy the Eel,"
a particularly unattractive jail snitch in the New York City trial of a jewel
fence replied, "that's all I've got." For me, it is reassuring when the stories
clients tell me about coercive control in the office have the same distinct
singularity of voice that I find in memoirs and the literary canon. Nothing
I am told isn't also given narrative form by authors like James T. Farrell,
Anna Burns, Tommy Orange, or DeShawn Charles Wilson. Conversely, we
know these real children have not taken their scripts from pop psychology
because, for better or worse, there is nothing about these experiences anywhere in the popular or research literature on child abuse or children's
health. When plaints resembling coercive control appear on Facebook,
they are put there by those who have experienced it and are almost immediately removed by perpetrators, parents, or censors. I also know the
stories are real, because while the plotlines of the abusive partners are almost identical, each script comes with a distinct twist. Most importantly,
I know coercive control is real because it is real in its consequences: Much
of what the children and adults in my forensic practice do in their families,
at school, with their friends, or alone they do in response to the constraints
on their rights and liberties. Children and adults act as if their memories
of oppression via coercive control are real. Most importantly, when I proceed as if the experiences of coercive control my clients recount are real, my
actions often have real consequences for helping them get a handle on their
lives. And justice in the Courts.

The fact that I am convinced that *The Children of Coercive Control* describes
a hidden substrata of everyday reality does not make it so. Unfortunately, the
only sure way to know if children are being entrapped with women in personal life is to create the conditions which can set them free, including laws

prohibiting coercive control that extend to children and the economic and social supports that restore their equality and autonomy as persons.

Children have been with us throughout the history of our movement, at our side during assaults, in the seat next to us and behind us as we fled by car or by bus, on the mattress on the floor of the refuge or nearby, on the picket lines, at the laundromats, at the funeral hall when our friend was buried, in the new home when we put the curtains up, installed the new locks, planted the new garden, everywhere we were, they were. And they are here still. We need to pay attention.

Notes

Introduction

1. I have altered the details of this case at my client's request.
2. "Study Finds China's Population Control Policy before the One Child Policy Was Responsible for 200,000 'Missing Girls,'" *Stanford Health Policy*, March 21, 2019.
3. "ACEs in Young Children Involved in the Child Welfare System," Retrieved from https://www.flcourts.org/content/download/215886/file/ACEsInYoungChildrenInvo lvedInTheChildWelfareSystem.pdf; Centers for Disease Control and Prevention (2016).
4. Andy Myhill, "Measuring Coercive Control: What Can We Learn From National Population Surveys?" *Violence against Women*, March 2015.
5. Sam Nevela, "Coercive Control and Its Impact on Intimate Partner Violence through the Lens of an EU-Wide Survey on Violence against Women," *Journal of Interpersonal Violence* 32, no. 12 (2017): 1792–1820
6. But cf. Emma Katz, *Coercive Control in Children's and Mother's Lives* (Oxford University Press, 2022).
7. David Gutterson, *The Final Case* (New York, 2022)
8. Most of my clients are charged with crimes secondary to the death of their partner or a child with harms to a third party in which they allegedly conspired. A small proportion of my caseload involves civil trials pursuant to divorce, personal injury, or libel.
9. Linda Gordon, *Heroes of Their Own Lives* (New York, 1985).

Chapter 1

1. I had a different experience in a Bergen County, New Jersey, courtroom, where a judge refused to admit photos of a woman's injuries that had accompanied a police report ("no charges filed") because, he told me, "I was a Trial Lawyer. Don't you think I know how photos can be doctored?" I offered to have the officer who took the photos testify to establish their validity. To which, he roared, "I WILL NEVER LET A POLICE OFFICER TESTIFY IN MY COURT!" The woman's claims of abuse were not found credible, and her husband was granted primary custody.
2. "2013 Daniel Pelka Murder: Social Worker Quits New Child Protection . . . ," *Guardian* (www.theguardian.com); "Magdelena Luczak: Mother Jailed for Murdering Four-Year-Old," *Independent* (www.independent.co.uk); "Killer Mum Magdalena Luczak Found Hanged Day before Murdered," *Mirror* (www.mirror.co.uk).

3. For instance, when reading about the case in chapter 9, it helps to know that the appalling bruises inflicted by Rachel's live-in partner were still visible to police as they pounded on the desk in front of her (as he had done numerous times) demanding that she "Confess!" "Confess!" (i.e., implicate him in hurting the children). By simultaneously demanding that Rachel acknowledge what they already knew (that he had abused both her and the children) and making it impossible for her to do so (or even to "know what she knew"), the police made her a "liar." This is a more subtle instance of abuse being made invisible in plain sight.

Chapter 2

1. As we will show in chapter 8, concerning the Nicholson case, the "recommendation" that Oyola seek counseling, if based solely on her being a victim of abuse, was contrary to a decision by the federal court for the 2nd District (including Connecticut) that it was unconstitutional for child welfare to mandate services for a nonoffending mother solely because of abuse. Although this was probably not the DCF intention, the recommendation to go into counseling communicated to Oyola that *she* was the problem to be fixed, not her husband, the same message he had sent her repeatedly. Moreover, what was the intent of counseling, since the DCF review had concluded she was doing "everything possible" to protect the child? In the past, DCF had employed an advocacy team that might have overridden the caseworker's poor practice. But a new commissioner with no previous experience in social work or child welfare had ended the contract with the advocacy group and restored the department's earlier emphasis on "family preservation."
2. State v. Miranda 41 Conn. App. 333 (1996) (14439) Appellate Court of Connecticut.
3. In Connecticut, I have been informed by the public defender in Juvenile Court that it is now DCF policy to bring a motion to terminate the rights of both parents if they suspect child abuse by an abusive husband, even if the wife had no knowledge of the abuse, was not present when it occurred, condemned it, and sought help promptly. I have a case which fit this fact pattern in which a woman was advised by her attorney to drop her claim that her husband's behavior after the incident pointed to his guilt for a child's injury and contest the medical evidence instead, lest his conviction result in the loss of both their parental rights.
4. Tondalo Hall's sentence of thirty years for not reporting her boyfriend's abuse was commuted and she was released from prison after serving fifteen years on November 19, 2019. Braxton, meanwhile, who pleaded guilty to abusing the children, was given a ten-year sentence, suspended after two. He never served a day of his sentence in jail. Although Hall testified at Braxton's sentencing that he beat her and choked her and she was afraid of him, the prosecutors insisted she deserved the longer sentence because she was "hiding something" and "trying to protect him."
5. "Unmasking Colorblindness in the Law: Lessons from the Formation of Critical Race Theory," in Kimberlé Williams Crenshaw, Luke Charles Harris, Daniel Martinez

HoSang, and George Lipsitz, eds., *Seeing Race Again: Countering Colorblindness across the Disciplines* (University of California Press, 2019); Katherine K. Barr, "Tondalo Hall Freed from Prison after Serving 15 Years," https://www.buzzfeednews.com (accessed November 16, 2021).

6. This does not mean that the man who "only" abuses his wife and not his child is a thereby a "good dad" or even "good enough." Both fathering and husbanding are here defined as subroles of a masculine identity or what same have called a hypermasculinity whereby children and women are prized "possessions" in whom one has vested property rights.

7. For summaries of the research, see Evan Stark and Anne Flitcraft, *Women at Risk: Domestic Violence and Women's Health* (Sage, 1996); Evan Stark, with Anne Flitcraft, "Failure to Protect: Resolving the Battered Mother's Dilemma," in C. Raghavan and S. J. Cohen, eds., *Intimate Partner Violence: Diverse Approaches in Dialogue* (Northeastern University Press, 2013), 200–223; "Child Custody Decisions in the Context of Coercive Control," in Mo Hannah and Barry Goldstein, eds., *Domestic Violence, Abuse and Child Custody: Legal Strategies and Policy Issues* (Civic Research Institute, 2009) (11-01-22-32); "The Battered Mother's Dilemma—Child Custody and Coercive Control," in E. Stark & E. Buzawa, eds., *The Family Context*, vol. 2 of *Violence against Women in Families and Relationships* (Praeger/Greenwood, 2009), 95–126; "Rethinking Custody Evaluations in Domestic Violence Cases," *Journal of Child Custody* 6 (2009): 287–321.

8. Evan Stark and Anne Flitcraft, "Women and Children at Risk: A Feminist Perspective on Child abuse," in R. Bergen, J. Edleson, and C. Renzetti, eds., *Violence against Women: Classic Papers* (Pearson, 2005), 244–268.

9. Kathleen Arnold, *Why Don't You Just Talk to Him?* (Oxford University Press, 2015).

10. Frank K. in the previous case was a Vietnam vet who had been diagnosed with PTSD, a psychiatric syndrome that can be combat-related and is associated with mood swings and outbursts of anger or violence. In the Yale culture in which Sarah sought help for herself and the girls, her decision to seek help was interpreted as a moral failure on her part to accept Frank's problems and if not to physically tolerate his abuse, then at least to acclimate the girls to the level of distress and disorder he brought to the table.

11. In later chapters, I discuss two cases in which abused women *did* hurt their children and so acknowledged, in one case, claiming to have inflicted "all" of the children's injuries, in both cases because they feared "worse would happen." Readers will be urged to mix sympathy with their skepticism of such protestations.

Chapter 3

1. See Evan Stark and Anne Flitcraft, *Women at Risk: Domestic Violence and Women's Health* (Sage, 1996); Evan Stark, with Anne Flitcraft, "Woman Battering," in J. M. Last, ed., *Maxcy-Rosenau: Public Health and Preventive Medicine*, 14th ed. (Appleton Century Crofts, 1998), 1040–1043; Evan Stark, with A. Flitcraft, "Violence among Intimates: An Epidemiological Review," in V. N. Hasselt et al., eds., *Handbook of*

Family Violence (Plenum, 1988), 293–319. The original work is A. H. Flitcraft, *Battered Women: An Emergency Room Epidemiology with a Description of a Clinical Syndrome and a Critique of Current Therapeutics* (Unpublished Doctoral Dissertation, Yale School of Medicine, 1977).

2. A summary of this evidence can be found in *Coercive Control: How Men Entrap Women in Personal Life* (Oxford University Press, 2007), 121–124.

3. Another important difference, little noted at the time, was that the New Hampshire sample consisted of couples that were "intact," though not necessarily legally married, whereas the women in the Yale sample had been in and out of relationships of all sorts throughout their medical careers and a majority were classified as "single, separated or divorced" at the time of abusive episodes. Considerable population evidence consistently reveals that "married" couples report lower levels of domestic violence than women who are single, separated, and divorced, with only "widows" reporting very low levels. This datum would lead to the realization that the form of abuse we were identifying in the Yale studies "crossed social space," though we had no idea what this meant at the time.

4. The Dart Team is a subgroup of pediatricians, nurses, and social workers who review all pediatric intakes for signs of child neglect and abuse.

5. E. McKibben, E. Devos, and E. Newberger, "Victimization of Mothers of Abused Children: A Controlled Study," *Pediatrics* 84 (1989): 531–535.

6. Remember, these are cases where researchers know about the history of domestic violence, but the pediatric service does not, at least not officially. Researchers can identify the abuser because they can match the children's records with the records of the mothers. Their identification of the mother's victimization is based on the presence of at least one episode of suspicion and so is extremely conservative. Note, excluded are the significant proportion of cases of abused mothers where there had been injurious violence brought to medical attention or where the predominant means of coercion and control were nonviolent.

7. C. Everett Koop, *Surgeon General's Workshop on Violence and Public Health Leesburg, Virginia October 27–29, 1985*, Report Published May 1986 by the Health Resources and Services Administration (HRSA), US Public Health Service, US Department of Health and Human Services (DHHS).

8. For a more detailed account of these developments, see Evan Stark, "Using Public Health to Reform the Legal and Justice Response to Domestic Violence," in John Colhoun, ed., *Reconsidering Law and Policy Debates: A Public Health Perspective* (Cambridge University Press, 2011), 125–152.

9. Jennifer Fauci and Lisa Goodman, "'You Don't Need Nobody Else Knocking You Down': Survivor-Mothers' Experiences of Surveillance in Domestic Violence Shelters," *Journal of Family Violence* 35, no. 6 (2019).

10. Paige Sweet, *The Politics of Surviving* (University of California Press, 2021).

11. For an uncritical summary of recent research in this area, see Miriam K. Ehrensaft and Jennifer Langhinrichsen-Rohlin, "Intergenerational Transmission of Intimate

Partner Violence: Summary and Current Research on Processes of Transmission," in *Handbook of Interpersonal Violence and Abuse across the Lifespan* (2022).

12. Clotilde Rougé-Maillart, Nathalie Jousset, Arnaud Gaudin, Brigitte Bouju, and Michel Penneaum, "Women Who Kill Their Children," *American Journal of Forensic Medicine and Pathology* 26, no. 4 (2005): 320–326.

Chapter 4

1. In a case I return to later in the book, in February 2020, Hannah Clark and her three children were fatally burned by her estranged husband Rowen in Brisbane, Australia. Mr. Clark had been recently convicted of kidnapping the children, but was released with no sentence because of his record and the belief that adequate protections were in place. Authorities attributed their failure to act despite the numerous warning signs to the absence of formal orders in the case—she feared he would harm the children—the man's legal right to see the children as their father, and the fact that domestic violence involves low-level policing not equipped to regulate protection orders. Suffice it to say here that given the high risk in this case and the complex issues involved in investigation and interdiction, this is an issue for specialized policing, not routine patrol work.

2. Susan Lynn Heward-Belle, L. Laing, C. Humphreys, and C. Toivonen, "Intervening with Children Living with Domestic Violence: Is the System Safe?," *Australian Social Work* (February 2018).

3. When we went to trial in 2004, roughly 58 percent of placements by ACS were made on an "emergency" basis without a court order. The vast majority of these involved children whose mothers has "engaged in domestic violence."

4. The possession of a firearm is illegal in New York City.

5. In several cases, ACS brought neglect proceedings against the batterer as an afterthought—only after they commenced proceedings against the victim.

6. In part, the high rates of child abuse and domestic violence in foster homes reflects the common practice of assessing only "mothers" in making placement decisions.

7. Colleen C. Katz, Mark E. Courtney, and Beth Sapiro, "Emancipated Foster Youth and Intimate Partner Violence: An Exploration of Risk and Protective Factors," *Journal of Interpersonal Violence* 35, no. 23–24 (2020).

8. 64@ <u>Id.</u> at 253; 9 F.2d 134 (2d Cir. 1981), cert. den. 404 U.S. 864 (1983).

9. *Nicholson vs. Scopetta.* The case was filed in the Eastern District of New York by the law firm Lansner & Kubitschek with the assistance of Jill Zuccardy, coordinator of legal services for Sanctuary for Families in New York. Based on the caseload of ACS and the proportion of cases estimated to involve domestic violence, the complaint alleged that the class represents more than 5,000 people in New York City and will increase by an additional 1,000 people each year.

10. An earlier case, *In re Lonell J.,* the New York state court held that the government did not have to offer expert testimony to prove harm to a child alleged to have been caused by witnessing domestic violence. *In re Lonell J, I 673, N.Y.S.2d 116 (app. Div.*

1998). New York courts interpreted this to mean that the existence of domestic violence was per se neglectful and that mothers so victimized could be charged with "failure to protect" without evidence establishing that a child had witnessed or been affected in any way by the abuse.

11. The analogy to indentured servitude is not far-fetched. The government's forced enslavement of indigenous youth goes back at least to the 1860s, when, "to kill the Indian and save the man," the US government "Indian schools" seized tens of thousands of Indian children to place in white homes and boarding schools. Until the 1920s, most "foster care" in the United States involved sending orphaned, abandoned, delinquent, or otherwise defective children, primarily from the homes of impoverished immigrant, Black, and poor white families to live as "free" "guest" family members on local farms where they became fully and often permanently integrated in the rural labor force. Many such arrangements were undoubtedly mutually beneficial, if only because the relocation reduced exposure to infectious and communicable diseases. Two things were notable, however. "Supply" was as much a function of the demand during harvest seasons as the reverse. More importantly, the placement system was unsupervised and ripe for exploitation, particularly within the combination of racial, religious, and patriarchal tyranny that governed rural life in much of the South and Midwest until well into the Depression. The novels, diaries, letters, and photo albums (e.g., Michel's Lesey's *Wisconsin Death Trip*) of the period are an eloquent record of physical and sexual abuse of children in these settings. One outcome was the gradual institutionalization of foster care and the current system of foster homes and kin care. But the endemic problem of entrusting children to an environment controlled by a male as the sole source of authority with a vested interest in hoarding familial resources, rights, and privileges in his own interest remains.

12. See for example, Sharah Shink, "Justice for Children: Justice for Change," *Duke University Law Review* 82, no. 4 (2005): 629–654; Leigh Goodmark, "From Property to Personhood: What the Legal System Should do for Children in Family Violence Cases," *West Virginia Law Review* 102 (1999): 237–294.

13. I draw this distinction here because the more affluent abused women found in family court often deploy the same evidence of how "witnessing" harms children that ACS mustered to charge the *Nicholson* mothers to discredit the custody claims of abusive fathers who insist all of their venom was reserved for their wives. In many US states, evidence of domestic violence conveys a presumption of custody to the victimized woman, the opposite of the effect such evidence was having on the low-income women who are the clients of the welfare system.

14. Note, though the threat Carl posed did not warrant a court order, it was sufficient to justify ACS's decision to keep the children out of her home. At trial, Nat Williams, the child protective manager who made the decision to place the children in foster care, acknowledged that it is common practice to remove children from battered mothers as a coercive measure, because "usually" battered mothers will agree to whatever services are demanded of them if their children are removed from them."

15. Nicholson v. Williams 203 F. Supp 2d 153 (E.D. NY) 2002.

16. Note, CPM Stewart filed a neglect petition against Rodriquez, although he had testified he did not believe she was neglectful, and took the children into ACS custody on January 28, 1999, though he knew ACS lacked judicial authorization to do so.

Chapter 5

1. As of this writing in 2022, I have ninety-three case reports in my forensic file (2006–2022). This includes criminal, family, and civil matters in which I've done at least an initial assessment to determine whether coercive control was present. In thirty-five of the cases where coercive control was present, minor and/or adult children were also victims. I interviewed the children in only three cases but reviewed narratives describing their experience (letters, a diary, text messages, emails, medical records, and social work and psychological reports in twenty-six cases. My clientele are extremely diverse, though only two of my clients were men.

2. Preethi Krishnan, "Measuring Violence, Erasing Struggles: Hermeneutical Injustice," *Domestic Violence Research Advances in Gender Research: Gender Visibility and Erasure* 33 (2022).

3. Emma Katz, *Coercive Control in Children's and Women's Lives* (Oxford University Press, 2022).

4. The three that have influenced me most are J. Davis and J. Dollard, *Children of Bondage* (Harper, 1964); G. Elder, *Children of the Great Depression*; and Oscar Lewis, *Children of Sanchez* (1974).

5. Among the novelists on whose portraits of children under family duress I relied are Chimamanda Ngozi Adiche, Patricia Engel, Brandon Hobson, Fernanda Melchor, Tommy Orange, Helen Philips, Douglas Stuart, Laurin Wilkinson, and C. Pam Zhang.

6. Currently, the model of service delivery for the group's treatment is an interagency collaborative model, which uses single-point access referral, through one group program coordinator, with the assistance of group cofacilitators from diverse member agencies. Groups are offered at different sites in the community at member agencies, including a child protective service, a children's mental health center, a center for preventative services for young children and their families, a women's shelter, a second-stage housing for women and children who have survived and left abusive relationships, and a youth detention facility. Approximately twenty-five groups are held per year, with an average of seven to eight participants per group. Children aged four to sixteen are accepted, and are grouped together by similar developmental level into four age groupings and teens, with gender balance in the preteen and teen groups. Critical is a pregroup with the mother present to give the child permission to talk about the violence and for the group leader to understand what the child will address. The group may be deferred if violence is ongoing, the child feels unsafe participating in the group, the child is denying the violence occurred in the past, or the child is in extreme turmoil with regard to their behavior and family situation. The topics addressed during the sessions include definitions of and language to describe violence, including emotional, physical, and sexual violence, with

terminology adapted to different developmental levels; recognizing, understanding, and communicating feelings; talking about violence in families; anger and conflict resolution; responsibility for violence and myths about family violence and woman abuse; power and control as they relate to different forms of abuse; safety planning; dating violence or sexual abuse prevention (depending on the child). A manual describes the procedures and exercises employed in the groups: Marlies Sudermann, Susan Loosley, Linda Bentley, Peter Lehmann, Larry Marshall, Stephanie Rabenstein, and Lori Milos, *Group Treatment for Children Who Witness Woman Abuse* (January 1, 1997).

7. Judith Hermann, *Trauma and Recovery* (1992).

8. John Berger, *Ways of Seeing* (1973).

9. I was fortunate to be at Washington University in St. Louis to observe one of the great ethnographic research teams in action studying the racial dynamics at the Pruitt-Igo Housing complex in St. Louis. Headed by the anthropologist Jules Henry and sociologist Lee Rainwater, their largely African American team of research assistants spent their days compiling diaries based largely on resident responses to a series of open-ended questions about their lives, a wonderful opportunity to bring new voices into sociology. Unfortunately for the residents (and so for the PhD candidates) the questionnaire was constructed around Henry's neo-Freudian belief that the folks in "the projects" had been sent into decline by "the death instinct," an insuperable force that the students could detect with appropriate probing. I will not pretend that the marijuana-induced entries with which we filled the diaries in my apartment were ethical. But they salved the choice they faced of being lynched by the residents or losing their support. For a very different view of this experience, see Joyce Ladner's marvelous study of black girls, *Pruitt Igoe Tomorrow's Tomorrow: The Black Woman* (University of Nebraska Press, 1971).

10. But cf. Margaret Mead's note on the relative absence of family violence in Samoa (male and female) which she attributes to the child-rearing.

11. Frances Power Cobbe, "Wife Torture in England," *Contemporary Review* (1873); Sylvia Walby and Jude Towers, "Untangling the Concept of Coercive Control: Theorizing Domestic Violent Crime," *Criminology and Criminal Justice* (January 2018).

12. Evan Stark and Anne Flitcraft, *Women at Risk* (Sage, 1995).

13. Stark and Flitcraft, *Women at Risk*.

14. Cited by Blake Edwards, "Alarming Effects of Children's Exposure to Domestic Violence," *Psychology Today*, February 26, 2019.

15. (L. Avery, K. Diane Hutchinson, and K. Whitaker, "Domestic Violence and Intergenerational Rates of Child Sexual Abuse: A Case Record Analysis," *Child and Adolescent Social Work Journal* 19, no. 1 (2002): 77–79.

16. Appel & Holden, 1998; Fantuzzo & Mohr, 1999; McCloskey, Figueredo, & Koss, 1995. Buzawa Responding to Domestic Violence, 401. Quoted in Massachusetts Executive Office of Public Safety and Security Research and Policy Analysis Division, "Youth Victims of Sexual Assault and Domestic Violence, 2001 to 2010," August 2011.

17. This is a conservative estimate because 24 to 40 percent of coercive control involves little or no physical violence (20%), repeated violence too low to be recorded as

"domestic violence," or late-onset domestic violence, as in the case where the boy was scapegoated.

18. Buzawa. Buzawa & Stark (2017), 395.

19. M. S. Yang, S. Y. Ho, and F. H. Chou "Physical Abuse during Pregnancy and Risk of Low Birthweight Infants among Aborigines in Taiwan," *Public Health* 120, no. 6 (2006): 557–562; Judith M. McFarlane and Barbara Parker, *Abuse during Pregnancy: A Protocol for Prevention and Intervention* (March of Dimes Nursing Module, 2007).

20. Casey Family Programs, "Domestic Violence," accessed at www.casey.org/child-pro tection-domestic-violence/–on February 27, 2021, and August 21, 2022. See also S. Hamby, D. Finkelhor, H. Turner, and R. Omrod, "Children's Exposure to Intimate Partner Violence and Other Family Violence," *Juvenile Justice Bulletin* (2011).

21. (O'Keefe & Lebovics, 1998; Straus & Gelles, 1990). J. Edleson, *Emerging Responses to Children Exposed to Domestic Violence: A Project of the National Resource Center on Domestic Violence/Pennsylvania Coalition against Domestic Violence* (2011), http:// www.vawnet.org/Assoc_Files_VAWnet/AR_ChildrensExposure.pdf.

   H. M. Hughes, S. A. Graham-Bermann, and G. Gruber, "Resilience in Children Exposed to Domestic Violence," in S. A. Graham-Bermann, ed., *Domestic Violence in the Lives of Children* (American Psychological Association, 2001), 67–90; K. L. Kilpatrick, M. Litt, and L. M. Williams, "Post-Traumatic Stress Disorder in Child Witness to Domestic Violence," *American Journal of Orthopsychiatry* 67, no. 4 (1997): 639–644; D. Siegel and M. Hartzell, *Parenting from the Inside Out: How a Deeper Self-Understanding Can Help You Raise Children Who Thrive* (2004).

22. A. Myhill, and Kelly, "Counting with Understanding? What Is at Stake in Debates on Researching Domestic Violence," *Criminology and Criminal Justice* 21, no. 3 (2021); A. Myhill, "Measuring Coercive Control: What Can We Learn from National Population Surveys?," *Violence against Women* 21, no. 3 (2015): 355–375.

23. Myhill, "Measuring Coercive Control."

24. Emma Katz, Anna Nikupeteri, and Merja Laitinen, "When Coercive Control Continues to Harm Children: Post-Separation Fathering, Stalking, and Domestic Violence," *Child Abuse Review* 29, no. 4 (2020): 310–324.

25. Ross, 1996.

26. Beck et al., 2009; Hamberger et al., 2017; Stark, 2017.

27. Straus and Gelles, 1990 p409.

28. McCloskey, et al., 1995.

29. Mbiliny et al., 2007.

30. Fantuzzo et al., 1997.

31. A year earlier, in 2021, in nearby Fort Lauderdale, a four-year-old boy, Greyson Kessler, was shot to death by his father after a long history of physical and psycholog-ical abuse of the mother. In this case, until he failed to return the child to school two days before he killed him, the father had done nothing to hurt the child and so posed no danger to the boy in the Court's eyes.

32. Sandra A. Graham-Bermann, Lana E. Castor, Laura E. Miller-Graff, and Kathryn H. Howell, "The Impact of Intimate Partner Violence and Additional Traumatic

Events on Trauma Symptoms and PTSD in Preschool-aged Children," *Journal of Traumatic Stress* (August 2012).

33. Meredith Bagwell-Gray, "Women's Experiences of Sexual Violence in Intimate Relationships: Applying a New Taxonomy," *Journal of Interpersonal Violence* (February 2019).

34. Oona Brooks, "Doing the 'Right Thing'? Understanding Why Rape Victim-Survivors Report to the Police," *Feminist Criminology* 15, no. 2 (2020).

35. Bagwell-Gray, "Women's Experiences"; Paige Hall Smith, Gloria E. Thornton, Robert F. DeVellis, et al. "A Population-Based Study of the Prevalence and Distinctiveness of Battering, Physical Assault, and Sexual Assault in Intimate Relationships," *Violence against Women* 8, no. 10 (2002): 1208–1232; B. B. B. Rossman, "Home Office Research Study: Children in Violent Families: Current Diagnostic and Treatment Considerations," *Family Violence and Sexual Assault Bulletin* 29 (1994): 276; "Domestic Violence, Sexual Assault and Stalking: Findings from the British Crime Survey," 192. "A Population-Based Study of the Prevalence and Distinctiveness of Battering, Physical Assault, and Sexual Assault in Intimate Relationships."

36. H. Turner, D Finkelhor, R. Ormrod, and M. Hunt, "Family Context, Victimization, and Child Trauma Symptoms: Variations in Safe, Stable, and Nurturing Relationships during Early and Middle Childhood," *American Journal of Orthopsychiatry* (2012).

37. S. Li, F. Zhao, and G. Yu, "A Meta-Analysis of Childhood Maltreatment and Intimate Partner Violence Perpetration," *Aggression and Violent Behavior* (2020); Stephanie Holt, Helen Buckley, and Sadhbh Whelan, "The Impact of Exposure to Domestic Violence on Children and Young People: A Review of the Literature," *Child Abuse and Neglect* 85, no. 8 (1989 or 2008???): 81–86, 89, 92.

38. Li et al., "A Meta-Analysis"; David Finkelhor, Richard Ormrod, and Heather Turner, "Poly-Victimization: A Neglected Component in Child Victimization," *Child Abuse and Neglect* (2007).

39. Gelinas, 1983.

40. Gordon (2002).

41. Paveza, 1988.

42. Li et al., "A Meta-Analysis"; Finkelhor et al., "Poly-Victimization."

43. Myers and Finkelhor, 1992.

44. Abusive men coercively controlling their children often derive secondary gains that are unrelated to their proximate effects on their partners. These gains may be material, for example, in the form of direct service (e.g., a "Fagin"-type relationship); psychosexual; or emotional and may continue to operate even when the abuse is no longer serving its primary function of controlling the mother. These secondary gains often come to the fore when the adult victim and/or one or more of the child victims "moves out" of the proximal control of the abuser. Keith continued to pursue Tiffany after she moved, with what effect we will see shortly. In fact, his predatory sexual pattern was independent of his control over her mother at this point and might have continued even if Tiffany had remained in the home.

45. Centers for Disease Control and Prevention, 2011.

46. Hamby, Finkelhor, Turner, & Ormrod, 2011.

47. Jaffe, Wolfe, and Wilson (1990) Leighton (1989).
48. O'Brien, John, Margolin, and Erel (1994).
49. Truesdell, McNeil, and Deschner (1986) O'Brien, John, Margolin, and Erel (1994).
50. Fantuzzo et al. 1997.
51. Bogat, DeJonghe, Levendosky, Davidson, & von Eye, 2005.
52. Enlow, 2012.
53. Holmes, 2013.
54. (Spilsbury et al., 2007).
55. Finkelhor and Browne, 1988.
56. Finkelhor, 1981.
57. Crooks, Jaffe and Balla. Bacha 2010.
58. (Peled, 1993, p. 122, as cited in Edleson, 1999).
59. Finkelhor, Turner, Ormrod, Hamby, & Kracke, 2009.

Chapter 6

1. After a child in a Connecticut family case described feeling that the "silent treatment" given to his mother by his father and his older brothers was "terrorism," the judge told me in an aside that he had suddenly recognized the same dynamic in his own childhood home.
2. With the author's permission.
3. I am talking here specifically about the intimidation of children secondary to woman abuse. Parents and other adults frequently use these and other tactics to frighten or control children with harmful effect, but "bad parenting" is not our topic.
4. MuriElse, K. AugustiElse, M, Augusti Margunn, M. et al., "Childhood Experiences of Companion Animal Abuse and Its Co-Occurrence with Domestic Abuse: Evidence from a National Youth Survey in Norway," *Journal of Interpersonal Violence* 37 (2022).
5. Callaghan et al.
6. Epstein and Goodman, 2018.
7. Trocmé & Bala, 2005.
8. (Rees et al., 2006; Tolman, 1989).
9. Bancroft and Silverman, 2002.

Chapter 7

1. I have borrowed concepts such as "identification with the aggressor" and "traumatic bond" from the psychoanalytic literature, where they appear to explain a behavior in its relational context better than other concepts at my disposal. While I have done my due diligence in the relevant literature, I make no pretext that my use is consistent with Anna Freud's intent, or Judy Hermann's, or takes into account the critical commentary in which these and related concepts have evolved. I could issue a similar

caveat regrading my use of "trauma" or other terms I adapt that have narrower and undoubtedly more precise definitions than I imply.

2. Katz, 2022.

3. Mary A. Kernic, Daphne J. Monary-Ernsdorff, Jennifer K. Koepsell, and Victoria L. Holt, "Children in the Crossfire: Child Custody Determinations among Couples with a History of Intimate Partner Violence. *Violence against Women* 11, no. 8 (2005): 991–1021.

4. Mariachiara Feresin, Federica Bastiani, and Lucia Beltramini, "The Involvement of Children in Postseparation Intimate Partner Violence in Italy: A Strategy to Maintain Coercive Control?" (2019)

5. I use "mother" throughout because more than 85 percent of my caseload consists of coercively controlled women. I have had four cases involving coercively controlled fathers in my practice where the dynamics of abuse have been similar, including high levels of physical, sexual, and economic exploitation, to those involving victimized mothers. Several of these cases involved multigenerational interventions, where the initial claim of abuse and custody came from the grandparents (fathers' parents).

6. In one case the man had so effectively and frequently denigrated the mother in front of her sons that they feared if they acknowledged seeing any abuse to the psychologist they would share a worse fate than she would ("Return to Italy without your cherry your children or your money"). The only evidence the father had hit the boys (whom he routinely beat with wooden boards) was an admission one of the boys had made to a friend, "My daddy has a big hand." When I brought this to the attention of the lawyer for the children, she was initially sympathetic. She turned however. The mother caught the son taping her phone calls for dad and threw a shoe at him, hitting him in the foot. The school reported "the minor bruise" to DCF; DCF opened a case against the mother; and the children's lawyer switched sides. The mother had been a maid at the Marriott, living in a bedroom above the kitchen of the man's pizza restaurant, where she cleaned the ovens before leaving for work. The husband stayed downstairs with his mistress. As he'd promised his sons, their mother was deported to Italy after the divorce with no money.

7. The secondary nature of much child abuse in coercively controlling relationships helps explain why so many abusive men are frankly shocked to learn how seriously they have harmed their children. It may also explain why so many women experiencing coercive control resist shifting the focus of intervention off themselves to their children.

8. We come across a similar "good girl" adaptation by a teen to a sexual abuse scenario.

9. M. H. Logan, "Stockholm Syndrome: Held Hostage by the One You Love," *Violence and Gender* 5, no. 2 (2018): 67–69, https//doi.org/10.1089/vio.2017.0076.

10. Anna Freud offers a brilliant analysis of the obsessively possessive husband as pathological extension of the same combination of projection and introjection found in identification with the aggressor. She writes, "when a husband displaces on this wife his own impulses to be unfaithful and then reproaches her passionately with unfaithfulness, he is really introjecting her reproaches and projecting part of his own id.

His intention, however, is not to protect himself from aggression from without but against the shattering of his positive libidinal fixation to her by disturbing forces from within . . . . Instead of an aggressive attitude towards some former external assailants, he develops an obsessional fixation to his wife, which takes the form of projected jealousy" (p. 130).

11. Anna Freud, "The Ego and the Mechanism of Defense," in *Identification with the Aggressor* (Routledge, 1966).

12. Elizabeth F. Howell, "A Ferenczi's Concept of Identification with the Aggressor: Understanding Dissociative Structure with Interacting Victim and Abuser Self-States," *American Journal of Psychoanalysis*, 74, no. 1 (2014): 48–59.

13. In Marx, the "alienation" has this double connotation. The primary alienation of man's labor (as industry) from his self-development sets capitalism in motion, in which persons becomes mere worker appendages of machines. But this alienation is what makes modern technology possible which, when shorn of the fetters of private ownership, then confronts "society" with its true potential as a fixed externality. Thus, "alienation" both denudes "man" of the capacity for self-reproduction and frees him from the bonds of necessary labor.

14. The documents reviewed included 5/11/09 Affidavit in Support of Shele COVLIN in action for divorce; 5/15/09 Temporary Order of Protection in action for divorce; 7/15/09 Affidavit in Support of Shele COVLIN in action for divorce; 7/28/09 NYC Children's Services report; 7/31/09 Temporary Order of Protection in action for divorce;8/13/09 Temporary Order of Protection in action for divorce; 11/24/09 Stipulation as to Supervised Visits in action for divorce; email correspondence of Shele COVLIN with her divorce attorney in action for divorce; Notes/Summary: Acts committed by R. COVLIN; 1/7/10 Affidavit of Hiacinth Sharpe; 4/9/10 Letter of the Chief Medical Examiner.

15. This psychologist's report was prepared at the request of the Covlins. I was told about the report, but it was not shared with me and I was not given access to the psychologist or his/her notes.

Chapter 8

1. The substance for this analysis is drawn from news reports of the killing, transcripts, and reports from the trial of Magdalena Luczak, who was also tried and convicted of the killing in 2013, and on a serious case review (SCR) of the professional involvement in the Pelka case completed during the Luczak-Krezolek trial.

2. British Home Office, "New Definition of Domestic Violence," GOV.UK, 2012.

3. A note to readers with an interest in policing or law. Coercively controlling men usually leave a broad trail of evidence, and multiple witnesses have seen or heard them describe their abusive conduct. They nonetheless appear behind a "cloak of invisibility" reinforced by friends or family of the victims who are suddenly dumb to

commonsense realities when cases are in court. My only advice is that persistence pays off.

4. Dr. C. Henry Kempe, who first described the battered child syndrome in 1962 *Archives of Pediatric and Adolescent Medicine* 165, no. 9 (2011): 778. https://doi.org/10.1001/archpediatrics.2011.146.

5. But cf. Herman, *Trauma and Recovery*.

6. Herbert Marcuse, "Repressive Tolerance," in *A Critique of Pure Tolerance* (Beacon Press, 1965).

7. For the first, see Lenore Walker, *Terrifying Love* (1990). For the view of DV as transitory couples violence, see Linda Mills, *Hidden Injuries* (Princeton University Press, 2006).

8. Evan Stark and Anne Flitcraft, *Women at Risk: Domestic Violence and Women's Health* (Sage, 1996).

9. Jim Scott, *Domination and the Art of Resistance; Hidden Transcripts* (Yale University Press, 1992).

10. Richard Stansfield and Kirk Williams, "Coercive Control between Intimate Partners: An Application to Nonfatal Strangulation," *Journal of Interpersonal Violence* (2018).

11. Evan Stark and Anne Flitcraft, "Woman Battering," in J. M. Last, ed., *Maxcy-Rosenau: Public Health and Preventive Medicine*, 14th ed. (Appleton Century Crofts, 1998).

12. Stark and Flitcraft, "Woman Battering."

13. Stark and Flitcraft, "Woman Battering."

14. Elizabeth Price, Leah Sharman, Heather Douglas, and Genevieve A. Dingle, "Experiences of Reproductive Coercion in Queensland Women," *Journal of Interpersonal Violence* (2019).

15. Stark and Flitcraft, *Women at Risk*.

Chapter 9

1. The discussion is based on Richard Sennett and Jonathan Cobbe, *Hidden Injuries of Class* (1993).

2. Several years after they separated, and Rachel was married, she ran into Roberto in a grocery store. He bowed deeply and addressed her as "Senora," the first time he used this term of respect. She was deeply moved.

3. These developments are reviewed in Evan Stark, "The Coercive Control Framework: What Makes the Law Work for Women?," in M. McMahon and P. McGorrery, eds., *Criminalising Non-Physical Family Violence: Coercive Control and Autonomy Crimes* (Springer International, 2019).

4. "Dangerousness-Lethality Assessment Guide," www.courtswv.gov/public-resources/CAN/2017GAL-training/.

5. Beth Richie, *Compelled to Crime: Gender Entrapment of Battered Black Women* (Routledge, 1996), 55–56.

6. It was only after the couple had been apart for some years and Rachel had remarried and ran into Roberto in a store where she was shopping with her sister-in-law that he first used this term of respect to address her directly. At that moment, she says, she felt "vindicated."

7. Kenneth Burke, *Attitudes Towards History* (Beacon Press, 197; Revised 2nd ed., 1959).

8. She told me she felt the same way when the psychiatrist who was interviewing Roberto at RWJ asked her if she would mind sitting in the room. "He's handcuffed to the chair," the psychiatrist assured her. She told him, "I don't care if he's handcuffed to the wall." She called her attorney, and the MD agreed to see them separately.

9. Carlos E. Sluzki and Donald C. Ransom. eds., *Double-Bind: A Foundation of a Communications Approach to the Family* (Gruen, 1976).

10. Anne Harrington, "The Fall of the Schizophrenogenic Mother," *Perspectives:|The Art of Medicine|* 379, no. 9823 (2012): 1292–1293.

11. Elaine (Hilberman) Carmen, P. P. Reiker, and T. Mills, "Victims of Violence and Psychiatric Illness," *AJP* 141 (1984): 378–383.

12. In the well-known case of "the burning bed," Francine Hughes set the fire that killed her husband after he burned her school books. For Hughes, school was a safety zone because it allowed her to think of a life beyond the relationship and to make friends. By closing her safety zone, burning Francine's books set the stage her to burn their bed. Faith McNulty, *The Burning Bed: The True Story of Francine Hughes—A Beaten Wife Who Rebelled* (1980).

13. This affirmative defense for the battered mother charged with "failure to protect" is not meant as an absolute standard. In some cases, the level of harms to the children by a victimized mother is so grossly disproportionate to the level of constraint on the woman that her accountability is merited. Even in these cases, however, the woman's liberty interest must be weighed seriously in her defense.

14. Evan Stark and Anne Flitcraft, "Killing the Beast Within: Woman Battering and Female Suicidality," *IJHS* 25 (1995): 45–64.

15. Judy Herman, *Trauma and Recovery: The Aftermath of Violence* (Beacon Hill, 1992).

Chapter 10

1. A variation on this scenario of "coercive control" is the classic con by a man (or woman) from a family of alcoholics, often suffering an undisclosed personality disorder, who ingratiates himself into high society, marries someone with wealth, elopes (isolates) to live out their fantasy, and embezzles their money. Sarma Melngalis, the former owner of Pure Food and Wine in New York, was a victim of "coercive control from below" by Antony Strangis, her con man ex-husband, who convinced her she could be "Queen" in another world; took her away from her friends, family, and

business associates; and embezzled more than $1.6 million of her savings. Sarma was convicted of fraud in 2016 and sentenced to four months in prison.

2. In 2022, ambiguous genitalia is recognized as a relatively rare development that can be identified early and addressed in a team approach in which cosmetic, surgical, and medical therapy (hormones, e.g.) are weighed in the context of the complex issues of children's autonomy that arise in gender assignment.

3. In the extent of professional scrutiny, this case resembles the level of professional involvement with the murder of Daniel Pelka in Coventry, England (chapter 8).

Conclusion

1. "Domestic-Violence-Child-Removal," janeprobstlaw.com (accessed September 24, 2022).

2. S. Hillis, J. Mercy, A. Amobi, and H. Kress, "Global Prevalence of Past-Year Violence against Children: A Systematic Review and Minimum Estimates," *Pediatrics* 137, no. 3 (2016).):

3. "Essentials for Childhood Framework: Steps To Create Safe, Stable, Nurturing Relationships and Environments for All Children," (2017), cdc.gov/violenceprevention/childmaltreatment/essentials.

4. For differing views, compare M. Tanha, C. J. A. Beck, A. J. Figueredo, and C. Raghavan, "Sex Differences in Intimate Partner Violence and the Use of Coercive Control as a Motivational Factor for Intimate Partner Violence," *Journal of Interpersonal Violence* (2009) (which shows an independent relation of psychological abuse), and M. L. Haselschwerdt, K. Hlavaty, C. Carlson, and M. Skipper, "Heterogeneity within Domestic Violence Exposure: Young Adults' Retrospective Experiences," *Journal of Interpersonal Violence* (2016), which shows no independent role of psychological abuse.

5. Office. 2015. "Controlling or Coercive Behaviour in an Intimate or Family Relationship: Statutory Guidance Framework," https://assets.publishing.service.gov.uk/government/uploads/system/uploads/attachment_data/file/482528/Controlling_or_coercive_behaviour_-_statutory_guidance.pdf; Jane Monckton Smith, "Intimate Partner Femicide: Using Foucauldian Analysis to Track an Eight Stage Relationship Progression to Homicide," *Violence against Women* 26, no. 11 (2020): 1267–1285, https://doi.org/10.1177/1077801219863876; Amanda Gearing,. "Reporting Child Sexual Abuse," in Ann Luce, ed., *Ethical Reporting of Sensitive Topics* (Routledge, 2019), 49–69; Amanda Gearing, "Reporting Disasters in the Digital Age," in Luce, *Ethical Reporting of Sensitive Topics*, 214–232; Amanda Gearing, "Coercive Control and Domestic Abuse: What Might Have Saved Hannah Clarke and Her Children?," *Guardian (Australia)*, 2020; Amanda Gearing, "Coercive Control: Hannah Clarke's Parents on the Abuse That Preceded Their Daughter's Murder," *Sydney: The Guardian*, 2020; *LAF v. AP* [2022] QDC, District Court of Queensland.

6. The United Nations Convention on the Rights of the Child (commonly abbreviated as the CRC or UNCRC) is an international human rights treaty that sets out the civil, political, economic, social, health, and cultural rights of children. The UN General Assembly adopted the Convention on November 20, 1989. As of October 1, 2022, 196 countries were party to it, including every member of the United Nations except the United States.

Index

For the benefit of digital users, indexed terms that span two pages (e.g., 52–53) may, on occasion, appear on only one of those pages.

Barahona, Carmen (*cont.*)
 Jorge's deterioration (1999-
  2009), 314–18
 marriage to Ray, 308–9
 relationship of Jorge and, 309–19
 sexual abuse of children, 342
 twins' withdrawal from school, 321–31
Barahona, Jorge
 coercive control by, 305
 control tactics of, 349
 deterioration (1999-2009), 314–18
 extermination business, 315–16, 321
 "ideal" family, 311, 312
 psychiatric condition, 313
 psychosis of, 304–5, 310
 relationship of Carmen and, 309–19
 restrictions on twins, 345–46
 See also Barahona, Carmen
Barahona, Nubia, 3
 death of, 341
 sexual abuse of, 342
battered child syndrome, 71–72, 85–
  86, 374n.4
battered wife, identity of, 52
battered women, 234–35
 alcohol and, 242
 failure to protect charge for mother,
  375n.13
 movement, 28–29, 77–78, 88
 practice of removing children from,
  366n.14
 syndrome, 85–86, 200
 urban study of, 138–40
Berger, John, 127
Berghdorf Health Center, 19
Berisha, Shipe, 111, 112–13
Berlin Zoo, 89
bespoke offence, coercive control, 155–56
Biden, Joe, 78
Big Country, The (film), 163–64
black list, dealing with children, 89
blackmail, abusers using children
  as, 174–75
Bond, James, 280–81
Boston Children's Hospital, 70–71
Branagh, Kenneth, 23
Brando, Marlon, 80–81
Braxton, Robert II

Hall and, 46–50, 51–52
 sentence of, 362n.4
Braxton, Tony, 132
British Crime Survey, 128, 135
British Home Office, 25–26, 226
Brothers Karamozov, The (film), 12
Brown, Nicole, 26, 227
Brownmiller, Susan, 61
bullying, 163–64
Bunker, Archie, 165–66
Burke, Kenneth, 288
"burning bed," case of, 375n.12
Burns, Anna, 359
Bush, George, 77–78

California, 6
 coercive control of children, 135–36
 definition of abuse, 277
 monographs on coercive control, 357
 out-of-state visitation, 191
Campbell, Jacqueline, 35–36
Campbell Dangerousness Assessment
  Scale (DAS), 277–78
Canada, 6, 7–8
 Divorce Act (1985), 357
 monographs on coercive control, 357
Canadian Incidence Study of Reported
  Child Abuse and Neglect, 186–87
Carroll, Patrick L. (Judge), 40–41
Casey Family Foundation, 131
Catholic patriarchy, 306
Centers for Disease Control and
  Prevention (CDC), 76–77,
  131, 153–55
Chamarro, Robert, 92–93, 112–13
Chaplin, Charlie, 165–66
child abuse, 1–2, 64, 74–75
 abuser forcing the role of "witness," 84
 coercive control, 355
 "coercive control of children," 85–86
 domestic violence and, 6–7, 8–9
 element of coercive control, 64
 experience of coercive control, 79–85
 false allegations of, 186–87
 fathers and, 363n.6
 leaving abuse, 81
 Pelka as tangential spouse
  abuse, 251–52

Honeymooners, The (television
series), 165–66
household pets, weaponization of, 172
Hughes, Francine, 375n.12
Hughes, Jeanette, 82–83, 133–34,
144, 149–53
isolating children, 347
killing abusive husband, 169–70
State of Penn. v. Jeanette Hughes, 144–49
Hughes, Keith, 131–32, 144–53, 332–
33, 346
intimidation, 166–67
sexual abuse of Tiffany, 342
Hughes, Tiffany, 82–83, 332–33
Hughes case
Brianne and Tiffany, 179–80
control, 185, 186
family pet, 172
harms of intimidation, isolation, and
control, 153–55
intimidation, 164, 166–67

identification with the aggressor,
201, 203–6
Anna Freud's theory, 203–4, 205–6,
371–72n.1, 372–73n.10
child victimization, 351–52
concept of, 371–72n.1
Samuel W. case, 203–4
video games, 206
incest, 147–48
indentured servitude, 7–8, 100–1, 366n.11
independence, beyond harms
reduction, 356–57
index of suspicion, 70, 74–75
indigenous youth, enslavement of, 366n.11
infanticide, 3–4
infants, coercive control of
children, 157–60
In re Lonell J., 365–66n.10
institutions of secondary
socialization, 90, 92
interagency collaborative model,
367–68n.6
intimidation, 161–62
children, 167–70, 172–75
children as secondary to women, 371n.3
coercive control of children, 162–75

coercive control of children
model, 343–46
harms beyond witnessing, 153–55
household pets, 172
Jonathan D. case, 171–72, 182–84
Samuel W. case, 170–71, 176–79
invisible man, 52–60
Frank K. case, 56–58
specter of, 55–56
IPSA (intimate partner sexual abuse), 149
Iraq, 354–55
Ireland, 357
isolation, 161–62
coercive control of children, 175–76
coercive control of children
model, 346–48
harms beyond witnessing, 153–55
homeschooling, 176–77, 178–79
Jonathan D. case, 182–84
Rachel and her children, 282–84
Samuel W. case, 176–79
sexual abuse of children as, 149–53
Izquierdo, Eliza, 95
child welfare in New York, 95–100
Izzy the Eel, testimony of, 359

James-Hanman, Davina, 25–26
Johns Hopkins University, 35–36
Johnson, Jeremiah "Ryder," 48–49
Johnson, Joyce, 61
Jonathan D. case
intimidation, 171–72, 182–84
isolation, 182–84, 348
Juan, Don, 280–81
justice, beyond harms reduction, 356–57
Juvenile Court, DCF recommending
parental right termination, 362n.3

Katz, Emma, 121–22, 161–62, 190, 357
Kempe, Henry, 72–73, 233
battered child syndrome, 71–72, 85–
86, 374n.4
population of "abused children," 70
Kessler, Greyson, death by father, 369n.31
Knock, Mariah, 188–89, 190, 192–93, 196,
197, 345–46
betrayal of mother, 196
child as weapon, 351

Pelka, Daniel, 3, 25–28, 123–24,
   291, 333–34
  abuse of, 26–27
  case background, 227–28
  case of, 130, 355–56
  child abuse as tangential spouse
     abuse, 251–52
  child's voice in assessment, 231–32
  coercive control by Krezolek, 244–50
  death of, 55, 341
  entering school , 253–54
  Krezolek and, 53, 54–55
  Krezolek as killer of, 226
  medical visit, 29
  murder of, 26, 27–28, 44–45,
     203, 225–26
  professional involvement with murder
     of, 376n.3
  reconstructing the Pelka case, 233–40
  serious case review, 228–31
  shaming, 344–45
Pennsylvania, Samuel W. case, 203–4
perspecticide, condition of, 44–45,
   310, 326
Petit, William, 41–42
pets, weaponization of, 172
Pinkus, Barry C. (Judge), 40, 42
  case of Aedan Moreno, 32–33
  Oyola's petition for restraining
     order, 37–40
Pizzey, Erin, 65–66
Poland, 7–8
pregnancy, risk point for physical
   violence, 247–48
preschool children, coercive control of
   children, 157–60
professionalism, pediatrician of
   Pelka's, 233
psychological abuse
  coercive control of children, 155–57
  coercive control of children model, 343
PTSD (posttraumatic stress disorder),
   56–57, 143–44, 262, 279–80, 319,
   363n.10

Queensland District Court, 357–58
Quixote, Don, 280–81

Rachel and her children, 3, 258–59, 305

background, 259–61
child abuse as tangential spouse
   abuse, 291–97
Claudia (David's child), 260, 268,
   269–71, 272, 273, 274–75, 277–79,
   281–82, 287, 288, 290–91, 294–95,
   297–300
closing the safety zone, 289–91
coercive control, 297–301
coercive control extending to children
   (Jan.-Sept. 2014), 270–77
control, 284–86
David (Claudia's father), 263, 266–67
entrapment and abuse of
   children, 286–89
escalation of violence and control (Sept.
   2013-Jan. 2014), 268–70
family background, 262–64
gender entrapment, 281–82
Head Start, 267–68, 269, 270, 278–
   80, 283–86
isolation, 282–84
New Jersey DCF, 259–60, 262, 275, 276,
   283–84, 289
onset of abuse (Feb.-Sept. 2013), 265–68
preconceptions of Rachel, 261–91
reframing the failure to protect, 280–82
relationship with Roberto, 264–77,
   374n.2, 375n.6, 375n.8
subjugation and entrapment, 279
tangential to spouse abuse, 259
violence for, 277–80
Radford, Lorraine, 161–62
Rainwater, Lee, 368n.9
rape as routine, 204–5
rape trauma victim, 234–35
Reagan, Ronald, 76–77, 78, 87–88
refuge movement, 77–78
refuge/shelter movement, 4–5
Regional Child Fatality Review Board,
   New Jersey, 62
Reyes, G., 108
Rhodes, Chrystal, 111, 113–14
risk assessment, child protection, 97–98
risk of injury, 45, 291
Robert Wood Johnson Hospital, 260
Rodriguez, April, 92–93, 100, 104–
   5, 113–14
  domestic violence hotline, 114–15